VDP.GROSSE LAGE® THE BOOK

Ahr · Baden · Franken · Mittelrhein · Mosel · Nahe · Pfalz · Rheingau · Rheinhessen · Sachsen S-U · Württemb.

1910

VDP. DIE PRÄDIKATSWEINGÜTER

IMPRINT

© VDP.Die Prädikatsweingüter
and Frankfurt Academic Press GmbH, 2019
www.frankfurt-academic-press.de
1st Edition. All rights reserved.

© Fotos Cover and Pages: VDP, except of:
© Foto Page 222, 423, 426, 438, 456, 459, 462: Andreas Durst
Page 412: P. Cebulla | devaton.de
© Page and Book Design: axel dielmann – verlag KG Frankfurt am Main

© All rights for contents and design, as well as the rights for graphic, text, image and map material belong, unless otherwise stated, to the copyright holder. Map material serves as information only. All representations made in the maps are provided without guarantee. The vineyard sites and the background maps make no claim of complete accuracy concerning vineyard boundaries. VDP.VINEYARD.ONLINE presents the discussion status quo of the current nearly 200 VDP.Vintners as of 30.11.2018. All boundaries are drawn in good conscience and according to our best knowledge. Boundaries and designations are often drawn from current wine law for protected designations of origin. The VDP.Classification makes no claims to be complete. It is a work in progress. We thank the DWI for their cooperation in creation of the maps, collection of data for the presentation and texts.—Concerning names of Vineyards:
[1] With reservation. Vineyard site is not yet authorised by German wine law.
[3] This vineyard is located in France. Therefore German wine estates are not allowed by German wine law to use the vineyard name on the label.
" " The name was selected by the wine maker. It usually refers to the small vineyard plot, the wine grows in.
®2018 mapz.com; Map Data: OpenStreetMap, Bundesamt für Kartografie
Cover photos show: Slate soil (© Reinhard Löwenstein) and VDP.GROSSE LAGE® BASSGEIGE KÄHNER (Baden). Back: VDP.GROSSE LAGE® UHLEN "LAUBACH" (Mosel) and VDP.GROSSE LAGE® SCHLOSSBERG, Rüdesheim (Rheingau).
Texts: Katja Apelt
Translations: Julia Sevenich, Paula Sidore
Production: Katja Apelt
Proof Reading: VDP.Team

ISBN 978 3 86983 022 3

CONTENTS

VDP.GROSSE LAGE®
The Book

Preface by Steffen Christmann, VDP.President	5
Index | VDP.GROSSE LAGE® Vineyards in Alphabetical Order	7
Index | VDP.WINERIES in Alphabetical Order & Their VDP.GROSSE LAGE® Vineyards	19
Who's Afraid of Terroir? by Reinhard Heymann-Löwenstein	31
The VDP.CLASSIFICATION Briefly Explained	37
VDP.GROSSE LAGE® | The Peak of the Pyramid	38
VDP.DIE PRÄDIKATSWEINGÜTER | Who We Are	40
Sound and Smoke | On Classified Vineyard Sites and Their Names by Dr. Daniel Deckers	41
Vineyard.Online | The Online Guide to Germany's Best Sites	49
Historical Vineyard Maps	50
The Wine Regions of Germany	51
The Region AHR & its VDP.GROSSE LAGE® Vineyards	52
The Region BADEN & its VDP.GROSSE LAGE® Vineyards	72
The Region FRANKEN & its VDP.GROSSE LAGE® Vineyards	120
The Region MITTELRHEIN & its VDP.GROSSE LAGE® Vineyards	146
The Region MOSEL-SAAR-RUWER & its VDP.GROSSE LAGE® Vineyards	156
The Region NAHE & its VDP.GROSSE LAGE® Vineyards	232

CONTENTS

VDP.GROSSE LAGE®
The Book

The Region PFALZ & its VDP.GROSSE LAGE® Vineyards	264
The Region RHEINGAU & its VDP.GROSSE LAGE® Vineyards	318
The Region RHEINHESSEN & its VDP.GROSSE LAGE® Vineyards	372
The Region SACHSEN/SAALE-UNSTRUT & its VDP.GROSSE LAGE® Vineyards	410
The Region WÜRTTEMBERG & its VDP.GROSSE LAGE® Vineyards	416
The VDP.REGIONAL OFFICES	468
The VDP.ESTATES | Addresses	469
The VDP.PARTNERS	489

FOREWORD

by
Steffen Christmann, VDP.President

Dear Friends of Great German Wine!

The German Renaissance of the 'Grand Cru' model of wine classification is well underway and rightfully basking in international attention. Yet the meaning and mechanisms behind this movement are less easily understood, making it difficult for observers to appreciate its distinctive elements and nuances.

The pages of this book gather together our most precious vineyards—the current roster of classified VDP.GROSSE LAGE® sites—together with a wealth of fascinating information. We hope to awaken your interest and inspire you to explore the extensive knowledge available at Vineyard.Online (www.vineyard-online.info).

We live in an age of digitization, yet good old-fashioned books can open up an effective channel to improving our understanding of our 'grand sites of origin'—in a form that is perhaps less ephemeral than online media. This book also provides an excellent forum for differing opinions, precisely the kind that might encourage deeper contemplation and foster more much-needed discussion within the VDP and the larger German winegrowing community.

Reinhard Löwenstein, Vice-President of the VDP, has put his thoughts to paper in an essay entitled "Who's Afraid of Terroir." He philosophizes about soil, nature and authenticity. For him, terroir is the basis for the true classification of wines. He retraces the path that brought us from Öchsle to vineyard and which led to a "provocative break from a system of wine classification that had been in place for a century and was ostensibly based on objective facts."

Daniel Deckers, journalist with the Frankfurter Allgemeine Zeitung and author of the book "The Sign of The Grape and Eagle," draws on Goethe as he ruminates on the thesis that vineyard sites are "sound and smoke." He follows historical clues and analyzes the rise of the famed classified site maps and site assessments that often oriented themselves by prices—and thus indirectly by demand and prestige on the market for the most renowned wines from German regions. He also casts a critical view over our current vineyard classification system.

We, the member estates of the VDP.Prädikatsweingüter, believe in the path we have chosen, and that Germany's finest classified sites are worthy of being restored to their former grandeur. But this kind of monumental achievement isn't built in a

FOREWORD

day. It is one step on a larger journey and needs constant review and optimization. As so the book in your hands can be understood as a slice in time, reflecting our current thoughts about Germany's GROSSE LAGEN.

We hope you enjoy your exploration of these many magnificent vineyards and join us on our shared journey along this highly promising path.

INDEX VDP.GROSSE LAGE® SITES

In Alphabetical Order

ABTSBERG (Mosel)	Page 158
ALTE LAY (Ahr)	Page 54
ALTENBERG, Strümpfelbach (Württemberg)	Page 419
ALTENBERG, Schnait (Württemberg)	Page 418
ALTENBERG, Kanzem (Mosel)	Page 159
"ALTTENBERG 1172"[1] (Franken)	Page 122
AM LUMPEN 1655® (Franken)	Page 123
AN DER RABENLEI (Mittelrhein)	Page 148
APOSTELGARTEN (Franken)	Page 124
APOTHEKE (Mosel)	Page 160
AUF DER HOHL (Pfalz)	Page 266
AUF DER LEY (Nahe)	Page 234
AUGENSCHEINER (Mosel)	Page 161
AULERDE (Rheinhessen)	Page 374
BADSTUBE (Mosel)	Page 162
BAIKENKOPF (Rheingau)	Page 320
BASSGEIGE KÄHNER (Baden)	Page 74
BASSGEIGE LEH (Baden)	Page 75
BASTEI (Nahe)	Page 235
BERG (Württemberg)	Page 420
BERG KAISERSTEINFELS (Rheingau)	Page 321
BERG ROSENECK (Rheingau)	Page 322
BERG ROTTLAND (Rheingau)	Page 323
BERG SCHLOSSBERG (Rheingau)	Page 324
BERNSTEIN - AM LAUERBAUM (Mittelrhein)	Page 149
BIENENBERG (Baden)	Page 77
BIENENBERG "WILDENSTEIN"[1] (Baden)	Page 76
BISCHOFSBERG (Franken)	Page 125
BOCKSTEIN (Mosel)	Page 163
BRAUNE KUPP (Mosel)	Page 164
BRAUNFELS (Mosel)	Page 165
BROTWASSER STEINGRUBE (Württemberg)	Page 421
BRÜCKE (Nahe)	Page 236
BRUDERBERG (Mosel)	Page 166
BRUDERSBERG (Rheinhessen)	Page 375
BRUNNENHÄUSCHEN (Rheinhessen)	Page 376

INDEX VDP.GROSSE LAGE® SITES

In Alphabetical Order

BURG WILDECK HERRSCHAFTSBERG (Württemberg) .... Page 422
BURGBERG (Nahe) .... Page 237
BÜRGEL (Rheinhessen) .... Page 377
BÜRGERGARTEN IM BREUMEL (Pfalz) .... Page 267
BURGGARTEN (Ahr) .... Page 55
BURGHALDE, Beutelsbach (Württemberg) .... Page 423
BURGHALDE, Schnait (Württemberg) .... Page 424
BURGWEG (Rheinhessen) .... Page 378
CENTGRAFENBERG (Franken) .... Page 126
CHORHERRNHALDE (Baden) .... Page 78
DAUBHAUS (Ahr) .... Page 56
DAUTENPFLÄNZER (Nahe) .... Page 238
DELLCHEN (Nahe) .... Page 239
DICKER FRANZ (Baden) .... Page 79
DOCTOR (Mosel) .... Page 167
DOKTORGARTEN (Baden) .... Page 80
DOMDECHANEY (Rheingau) .... Page 325
DOMHERR (Mosel) .... Page 168
DOMPROBST (Mosel) .... Page 169
DOOSBERG, (Rheingau) .... Page 326
ECK (Ahr) .... Page 57
EDELACKER (Saale-Unstrut) .... Page 412
EICHBERG (Baden) .... Page 81
EICHELBERG (Baden) .... Page 82
EILFINGERBERG KLOSTERSTÜCK (Württemberg) .... Page 425
ENSELBERG (Baden) .... Page 83
ENGELSTEIN (Mittelrhein) .... Page 150
FALKENBERG (Rheinhessen) .... Page 379
FEILS (Mosel) .... Page 170
FELSENBERG, Schloßböckelheim (Nahe) .... Page 240
FELSENBERG, Leistadt (Pfalz) .... Page 268
FELSENECK, Bockenau (Nahe) .... Page 241
FELSENECK, Wallhausen (Nahe) .... Page 242
FELSENKOPF (Mosel) .... Page 171
FEUERBERG HASLEN (Baden) .... Page 84
FEUERBERG KESSELBERG (Baden) .... Page 85

INDEX VDP.GROSSE LAGE® SITES

In Alphabetical Order

FORSTBERG (Württemberg)	Page 426
FÖRSTERLAY (Mosel)	Page 172
FRAUENBERG, Nieder-Flörsheim (Rheinhessen)	Page 380
FRAUENBERG, Mauchen (Baden)	Page 86
FREUNDSTÜCK (Pfalz)	Page 269
FRÜHLINGSPLÄTZCHEN (Nahe)	Page 243
FÜRSTLICHER KALLMUTH® (Franken)	Page 127
GAISBÖHL (Pfalz)	Page 270
GAISSBERG (Württemberg)	Page 427
„GANZ HORN" (IM SONNENSCHEIN) (Pfalz)	Page 279
GÄRKAMMER (Ahr)	Page 58
GEHRN KESSELRING (Rheingau)	Page 327
GEIERSBERG (Rheinhessen)	Page 381
GIPS (Württemberg)	Page 429
GIPS MARIENGLAS® (Württemberg)	Page 428
GLÖCK (Rheinhessen)	Page 382
GOLDBERG (Mosel)	Page 173
GOLDENES LOCH (Baden)	Page 87
GOLDLOCH (Nahe)	Page 244
GOLDTRÖPFCHEN (Mosel)	Page 174
GOTTESFUSS (Mosel)	Page 175
GÖTZENBERG, Kleinbottwar (Württemberg)	Page 430
GÖTZENBERG, Uhlbach (Württemberg)	Page 431
GRABEN (Mosel)	Page 176
GRAFENBERG (Mosel)	Page 177
GRÄFENBERG (Rheingau)	Page 328
GRAINHÜBEL (Pfalz)	Page 271
GREIFFENBERG (Rheingau)	Page 329
HALENBERG (Nahe)	Page 245
HARDTBERG (Ahr)	Page 59
HASENSPRUNG (Rheingau)	Page 330
HASSEL (Rheingau)	Page 331
HEERKRETZ (Rheinhessen)	Page 383
HEINBERG (Baden)	Page 88
HENKENBERG (Baden)	Page 89
HERMANNSBERG (Nahe)	Page 246

INDEX VDP.GROSSE LAGE® SITES

In Alphabetical Order

HERMANNSHÖHLE (Nahe)	Page 247
HERRENBERG, Rech (Ahr)	Page 60
HERRENBERG, Ungstein (Pfalz)	Page 272
HERRENBERG, Oppenheim (Rheinhessen)	Page 384
HERRENBERG, Mertesdorf (Mosel)	Page 178
HERRENBERG, Serrig (Mosel)	Page 179
HERRENBERG LANGE WINGERT (Baden)	Page 90
HERRENBERGER (Mosel)	Page 180
HERRENTISCH (Baden)	Page 91
HERZOGENBERG (Württemberg)	Page 432
HEYDENREICH³ (Pfalz)	Page 273
HIMMELREICH, Gundelsheim (Württemberg)	Page 433
HIMMELREICH, Graach (Mosel)	Page 181
HIMMELSPFAD (Franken)	Page 128
HIPPING (Rheinhessen)	Page 385
HOFBERGER (Mosel)	Page 182
HOHE GRÄTE (Saale-Unstrut)	Page 413
HOHELEITE¹ (Franken)	Page 129
HOHENMORGEN (Pfalz)	Page 274
HOHENRAIN (Rheingau)	Page 332
HOHENROTH¹ (SONNENSTUHL) (Franken)	Page 141
HÖLLBERG (Rheinhessen)	Page 386
HÖLLE, Johannisberg (Rheingau)	Page 333
HÖLLE, Wiltingen (Mosel)	Page 183
HÖLLE, Hochheim am Main (Rheingau)	Page 334
HÖLLE - UNTERER FAULENBERG (Pfalz)	Page 275
HÖLLENBERG (Rheingau)	Page 335
HÖRECKER (Mosel)	Page 184
HORN (Rheinhessen)	Page 387
HUBACKER (Rheinhessen)	Page 388
HUNDSRÜCK (Franken)	Page 130
HUNGERBERG (Württemberg)	Page 434
HUSARENKAPPE (Baden)	Page 92
HÜTTE (Mosel)	Page 185
IDIG (Pfalz)	Page 276
IM GOLDENEN JOST (Pfalz)	Page 277

INDEX VDP.GROSSE LAGE® SITES

In Alphabetical Order

IM GROSSEN GARTEN (Pfalz)	Page 278
IM HAHN (Mittelrhein)	Page 151
IM KAHLENBERG (Nahe)	Page 248
IM LANGENBERG (Nahe)	Page 249
IM MÜHLBERG (Nahe)	Page 250
IM PITTERBERG (Nahe)	Page 251
IM ROTHENBERG (Rheingau)	Page 336
(IM SONNENSCHEIN) "GANZ HORN"[1] (Pfalz)	Page 279
IM SONNENSCHEIN, (Pfalz)	Page 280
JESUITENGARTEN, Forst an der Weinstr. (Pfalz)	Page 281
JESUITENGARTEN, Oestrich-Winkel, Geißenheim (Rheingau)	Page 337
JOHANNISBERG (Nahe)	Page 252
JOHANNISBRÜNNCHEN (Mosel)	Page 186
JOSEPHSHÖFER (Mosel)	Page 187
JUFFER (Mosel)	Page 188
JUFFER SONNENUHR (Mosel)	Page 189
JULIUS-ECHTER-BERG (Franken)	Page 131
JUNGFER (Rheingau)	Page 338
KALKBERG (Pfalz)	Page 282
KALKOFEN (Pfalz)	Page 283
KALMIT (Pfalz)	Page 284
KAMMERBERG[3] (Pfalz)	Page 285
KAPELLENBERG, Eichelberg (Baden)	Page 93
KAPELLENBERG, Lorch (Rheingau)	Page 339
KARTHÄUSER (Franken)	Page 132
KARTHÄUSERHOFBERG (Mosel)	Page 190
KÄSBERG (Württemberg)	Page 435
KASTANIENBUSCH (Pfalz)	Page 286
KASTANIENBUSCH-"KÖPPEL"[1] (Pfalz)	Page 287
KEHRNAGEL (Mosel)	Page 191
KIESELBERG (Pfalz)	Page 288
KIRCHBERG, Ilbesheim b. Landau/Pf, Landau i. d. Pfalz (Pfalz)	Page 289
KIRCHBERG, Bingen am Rhein (Rheinhessen)	Page 389
KIRCHBERG, Oberrotweil (Baden)	Page 94
KIRCHBERG, Hatzenport (Mosel)	Page 192
KIRCHENPFAD (Rheingau)	Page 340

INDEX VDP.GROSSE LAGE® SITES

In Alphabetical Order

KIRCHENSTÜCK, Forst an der Weinstr. (Pfalz) .... Page 290
KIRCHENSTÜCK, Hohen-Sülzen (Rheinhessen) .... Page 390
KIRCHENSTÜCK, Hochheim am Main (Rheingau) .... Page 341
KIRCHGASSE (Baden) .... Page 95
KIRCHSPIEL (Rheinhessen) .... Page 391
KIRCHTÜRMCHEN (Ahr) .... Page 61
KIRSCHGARTEN (Pfalz) .... Page 291
KIRSCHHECK (Nahe) .... Page 253
KLAMM (Nahe) .... Page 254
KLAUS (Rheingau) .... Page 342
KLÄUSERWEG (Rheingau) .... Page 343
KLOPPBERG (Rheinhessen) .... Page 392
KÖNIGIN VIKTORIABERG (Rheingau) .... Page 344
KÖNIGLICHER WEINBERG (Sachsen) .... Page 414
KÖNIGSBECHER (Baden) .... Page 96
KRANZBERG (Rheinhessen) .... Page 393
KRÄUTERBERG (Ahr) .... Page 62
KREUZ (Rheinhessen) .... Page 394
KREUZWINGERT (Mosel) .... Page 193
KROHNENBÜHL GOTTSACKER (Baden) .... Page 97
KRÖTENPFUHL (Nahe) .... Page 255
KRONSBERG KAMMER (Franken) .... Page 133
KUPFERGRUBE (Nahe) .... Page 256
KUPP, Saarburg (Mosel) .... Page 197
KUPP, Wiltingen (Mosel) .... Page 198
KUPP, Ayl (Mosel) .... Page 196
KUPP "NEUENBERG"[1], Ayl (Mosel) .... Page 194
KUPP "UNTERSTENBERG"[1], Ayl (Mosel) .... Page 195
LÄMMLER (Württemberg) .... Page 436
LANDSKRONE (Ahr) .... Page 63
LANGENBERG (Rheingau) .... Page 345
LANGENMORGEN (Pfalz) .... Page 292
LAURENTIUSLAY (Mosel) .... Page 199
LAY (Mosel) .... Page 200
LAYET (Mosel) .... Page 201
LECKERBERG (Rheinhessen) .... Page 395

INDEX VDP.GROSSE LAGE® SITES

In Alphabetical Order

LEISTENBERG (Nahe)	Page 257
LEITERCHEN (Mosel)	Page 202
LENCHEN (Rheingau)	Page 346
LIEBFRAUENSTIFT-KIRCHENSTÜCK (Rheinhessen)	Page 396
LINNENBRUNNEN (Württemberg)	Page 437
LÖCHLE (Baden)	Page 98
MANDELBERG "AM SPEYRER WEG"[1] (Pfalz)	Page 293
MANDELBERG (Pfalz)	Page 294
MANDELPFAD (Pfalz)	Page 295
MARCOBRUNN (Rheingau)	Page 347
MARIENBURG (Mosel)	Page 203
MAUERBERG "MAUERWEIN" (Baden)	Page 99
MÄUERCHEN (Rheingau)	Page 348
MAUSTAL (Franken)	Page 134
MEERSPINNE-IM MANDELGARTEN (Pfalz)	Page 296
MICHAELSBERG (Württemberg)	Page 438
MICHELSBERG (Pfalz)	Page 297
MITTELHÖLLE (Rheingau)	Page 349
MÖNCHBERG, Mayschoß (Ahr)	Page 64
MÖNCHBERG, Untertürkheim (Württemberg)	Page 442
MÖNCHBERG "BERGE", Stetten (Württemberg)	Page 439
MÖNCHBERG "GEHRNHALDE", Stetten (Württemberg)	Page 440
MÖNCHBERG "ÖDE HALDE", Stetten (Württemberg)	Page 441
MÖNCHBERG "SCHALKSBERG", Stetten (Württemberg)	Page 442
MÖNCHSHOF (Franken)	Page 135
MORSTEIN (Rheinhessen)	Page 397
MÜHLBERG, Pfaffenhofen (Württemberg)	Page 444
MÜHLBERG, Traisen (Nahe)	Page 258
MÜNZBERG (Pfalz)	Page 298
NIEDERBERG HELDEN (Mosel)	Page 204
NIEDERNBERG (Württemberg)	Page 445
NIES'CHEN (Mosel)	Page 205
NONNBERG FUSSHOL (Rheingau)	Page 350
NONNBERG VIER MORGEN (Rheingau)	Page 351
NONNENGARTEN (Mosel)	Page 206
NUSSBRUNNEN (Rheingau)	Page 352

INDEX VDP.GROSSE LAGE® SITES

In Alphabetical Order

OBERER BERG (Württemberg) .... Page 446
OBERER FIRST (Baden) .... Page 100
OCHSENBERG (Württemberg) .... Page 447
OHLIGSBERG (Mosel) .... Page 207
ÖLBERG (Rheinhessen) .... Page 398
ÖLBERG-HART (Pfalz) .... Page 299
OELSBERG (Mittelrhein) .... Page 152
ORBEL (Rheinhessen) .... Page 399
PARES (Rheinhessen) .... Page 400
PATERBERG (Rheinhessen) .... Page 401
PECHSTEIN (Pfalz) .... Page 300
PETTENTHAL (Rheinhessen) .... Page 402
PFAFFENWIES RÖDER (Rheingau) .... Page 353
PFARRWINGERT (Ahr) .... Page 65
PFÜLBEN (Franken) .... Page 136
PITTERMÄNNCHEN (Nahe) .... Page 259
POSTEN (Mittelrhein) .... Page 153
PRÄLAT (Mosel) .... Page 208
PULCHEN (Mosel) .... Page 209
PULVERBUCK (Baden) .... Page 101
PULVERMÄCHER "BERGE" (Württemberg) .... Page 448
PULVERMÄCHER (Württemberg) .... Page 449
RATSHERR (Franken) .... Page 137
RAUSCH (Mosel) .... Page 210
REICHESTAL (Rheingau) .... Page 354
REITERPFAD-ACHTMORGEN (Pfalz) .... Page 301
REITERPFAD-HOFSTÜCK (Pfalz) .... Page 302
REITERPFAD-IN DER HOHL (Pfalz) .... Page 303
RITTERPFAD (Mosel) .... Page 211
RITTERBERG (Württemberg) .... Page 450
RÖDCHEN (Rheingau) .... Page 355
ROSENBERG (Mosel) .... Page 212
ROSENGARTEN, Oestrich-Winkel (Rheingau) .... Page 356
ROSENGARTEN, Rüdesheim (Rheingau) .... Page 357
ROSENKRANZ-IM UNTERN KREUZ (Pfalz) .... Page 304
ROSENKRANZ-ZINKELERDE (Pfalz) .... Page 305

INDEX VDP.GROSSE LAGE® SITES

In Alphabetical Order

ROSENTHAL (Ahr)	Page 66
ROTENBERG (Nahe)	Page 260
ROTER BERG (Württemberg)	Page 451
ROTHENBERG, Geisenheim (Rheingau)	Page 358
ROTHENBERG, Nackenheim (Rheinhessen)	Page 403
ROTHLAUF (Franken)	Page 138
RÖTTGEN (Mosel)	Page 213
RUTHE (Württemberg)	Page 452
SACKTRÄGER (Rheinhessen)	Page 404
SANKT PAUL (Pfalz)	Page 306
SAUMAGEN (Pfalz)	Page 307
SCHARLACHBERG (Rheinhessen)	Page 405
SCHARZHOFBERGER (Mosel)	Page 214
SCHARZHOFBERGER PERGENTSKNOPP (Mosel)	Page 215
SCHÄWER (Pfalz)	Page 308
SCHELLENBRUNNEN (Baden)	Page 102
SCHEMELSBERG (Württemberg)	Page 453
SCHEUERBERG ORTHGANG (Württemberg)	Page 454
SCHEUERBERG STEINKREUZ (Württemberg)	Page 455
SCHIEFERLAY (Ahr)	Page 67
SCHLENZENBERG (Rheingau)	Page 359
SCHLIPSHÄLDE (Württemberg)	Page 456
SCHLOSS JOHANNISBERG (Rheingau)	Page 360
SCHLOSS PROSCHWITZ (Sachsen)	Page 415
SCHLOSS SAARFELSER SCHLOSSBERG (Mosel)	Page 216
SCHLOSS SAARSTEIN (Mosel)	Page 217
SCHLOSS WESTERHAUS (Rheinhessen)	Page 406
SCHLOSSBERG, Achkarren (Baden)	Page 104
SCHLOSSBERG, Castell (Franken)	Page 140
SCHLOSSBERG, Freiburg (Baden)	Page 105
SCHLOSSBERG, Hecklingen (Baden)	Page 106
SCHLOSSBERG, Klingenberg (Franken)	Page 139
SCHLOSSBERG, Neipperg (Württemberg)	Page 457
SCHLOSSBERG, Schloss Vollrads (Rheingau)	Page 361
SCHLOSSBERG MARIENBERG (Baden)	Page 103
SCHLOSSGARTEN VILLINGER (Baden)	Page 107

INDEX VDP.GROSSE LAGE® SITES

In Alphabetical Order

SCHLOSSWENGERT (Württemberg) .... Page 458
SCHONFELS (Mosel) .... Page 218
SCHÖNHELL (Rheingau) .... Page 362
SCHUBERTSLAY (Mosel) .... Page 219
SCHUPEN (Württemberg) .... Page 459
SCHWARZER HERRGOTT (Pfalz) .... Page 309
SELIGMACHER (Rheingau) .... Page 363
SIEGELSBERG (Rheingau) .... Page 364
SILBERBERG (Ahr) .... Page 68
SOMMERHALDE (Baden) .... Page 108
SONNENBERG, Bad Neuenahr (Ahr) .... Page 69
SONNENBERG, Leinsweiler (Pfalz) .... Page 312
SONNENBERG, Schweigen-Rechtenbach (Pfalz) .... Page 313
SONNENBERG "KOSTERT" [1][3] (Pfalz) .... Page 310
SONNENBERG "RÄDLING" [1][3] (Pfalz) .... Page 311
SONNENSTÜCK (Baden) .... Page 109
(SONNENSTUHL) HOHENROTH[1] (Franken) .... Page 141
SONNENUHR, Wehlen (Mosel) .... Page 221
SONNENUHR, Zeltingen (Mosel) .... Page 222
SPIEGELBERG (Baden) .... Page 110
ST. JOST (Mittelrhein) .... Page 154
ST. NIKOLAUS (Rheingau) .... Page 365
STAHLBÜHL (Württemberg) .... Page 460
STEIN, Stetten (Franken) .... Page 142
STEINBERG, Niederhausen (Nahe) .... Page 161
STEINBERG, Traisen (Nahe) .... Page 162
STEIN-BERG[1], Würzburg (Franken) .... Page 143
STEINBERGER (Rheingau) .... Page 366
STEINBUCKEL (Pfalz) .... Page 314
STEINGRUBE (Württemberg) .... Page 461
STEINGRÜBEN (Württemberg) .... Page 462
STEIN-HARFE, Würzburg (Franken) .... Page 144
STIFTBERG HUNSPERG (Württemberg) .... Page 463
STIFTSBERG KLINGE (Württemberg) .... Page 464
STOLZENBERG (Mosel) .... Page 223
STROMBERG (Nahe) .... Page 163

INDEX VDP.GROSSE LAGE® SITES

In Alphabetical Order

SÜSSMUND (Württemberg) .... Page 465
TAFELSTEIN (Rheinhessen) .... Page 407
TREPPCHEN (Mosel) .... Page 224
TROTZENBERG (Ahr) .... Page 70
UHLEN (Mosel) .... Page 228
UHLEN „BLAUFÜSSER LAY"[1] (Mosel) .... Page 225
UHLEN „LAUBACH"[1] (Mosel) .... Page 226
UHLEN „ROTH LAY"[1] (Mosel) .... Page 227
UNGEHEUER (Pfalz) .... Page 315
UNTERER BISCHOFSBERG (Rheingau) .... Page 367
VERRENBERG (Württemberg) .... Page 466
VOLZ (Mosel) .... Page 229
VORDERER WINKLERBERG (Baden) .... Page 111
WALKENBERG (Rheingau) .... Page 368
WARTBERG SONNENSTRAHL® (Württemberg) .... Page 467
WEILBERG (Pfalz) .... Page 316
WEISS ERD (Rheingau) .... Page 369
WIGOLDESBERG (Baden) .... Page 112
WINGERTE (Baden) .... Page 113
WINKLEN (Baden) .... Page 114
WINKLERBERG "FOHRENBERG" (Baden) .... Page 115
WINKLERBERG HINTER WINKLEN (Baden) .... Page 116
WINKLERBERG WANNE (Baden) .... Page 117
WINKLERBERG WINKLERFELD (Baden) .... Page 118
WISSELBRUNNEN (Rheingau) .... Page 370
WOLFSHÖHLE (Mittelrhein) .... Page 155
WORMSBERG (Baden) .... Page 119
WÜRTZBERG (Mosel) .... Page 230
WÜRZGARTEN (Mosel) .... Page 231
ZEHNMORGEN (Rheinhessen) .... Page 408
ZELLERWEG AM SCHWARZEN HERRGOTT (Rheinhessen) .... Page 409

What is the VDP?

200 WINE GROWERS · 13 WINE REGIONS

VDP.GROSSE LAGE® · AUTHENTIC

INNOVATIVE WINES

 *Germany's elite estates*

HANDMADE IN GERMANY

VDP.GROSSES GEWÄCHS® · 13 WINE

HIGH QUALITY STANDARDS · REGIONS

PASSION · VDP.ERSTE LAGE®

200 WINE · SITE CLASSIFICATION

GROWERS · VDP.ORTSWEIN

INDIVIDUALISTS · ORIGIN

TRADITION · ASSOCIATION FOUNDED 1910

EAGLE AND GRAPES BOTTLE CAPSULE

VDP.GUTSWEIN · Artisanal

INDEX VDP.WINERIES

In Alphabetical Order With Their
VDP.GROSSE LAGE® Vineyards

Acham-Magin | Pfalz	KIRCHENSTÜCK (Forst), PECHSTEIN,
	JESUITENGARTEN, UNGEHEUER
Adelmann, Graf | Württemberg	OBERER BERG, GÖTZENBERG
	(Kleinbottwar), SÜSSMUND
Adeneuer, J. J. | Ahr	BURGGARTEN (Heimersheim),
	GÄRKAMMER, KRÄUTERBERG,
	LANDSKRONE, ROSENTHAL, SCHIEFERLAY,
	SILBERBERG (Ahrweiler), SONNENBERG
	(Bad Neuenahr)
Aldinger | Württemberg	LÄMMLER, GIPS "MARIENGLAS®",
	GÖTZENBERG (Uhlbach), PULVERMÄCHER
Allendorf, Fritz | Rheingau	JESUITENGARTEN (Winkel), HASENSPRUNG,
	BERG ROSENECK, BERG ROTTLAND,
	HÖLLENBERG, SCHÖNHELL, JUNGFER,
	DOOSBERG, LENCHEN, KLÄUSERWEG,
	ST. NIKOLAUS
Arnold, Johann | Franken	KAMMER
Arnold, Wilhelm | Franken	PFÜLBEN, HOHENROTH[1]
Baltes, Benedikt | Franken	SCHLOSSBERG (Klingenberg), BISCHOFSBERG
Barth | Rheingau	WISSELBRUNNEN, HASSEL, SCHÖNHELL
	KRANZBERG, ZEHNMORGEN, ROTHENBERG
	(Geisenheim)
Bassermann-Jordan, Geh. Rat Dr. von | Pfalz	KIESELBERG, HOHENMORGEN, KALKOFEN,
	GRAINHÜBEL, LANGENMORGEN,
	KIRCHENSTÜCK (Forst), JESUITENGARTEN
	(Forst), PECHSTEIN, UNGEHEUER,
	FREUNDSTÜCK, ÖLBERG "HART"
Bastian | Mittelrhein	WOLFSHÖHLE, POSTEN, ST. JOST, OELSBERG
Battenfeld Spanier | Rheinhessen	FRAUENBERG, KIRCHENSTÜCK
	(Hohen-Sülzen), ZELLERWEG AM
	SCHWARZEN HERRGOTT
Becker, Brüder Dr. | Rheinhessen	TAFELSTEIN, FALKENBERG
Becker, Friedrich | Pfalz	HEYDENREICH, SANKT PAUL (SP),
	KAMMERBERG (KB)
Bentzel-Sturmfeder, Graf von | Württemberg	ROTER BERG

INDEX VDP.WINERIES

In Alphabetical Order With Their VDP.GROSSE LAGE® Vineyards

Winery	Vineyards
Bercher | Baden	FEUERBERG HASLEN, FEUERBERG KESSELBERG, SCHLOSSGARTEN VILLINGEN
Bergdolt - Klostergut St. Lamprecht | Pfalz	KALKBERG, MANDELBERG "AM SPEYRER WEG", REITERPFAD-ACHTMORGEN
Bernhart | Pfalz	SONNENBERG (Schweigen), SONNENBERG "KOSTERT", SONNENBERG "RÄDLING"
Beurer | Württemberg	PULVERMÄCHER, MÖNCHBERG (Stetten)
Bickel-Stumpf | Franken	MÖNCHSHOF, ROTHLAUF
Blankenhorn | Baden	SONNENSTÜCK
Buhl, Reichsrat von | Pfalz	KIESELBERG, KALKOFEN, REITERPFAD - IN DER HOHL, REITERPFAD-HOFSTÜCK, UNGEHEUER, PECHSTEIN, JESUITENGARTEN (Forst), FREUNDSTÜCK, KIRCHENSTÜCK (Forst)
Bürgerspital zum Hl. Geist | Franken	STEIN-BERG[1], STEIN-HARFE (Monopollage), PFÜLBEN
Bürklin-Wolf, Dr. | Pfalz	KIRCHENSTÜCK (Forst), JESUITENGARTEN (Forst), PECHSTEIN, UNGEHEUER, HOHENMORGEN, LANGENMORGEN, KALKOFEN
Busch, Clemens | Mosel-Saar-Ruwer	MARIENBURG, NONNENGARTEN
Castell'sches Domänenamt, Fürstliches | Franken	SCHLOSSBERG (Castell)
Christmann, A. | Pfalz	IDIG, ÖLBERG-HART, MEERSPINNE-IM MANDELGARTEN, REITERPFAD-HOFSTÜCK, REITERPFAD-IN DER HOHL, LANGENMORGEN
Crusius, Dr. | Nahe	BASTEI, MÜHLBERG, STEINBERG (Traisen), KIRSCHHECK, FELSENBERG (Schloßböckelheim), KUPFERGRUBE,
Dautel | Württemberg	SCHLIPSHÄLDE, SCHUPEN, STEINGRÜBEN, MICHAELSBERG, FORSTBERG
Deutzerhof - Cossmann-Hehle | Ahr	ECK, MÖNCHBERG (Mayschoss), KIRCHENTÜRMCHEN, SCHIEFERLAY, LANDSKRONE, DAUBHAUS, HERRENBERG
Diefenhardt | Rheingau	LANGENBERG (Martinsthal), SCHLENZENBERG

INDEX VDP.WINERIES

In Alphabetical Order With Their VDP.GROSSE LAGE® Vineyards

Diel, Schlossgut | Nahe	GOLDLOCH, BURGBERG, PITTERMÄNNCHEN
Dönnhoff, H. | Nahe	BRÜCKE, LEISTENBERG, HERMANNSHÖHLE,
	KLAMM, KIRSCHHECK, DELLCHEN,
	FELSENBERG (Schloßböckelheim),
	IM KAHLENBERG, KRÖTENPFUHL,
	IM MÜHLENBERG
Drautz-Able | Württemberg	STIFTSBERG, SCHEUERBERG
Ellwanger, Jürgen | Württemberg	ALTENBERG (Schnait), LICHTENBERG,
	HUNGERBERG
Emrich-Schönleber | Nahe	HALENBERG, FRÜHLINGSPLÄTZCHEN,
	AUF DER LAY
Eser, August | Rheingau	LENCHEN, DOOSBERG, SIEGELSBERG,
	NUSSBRUNNEN, WISSELBRUNNEN, HASSEL,
	HASENSPRUNG, JESUITENGARTEN
	(Oestrich-Winkel), SCHÖNHELL, JUNGFER,
	ST. NIKOLAUS
Fendel, Friedrich | Rheingau	BERG SCHLOSSBERG, BERG ROSENECK,
	BERG ROTTLAND, HÖLLENBERG
Fischer, Dr. - Hofstätter Weis | Mosel-Saar-Ruwer	BOCKSTEIN, KUPP (Saarburg)
Fitz-Ritter | Pfalz	MICHELSBERG, HERRENBERG (Ungstein)
Flick, Joachim | Rheingau	NONNBERG "VIER MORGEN",
	NONNBERG "FUSSHOHL", HÖLLE
	(Hochheim), KÖNIGIN VIKTORIABERG
Franckenstein, Freiherr von und zu | Baden	ABTSBERG "PFAFFENGÄSSLE"[1], NEUGESETZ
	"MARIENQUELLE"[1], SCHÜTZENBERG "IM
	HIMMELREICH" (not yet defined)
Freimuth | Rheingau	KLÄUSERWEG, MÄUERCHEN
Fröhlich, Michael | Franken	AM LUMPEN 1655®
Fürst, Rudolf | Franken	CENTGRAFENBERG, HUNDSRÜCK,
	KARTHÄUSER, SCHLOSSBERG (Klingenberg)
Gallais, Le | Mosel-Saar-Ruwer	BRAUNE KUPP (Monopole Site)
Geisenheim Hochschule University | Rheingau	ROTHENBERG (Geisenheim), KLÄUSERWEG
Geltz-Zilliken, Forstmeister | Mosel-Saar-Ruwer	RAUSCH, BOCKSTEIN
Glaser-Himmelstoss | Franken	keine VDP.GROSSE LAGE®
Grans-Fassian | Mosel-Saar-Ruwer	LAURENTIUSLAY, APOTHEKE, HOFBERGER,
	GOLDTRÖPFCHEN

INDEX VDP.WINERIES

In Alphabetical Order With Their VDP.GROSSE LAGE® Vineyards

Winery	Vineyards
Groebe, K. F. | Rheinhessen	AULERDE, KIRCHENSPIEL, MORSTEIN
Gunderloch | Rheinhessen	ROTHENBERG (Nackenheim), PETTENTHAL, HIPPING, ÖLBERG
Gut Hermannsberg | Nahe	KUPFERGRUBE, FELSENBERG, (Schloßböckelheim), HERMANNSBERG, (Monopole Site), KLAMM, STEINBERG, (Niederhausen), KERTZ, ROTENBERG, BASTEI
Gutzler | Rheinhessen	MORSTEIN, BRUNNENHÄUSCHEN, LIEBFRAUENSTIFT-KIRCHENSTÜCK
Haag, Fritz | Mosel-Saar-Ruwer	JUFFER, JUFFER - SONNENUHR
Haag, Willi | Mosel-Saar-Ruwer	JUFFER, JUFFER - SONNENUHR, GOLDTRÖPFCHEN
Haart | Mosel-Saar-Ruwer	GOLDTRÖPFCHEN, GRAFENBERG, KREUZWINGERT, DOMHERR, OHLIGSBERG
Haidle, Karl | Württemberg	PULVERMÄCHER, MÖNCHBERG (Stetten), MÖNCHBERG "BERGE"[1], MÖNCHBERG "GEHRNHALDE"[1], BURGHALDE (Schnait)
Hamm | Rheingau	JESUITENGARTEN (Winkel), HASENSPRUNG
Heger, Dr. | Baden	WINKLEN, WINKLERBERG HINTER WINKLEN, WINKLERBERG WANNE, VORDERER WINKLERBERG, SCHLOSSBERG (Achkarren)
Heid | Württemberg	LÄMMLER, PULVERMÄCHER
Heitlinger | Baden	SCHELLENBRUNNEN, WORMSBERG, SPIEGELBERG, KÖNIGSBECHER, EICHELBERG, WIGOLDESBERG
Hessen, Prinz von | Rheingau	KLAUS, JESUITENGARTEN (Winkel), HASENSPRUNG, KLÄUSERWEG, DOOSBERG
Heymann-Löwenstein | Mosel-Saar-Ruwer	KIRCHBERG (Hatzenport), STOLZENBERG, UHLEN, UHLEN "BLAUFÜSSER LAY"[1], UHLEN "LAUBACH"[1], UHLEN "ROTH LAY"[1], RÖTTGEN
Höfler, Bernhard | Franken	APOSTELGARTEN
Hohenbeilstein, Schlossgut | Württemberg	SCHLOSSWENGERT (Monopole Site), STAHLBÜHL
Hohenlohe Oehringen, Fürst | Württemberg	VERRENBERG (Monopole Site)
Hövel, von | Mosel-Saar-Ruwer	HÜTTE (Monopole Site), SCHARZHOFBERGER, HÖRECKER

INDEX VDP.WINERIES

In Alphabetical Order With Their
VDP.GROSSE LAGE® Vineyards

Winery	Vineyards
Huber, Bernhard	Baden	BIENENBERG, BIENENBERG "WILDENSTEIN"[1], SOMMERHALDE, SCHLOSSBERG (Hecklingen)
Johannisberg, Domäne Schloss	Rheingau	SCHLOSS JOHANNISBERG
Johannishof	Rheingau	BERG ROTTLAND, HÖLLE (Johannisberg), KLÄUSERWEG
Jost, Toni	Mittelrhein / Rheingau	IM HAHN, ST. JOST, WOLFSHÖHLE, WALKENBERG
Juliusspital Würzburg	Franken	STEIN-BERG[1], JULIUS-ECHTER-BERG, PFÜLBEN, KARTHÄUSER
Jung, Jakob	Rheingau	HOHENRAIN, SIEGELSBERG
Kanitz, Graf von	Rheingau	PFAFFENWIES RÖDER, KAPELLENBERG
Karthäuserhof	Mosel-Saar-Ruwer	KARTHÄUSERHOFBERG (Monopole Site)
Kaufmann	Rheingau	WISSELBRUNNEN, HASSEL, SCHÖNHELL
Keller, Franz	Baden	SCHLOSSBERG (Achkarren), EICHBERG, KIRCHBERG (Oberrotweil), ENSELBERG, BASSGEIGE KÄHNER, BASSGEIGE LEH
Keller	Rheinhessen	HUBACKER, BÜRGEL, FRAUENBERG (Nieder-Flörsheim), KIRCHSPIEL, MORSTEIN, BRUNNENHÄUSCHEN, AULERDE, PETTENTHAL, HIPPING
Kesseler August	Rheingau	HÖLLENBERG, BERG SCHLOSSBERG, BERG ROSENECK, BISCHOFSBERG (Rüdesheim), SEELIGMACHER
Kesselstadt, Reichsgraf von	Mosel-Saar-Ruwer	JOSEPHSHÖFER (Monopole Site), DOMPROBST, JUFFER, JUFFER-SONNENUHR, DOMHERR, GOLDTRÖPFCHEN, SONNENUHR (Wehlen), SCHARZHOFBERGER, SCHARZHOFBERGER, PERGENTSKNOPP, GOTTESFUSS, BRAUNFELS, VOLZ, NIES'CHEN, KEHRNAGEL
Kistenmacher-Hengerer	Württemberg	STIFTSBERG, STIFTSBERG KLINGE, WARTBERG SONNENSTRAHL®
Knebel	Mosel-Saar-Ruwer	UHLEN, UHLEN "BLAUFÜSSER LAY"[1], UHLEN "LAUBACH"[1], UHLEN "ROTH LAY"[1], RÖTTGEN
Knipser	Pfalz	KIRSCHGARTEN, STEINBUCKEL, IM GROSSEN GARTEN, MANDELPFAD

INDEX VDP.WINERIES

In Alphabetical Order With Their
VDP.GROSSE LAGE® Vineyards

Winery	Vineyards
Knyphausen, Baron | Rheingau	MARCOBRUNN, HOHENRAIN, SIEGELSBERG, WISSELBRUNNEN
Kranz | Pfalz	KALMIT, KIRCHBERG (Ilbesheim)
Kreuzberg, H. J. | Ahr	PFARRWINGERT, HARDTBERG, ROSENTHAL, SILBERBERG (Ahrweiler) SONNENBERG (Bad Neuenahr), SCHIEFERLAY, KIRCHTÜRMCHEN, TROTZENBERG, ALTE LAY
Krone Assmannshausen | Rheingau	HÖLLENBERG, SCHÖNHELL
Kruger-Rumpf | Nahe/Rheinhessen	IM LANGENBERG, IM PITTERBERG, DAUTENPFLÄNZER, GOLDLOCH, BURGBERG, SCHARLACHBERG
Kühling-Gillot | Rheinhessen	ROTHENBERG (Nackenheim), PETTENTHAL, ÖLBERG, HIPPING, ORBEL, KREUZ, SACKTRÄGER, BURGWEG
Kühn, Peter Jakob | Rheingau	LENCHEN, DOOSBERG, ST. NIKOLAUS, JUNGFER, SCHÖNHELL
Kuhn, Philipp | Pfalz	KIRSCHGARTEN, STEINBUCKEL, SAUMAGEN, SCHWARZER HERRGOTT, IM GROSSEN GARTEN
Künstler | Rheingau	HÖLLE (Hochheim), KIRCHENSTÜCK (Hochheim), REICHESTAL, DOMDECHANEY, WEISS ERD, BERG ROTTLAND, BERG SCHLOSSBERG, HÖLLENBERG
Laible, Andreas | Baden	PLAUELRAIN AM BÜHL, PLAUELRAIN STOLLENBERG (not yet defined)
Lämmlin-Schindler | Baden	FRAUENBERG (Mauchen)
Lanius-Knab | Mittelrhein	BERNSTEIN-LAUERBAUM, OELSBERG
Lauer, Peter | Mosel-Saar-Ruwer	SAARFEILSER, FEILS, KUPP (Ayl), KUPP "NEUENBERG"[1], KUPP "UNTERSTENBERG"[1], SCHONFELS
Leitz | Rheingau	BERG SCHLOSSBERG, BERG ROSENECK, BERG ROTTLAND, BERG KAISERSTEINFELS, ROSENGARTEN (Rüdesheim) (Monopol)
Lieser, Schloss - Thomas Haag | Mosel-Saar-Ruwer	NIEDERBERG HELDEN, JUFFER SONNENUHR, JUFFER, SONNENUHR (Wehlen), HIMMELREICH (Graach), DOCTOR, GOLDTRÖPFCHEN

INDEX VDP.WINERIES

In Alphabetical Order With Their VDP.GROSSE LAGE® Vineyards

Winery	Vineyards
Loosen, Dr. | Mosel-Saar-Ruwer	TREPPCHEN, PRÄLAT, WÜRZGARTEN, SONNENUHR (Wehlen), LAY, HIMMELREICH (Graach), DOMPROBST, FÖRSTERLAY, ROSENBERG
Löwenstein, Fürst | Franken	FÜRSTLICHER KALLMUTH®, JUNGFER, SCHÖNHELL
Lützkendorf | Saale-Unstrut	HOHE GRÄTE
Markgraf von Baden | Baden	CHORHERRNHALDE, SCHLOSSBERG, MARIENBERG
Maximin Grünhaus | Mosel-Saar-Ruwer	ABTSBERG (Monopole Site), HERRENBERG (Mertesdorf, Monopole Site), BRUDERSBERG (Monopole Site)
May, Rudolf | Franken	ROTHLAUF, HIMMELSPFAD
Meßmer, Herbert | Pfalz	SCHÄWER, IM GOLDENEN JOST, AUF DER HOHL
Meyer-Näkel | Ahr	PFARRWINGERT, HARDTBERG, KRÄUTERBERG, SONNENBERG (Bad Neuenahr), TROTZENBERG, DAUBHAUS, ROSENTHAL, LANDSKRONE, BURGGARTEN
Michel | Baden	SCHLOSSBERG (Achkarren)
Milz, Josef | Mosel-Saar-Ruwer	LEITERCHEN, FELSENKOPF, APOTHEKE, HOFBERGER
Minges Theo | Pfalz	HÖLLE - UNTERER FAULENBERG, ROSENKRANZ - IM UNTERN KREUZ, ROSENKRANZ - ZINKELERDE, SCHÄWER
Mosbacher, Georg | Pfalz	JESUITENGARTEN (Forst), UNGEHEUER, PECHSTEIN, FREUNDSTÜCK, KIESELBERG, KALKOFEN
Müller, Egon - Scharzhof | Mosel-Saar-Ruwer	SCHARZHOFBERGER, BRAUNE KUPP, KUPP
Müller Stiftung, Georg | Rheingau	WISSELBRUNNEN, NUSSBRUNNEN, HASSEL, JUNGFER
Müller, Matthias | Mittelrhein	ENGELSTEIN, AN DER RABENLAY
Müller-Catoir | Pfalz	BÜRGERGARTEN IM BREUMEL, MEERSPINNE - IM MANDELGARTEN
Münzberg, Gunter Keßler | Pfalz	MÜNZBERG
Neipperg, Graf | Württemberg	RUTHE, SCHLOSSBERG (Neipperg)

INDEX VDP.WINERIES

In Alphabetical Order With Their VDP.GROSSE LAGE® Vineyards

Winery	Vineyards
Nelles | Ahr	LANDSKRONE, BURGGARTEN, SONNENBERG (Bad Neuenahr), SCHIEFERLAY
Neus, J. | Rheinhessen	PARES, HORN
Neuweier, Schloss - Robert Schätzle | Baden	MAUERBERG "MAUERWEIN"[1], GOLDENES LOCH
Nik Weis - St. Urbans-Hof | Mosel-Saar-Ruwer	LAURENTIUSLAY, GÖLDTRÖPFCHEN, BOCKSTEIN, SAARFEILSER, FEILS, LAYET
Othegraven, von | Mosel-Saar-Ruwer	ALTENBERG (Kanzem), HERRENBERGER BOCKSTEIN, KUPP (Wiltingen)
Pawis | Saale-Unstrut	EDELACKER
Pfeffingen | Pfalz	WEILBERG, HERRENBERG (Ungstein)
Piedmont | Mosel-Saar-Ruwer	PULCHEN
Prinz | Rheingau	JUNGFER, SCHÖNHELL, JESUITENGARTEN (Winkel)
Prinz Salm | Nahe / Rheinhessen	JOHANNISBERG, FELSENECK (Wallhausen), SCHARLACHBERG, KIRCHBERG
Prüm, Joh. Jos | Mosel-Saar-Ruwer	SONNENUHR (Wehlen), HIMMELREICH (Graach), SONNENUHR (Zeltingen), LAY, BADSTUBE, JOHANNISBRÜNNCHEN
Prüm, S. A. | Mosel-Saar-Ruwer	SONNENUHR (Wehlen), DOMPROBST, HIMMELREICH (Graach), LAY, GRABEN, WÜRZGARTEN, TREPPCHEN
Rappenhof | Rheinhessen	PETTENTHAL, ÖLBERG, SACKTRÄGER, HERRENBERG (Oppenheim)
Ratzenberger | Mittelrhein	WOLFSHÖHLE, POSTEN, ST. JOST, OELSBERG
Ravensburg, Burg | Baden	HUSARENKAPPE, LÖCHLE, DICKER FRANZ, KAPELLENBERG (Eichelberg)
Rebholz, Ökonomierat | Pfalz	KASTANIENBUSCH, KASTANIENBUSCH-"KÖPPEL"[1], MANDELBERG, IM SONNENSCHEIN, "GANZ HORN"[1]
Ress, Balthasar | Rheingau	NUSSBRUNNEN, WISSELBRUNNEN, MARCOBRUNN, BERG SCHLOSSBERG, BERG ROTTLAND, HÖLLENBERG, DOOSBERG, JUNGFER

INDEX VDP.WINERIES

In Alphabetical Order With Their VDP.GROSSE LAGE® Vineyards

Winery	Vineyards
Rings	Pfalz	SAUMAGEN, WEILBERG
Ruck, Johann	Franken	JULIUS-ECHTER-BERG
Roth	Franken	keine VDP.GROSSE LAGE®
Saarstein, Schloss	Mosel-Saar-Ruwer	SCHLOSS SAARSTEINER (Monopole Site)
Salwey	Baden	HENKENBERG, EICHBERG, KIRCHBERG (Oberrotweil)
Sauer, Horst	Franken	AM LUMPEN 1655®
Sauer, Rainer	Franken	AM LUMPEN 1655®
Schaefer, Karl	Pfalz	PECHSTEIN, MICHELSBERG, WEILBERG, HERRENBERG (Ungstein)
Schaefer, Willi	Mosel-Saar-Ruwer	HIMMELREICH (Graach), DOMPROBST, SONNENUHR (Wehlen)
Schäfer, Joh. Bapt	Nahe	PITTERMÄNNCHEN, GOLDLOCH
Schäfer-Fröhlich	Nahe	FELSENECK (Bockenau), STROMBERG, FRÜHLINGSPLÄTZCHEN, HALENBERG, KUPFERGRUBE, FELSENBERG (Schloßböckelheim)
Schäffer, Egon	Franken	AM LUMPEN 1655®
Schätzel	Rheinhessen	PETTENTHAL, HIPPING, ÖLBERG
Schlör	Baden	OBERER FIRST
Schloss Proschwitz - Prinz zur Lippe	Sachsen	SCHLOSS PROSCHWITZ (Monopole Site)
Schlumberger, H.	Baden	WINGERTE
Schmitt's Kinder	Franken	PFÜLBEN, HOHENROTH[1]
Schnaitmann, Rainer	Württemberg	LÄMMLER, GÖTZENBERG (Uhlbach), ALTENBERG (Schnait)
Schönleber, F. B.	Rheingau	ST. NIKOLAUS, JESUITENGARTEN (Winkel), HASENSPRUNG, DOOSBERG, LENCHEN
Schwab, Gregor	Franken	ROTHLAUF
Schwane, Zur	Franken	RATSHERR, AM LUMPEN 1655®
Seeger	Baden	HERRENBERG OBERKLAMM, HERREBERG SPERMEN, BURG (not yet defined), HERRENBERG LANGE WINGERTE
Siben, Georg - Erben	Pfalz	GRAINHÜBEL, KALKOFEN, KIESELBERG, LANGENMORGEN, HOHENMORGEN, UNGEHEUER
Siegrist	Pfalz	SONNENBERG (Leinsweiler), KALMIT

INDEX VDP.WINERIES

In Alphabetical Order With Their VDP.GROSSE LAGE® Vineyards

Winery	Vineyards
Sommerhausen, Schloss | Franken	"ALTTENBERG 1172"
Spreitzer, Josef | Rheingau	ROSENGARTEN (Oestrich), LENCHEN, DOOSBERG, WISSELBRUNNEN, ST. NIKOLAUS, JESUITENGARTEN (Winkel), SCHÖNHELL, JUNGFER
St. Antony | Rheinhessen	PETTENTHAL, ÖLBERG, HIPPING, ORBEL, PATERBERG, BRUDERSBERG, KRANZBERG, ZEHNMORGEN, ROTHENBERG (Nackenheim)
Staatliche Weinbaudomäne Oppenheim | Rheinhessen	ÖLBERG, GLÖCK, PETTENTHAL, ROTHENBERG (Nackenheim), HERRENBERG (Oppenheim), SACKTRÄGER
Staatlicher Hofkeller Würzburg | Franken	STEIN-BERG[1], PFÜLBEN, BISCHOFSBERG (Großheubach)
Staatsweingut Freiburg | Baden	SCHLOSSBERG (Freiburg), DOKTORGARTEN
Staatsweingut Weinsberg | Württemberg	BURG WILDECK, HIMMELREICH (Gundelsheim), SCHEMELSBERG
Staatsweingüter, Hessische - Kloster Eberbach | Rheingau	STEINBERGER (Monopole Site), HÖLLE (Hochheim), DOMDECHANEY, KIRCHENSTÜCK (Hochheim), BAIKENKOPF, GEHRN KESSELRING, MARCOBRUNN, SIEGELSBERG, BERG SCHLOSSBERG, BERG ROSENECK, BERG ROTTLAND, HÖLLENBERG
Stein, Am - Ludwig Knoll | Franken	STEIN (Stetten), PFÜLBEN, STEIN-HARFE, STEIN-BERG[1], HOHENROTH[1]
Stiftungsweingut Vereinigte Hospitien | Mosel-Saar-Ruwer	GOLDTRÖPFCHEN, SCHUBERTSLAY, DOMHERR, HÖLLE (Wiltingen - Monopole), SCHARZHOFBERGER, KUPP (Wiltingen), AUGENSCHEINER (Monopole Site), SCHLOSS SAARFELSER SCHLOSSBERG (Monopole Site), ALTENBERG (Kanzem)
Stigler | Baden	VORDERER WINKLERBERG, WINKLERBERG WINKLEN, WINKLERBERG

INDEX VDP.WINERIES

In Alphabetical Order With Their VDP.GROSSE LAGE® Vineyards

....	FOHRENBERG, WINKLERBERG
....	WINKLERFELD, SCHLOSSBERG (Freiburg),
....	EICHBERG
Stodden, Jean | Ahr	HERRENBERG (Rech), ROSENTHAL,
....	SONNENBERG (Bad Neuenahr),
....	MÖNCHBERG (Mayschoss), HARDTBERG
Störrlein Krenig | Franken	HOHENROTH[1]
Thanisch, Wwe. Dr. H. - Erben Thanisch | Mosel-Saar-Ruwer	
....	GRABEN, LAY, BADSTUBE, DOCTOR,
....	NIEDERBERGER HELDEN, JUFFER, JUFFER
....	SONNENUHR, DOMPROBST
Vollrads, Schloss | Rheingau	SCHLOSSBERG (Schloss Vollrads),
....	GREIFFENBERG
Volxem, Van | Mosel-Saar-Ruwer	SCHARZHOFBERGER, SCHARZHOFBERGER
....	PERGENTSKNOPP, BRAUNFELS,
....	GOTTESFUSS, VOLZ, KUPP (Wiltingen),
....	ALTENBERG (Kanzem), GOLDBERG,
....	RITTERPFAD
von Oetinger | Rheingau	MARCOBRUNN, SIEGELSBERG, HOHENRAIN
Wachtstetter | Württemberg	STEINGRUBE, OCHSENBERG, MÜHLBERG,
....	GAISSBERG
Wagner, Dr. | Mosel-Saar-Ruwer	RAUSCH, KUPP (Saarburg), BOCKSTEIN
Wagner-Stempel | Rheinhessen	HÖLLBERG, HEERKRETZ
Wegeler, Geheimrat J. | Mosel-Saar-Ruwer	DOCTOR, LAY, GRABEN, BADSTUBE,
....	SONNENUHR (Wehlen), HIMMELREICH
....	(Graach)
Wegeler, Geheimrat J. | Rheingau	BERG SCHLOSSBERG, BERG ROSENECK,
....	BERG ROTTLAND, ROTHENBERG
....	(Geisenheim), KLÄUSERWEG, HÖLLE
....	(Johannisberg), HASENSPRUNG,
....	JESUITENGARTEN (Winkel), ST.NIKOLAUS,
....	LENCHEN, ROSENGARTEN (Oestrich),
....	DOOSBERG, SCHÖNHELL, HÖLLENBERG
Wehrheim, Dr. | Pfalz	KASTANIENBUSCH,
....	KASTANIENBUSCH "KÖPPEL"[1], MANDELBERG
Weil, Robert | Rheingau	GRÄFENBERG

INDEX VDP.WINERIES

In Alphabetical Order With Their VDP.GROSSE LAGE® Vineyards

Weltner, Paul | Franken	HOHELEITE, JULIUS-ECHTER-BERG
Werner, Domdechant | Rheingau	DOMDECHANEY, KIRCHENSTÜCK
	(Hochheim), HÖLLE (Hochheim),
	REICHESTAL
Westerhaus, Schloss | Rheinhessen	SCHLOSS WESTERHAUS (Monopole Site)
Winning, von | Pfalz	KALKOFEN, GRAINHÜBEL, KIESELBERG,
	HOHENMORGEN, LANGENMORGEN,
	UNGEHEUER, JESUITENGARTEN (Forst),
	KIRCHENSTÜCK (Forst), PECHSTEIN
Winter | Rheinhessen	GEYERSBERG, LECKERBERG, KLOPPBERG
Wirsching, Hans | Franken	JULIUS-ECHTER-BERG, KRONSBERG KAMMER
Wittmann | Rheinhessen	MORSTEIN, BRUNNENHÄUSCHEN,
	KIRCHSPIEL, AULERDE
Wöhrle | Baden	HERRENTISCH, KRONENBÜHL GOTTSACKER,
	KIRCHGASSE
Wöhrwag | Württemberg	HERZOGENBERG, ALTENBERG
	(Untertürkheim)
Württemberg, Herzog von | Württemberg	EILFINGERBERG KLOSTERSTÜCK,
	BROTWASSER, MÖNCHBERG
	(Untertürkheim), KÄSBERG
Zehnthof, Theo Luckert | Franken	MAUSTAL
Zimmerling, Klaus | Sachsen	KÖNIGLICHER WEINBERG

WHO's AFRAID OF TERROIR?

by
Reinhard Heymann-Löwenstein

Selektion J, Cuvee Max, Spätlese***, Alte Reben, Reserve ... let's take a little journey back to the wine world of the 1990s. To an era when the names of world-famous communities and classified sites lost much of their radiance and their bottles were exiled, at best dolled up with a Spätlese Prädikat, to the lower shelves of discount supermarkets. A time when all that had elevated German wine to the absolute pinnacle of popularity during the belle époque was now burned on the altar of cheap marketing to fuel the post-war boom. A period when high-quality wines were fundamentally defined by the names of their famous winegrowing estates. Usually in connection with a few trendy terms like "dry" and "organic" and some catchy suffix.

The 90s also marked the start of the decade of biotechnology. After years of yield stimulation, concentration and hygiene, the so-called "new enological procedures," combined with cultured yeasts, enzymes and the like, rang in a new age of wine. The techniques of modern food design allowed for previously inconceivable options for improving or—depending on your point of view—manipulating tastes. And the winemaker? Was he to play the role of Miraculix, brewing a fine-tasting magic potion to fend off the wine invaders from Roman fields, or was he instead more an incarnation of Frankenstein, sinning against creation by making monsters? Whatever your view ... there's no denying that wine was slowly but surely assuming its place in a globalized industrial world. "Optimization of taste!" the enological zeitgeist proclaimed.

And then, suddenly, came the "T" word. TERROIR. And what a word! What a sound, or better "quel son magnifique," since everything sounds more mellifluous in French. The T word resonates with earth, nature and authenticity. Nebulous and secretive, it also plays on the growing yen for spirituality. While wine production has catapulted into the industrial age on the back of the sober spirit of

Back-breaking Work or Magic

science, that Enlightenment ends in the marketing department. Nobody sells wine based on analytical data. The product is pitched using emotions tuned to the target audience. As befits the zeitgeist. Socialism may have ultimately relinquished its claim

WHO's AFRAID OF TERROIR?

Will-o'-the-wisps in the Vineyard

to societal utopia and right now the civic ideal of "liberté, égalité, fraternité" can muster little more than a tired smile. Our concerns are primarily about sea levels and hermit beetles and, increasingly, the search for regional identity, the longing for a homeland. Reunification has restored the word "Germany" for use in polite company and, truly, we owe a great deal to a young generation of winemakers who have done so much to rejuvenate the musty image of German wines. Brimming with positivity, their bottles are conquering the menus of star restaurants and the hearts of wine geeks. And they taste good! And they keep getting better! Red grapes have been liberated from their fetters and are blossoming into fantastic red wines, while fat Ruländers have pupated into gossamer Pinot Gris. Baroque Silvaners have transformed into fleet-footed ballerinas and formerly syrupy Rieslings now radiate elegance, power and electric minerality.

If only it weren't for all those odd names. Spätlese trocken, Auslese trocken… what works at least to some degree on the German market leaves the rest of the world shaking its head. After all, hadn't they just learned that "Spätlese" and "Auslese" were synonyms for residually sweet wines? And now these same wines were all supposed to be dry?

What was going on here? Concerned visionaries came together to brainstorm… and thus emerged the concept of the "Erstes Gewächs." It drew on the old English label of "first growth," with the premium dry wines from the VDP now given not just a new name, but also a sensible context: classification of the vineyards. From Öchsle to the vineyard! What a provocative break from a system of wine classification that had been in place for a century and was ostensibly based on objective facts.

The classification movement gained momentum within the VDP. For wine legislation reasons, the Erstes Gewächs ('first growths') made its way to the Rheingau, while other regions proclaimed Grosses Gewächs ('great growths') and the Mosel sublimated their finest vineyards with the title of Erste Lage ('premier cru'). Chaos all the way down the line. The new millennium began with hard discussions within the VDP. The difficult and wearisome process of ratifying new classifications lasted until 2012: Estate-level "Gutswein" as the solid foundation, village-level "Ortswein" as a

WHO's AFRAID OF TERROIR?

more upscale option, followed by high-end Erste Lage and ultimately crowned by the crème de la crème Grosse Lage. The names of a thousand single sites deemed unworthy of classification were made to disappear; Kabinett, Spätlese and Auslese would now communicate a fruity taste profile, while dry high-end wines would bear the names Erstes Gewächs and Grosses Gewächs, respectively.

So far, so good. More than good, in fact. Very good. Because a uniform, origin-based system for communicating wine across an entire country, in 13 different growing regions with different histories and sensibilities, is a formidable task indeed! Without any intervention by state institutions, the VDP delivered a monumental achievement in wine culture, one that might well be seen as the first truly successful economic innovation of a reunited Germany's wine world. And indeed, Germany's finest classified single sites are now shining all the brighter in the wine firmament. And Grosses Gewächs wines, popularly known as "GG," are in international demand, with prices rising.

Stones or Terroir

There are still open questions, naturally. Have all vineyards been sensibly delineated, and have the best varieties been approved for them? A Grosses Gewächs from a Grosse Lage—isn't that a bit of a tautology? How restrictive should the requirements for vine density, yield volumes and taste profiles be? How ecological, how sustainable should and must terroir wines be? And, since the word is already on our lips: when does a wine really become a 'terroir wine'?

Vineblot Test

The French word encompasses not just a great deal of soil and region, but also, depending on how you interpret it, the winemaker and a bit of what Germans

WHO's AFRAID OF TERROIR?

call 'Heimat,' or 'homeland.' A terroir wine is a wine where these dimensions are there in the glass to be discovered. At first blush, sounds fine. Terroir is origin. OK. But what does a vineyard taste like? How about a region?

Changing climate, new grape varieties, cultural taboos, technical innovations ... wine has always been in a state of flux. In Europe, 'typical' and 'traditional' only function as taste guidelines if the terms are limited to a relatively brief window of time. And what do we do with California? Are they not allowed to have terroir wines? And what about a Yellow Tail that tastes like Australia, or a glass of Blue Nun that tastes like Rheinhessen? Those ARE wines with a typical regional character. Which makes them terroir wines too, right? And then what? Maybe we're better off just forgetting the T word? Right?

No. We shouldn't forget about it. We should refine it.

What do modern interpretations of original sin, feminist dreams of the matriarchy, kitsch economic romanticism and natural wine propaganda have in common? The concept of Mother Nature as good and egoistic humans as evil. This ideologically dangerous refrain has more than just a bit of Pied Piper to it, but it absolutely reflects the current foggy-brained zeitgeist. In reality, vineyards are not a natural landscape and wine is anything but a natural product. Vineyards and wines need to be wrested out of nature. They are the children of civilization and belong to the realm of agriculture—probably the oldest form of productive interaction between man and nature.

A Matter of Perspective ...

And this is where a contemporary approach begins. With a culture that questions what might represent a sensible interaction between man and nature. Where does the loving treatment end, where does violence begin? Where does ecologically responsible action turn into the annihilation of our means of livelihood? When does agricultural industriousness tip into outright industry? How much individualism can be sustained within a taste-based interpretation of a vineyard? Or, posed a different way: How much acoustic amplification is acceptable for an opera? How much retouching work in photography? What remains of "the work of art in the age of mechanical reproduction" (Walter Benjamin)?

WHO's AFRAID OF TERROIR?

Let's move to the concrete and explore a specific aspect, namely the category of so-called 'cultured yeasts.' Good or bad? Naturally good, the medical world says, since it helps reduce the amount of sulfur and produces fewer allergic histamines. Works for us, the organic movement says—as long as there's no genetic manipulation. No problem, say the Orthodox Jews—as long as it's processed kosher. Bad, say the Anthroposophists—alcohol should disappear from our lives one way or the other. We don't need it, says tradition—after all, we've gotten by just fine without it for millennia. Absolutely not, says consistency—because the various different wild yeasts are precisely what is responsible for the taste of authenticity, beyond soil of course. Absolutely, says the Controlling department—otherwise the risks are too great. Don't care, says Ignorance—as long as it tastes good. Super, says Marketing—because if we select the right kind of yeast, then I can pursue precisely the tastes my customers want.

And the yeast itself? Was it injected with foreign DNA? Did the gene scalpel do some nipping and tucking? Or was it bred in the classic manner, selecting for specific characteristics? Did it originally come from the region's vineyards? Or even from the winegrower's own vineyard? Or was it fished out from the grower's own wine and then painstakingly cultured and reproduced?

And what about when the yeast is stirred multiple times during vinification, and the wine sees significant oxygen and almost no sulfur, and the taste of the vineyard can only be guessed at?

Just like so many other aspects of terroir, there is no right or wrong here, just sensibility, perspective and a cultured attitude. (And thank the gods that we live in a relatively pluralistic society!) Terroir is bound up with complexity and prefers being conceived and perceived systematically. Terroir is contradictory and disruptive.

Homeland

Is this all too complex, uncertain or just annoying? Prefer industrial wine? Fine, no problem. The globalized wine market offers a hawker's delight of reproduceable taste experiences, with the right feeling for every target audience, all in the right price segment.

WHO's AFRAID OF TERROIR?

Terroir wines are the cultural alternative. They invite you on a trip into the space between structure and chaos, into uncertainty and surprise, toward provocation and authentic enjoyment. Terroir wines guide us through various regions, geological formations and climatic conditions. And they accompany us through different cultures, people, dreams and fantasies. Terroir wines reflect the state of our souls and expand our consciousness. They are perhaps the most pleasurable aspect of emancipation.

The VDP.CLASSIFICATION

VDP. DIE PRÄDIKATSWEINGÜTER

Since vintage 2012, all members of the VDP.Prädikatsweingüter have been in the process of reorganizing their portfolios to conform with the classification.

The classification of the VDP.Prädikatsweingüter is based on the significance of the vineyard as the decisive mark of quality for top-quality wines. Henceforth, only wines that express site-specific characteristics will bear a vineyard designation on their labels. The goal of the VDP.Classification is to assess the quality potential of Germany's very best vineyard sites; secure the future of Germany's viticultural landscape; restore esteem for Germany's outstanding dry wines; and underscore the significance of traditional Prädikat wines with natural, ripe sweetness. The implementation of the four-tier VDP.CLASSIFICATION began with vintage 2012.

The VDP
CLASSIFICATION PYRAMID

	DRY:	NATURAL RIPE SWEETNESS:
VDP. GROSSE LAGE®	VDP. GROSSES GEWÄCHS®	traditional Prädikats®
VDP. ERSTE LAGE®	Qualitätswein	traditional Prädikats®
VDP. ORTSWEIN	Qualitätswein	traditional Prädikats®
VDP. GUTSWEIN	Qualitätswein	Qualitätswein & traditional Prädikats®

VDP.GROSSE LAGE®

The Peak of the Pyramid

SITE CLASSIFICATION CRITERIA
In 2012, a procedure was ratified for determining eligibility for potential VDP.GROSSE LAGE® sites. It called for an in-depth review of all existing Erste Lage sites. The new VDP.GROSSE LAGE® sites can be carved out of larger vineyards that had been drawn overly broad or which were topographically heterogeneous. They can now also be registered by their geographical designations of origin (protected designation of origin or PDO) or, thanks to a modification to wine law, by their lieu-dit. This process remains a work in progress, as the list of sites can be expected to change periodically through new members and changes in ownership.

GRAPE VARIETIES
Restricted to varieties defined by the regional association as suitable for the specific vineyard.

MAXIMUM YIELDS
Yield volumes are restricted to a maximum of 50 hl/ha.

HARVEST
Grapes are harvested selectively, by hand. The harvest fruit must be physiologically fully ripe.

VINIFICATION
The wines are produced exclusively using traditional methods and techniques.

CERTIFICATION
Beyond the standard operations audits for VDP.Members, wines from VDP.GROSSE LAGE® sites are also subject to additional inspections and monitoring: quality-oriented work in the vineyard and, in particular, yield volumes are monitored for each vineyard throughout the entire growing season and in the weeks prior to harvest. The wines are audited and certified by a testing commission before and after bottling.

TASTE PROFILES
Wines meeting the legal criteria for dry are designated as VDP.GROSSES GEWÄCHS®. Labelling as "trocken" (dry) is legally mandatory. Wines that are legally classified as halbtrocken (semi-dry) and feinherb (off-dry) do not receive additional labelling. Wines with higher levels of residual sugar are classified based on the classic Prädikat

VDP.GROSSE LAGE®

categories: Kabinett, Spätlese, Auslese, Beerenauslese, Trockenbeerenauslese and Eiswein. The regional associations bear responsibility for establishing appropriate taste profiles, although Spätlese wines must have at least 18 g/l of residual sugar.

LABELLING
The site—without the name of the village—is indicated on the front and decorative label in capital letters. The term VDP.GROSSE LAGE® must be implemented as a circumferential band on the capsule below the VDP.Traubenadler logo. VDP.GROSSES GEWÄCHS® wines are filled in special bottles with the "GG Grape Cluster" logo embossed on the glass. In exceptional cases, the "GG Grape Cluster" logo and the term VDP.GROSSE LAGE® can be placed on the label.

RELEASE DATES
Naturally and nobly sweet wines from VDP.GROSSE LAGE® are released onto the market on 1 May. VDP.GROSSES GEWÄCHS® wines are not to be marketed before 1 September of the year following the harvest. Red wines mature for at least 12 months in wood casks and are released two years after the harvest on 1 September.

USE OF THE SITE NAME
All wines from a VDP.GROSSE LAGE® to be marketed with site names must fulfil the criteria for this quality tier. No estate may produce more than one VDP.GROSSES GEWÄCHS® per site and variety. VDP.GROSSE LAGE®—THE PEAK OF THE PYRAMID.

VDP.DIE PRÄDIKATSWEINGÜTER

VDP. DIE PRÄDIKATSWEINGÜTER

The VDP.Prädikatsweingüter is the world's oldest national association of top-quality wine estates. In 1910, four regional associations joined forces to form the Verband Deutscher Naturweinversteigerer (VDNV). Today, more than a century later, the VDP unites some 200 leading wine estates from all German wine-growing regions. The VDP (Association of German Prädikat Wine Estates) works according to stringent, self-imposed quality standards—from the grape to the bottle.

→ Cultivation of the best vineyard sites, based on soil, topography, and microclimate

→ Production in harmony with nature to foster individualistic wines

→ Preservation of unique cultural landscapes

→ Cultivation of traditional grape varieties, particularly Riesling, Silvaner, and Pinots

→ Reduction of yields to foster the highest quality

→ Care and passion in winemaking to bring forth the best of the grape into the bottle

The "VDP.Eagle"—a stylized eagle bearing a cluster of grapes—on the capsule is the seal of quality of VDP.Wines. It stands for handcrafted wines made from grapes grown in excellent vineyard sites.

SOUND AND SMOKE?

On Classified Vineyard Sites and Their Names
by Dr. Daniel Deckers

"There may well be few tasks more difficult than creating a precise, all-encompassing cartographic representation of a parcel of agriculturally active land within a large district, assessed based on the quality of the product grown there under varying conditions. This applies in particular for agriculture involving grapevines, where the site, soil conditions, age and management technique, selection of variety, etc. have such a major impact on the quality of the product in ways that are barely imaginable in other settings. It is, however, sufficiently acknowledged that the finest of vineyards often sit in immediate proximity to the meanest and that individual vineyards that represent one part of a larger complex can often produce extreme differences in the wines made within them. A vineyard that sits in a district primarily notable for including an illustrious block name can produce relatively poor wine even in good years."

Heinrich Wilhelm Dahlen,
Secretary General of the German Winegrowing Association, 1885

Teufelskeller, Lämmler, Winklerberg, Domdechaney—what do these and hundreds of other "illustrious" (Dahlen) names mean? If we are to believe Goethe's Mephistopheles, then these site appellations could have the same relationship as God has to religion: "Feeling is all. The name but sound and smoke." And it is true: If site names were little more than pure geographic indicators, then there would be little ado about them. But site names do in fact indicate far more than location alone. Pull out a copy of Article 6 Paragraph 1 of the Wine Act of 1909 and you'll find the following: "For commercial transactions with wine, geographical designations may only be used to denote the origin of the wine." Origin?

Mephistopheles didn't just make Gretchen's head spin, he quite literally drove her mad. What is 'origin' other than a long-term symbiosis of names and feelings that can be tasted in the product that man has wrested from nature. Yet nature is not nature. The better the site, the greater the potential for the wine, and the more vehement the feelings. That is wine culture. Which is precisely why site names may not be just sound and smoke—neither in theory nor in practice.

SOUND AND SMOKE?

On Classified Vineyard Sites and Their Names

The two dimensions seem to have reached peak clarity at present—that, at least, is the theory behind the practice of the almost 200 members of the Verband der Prädikatsweingüter (VDP). Within this association of premium winegrowing estates, the oldest of its ilk in the world, a decision was taken roughly twenty years ago that the use of names of vineyard sites would gradually be reduced: grand names solely for grand wines, one might say in summary, and even that not left to the discretion of the individual, but rather as an objective coronation of the best-possible work in vineyard and in cellar.

This might seem like a clear dictum of quality, but it also presupposes the theory of a "grand site"—one that upon closer inspection seems thoroughly questionable. After all, what character should and must a site evince for it to be described as "grand"? It cannot be the size of the parcel itself—as this says nothing about the minimum or maximum scope, or even an ideal size, for a "grand" site. "Grand" sites may encompass a mere few hectares, or several dozen. Yet where and how is a border to be drawn between sites of different quality and which criteria are to be used to make that differentiation?

At the very least, one potential—even mandatory—border comes at the linguistic level. No concept could possibly be more homophonic yet diametrically opposed to that of a "Große Lage" (Grand Cru site) then the "Großlage" (collective site). German wine law also primarily regards the two types of agricultural space as being largely the same. From a historical standpoint, the collective site generally derived from a famous single site—such as in the case of the "Freyburger Schweigenberg" in the Saale-Unstrut region, which after Reunification was mutated from a classified single site into a collective site; or the "Johannisberger Erntebringer," which as part of the Wine Act of 1971 became "THE" Rheingau collective site. Looking further back into the past, the concept of the collective site appears to be a distant echo of the procedure, explicitly allowed since the Wine Act of 1909, of "using the name of individual blocks or vineyard sites that belong to more than one block to describe products of similar type and quality from neighboring or nearby blocks or sites." [1] Similar types, similar quality, neighboring, nearby—anyone who failed to exploit the opportunity to ennoble wines of poor repute by slapping a more illustrious name on them clearly hadn't grasped the point of this regulation.

Yet whatever the logic behind these specifications and the fact that they remain at least in part a shaping force in the winegrowing mentality: The concept of the "collective block" is deceptive advertising of the crassest kind. It uses language to suggest to buyers an origin that does not in fact exist. At the same time, the feeling is

SOUND AND SMOKE?

On Classified Vineyard Sites and Their Names

supposed to be awakened in the consumer that this wine has the same specific origin as wines from a single classified site. Names are not just sound and smoke. That's always been clear.

And yet doesn't the world seem to want to be fooled? Even as the number of site names both in common use and officially codified in wine law have shrank since the early 20th century, including a reduction to roughly 5 000 with the advent of the Wine Act of 1971, this number is more than enough to instill general confusion. It is true that most historically established "grand" sites have avoided being subsumed into collective sites. But they did have to endure being lumped together with neighboring or nearby plots whose soil quality and other parameters are inferior to those of the "classic" parcels.

The logic behind this procedure is entirely comprehensible. Back in the early 1960s, the various stakeholders in winegrowing were tasked with forming "classified site committees" to redraw sites and districts. These groups were responsible for establishing the vineyard rolls that are still in effect today [2], and make no doubt that they were well aware of where the best wines had been made for decades. If many small individual sites had to be fused into a single classified site of at least five hectares, the wine legislation of 1971 declared, then the name of the finest of the old single sites could be used to ennoble the meaner ones—ostensibly to prevent better sites from being debased with the name of the poorer ones.

At the same time, many sites that for centuries had proven their worth as cradles of high-quality wines did manage to retain their aura. And wines continued to be created from 'classic' parcels that lived up to the implicit promise of quality tied up with their site names, many of which had been in place since time immemorial. Yet the risk that this aura might vanish continues to loom above these sites, even today. For in a world with changing climatic conditions, the probability is not low that wines labeled with a "grand" name might slide into the mediocre—too heterogeneous to maintain, let alone expand, their site's reputation.

Even wines that come onto the market from "Grand Cru" sites under the symbol of the VDP's Traubenadler are not immune to this danger. Only a few historically maintained "grand" sites, such as the Steinberger in the Rheingau, were not enlarged in 1971. Bottles sold today under "illustrious" site names may potentially contain wine from parcels that could have only been marketed under much less impressive names prior to the re-composition of the vineyard rolls in 1971. The legislators who revised the Wine Act were not concerned with this issue. The legal proclamation from 1969 stated: "units of land and names are desired that allow for the marketing of the wine,

SOUND AND SMOKE?

On Classified Vineyard Sites and Their Names

even under changes to the competitive conditions, based on size and informative value"—whatever that was supposed to mean. A generous reading, one that persists even today, sees the legislators as having tried to simplify a set of labeling laws that were the most complicated in the world, making them not only clearer and more comprehensible, but also "more democratic." For those lawmakers, names were perhaps little more than sound and smoke. What really mattered was what was in the glass. If the world was going to be tricked, then it should at least feel good in the process.

So what can be done if the law sees all sites and the wines created thereon as per se equal? Legislators cannot be forced to care whether a wine comes from the original, historically justified section of a grand site or from lesser-valued parcels that were added to the other site during the last fundamental reconfiguration of German wine law in 1971. The commission that assigns official testing numbers works behind a similar veil of ignorance: all that matters to them is that the grapes from which the respective wine was created grew on vines planted on the parcel that provides the name; and that an analysis by a government accredited lab finds the wine to be acceptable; and that the wine attains a certain minimum score from the members of the official testing commission during a sensory examination of its smell, taste and balance.

For many years now the VDP has been moving in a different direction. The narrower the origin, the higher the expectations of quality—that is the motto of the association's internal labeling rules. Thus it audits parcels intended for the finest dry wines ("Grosses Gewächs," or GG) prior to harvest; thus the exclusion of wines intended as GG if they cannot pass the association's mandatory internal sensory review; thus the restriction of site name usage to a producer's better and best wines.

Yet as coherent as this concept might seem against the significantly vaguer Wine Act, the VDP quality pyramid itself is not chiseled in stone. "Work in progress" might be a more accurate description. The lowest level, known as VDP.GUTSWEIN (estate-level wine), is intended for "light, lively and fruit-forward wines that bear the signature of the winemaker and which have the kind of uncomplicated character that fits with many daily events." These "handcrafted wines for daily enjoyment" are distinguished from the VDP.ORTSWEIN (village-level wine). They are defined as "accessible wines whose taste profile reveals their regional heritage, which pair well with food and which reach a broad public."

Site descriptions are then typically employed by the VDP only upon reaching the realm of high-end wines. "Discerning wines with aging potential" come solely from

SOUND AND SMOKE?

On Classified Vineyard Sites and Their Names

"special sites" that fulfill the necessary requirements for their wines to be "shaped significantly by the terroir at a sensory level." Wines with the "VDP.Erste Lage" signet on the neck of the bottle are intended to enliven "special occasions" and "win the heart and mind of every wine fan and aficionado." The last category are wines from a "VDP.GROSSE LAGE" These are the "finest, most complex and multifaceted wines with enormous aging potential" and originate from "unique sites."

The difference between "grand" and "premiere" sites is anything but clear at a linguistic level. Without context it is not self-evident whether "grand" sites are higher quality than "premiere" sites, or vice versa. Beyond this, the criteria applied to differentiate between grand ("unique") and premiere ("special") sites is itself hardly unambiguous.

The difficulty in establishing these kinds of delineations was already described back in 1885 by the aforementioned Secretary General of the German Winegrowing Association. Little has changed since that time in this regard. Even the "terroir" term that is gladly applied in relationship to the quality of the vineyard sites is not always an aid; one need only look at how individual sites were elevated by the wine law when the category of "Erstes Gewächs" was first introduced to the Rheingau in 1999 for Riesling and Spätburgunder wines. The quality map that served to delineate the "Erstes Gewächs vineyard sites" was based on the presumption that not only "suitable soil" and "continuity of quality," but also the potential must weight (calculated based on the average number of sunny hours per year and other agro-metereological values) served as the sole scientific (and hence objectively decisive) parameter for determining the quality of a vineyard parcel.

But what if a high number of sunny hours is solely a primary, but not necessarily determinative, factor in the production of high-end wines? By this theory, after all, shouldn't the world's finest Rieslings come not from the Rhine and its tributaries but rather from Sicily? No. In truth, the Riesling vine does not design to produce fruit with both the necessary sugar levels and the desirable acidity when placed under the Mediterranean sun. Furthermore, the reverse also holds true: the quality of a vineyard site has no absolute value, but is rather by definition a relational one, in this case related to the varieties Spätburgunder and Riesling. Yet even this objective "scientific" criteriology cannot be said to be free of criticism.

Because it is based on the fallacy that Riesling wines in particular are better as their must weight rises. When it comes to the way society esteems wine, certain fashions and changes to wine stylistics on the part of the producer both shape and react to trends and changes in the preferences of the consumers. The fixation on

SOUND AND SMOKE?

On Classified Vineyard Sites and Their Names

high must weights and correspondingly alcohol-rich wine can be interpreted as an outflow of the globally prevalent "Parkerization" of wine tastes in the 1990s—and with it a tendency that, in Germany at least, has long been in retreat. While "GG" wines with alcohol levels below 13 percent were an exception even just a few years ago, a growing number of VDP estates appear to have regained a sense that white wines with moderate alcohol levels often have a better "momentum."

It was no accident that the vineyards selected in the Rheingau for the production of "prémier Cru" wines were already highlighted in the world's oldest classification map for a specific growing region from 1867 as being sites of I or II class. Friedrich Wilhelm Dünkelberg, the creator of the "Map of Vineyard Sites in the Nassau Rheingau," really ought to be recorded in the annals of agricultural science as a "cultural engineer." Dünkelberg did not base his colored gradations for the vineyard sites on objective parameters such as the share of mineral or stone in the soil, despite the fact that the era's increasingly refined understanding of organic chemistry was perfectly capable of delivering the precise chemical composition of the soil, must and wines. Dünkelberg in fact had access neither to soil analysis for the overall Rheingau nor property tax rolls; he had solely the (officially recorded) prices that the wines from the individual sites had earned over the course of many years.

He used this information to apply a process that was not unusual for the wine world of the early 19th century. The classification of the red wines of Médoc and the whites of Sauternes, which had been created with a view towards the 1855 World Exhibition in Paris, had also been oriented toward prices—and thus indirectly on market demand—for the region's most renowned wines. [3] For the Rheingau as well, one must accept that demand for the prestigious wines was one of the decisive determinants for pricing. Yet the elements that helped sustain the prestige of Rheingau wines were different from those that helped position the pricing trends for the famous chateaux of Médoc. In France, the name of the producer—not the origin of the grapes—was the sole guarantor of quality, at least in any direct way. This was different in the Rheingau: in the mid-19th century, the connection between a prestigious producer and a vineyard site of renowned historical quality was precisely what played a decisive role.

This combination makes it difficult to transfer the concept of the I and II class sites into solid starting points for differentiation between Grosse Lage and Erste Lage sites—and furthermore requires that one conveniently ignore the fact that this sort of map exists only for the Rheingau. Because at that time the lack of a good or, at the very least, prestigious producer on a good vineyard site was enough to hinder

SOUND AND SMOKE?

On Classified Vineyard Sites and Their Names

its potential on the market. The same problem was also present in the system used for the site classification map for the Prussian Rhine province, covering the modern growing regions of Mosel, Mittelrhein, Ahr and Nahe (left bank). It is true that the protagonist of that map, Royal Government and Department Council for Land Improvement and Statistics Otto Beck, applied a different approach than Dünkelberg. Beck based his 1868 vineyard classifications for the administrative district of Trier not on auction or other sales proceeds, but rather on the net property tax totals. Yet property taxes themselves remain based in large part on the prices of wines grown on those respective parcels. Those prices in turn reflect not only the potential of the site and the quality of the wine produced there, but also the prestige of the producer.

Any attempt to use the historical site classification maps as a starting point to differentiate between "Erste Lage" and "Grosse Lage" sites eventually must acknowledge that while they offer a basic sense of orientation, they are not appropriate as objective measurements. And while it is hardly possible to produce outstanding wines from low-quality parcels, it is entirely possible over decades, if not centuries, to create mere mediocre wine from parcels of above average, or even outstanding potential. Beyond this, it is also conceivable that a vineyard site that was held in the highest regard in the 19th century might no longer be counted among the grand vineyard sites under the climatic conditions of the 21st century. Finally, it must be remembered that this kind of procedure is only appropriate for a few winegrowing regions. Pfalz, Rheinhessen, Franken, Baden, Württemberg, Hessische Bergstrasse, Saale-Unstrut and Sachsen have only cadastral charts and historical records of levied property or other taxes—but no classification charts.

There can be little claim to objective, let alone scientific, criteria for the differentiation of sites of first and second quality. With that said, the VDP still bears responsibility for establishing robust criteria for differentiation between various hierarchical levels and for applying those criteria consistently and without objection. This is necessary to ensure that wines from the same site but different estates are not marketed as "Erste Lage" by one and then "Grosse Lage" by the other. What cannot be avoided, by contrast, is the need for a review of the accuracy of the initial assessment of sites as "Grosse Lage" or "Erste Lage," and with corrections undertaken as necessary. And should a site, based on the wines marketed explicitly with its name, not prove to be "special" or even "outstanding," then it is in the interest of all to lower the classification of that site. By the same token, it may be possible to elevate other vineyard sites to a higher category if it is determined that the conditions of the 21st century allow for the production of wines that stand shoulder to shoulder with

SOUND AND SMOKE?

On Classified Vineyard Sites and Their Names

the better, and perhaps even the best, of what the world has to offer. "The vineyard binds both its master and its servant." This wisdom was clear as far back as 1869, when it was published in a text about "Winegrowing on the Mosel and Saar" that accompanied the Saar-Mosel Winegrowing Map published shortly before.

Footnotes:
[1] Wine Act of 25 July 1930 alongside export specifications, published and commentated by Consul Fritz Goldschmidt, Mainz: Diemer 1930, 179ff.
[2] See for example regarding Rheinland-Pfalz the „Entwurf eines Landesgesetzes über die Neufestsetzung von Lagen und Bereichen und über die Weinbergsrolle" of 19 July 1969, in: Deutsche Weinzeitung 105 (1969), 876ff.
[3] Markham

GLOSSARY

Classified Grape Varieties & their International Designation

WHITE
Weißburgunder	Pinot Blanc
Grauburgunder	Pinot Gris

RED
Spätburgunder	Pinot Noir
Frühburgunder	Pinot Noir Précroce
Lemberger	Blaufränkisch

HISTORICAL WINE MAPS

The oldest known vineyard classification maps (circa 1867) offer detailed insights into the official 19th century assessment of viticulture along the Rhine and Mosel rivers. There was more than just prestige at stake; the maps served as a formal survey of which vineyards and which wines could be expected to earn the highest market prices, and thus could be taxed at a higher rate. The resulting property tax brackets, visible on the maps as gradated color zones, formed the heart of the new site classification system. The Prussian vineyard site classification maps remain unique even today for their beautiful and effective handling of a dual task: indexing property tax assessments on the one hand and overtly advertising the quality of the very good and absolute finest vineyard sites as a product of cultural history on the other. Are you interested in the maps? The VDP offers reprints on their website: bit.ly/vineyard_maps.

Viticultural Map of the Nassau Rheingau in 1867

Mosel Viticultural Map of 1897

Rhine Viticultural Map covering Rüdesheim – Coblenz from 1902

Rhine Viticultural Map covering Coblenz – Bonn from 1904

Nahe Viticultural Map of 1900

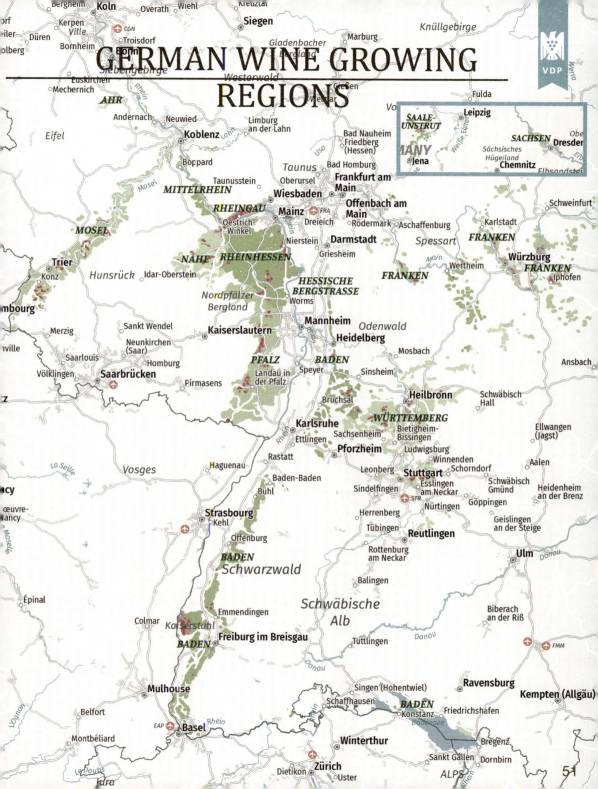

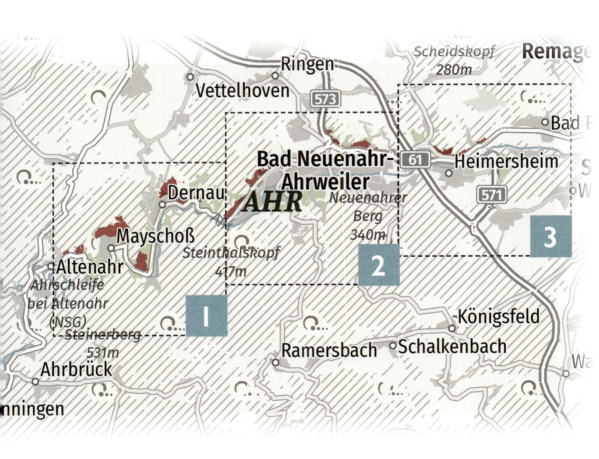

AHR

The Ahr is one of the smaller German wine regions and follows the river for 25 kilometres from southwest to northeast. 560 hectares are planted with vines. Black grape varieties make up the lion's share on the Ahr and it is considered the red wine paradise of Germany. The predominant grape variety is Spätburgunder. The vineyard slopes are particularly rocky and steep in the upper and middle Ahr and usually face south. The protected and often very narrow valley provides a mild microclimate that lens wines elegance and good structure. The lower Ahr Valley becomes flatter and the landscape around Heimersheim is marked by volcanic soils and basalt hills.

Region:	VDP.GROSSE LAGE®:
560 ha	224 ha
VDP.Wineries:	VDP.GROSSE LAGE® Sites:
6	17

ALTE LAY

Walporzheim | Ahr
VDP.GROSSE LAGE®

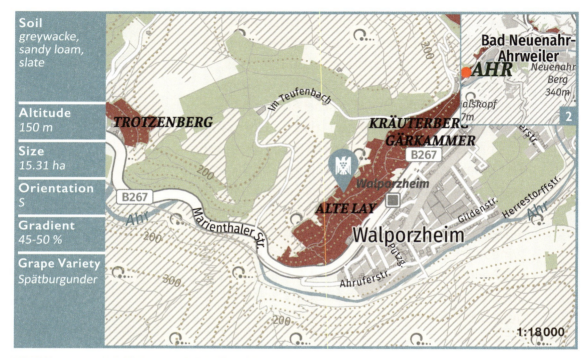

Soil
greywacke, sandy loam, slate

Altitude
150 m

Size
15.31 ha

Orientation
S

Gradient
45-50 %

Grape Variety
Spätburgunder

VDP.Estates: J. J. Adeneuer, H. J. Kreuzberg

Numerous small and tiny terraces braced with slate walls determine the appearance of the VDP.GROSSE LAGE® ALTE LAY. It is located above the village Walporzheim at 150 metres above sea level. It faces south to southeast toward the Ahr River at an up to 50 percent gradient. Spätburgunder is cultivated here in the weathered slate and greywacke soil.

History: The word "Lay" stems from the Celts and means "rock" or "slate rock". A prominent rock crag protrudes in this vineyard.

BURGGARTEN

Heimersheim | Ahr
VDP.GROSSE LAGE®

Soil
basalt, stony-loamy clay, greywacke

Altitude
125 m

Size
8.78 ha

Orientation
S

Gradient
50 %

Grape Variety
Spätburgunder

VDP.Estates: J. J. Adeneuer, Meyer-Näkel, Nelles

The diversity of its soil structure is one of the things that makes the VDP.GROSSE LAGE® BURGGARTEN so noteworthy. Greywacke and greywacke slate, loess and loess loam, and even basalt from the conical basalt hill above Heimersheim are all found in the approximately 9-hectare vineyard. Each of these soil types mark the Spätburgunder wines that grow here quite differently—from spicy-fruity (greywacke) to full-bodied and generous (loess, loam) to deep and powerful wines (basalt). The BURGGARTEN GL faces south and rises to 125 metres above sea level.

History: The name Burggarten stems from the fortress (Burg) that King Philipp of Swabia had built here.

DAUBHAUS

Ahrweiler | Ahr
VDP.GROSSE LAGE®

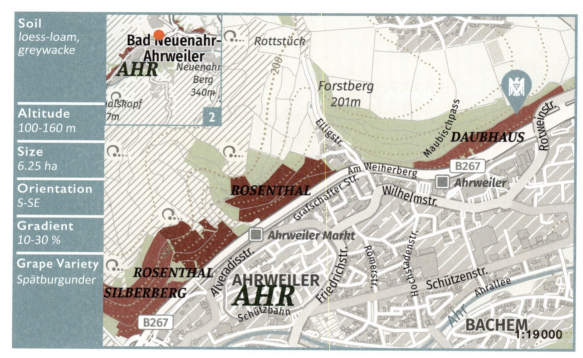

Soil
loess-loam, greywacke

Altitude
100-160 m

Size
6.25 ha

Orientation
S-SE

Gradient
10-30 %

Grape Variety
Spätburgunder

VDP.Estates: Deutzerhof - Cossmann-Hehle, Meyer-Näkel

The VDP.GROSSE LAGE® DAUBHAUS rises above Ahrweiler from 100 to 160 metres above sea level. Due to its south to southeast aspect, it collects the warmth of the day and releases it into the vines. The soils are mostly loess loam with good water storage capacity and a share of greywacke. The slope gradient is 10 to 30 percent. The GL DAUBHAUS was classified as a VDP.GROSSE LAGE® in 2017.

History: "Daube" is the German word for a barrel stave. It is assumed that barrel staves were produced in the vicinity in the past.

ECK

Altenahr | Ahr
VDP.GROSSE LAGE®

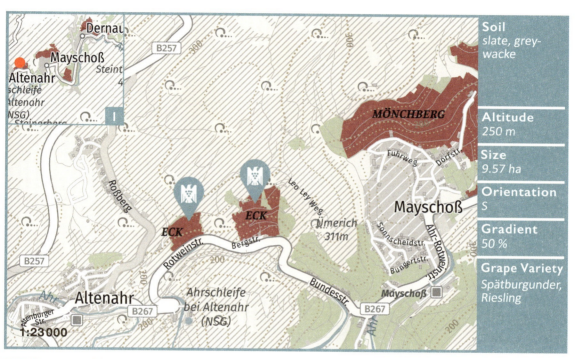

Soil
slate, greywacke

Altitude
250 m

Size
9.57 ha

Orientation
S

Gradient
50 %

Grape Variety
Spätburgunder, Riesling

VDP.Estates: Deutzerhof - Cossmann-Hehle

The VDP.GROSSE LAGE® ECK is a south facing slope, devided by a slate formation. It rises to 250 metres above sea level in a very narrow section of the Ahr Valley. The 50 percent gradient exposes the site to plenty of sunshine throughout the day. The soil of dark greywacke and weathered slate debris has a high share of rock and stores the sun's warmth, radiating it into the vines in the night like natural floor heating. The summer microclimate of the GL ECK is nearly Mediterranean. Predominantly Riesling and Spätburgunder grow here.

GÄRKAMMER

Walporzheim | Ahr
VDP.GROSSE LAGE®

Soil
greywacke, sandy loam, slate

Altitude
150 m

Size
0.67 ha

Orientation
S

Gradient
50 %

Grape Variety
Spätburgunder

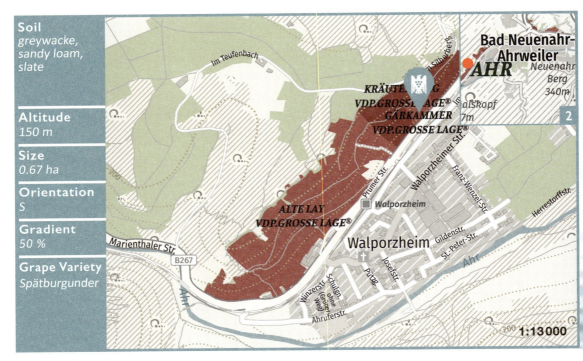

VDP.Estates: J. J. Adeneuer

At only 0.67 hectare, the VDP.GROSSE LAGE® GÄRKAMMER is one of the smallest vineyards in Germany and the smallest in the Ahr region. Dark greywacke and weathered slate with sandy loam dominate the site. The south facing slope is well bedded in the hillside and protected by a high slate wall lending logical testimony to the name "Gärkammer". Heat is trapped in the GÄRKAMMER GL particularly in summer and is stored in the dark rock until late into the evening. With a 50 percent slope, the terraced site is quite steep. It rises to 150 metres above the Ahr. The site is planted exclusively with Spätburgunder – a portion of which is not grafted.

History: The GÄRKAMMER GL is so named due to its rather high temperatures, particularly in summer. The well-known German writer and politician Johann Gottfried Kinkel (1815-1882) described the site as "the most precious vineyard in the entire Ahr Valley".

HARDTBERG

Dernau | Ahr
VDP.GROSSE LAGE®

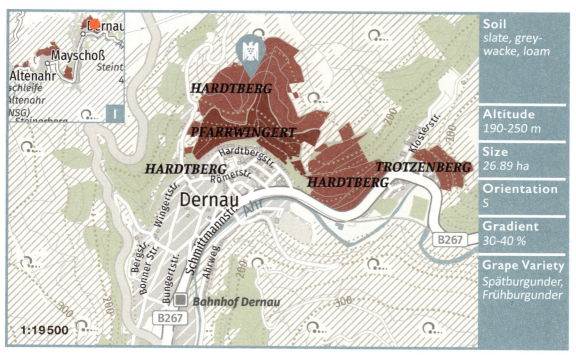

Soil
slate, greywacke, loam

Altitude
190-250 m

Size
26.89 ha

Orientation
S

Gradient
30-40 %

Grape Variety
Spätburgunder, Frühburgunder

VDP.Estates: H. J. Kreuzberg, Meyer-Näkel, Jean Stodden

Spätburgunder and Frühburgunder grow in the VDP.GROSSE LAGE® HARDTBERG in the Dernau community on the Ahr River. The vineyard is braced with dry stone terrace walls and rises at a 60 percent slope gradient up to 250 metres above sea level. The soils are slate and greywacke, a type of sandstone with feldspar content. Loam appears in the lower part of the vineyard. The GL HARDTBERG faces south and is interrupted by the small side valleys Albental, Eigelstal and Rötzeltal.
History: There was once an alternative location for the constitutional organs of the Federal Republic of Germany, nicknamed "government bunker" at the foot of the vineyard. It was built between 1958 and 1972, but abandoned by the federal government in 1997 and dismantled in 2001. A remaining part of the buildings can be seen in Ahrweiler as a documentation centre. The "Hardthöhe" is still the headquarters of the Federal Ministry of Defence (BMVg).

HERRENBERG

Rech | Ahr
VDP.GROSSE LAGE®

Soil
greywacke, loam

Altitude
170-190 m

Size
20.42 ha

Orientation
S

Gradient
45 %

Grape Variety
Spätburgunder, Frühburgunder

VDP.Estates: Deutzerhof - Cossmann-Hehle, Jean Stodden

The steep, terraced VDP.GROSSE LAGE® HERRENBERG is a sunny south facing slope between 170 and 190 metres above sea level The top section of the site has a slope gradient of 45 percent. The soil is stony and of volcanic origin with slate and greywacke. Spätburgunder is the preferred variety in this vineyard and many of the vines are ungrafted. The HERRENBERG is the only GROSSE LAGE® around Rech, which has not been consolidated, because no wine estate was willing to exchange vineyards.

History: The name Herrenberg can be traced to the Grafen of Saffenburg. Their fortress ruin on the slope opposite is easily viewed from the vineyard. The aristocracy of Saffenburg were the lords of the village Rech and the surrounding vineyards.

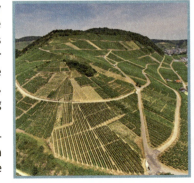

KIRCHTÜRMCHEN

Bad Neuenahr | Ahr
VDP.GROSSE LAGE®

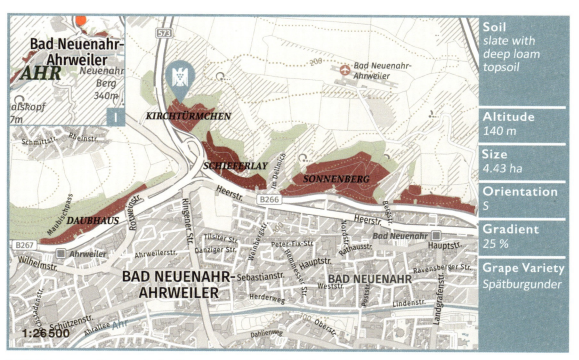

Soil
slate with deep loam topsoil

Altitude
140 m

Size
4.43 ha

Orientation
S

Gradient
25 %

Grape Variety
Spätburgunder

VDP.Estates: Deutzerhof - Cossmann-Hehle, H. J. Kreuzberg

The VDP.GROSSE LAGE® KIRCHTÜRMCHEN in Bad Neuenahr lies at 140 metres above sea level on the Ahr River. The vineyards face the sun in the south at a 25 percent gradient. Spätburgunder grows here in slate soils with a deep loam topsoil.

History: The vineyard is found in old maps as "An dem Kirchtürmchen", which translates to "near the little church steeple". The name probably comes from the church estates in the old wine villages Hemmessen, Beul and Wadenheim. One also has a good view of the steeple of the Catholic church in Bad Neuenahr from here. The vineyard was once larger, but several hectares had to be sacrificed for a highway.

KRÄUTERBERG

Walporzheim | Ahr
VDP.GROSSE LAGE®

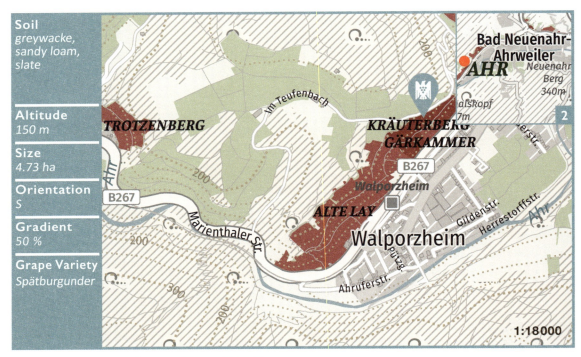

Soil
greywacke, sandy loam, slate

Altitude
150 m

Size
4.73 ha

Orientation
S

Gradient
50 %

Grape Variety
Spätburgunder

VDP.Estates: J. J. Adeneuer, Meyer-Näkel

The vineyard terraces that climb the steep slope are a significant feature of the VDP.GROSSE LAGE® KRÄUTERBERG northeast of Walporzheim. This vineyard surrounds the GL GÄRKAMMER, which is known for its warm climate. Its protected position in the valley and the intensity of the sun in a steep south facing aspect create a nearly Mediterranean microclimate. The slope climbs to 150 metres above sea level at a 50 percent gradient. The soils are greywacke, sandy loam and slate.

History: The name possibly stems from Roman times when not only wine, but also herbs (Kräuter) were cultivated here.

LANDSKRONE

Heimersheim | Ahr
VDP.GROSSE LAGE®

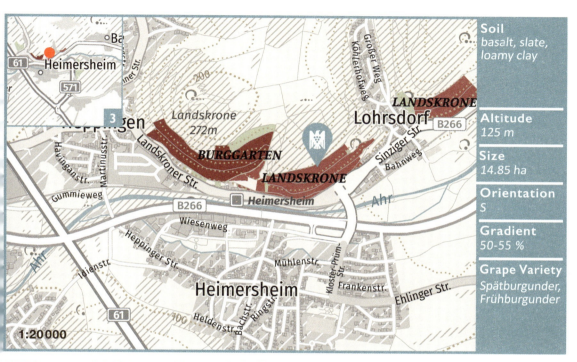

Soil
basalt, slate, loamy clay

Altitude
125 m

Size
14.85 ha

Orientation
S

Gradient
50-55 %

Grape Variety
Spätburgunder, Frühburgunder

VDP.Estates: J. J. Adeneuer, Deutzerhof - Cossmann-Hehle, Meyer-Näkel, Nelles

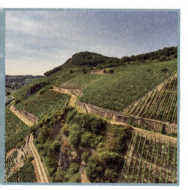

The VDP.GROSSE LAGE® LANDSKRONE is an extinct volcanic cone that rises to 125 metres above sea level overlooking the village of Heimersheim. Its high vineyard walls brace the rocky, steep 50 to 55 percent slope. When travelling from the Rhine down the Ahr River, this is the first vineyard of the Ahr Valley. Typical for its volcanic origin, the soils are basalt, slate and loamy clay. The soils and terrace walls of this south-facing vineyard store the sun's intense warmth during the day and release it into the vines at night.

History: King Philip of Swabia took advantage of the prominent mountain cone to build a fortress to guard the Frankfurt-Aachen army road in 1206. He gifted it to his wife as the "crown of the country".

MÖNCHBERG

Mayschoß | Ahr
VDP.GROSSE LAGE®

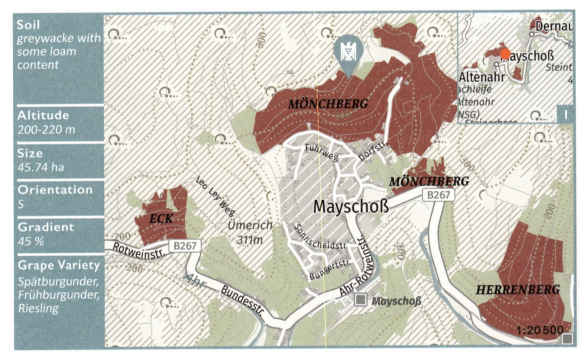

Soil
greywacke with some loam content

Altitude
200-220 m

Size
45.74 ha

Orientation
S

Gradient
45 %

Grape Variety
Spätburgunder, Frühburgunder, Riesling

VDP.Estates: Deutzerhof - Cossmann-Hehle, Jean Stodden

With 46 hectares of classified vineyard area, the VDP.GROSSE LAGE® MÖNCHBERG is the largest VDP.GROSSE LAGE® in the Ahr region. It lies at 200 to 220 metres above sea level above the Mayschoss community. The forest that borders it to the north protects it from cold winds. The steep, south-facing slope is braced with slate terrace walls. The convex form of the site captures solar radiation like a satellite dish. The soil is greywacke, a type of sandstone, with a small portion of loam. Spätburgunder and Frühburgunder are cultivated here.

PFARRWINGERT

Dernau | Ahr
VDP.GROSSE LAGE®

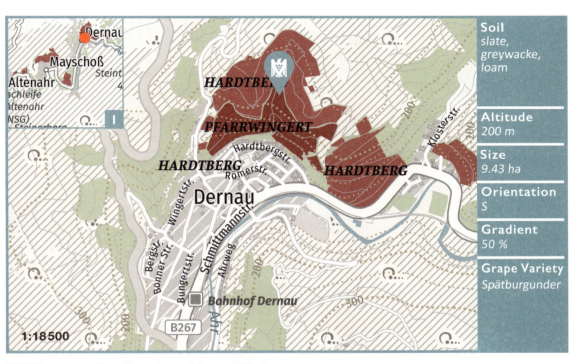

Soil
slate, greywacke, loam

Altitude
200 m

Size
9.43 ha

Orientation
S

Gradient
50 %

Grape Variety
Spätburgunder

VDP.Estates: H. J. Kreuzberg, Meyer-Näkel

The VDP.GROSSE LAGE® PFARRWINGERT is a convex site that faces southeast, south and southwest making it well protected from winds in the lower reaches. The site rises from 125 to 200 metres above sea level directly behind the city Dernau. The soils are grainy greywacke and weathered slate with a share of argillaceous slate, which are easily warmed and make the PFARRWINGERT GL one of the hottest vineyards in the Ahr. The PFARRWINGERT GL measures 10 hectares and with an up to 50 percent slope, it is very steep in the most elevated section.

History: "Pfarr" means "parish" and "Wingert" is an old name for vineyard. The catholic parish church in Dernau once owned this vineyard and continues to own a few parcels here.

ROSENTHAL

Ahrweiler | Ahr
VDP.GROSSE LAGE®

Soil
greywacke, sandy loam loess

Altitude
130-160 m

Size
15.25 ha

Orientation
S

Gradient
45 %

Grape Variety
Spätburgunder

VDP.Estates: J. J. Adeneuer, H. J. Kreuzberg, Meyer-Näkel, Jean Stodden

The prime vineyard site of Ahrweiler, the VDP.GROSSE LAGE® ROSENTHAL, rises above the roofs of the old town. Facing south and strikingly braced with high retaining walls, the 45 percent slope gradient rises from 130 to 160 metres above sea level. Remains of an old viaduct lend the vineyard a wild-romantic appearance. Greywacke and sandy loess-loam comprise the soil.

History: The origin of the name is uncertain, but could possibly indicate that roses were also planted here in the past.

SCHIEFERLAY

Bad Neuenahr | Ahr
VDP.GROSSE LAGE®

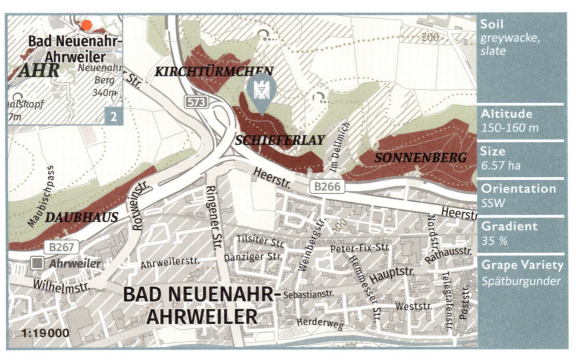

Soil
greywacke, slate

Altitude
150-160 m

Size
6.57 ha

Orientation
SSW

Gradient
35 %

Grape Variety
Spätburgunder

VDP.Estates: J. J. Adeneuer, Deutzerhof - Cossmann-Hehle, H. J. Kreuzberg, Nelles,

The VDP.GROSSE LAGE® SCHIEFERLAY in Bad Neuenahr faces south-southwest and is bordered to the east and west by side valleys. The vineyard climbs from 150 to 160 metres above sea level at a 35 percent slope gradient. The soils vary, but Devon slate and greywacke, a grey-greenish type of sandstone with high feldspar content, dominate. Loess and loam are also found. Spätburgunder is the main grape variety.

History: The word "Lay" stems from the Celts and means "rock" or "slate rock".

SILBERBERG

Ahrweiler | Ahr
VDP.GROSSE LAGE®

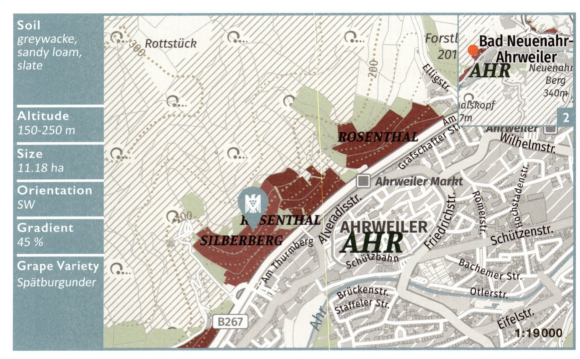

Soil
greywacke, sandy loam, slate

Altitude
150-250 m

Size
11.18 ha

Orientation
SW

Gradient
45 %

Grape Variety
Spätburgunder

VDP.Estates: J. J. Adeneuer, H. J. Kreuzberg

Steep slopes with up to 45 percent gradient, the long hours of sunshine due to the southwest exposition, and elevation of 150 to 250 metres above sea level are the attributes that characterise the VDP.GROSSE LAGE® SILBERBERG. The 11-hectare vineyard is planted mostly with Spätburgunder. The soils vary with different areas dominated by greywacke, slate, or loam. Each soil type lends the wine a different character: greywacke brings fine fruit, while loam yields generous body.

History: The Silberberg is located above an old Roman villa. Archaeological diggings revealed old melting ovens, which indicate the mining of silver ore. This is one logical conclusion for the name. Another plausible variation is that the name comes from "Selberberg", referring to a mountain on which wild sage grew.

SONNENBERG

Bad Neuenahr | Ahr
VDP.GROSSE LAGE®

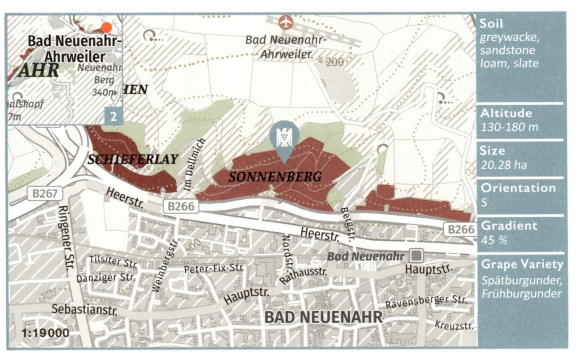

Soil
greywacke, sandstone loam, slate

Altitude
130-180 m

Size
20.28 ha

Orientation
S

Gradient
45 %

Grape Variety
Spätburgunder, Frühburgunder

VDP.Estates: J. J. Adeneuer, H. J. Kreuzberg, Meyer-Näkel, Nelles, Jean Stodden

The VDP.GROSSE LAGE® SONNENBERG belongs to Bad Neuenahr and lies in the part of the Ahr region where the river valley is wider. The 45 percent slope gradient benefits from a south aspect. The soils are predominantly sandstone-loam and slate, but greywacke, a type of grey to greenish sandstone with high feldspar content, is also present. Spätburgunder and Frühburgunder are cultivated here. Several of the vineyard terraces are protected as historic monuments. A special type of wild bee that is a protected species has also settled here.

History: "Sonnenberg" is a common vineyard name in Germany that is found around 40 times. It denotes that the vineyard faces towards the sun and therefore is an advantageous site.

TROTZENBERG

Marienthal | Ahr
VDP.GROSSE LAGE®

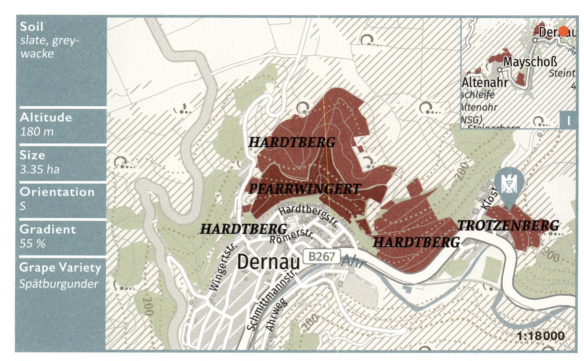

Soil
slate, greywacke

Altitude
180 m

Size
3.35 ha

Orientation
S

Gradient
55 %

Grape Variety
Spätburgunder

VDP.Estates: H. J. Kreuzberg, Meyer-Näkel

The VDP.GROSSE LAGE® TROTZENBERG curves around the village of Marienthal and faces south to southwest toward a bend in the Ahr River. The vineyard slope has a gradient of up to 55 percent and lies at 180 metres above sea level. Spätburgunder grows on the typical Ahr soils, slate and greywacke. The Marienthal monastery ruin borders the GL TROTZENBERG to the west.

THE AROMA
REVOLUTION

SENSA. ALWAYS THE PERFECT GLASS.

ENJOYING WINE CAN BE THAT EASY.

SENSA takes the complexity out of modern wine enjoyment because every glass shape fits exactly one aroma or wine style.

With only four glass sizes, SENSA makes it uniquely uncomplicated to serve light-fresh, fruity-refined, velvety-rich or strong-spicy wines, covering the most important wines of the world. Another glass shape for sparkling wine and champagne completes the collection.

Regardless of whether you are serving red wine, white wine or rosé. Only the character, aroma, flavour and taste of a wine decide.

www.schott-zwiesel.com

The glass of the professional.

SCHOTT ZWIESEL
Tritan® protect

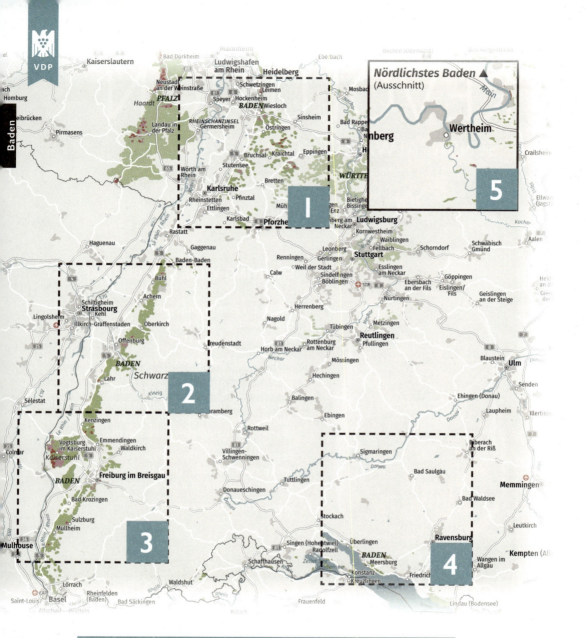

Region:	VDP.GROSSE LAGE®:
16 000 ha	446 ha
VDP.Wineries:	VDP.GROSSE LAGE® Sites:
20	46

BADEN

Baden is a wine universe of its own, embedded in a rich cultural landscape. On one side, there is the Bodensee (Lake Constance), with its view of the Alps; on the other side, the wonderful landscape of the Tauber River Valley. Here, the gently rounded hills of Heidelberg; there, the massif of the Kaiserstuhl that majestically overlooks the Rhine Valley. Viticultural diversity here is not merely a whim of the times, but rather something that has evolved naturally, as have its climatic and geological differences.

Such extreme differences in landscape naturally result in very distinctive microclimates, soil conditions and levels of inclination. The subsoils, for example, range from gravel to limestone, shell-limestone, loess, volcanic stone, granite, gneiss and keuper. The climate in a region whose vineyards are up to 400 km (250 miles) apart is no less diverse than the soils. Baden's leading producers are savvy enough to regard viticulture from both a Romance and Germanic perspective. They have long been as familiar with cultivating Pinot grapes as with dealing with Riesling. Baden is Pinot country. Led by Spätburgunder, the main grape variety, the Pinot family accounts for over half of Baden's total vineyard area. Although Riesling accounts for only about 8 percent of the growing area, it is no less significant. Riesling wines of exceptional quality are produced in the Riesling enclaves of the Ortenau, Kraichgau and Kaiserstuhl. With the Pinots, they are the center of Baden's wine character.

BASSGEIGE KÄHNER

Oberbergen | Baden
VDP.GROSSE LAGE®

Soil
loess, volcanic soil

Altitude
300–360 m

Size
3.02 ha

Orientation
SW

Gradient
20 %

Grape Variety
Grauburgunder

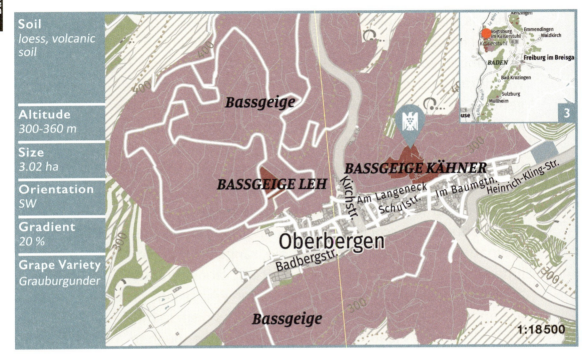

1:18 500

VDP.Estates: Franz Keller

The VDP.GROSSE LAGE® BASSGEIGE KÄHNER is a prime parcel in the Bassgeige vineyard in the Oberbergen community on the Kaiserstuhl. It is located in the southeast section and comprises a set of long terraces at 300 to 360 metres above sea level. The soil is loess over volcanic rock. VDP.Estate Franz Keller cultivates Grauburgunder in this monopole site. Where this variety can elsewhere have the tendency to become rather voluptuous, here in this rocky, often meagre soil, it achieves marked structure.

History: The name "Bassgeige" stems from the original shape of this vineyard, which resembled a double bass. Since the Flurbereinigung (land consolidation) of 1971, this shape is no longer discernable. "Kähner" is local German dialect for a rain gutter, which indicates that the parcel once acted as a drainage.

BASSGEIGE LEH

Oberbergen | Baden
VDP.GROSSE LAGE®

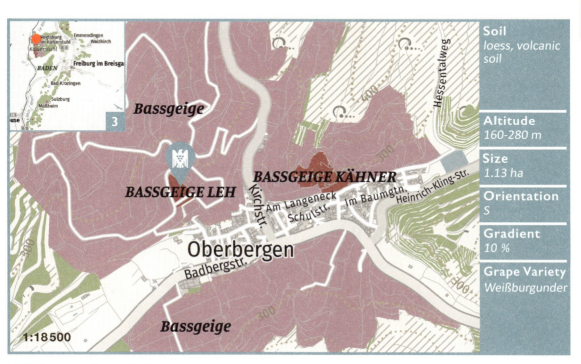

Soil
loess, volcanic soil

Altitude
160-280 m

Size
1.13 ha

Orientation
S

Gradient
10 %

Grape Variety
Weißburgunder

VDP.Estates: Franz Keller

The VDP.GROSSE LAGE® BASSGEIGE LEH is a parcel in the Bassgeige vineyard in the community of Oberbergen on Kaiserstuhl. It lies at 160 to 280 metres above sea level and faces south. The soil is calcareous loess and volcanic soil. VDP.Estate Franz Keller cultivates Weissburgunder here.

History: The name "Bassgeige" stems from the original shape of this vineyard, which resembled a double bass. Since the Flurbereinigung (land consolidation) of 1971, this shape is no longer discernable. The name "Leh" refers to a tumulus grave from the Hallstatt culture in the Early Iron Age Europe around 800 B.C., which documents the early settlers of this region.

BIENENBERG "WILDENSTEIN"

Malterdingen | Baden
VDP.GROSSE LAGE®

Soil
weathered red shell limestone

Altitude
240-260 m

Size
1.4 ha

Orientation
S-SW

Gradient
30-40 %

Grape Variety
Spätburgunder

VDP.Estates: **Bernhard Huber**

The prominent, terraced VDP.GROSSE LAGE® BIENENBERG "WILDENSTEIN" can be seen from a distance. This famous vineyard slope climbs at an up to 40 percent gradient from 240 to 260 metres above sea level. Its 1.4 hectare have a south to southwest aspect. The site is predestined for the cultivation of Spätburgunder and the vines root in reddish, weathered shell limestone. The soil is very rocky and vines must dig deep below the surface to attain sufficient moisture and nourishment.

History: Cistercian monks already cultivated Pinot Noir in this vineyard in the 14th century.

BIENENBERG

Malterdingen | Baden
VDP.GROSSE LAGE®

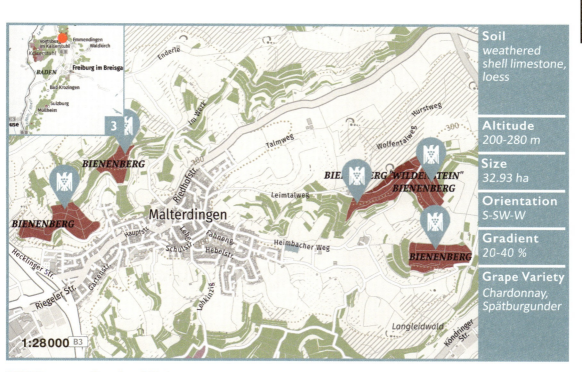

Soil
weathered shell limestone, loess

Altitude
200-280 m

Size
32.93 ha

Orientation
S-SW-W

Gradient
20-40 %

Grape Variety
Chardonnay, Spätburgunder

VDP.Estates: Bernhard Huber

The VDP.GROSSE LAGE® BIENENBERG rises up out of the Upper Rhine Plain in Malterdingen. Spätburgunder and Chardonnay are cultivated here on weathered shell limestone. Iron deposits cause the soil to appear yellowish-red in some places. Because the soil is often quite rocky, vines are forced to drive their roots deep. The south to southwest facing vineyard has a steep slope gradient of up to 40 percent and is partially terraced.

History: Cistercian monks from Burgundy cultivated Pinot Noir in this vineyard in the 14th century. They were already familiar with shell limestone soils from their home. The local synonym for Pinot Noir "Malterdinger" stems from this time. This synonym was also exported with the vines into Bavaria and Switzerland and is occasionally listed in wine encyclopaedias.

CHORHERRNHALDE

Meersburg | Baden
VDP.GROSSE LAGE®

Soil
moraine

Altitude
400-460 m

Size
11.23 ha

Orientation
S

Gradient
60 %

Grape Variety
Riesling

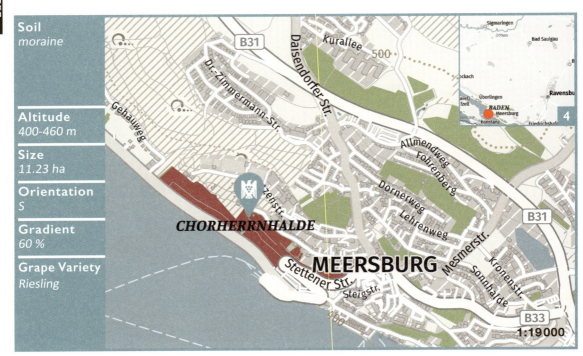

VDP.Estates: **Markgraf von Baden**

The VDP.GROSSE LAGE® CHORHERRNHALDE lies directly above Lake Constance in Meersburg. The conditions are nearly maritime and vines benefit from abundant solar radiation due to the reflection of light from the surface of the lake. Light is further intensified with the vineyard's steep 60 percent slope gradient and orientation toward the south. Lake Constance stores warmth and moderates the climate, particularly in winter. The GL CHORHERRNHALDE lies at 400 to 460 metres above sea level. Vines root in molasse and moraine soils.

DICKER FRANZ

Sulzfeld | Baden
VDP.GROSSE LAGE®

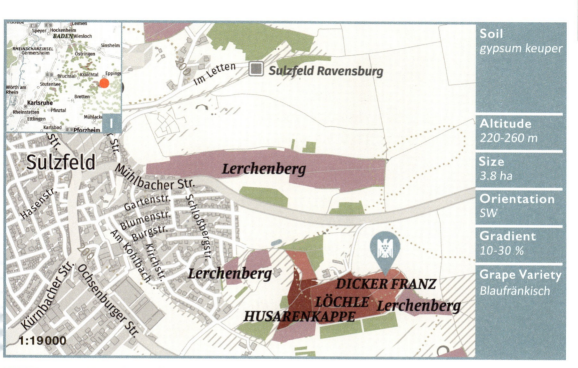

Soil
gypsum keuper

Altitude
220-260 m

Size
3.8 ha

Orientation
SW

Gradient
10-30 %

Grape Variety
Blaufränkisch

VDP.Estates: **Burg Ravensburg**

The VDP.GROSSE LAGE® DICKER FRANZ is located in Sulzfeld in Kraichgau and is situated at 220 to 260 metres above sea level This Blaufränkisch vineyard has a slope gradient of up to 30 percent and faces southwest. Deep, gypsum marl soil with high mineral content distinguishes this site, which is a monopole vineyard of the VDP.Estate Burg Ravensburg.

History: The vineyard is named after Baron Göler von Ravensburg (1701-1765). He was referred to as the "Dicker Herr" (Big Gentleman) in family history and was a reputed gourmand.

DOKTORGARTEN

Blankenhornsberg | Baden
VDP.GROSSE LAGE®

Soil
volcanic soil

Altitude
180-310 m

Size
28.26 ha

Orientation
W-E

Gradient
30-50 %

Grape Variety
Weißburgunder, Grauburgunder, Chardonnay, Spätburgunder

VDP.Estates: Staatsweingut Freiburg

The VDP.GROSSE LAGE® DOKTORGARTEN geologically belongs to the Ihringer Winklerberg on the Kaiserstuhl and has the same black weathered volcanic soil. A unique characteristic of the volcanic rock are the lime inclusions. The vineyard descends toward the east, south and west with the Staatsweingut – Gutsbetrieb Blankenhornsberg crowing the top of the hill like a fortress. Slopy with a gradient of 30 to 50 percent, the GL DOKTORGARTEN is situated at 180 to 310 metres above sea level The soil warms quickly due to its black colour and stores this warmth, which benefits the vines.

History: The site was named after the viticulture researcher and viticulture association president, Prof. Dr. Adolph Blankenhorn, who conducted research and experimentation on the slope. His family reclaimed the vineyard in 1842 and commenced replanting in 1844. Family Blankenhorn sold the vineyard to the Agricultural Chamber of Baden in 1919. It was transferred to Staatliches Weinbauinstitut in 1954.

EICHBERG

Oberrotweil | Baden
VDP.GROSSE LAGE®

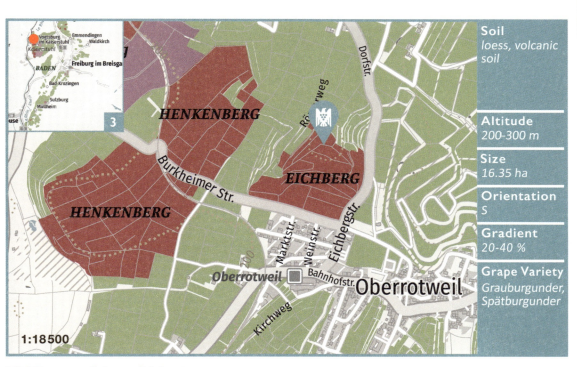

Soil
loess, volcanic soil

Altitude
200-300 m

Size
16.35 ha

Orientation
S

Gradient
20-40 %

Grape Variety
Grauburgunder, Spätburgunder

VDP.Estates: Salwey, Stigler

The VDP.GROSSE LAGE® EICHBERG is located in the warmest part of Germany, where balmy Mediterranean air masses flow through the "Burgundian gates" directly into the Rhine Valley. Situated in the Kaiserstuhl above Oberrotweil, the site rises from 200 to 300 metres above sea level at a 20 to 40 percent gradient. Dark volcanic soils enhance the sun exposition in this south facing site and increase temperatures on summer days, which continue to provide vines with warmth in the night. The vineyard encompasses around 16 hectares.

EICHELBERG

Hilsbach | Baden
VDP.GROSSE LAGE®

Soil
white limestone

Altitude
270-320 m

Size
5,3 ha

Orientation
SE

Gradient
30-50 %

Grape Variety
Pinot Blanc, Chardonnay

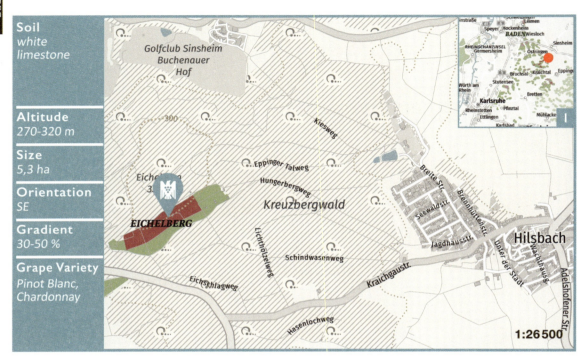

VDP.Estates: Heitlinger

The south and southeast facing VDP.GROSSE LAGE® EICHELBERG is protected by a forested peak and warms well during the day. It is located west of Heilbronn. The GL EICHELBERG rises from 270 to 320 metres above sea level at an incline of 30 to 50 percent. White limestone and marl dominate the soils of the 5,3 hectare vineyard site. The site is completely surrounded by forest and therefore has a very special microclimate with cool nights and hot days in the summertime.

ENSELBERG

Jechtingen | Baden
VDP.GROSSE LAGE®

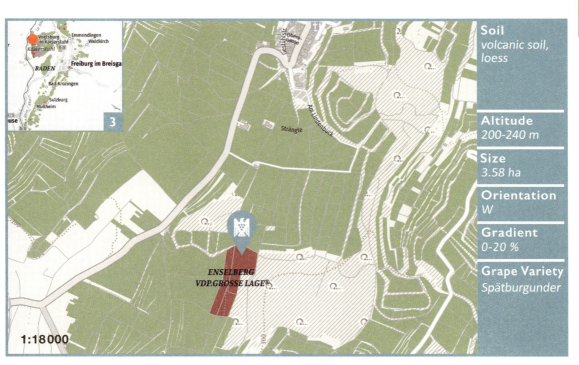

Soil
volcanic soil, loess

Altitude
200-240 m

Size
3.58 ha

Orientation
W

Gradient
0-20 %

Grape Variety
Spätburgunder

VDP.Estates: Franz Keller

The VDP.GROSSE LAGE® ENSELBERG is in the northern section of the Kaiserstuhl. With inclines measuring up to 20 percent, it is fairly moderate by Kaiserstuhl standards. The site looks out west toward the Rhine and rises from 200 to 240 meters in elevation. The vines are rooted in loess and the region's characteristic volcanic soils. The 3.5 hectare GL is primarily planted with Spätburgunder.

FEUERBERG HASLEN

Burkheim | Baden
VDP.GROSSE LAGE®

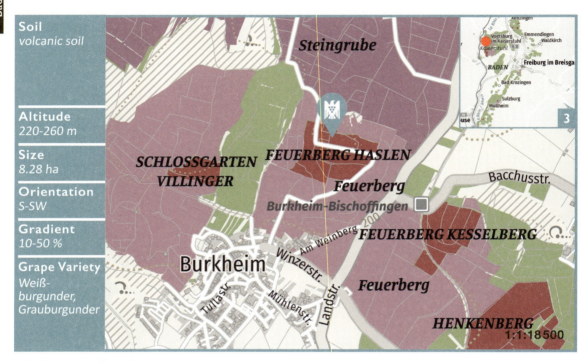

Soil
volcanic soil

Altitude
220-260 m

Size
8.28 ha

Orientation
S-SW

Gradient
10-50 %

Grape Variety
Weiß-burgunder, Grauburgunder

1:1:18 500

VDP.Estates: Bercher

Overlooking Burkheim at the western rim of the Kaiserstuhl, the VDP. GROSSE LAGE® FEUERBERG HASLEN lies between 220 and 260 meters above sea level with a gradient ranging from 10 to 50 percent. It used to be its own single vinyard called Burkheimer Haselberg before 1971. The very dry and stony soil consists of eroded volcanic rock, wheatered by the elements. This terroir imprints on the wines impressively, especially on the varieties Grauburgunder and Weißburgunder that are being cultivated here.

History: The vineyards name Haslen refers to the many hazelnut-bushes that used to be growing on the top of the Feuerberg.

FEUERBERG KESSELBERG

Burkheim | Baden
VDP.GROSSE LAGE®

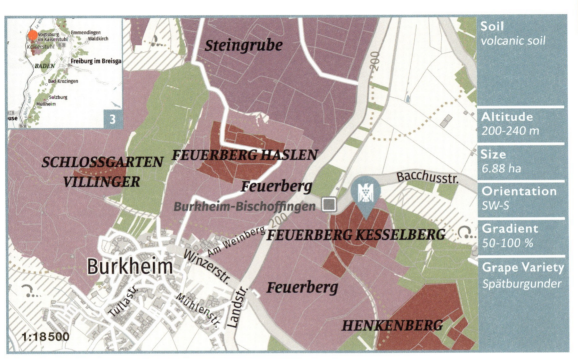

Soil
volcanic soil

Altitude
200-240 m

Size
6.88 ha

Orientation
SW-S

Gradient
50-100 %

Grape Variety
Spätburgunder

VDP.Estates: Bercher

Located east from Burkheim at the western rim of the Kaiserstuhl, the VDP.GROSSE LAGE® FEUERBERG KESSELBERG is exposed from south to south-west. It lies between 200 and 240 meters above sea level and has a steep gradient ranging from 50 to 100 percent. It is protected by a wooded area that shields it from the cold winds of the north. The many volcanic stones in its dark weathered soil store the sun's warmth in the daytime and radiate it into the vines. Spätburgunder is grown here.

History: The vineyards name refers to the perfectly round hill it is situated on, which looks like a toppled over kettle (Kessel) from afar.

FRAUENBERG

Mauchen | Baden
VDP.GROSSE LAGE®

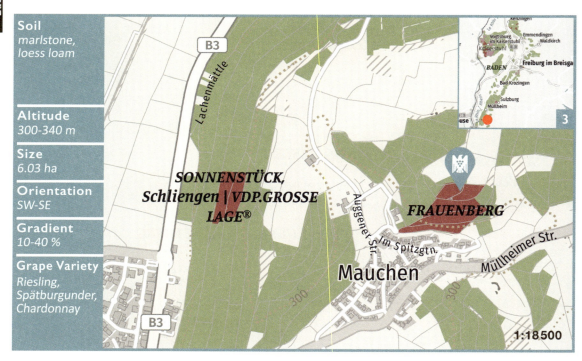

Soil
marlstone, loess loam

Altitude
300-340 m

Size
6.03 ha

Orientation
SW-SE

Gradient
10-40 %

Grape Variety
Riesling, Spätburgunder, Chardonnay

VDP.Estates: **Lämmlin-Schindler**

Calcareous loess loam and marl determine the soil of the VDP.GROSSE LAGE® FRAUENBERG, located in the Mauchen district of Schliengen in Markgräflerland. The slopes face southwest to southeast and have a slope gradient of 10 to 40 percent. Riesling, Spätburgunder and Chardonnay are cultivated here.

GOLDENES LOCH

Neuweier | Baden
VDP.GROSSE LAGE®

Soil
sandstone, clay, slate

Altitude
200-230 m

Size
0.85 ha

Orientation
SW

Gradient
30-60 %

Grape Variety
Riesling

VDP.Estates: Robert Schätzle - Schloss Neuweier

The VDP.GROSSE LAGE® GOLDENES LOCH is extremely steep with up to 60 percent slope gradient. The approximately one-hectare vineyard is located in the Neuweier district of Baden-Baden. It forms a southwest-facing amphitheatre and captures the evening sunshine like a concave mirror. The reflection of light causes vine leaves to turn golden in autumn. Riesling grows here on clay, sandstone and slate. This VDP.GROSSE LAGE® is a monopole vineyard of the VDP.Estate Schloss Neuweier.

History: After lying fallow for decades, horizontal terraces were constructed in 1993 to render it suitable for cultivation.

HEINBERG

Tiefenbach | Baden
VDP.GROSSE LAGE®

Soil
middle keuper

Altitude
240-265 m

Size
2.49 ha

Orientation
S-SW

Gradient
20-40 %

Grape Variety
Chardonnay

VDP.Estates: Heitlinger

The VDP.GROSSE LAGE® HEINBERG is located on the steeply rising slope of the Heinberg Mountain, just one hill away from Tiefenbach. With a 40 percent slope gradient the 2.5-hectare site lies at 240 to 265 metres above sea level. The Keuper marl is pale in colour. The site turns from southwest to south and benefits fully from the sunshine from midday onwards. The forested area on the Heinberg protects this site from cold north winds and helps mitigate the risk of frost.

HENKENBERG

Oberrotweil | Baden
VDP.GROSSE LAGE®

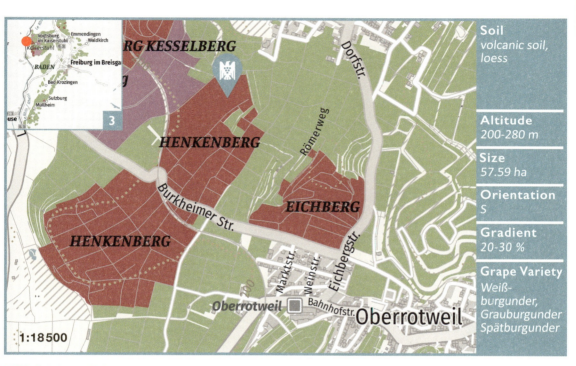

Soil
volcanic soil, loess

Altitude
200-280 m

Size
57.59 ha

Orientation
S

Gradient
20-30 %

Grape Variety
Weißburgunder, Grauburgunder, Spätburgunder

VDP.Estates: **Salwey**

The VDP.GROSSE LAGE® HENKENBERG lies in the steepest part of the Henkenberg, a mountain ridge of volcanic origin located between Oberrrotweil and Burkheim. Weathered volcanic rock determines the soils here at 200 to 280 metres above sea level. The soil is quite skeletal and examples of garnet gemstones can even be found. The HENKENBERG GL stretches to the south and is not only warmed by long direct solar radiation, but also from Mediterranean winds that make their way from the Rhône to the Upper Rhine Plain through the Saône Valley.

History: "Henken" means "to hang". The name refers to the location of a gallows belonging to early rulers of the region.

HERRENBERG LANGE WINGERT

Leimen | Baden
VDP.GROSSE LAGE®

Soil
loess, shell limestone

Altitude
180 m

Size
2.7 ha

Orientation
SW

Gradient
10-20 %

Grape Variety
Spätburgunder

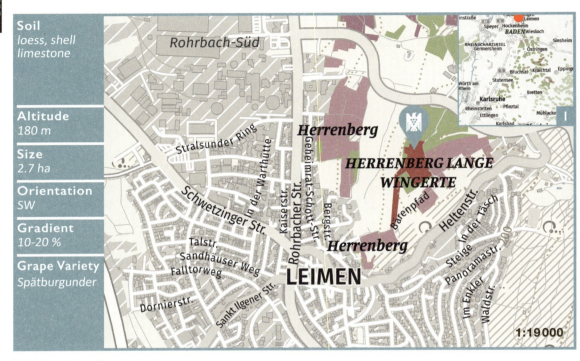

VDP.Estates: **Seeger**

Loess, shell limestone and coloured sandstone distinguish the soils of the VDP.GROSSE LAGE® HERRENBERG LANGE WINGERTE, located in Leimen on the Badische Bergstrasse. The vineyard faces southwest and has a slope gradient of up to 20 percent. One enjoys a view of the southern foothills of the Odenwald Mountains. VDP.GROSSE GEWÄCHSE® from Spätburgunder are cultivated here.

History: The Herrenberg vineyard was first documented in the 16th century as a vineyard belonging to the Catholic Teutonic Order. According to recorded history tithes were paid to the Prince Elector cellar in Heidelberg in the form of wine instead of money.

HERRENTISCH

Lahr | Baden
VDP.GROSSE LAGE®

Soil	loess
Altitude	240-280 m
Size	0.50 ha
Orientation	W-SE
Gradient	10-50 %
Grape Variety	Weiß-burgunder, Grauburgunder

VDP.Estates: Wöhrle

The VDP.GROSSE LAGE® HERRENTISCH is the most highlight elevated, south-facing vineyard on the Schutterlindenberg, a conical foothill of the Black Forest in the community of Lahr in Breisgau. This vineyard has a view of the Vosges Mountains to the west and of the Kaiserstuhl to the south. The vineyard is partially terraced and has a slope gradient of up to 50 percent. The vineyard benefits from abundant sunshine and cool breezes from the east and north that frequently waft though the vines. Weissburgunder is cultivated here on fertile loess loam.

History: The top of the hill is capped with a linden forest. Local aristocrats once celebrated evening meals here, lending the vineyard its name, which means "Gentlemen's Table".

HUSARENKAPPE

Sulzfeld | Baden
VDP.GROSSE LAGE®

Soil
gypsum marl

Altitude
220-260 m

Size
2.83 ha

Orientation
SW

Gradient
10-40 %

Grape Variety
Riesling

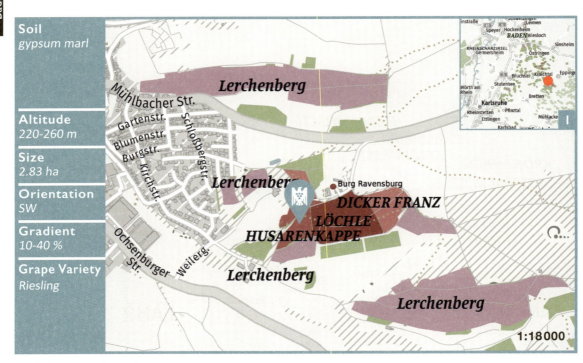

VDP.Estates: Burg Ravensburg

The VDP.GROSSE LAGE® HUSARENKAPPE is situated on the southwest facing slopes of the hill beneath the Ravensburg fortress. The vineyard slopes gently at 10 to 40 percent. Gipskeuper (gypsum marl) and marl comprise the soils of the GL HUSARENKAPPE. The site is close to three hectares in size and lies at 220 to 260 metres above sea level The GL HUSARENKAPPE is planted exclusively with Riesling.

History: The name Husarenkappe is attributed to the supposed means of transportation of the vineyard's first Riesling scions. The vines were a gift to the former owner of the fortress, commander of the Baden Hussar regiment Baron Göler von Ravensburg from the supreme commander Margrave Friedrich von Baden. The lord of the fortress carried the scions to Sulzfeld in his uniform hat (Kappe) and planted them on the fortress hill.

KAPELLENBERG

Eichelberg | Baden
VDP.GROSSE LAGE®

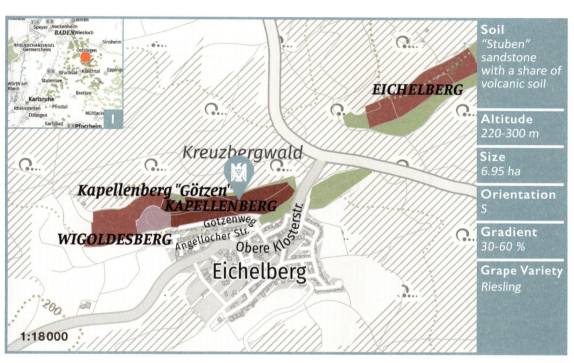

Soil
"Stuben" sandstone with a share of volcanic soil

Altitude
220-300 m

Size
6.95 ha

Orientation
S

Gradient
30-60 %

Grape Variety
Riesling

VDP.Estates: **Burg Ravensburg**

The VDP.GROSSE LAGE® KAPELLENBERG lies above the wine village Eichelberg. The 7-hectare vineyard is steep and rises from 220 to 300 metres above sea level at an up to 60 percent slope gradient with a south aspect. The soils are "Stuben" sandstone with a share of volcanic soil that provide sufficient water availability. The pale colour of the soil reflects sunlight back into the vine rows allowing ripening grape bunches to benefit from light on all sides.

History: The Romans were the first to discover the potential of the Kapellenberg for wine cultivation. The site gets its name from the St. Michael Chapel that was built there in 1748.

KIRCHBERG

Oberrotweil | Baden
VDP.GROSSE LAGE®

Soil
volcanic soil

Altitude
220-260 m

Size
7.75 ha

Orientation
W-SW

Gradient
20-40 %

Grape Variety
*Weiß-
burgunder,
Grauburgunder,
Spätburgunder*

VDP.Estates: **Salwey**

The VDP.GROSSE LAGE® KIRCHBERG in Oberrotweil in southern Baden slopes southwest toward the Upper Rhine Plain. It lies at 220 to 260 metres above sea level in an exposed concave slope of the Kaiserstuhl, where grapes enjoy optimal solar radiation. The rocky volcanic soil stores warmth and releases it into the vines during the night. Black granite and melanite can occasionally be found in the soil. The forest to the north protects the vines from wind. Weissburgunder, Grauburgunder and Spätburgunder are cultivated here.
History: The name of this vineyard stems from the church (Kirche) of a women's cloister that was settled in this valley the middle ages.

KIRCHGASSE

Lahr | Baden
VDP.GROSSE LAGE®

Soil
loess

Altitude
230-270 m

Size
4.41 ha

Orientation
SE

Gradient
30-60 %

Grape Variety
Weiß-burgunder, Grauburgunder, Spätburgunder

VDP.Estates: **Wöhrle**

The VDP.GROSSE LAGE® KIRCHGASSE lies on the south side of the Schutterlindenberg, a foothill of the Black Forest near Lahr in Breisgau. Grauburgunder and Spätburgunder grow here on fertile loess over mineral-rich limestone. The vines grow in terraces that form a horseshoe shape on a south-facing slope. The vineyard is quite steep in parts with a slope gradient ranging from 30 to 60 percent. The concave shape of the site allows the sun to warm the soil intensely. Warm south to southwest winds blow through the so-called "Burgundian Gates" into this site.

History: Evidence of wine cultivation in this vineyard exists from the year 1114. Up into the 19th century, the main access to this vineyard was an erosion channel that emptied into the village near the St. Martin church.

KÖNIGSBECHER

Odenheim | Baden
VDP.GROSSE LAGE®

Soil
red marl

Altitude
180-200 m

Size
4.57 ha

Orientation
S-SE

Gradient
15-35 %

Grape Variety
Pinot Noir

VDP.Estates: Heitlinger

The VDP.GROSSE LAGE® KÖNIGSBECHER lies on a steep site that is well protected to the south and west. The vineyard descends toward Odenheim at a slope of 35 percent between 180 and 200 metres above sea level The vineyard is found on chalky red marl. The main variety is Spätburgunder.

History: The name Königsbecher translates into Kings' goblet meaning, that the wines from this vineyard site have a royal quality.

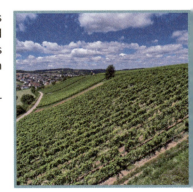

KROHNENBÜHL GOTTSACKER

Lahr | Baden
VDP.GROSSE LAGE®

Soil	loess
Altitude	180-200 m
Size	0.66 ha
Orientation	SW
Gradient	10-20 %
Grape Variety	Chardonnay

VDP.Estates: Wöhrle

The VDP.GROSSE LAGE® KROHNENBÜHL GOTTSACKER is situated on a small plateau on the Schutterlindenberg, a foothill of the Black Forest near Lahr in Breisgau. It is a prime parcel in the VDP.ERSTE LAGE® KRONENBÜHL. Chardonnay thrives here on deep, calcareous loess soil. The vineyard has a gentle slope of 10 to 20 percent gradient that faces southwest. The microclimate here allows a long vegetation period in which grapes benefit from gradual ripening.

LÖCHLE

Sulzfeld | Baden
VDP.GROSSE LAGE®

Soil
gypsum marl

Altitude
240-280 m

Size
6.18 ha

Orientation
SW-S

Gradient
10-40 %

Grape Variety
Weißburgunder, Grauburgunder, Spätburgunder

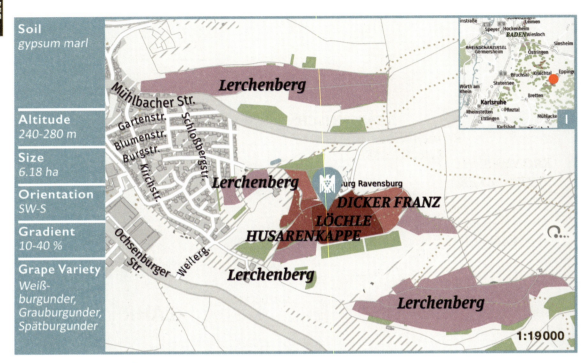

VDP.Estates: **Burg Ravensburg**

The VDP.GROSSE LAGE® LÖCHLE is a south-facing slope below the visibly prominent Burg Ravensburg. The slope is concave like a parabolic mirror, which creates a warm, well-protected microclimate. It climbs from 240 to 280 metres above sea level at a 10 to 40 percent gradient. The soils are dominated by gypsum marl. The GL LÖCHLE is a monopole vineyard of the VDP.Estate Burg Ravensburg.

MAUERBERG "MAUERWEIN"[1]

Neuweier | Baden
VDP.GROSSE LAGE®

Soil
Carbon

Altitude
200-300 m

Size
0.80 ha

Orientation
W-SW

Gradient
40-60 %

Grape Variety
Riesling

VDP.Estates: Robert Schätzle - Schloss Neuweier

The VDP.GROSSE LAGE® MAUERBERG "MAUERWEIN"[1] is located above the wine village Neuweier and is extremely steep. Horizontal terrace walls climb the 60 percent slope gradient from 200 to 300 metres above sea level. The little 0.8-hectare vineyard has a southwest aspect. The name "Mauerberg" (wall mountain) stems from the dry stacked terrace walls that cross the site. The walls store the warmth of the day and release it into the vines at night, thus extending the daily grape ripening period. The geology of the GL contains interstratifications from the Upper Carboniferous period – carbon therefore plays an important role in the rocks present in this site.

Information: Although this site belongs to the Baden wine region and not to Franken, an exception is made in packaging the wines. Due to a standing tradition since the 19th century, these wines may be filled in Bocksbeutel bottles.

OBERER FIRST

Reicholzheim | Baden
VDP.GROSSE LAGE®

Baden

Soil
shell limestone

Altitude
280-320 m

Size
3.72 ha

Orientation
S-SE

Gradient
20-30 %

Grape Variety
Weiß-burgunder, Spätburgunder

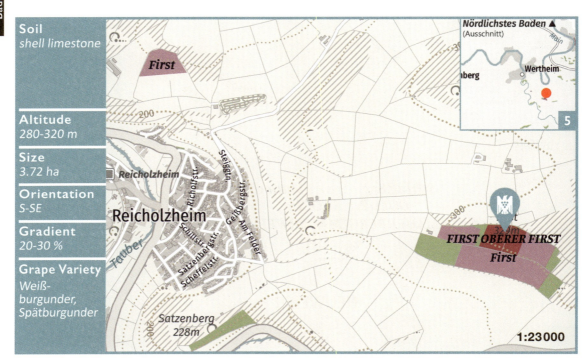

VDP.Estates: Schlör

The VDP.GROSSE LAGE® OBERER FIRST lies on the slopes of the Tauber Valley and is the northernmost VDP.GROSSE LAGE® in Baden. It is found in the upper half of the First vineyard at 280 to 320 metres above sea level Predominantly Spätburgunder and Weißburgunder are planted on a slope of around 20 to 30 percent gradient. The soils are mostly rocky lower shell limestone and Wellenkalk. Variegated sandstone and friable loam are also found – therefore the vines have a good mineral supply. Also the soil warms up easily und cools out slowly. With over 1370 hours of sunshine during vegetation the OBERER FIRST is sundrenched. It lies in the rain shade of the Odenwald and Spessart which can cause rather dry summers. Therefore the vines need long roots to reach the needs water.

PULVERBUCK

Oberbergen | Baden
VDP.GROSSE LAGE®

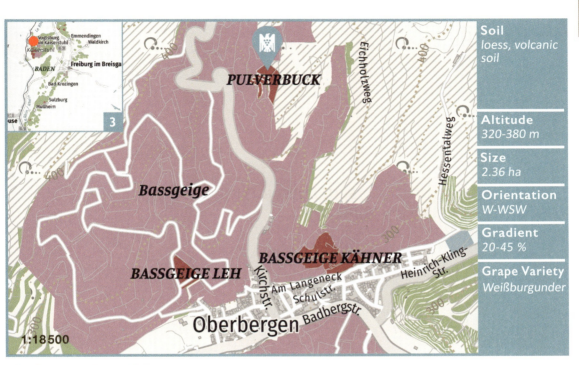

Soil
loess, volcanic soil

Altitude
320-380 m

Size
2.36 ha

Orientation
W-WSW

Gradient
20-45 %

Grape Variety
Weißburgunder

VDP.Estates: Franz Keller

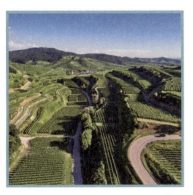

At 380 metres above sea level, the VDP.GROSSE LAGE® PULVERBUCK is the most highly elevated parcel within the VDP.ERSTE LAGE® Bassgeige. The vineyard is moderately steep with up to a 45 percent gradient. The vines root in vulcanite and very fine-grained loess. The GL PULVERBUCK has a concave shape and west to west-southwest aspect that captures the midday and evening sunshine. The dark soil stores the heat and releases it into the vines at night, thus prolonging the daily ripening period of the grapes.

SCHELLENBRUNNEN

Tiefenbach | Baden
VDP.GROSSE LAGE®

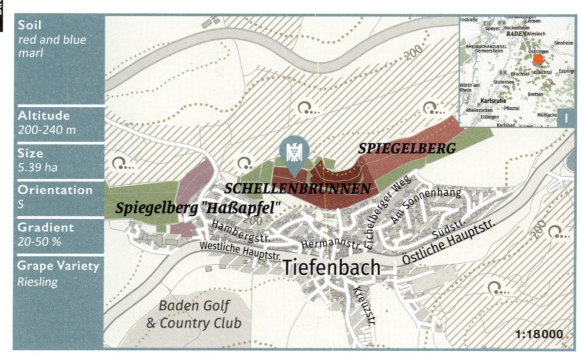

Soil
red and blue marl

Altitude
200-240 m

Size
5.39 ha

Orientation
S

Gradient
20-50 %

Grape Variety
Riesling

VDP.Estates: Heitlinger

The VDP.GROSSE LAGE® SCHELLENBRUNNEN is located above the little wine city Tiefenbach just below the GL WORMSBERG. The red and blue marl that dominates the soil reflect the sunlight and enhances photosynthesis and grape ripening. The 5.4-hectare GL rises from 200 to 240 metres above sea level at a steep slope gradient of 50 percent. Temperatures cool significantly at night, which helps preserve acidity in the grapes.

SCHLOSSBERG MARIENBERG

Durbach | Baden
VDP.GROSSE LAGE®

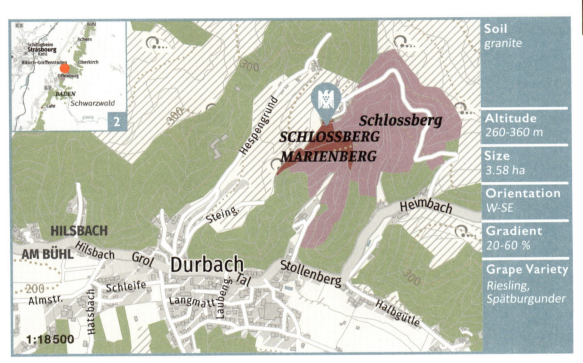

Soil
granite

Altitude
260-360 m

Size
3.58 ha

Orientation
W-SE

Gradient
20-60 %

Grape Variety
Riesling, Spätburgunder

VDP.Estates: **Markgraf von Baden**

The VDP.GROSSE LAGE® SCHLOSSBERG MARIENBERG is located on the Staufenberg hill in Durbach in Ortenau Valley. The small vineyard parcel is located in the upper section of the Schlossberg vineyard, below and northeast of Schloss Staufenberg. It has a slope gradient of up to steep 60 percent. Vines root deeply in the weathered granite soil. The southeast aspect provides optimal solar radiation. Night temperatures in this elevated site are quite cool and prolong the ripening period of grapes. Riesling and Spätburgunder are cultivated here. This VDP.GROSSE LAGE® is a monopole vineyard of the VDP. Estate Markgraf von Baden, which is housed in Schloss Staufenberg.

History: Earliest evidence of viticulture in the Schlossberg vineyard stems from the year 1399. Schloss Staufenberg, the castle that thrones above the vineyard, was built in the 11th century.

SCHLOSSBERG

Achkarren | Baden
VDP.GROSSE LAGE®

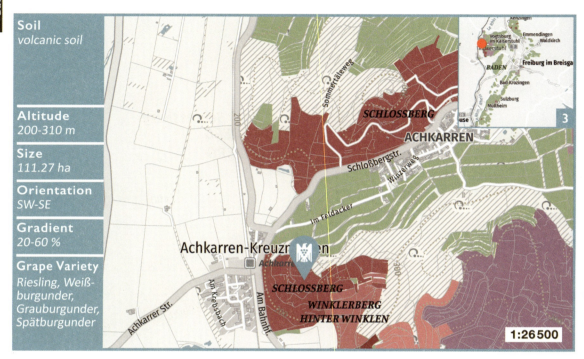

Soil
volcanic soil

Altitude
200-310 m

Size
111.27 ha

Orientation
SW-SE

Gradient
20-60 %

Grape Variety
Riesling, Weißburgunder, Grauburgunder, Spätburgunder

VDP.Estates: Dr. Heger, Franz Keller, Michel

The VDP.GROSSE LAGE® SCHLOSSBERG rises up to 310 metres above sea level north of Achkarren on the Kaiserstuhl. It looks over the Upper Rhine and Breisach on the German-French border and on into Alsace and the Vosges Mountains. With a slope gradient ranging from 20 to 60 percent, the vineyard is extremely steep in parts. Riesling, Weissburgunder, Grauburgunder and Spätburgunder grow here on rocky volcanic soil. The soil is capable of storing the sun's warmth well, which is further enhanced by the concave shape of the slope.

History: "Schlossberg" is a common name for a vineyard in Germany and refers to a vineyard that is adjacent to a castle. Remnants of the walls of the 13th century Schloss Höhingen can be found in the vineyard. Rock below the castle ruin was blasted in the year 1819 to prepare the area for vine cultivation.

SCHLOSSBERG

Freiburg | Baden
VDP.GROSSE LAGE®

Soil
gneiss

Altitude
300-360 m

Size
3.98 ha

Orientation
S

Gradient
40-60 %

Grape Variety
Spätburgunder

VDP.Estates: Staatsweingut Freiburg, Stigler

The steep VDP.GROSSE LAGE® SCHLOSSBERG rises over the city of Freiburg up to 360 metres above sea level Spätburgunder is cultivated in this south-facing vineyard. Gneiss, a mineral-rich metamorphic rock, dominates the soil of this site. Average precipitation here is twice as high as on the Kaiserstuhl. The cool Höllentäler wind from the Black Forest frequently wafts over the city and through the vineyard.
History: According to recorded history, wine has been cultivated here for more than 1000 years. At the end of the 17th century, Freiburg was seized by troops led by the Sun King Ludwig XIV of France, who then made the city a fortress. Strongholds were also built on this hill. Before the French took the city in the middle of the 18th century, the strongholds were destroyed. Remnants of these bastions were then used to build vineyard walls that continue to brace the small terraces of the Schlossberg vineyard.

SCHLOSSBERG

Hecklingen | Baden
VDP.GROSSE LAGE®

Soil
weathered white shell limestone

Altitude
200-280 m

Size
5.54 ha

Orientation
W-SW

Gradient
80-90 %

Grape Variety
Chardonnay, Spätburgunder

VDP.Estates: **Bernhard Huber**

The Lichteneck castle ruin thrones above the VDP.GROSSE LAGE® SCHLOSSBERG, which makes it easily recognisable from a distance. The vineyard soil is unusual for the region here in the foothills of the Black Forest: fossil-rich, weathered shell limestone that appears white to yellowish. Chardonnay and Spätburgunder grow here on a steep, west to southwest-facing slope with a 80 to 90 percent gradient.

History: Cultivation of this vineyard is first mentioned in documents dating 1492. "Schlossberg" is a common name for a vineyard in Germany and refers to a vineyard that is adjacent to a castle. The Count of Freiburg built the Lichteneck castle in the 13th century. The building was eventually destroyed in the Franco-Dutch War by French troops led by General Nicolas de Bautru, Marquis de Vaubrun in 1675. Today it is owned privately.

SCHLOSSGARTEN VILLINGER

Burkheim | Baden
VDP.GROSSE LAGE®

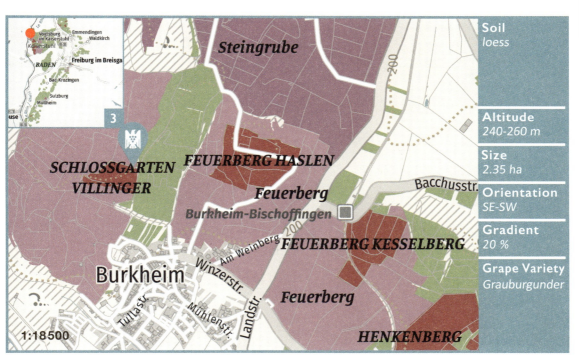

Soil	loess
Altitude	240-260 m
Size	2.35 ha
Orientation	SE-SW
Gradient	20 %
Grape Variety	Grauburgunder

VDP.Estates: Bercher

The VDP.GROSSE LAGE® SCHLOSSGARTEN VILLINGER is located in Burkheim at the western rim of the Kaiserstuhl and extends from the ruin of the Burkheim castle towards the west. This traditionally terraced vineyard has a 20 percent slope gradient and faces southeast to southwest. The soil consists of volcanic tuff with a covering of loess deposit. It is rich in nutrients and has a good water storage capacity. Grauburgunder is planted here.

History: Vine cultivation on terraces was documented here during the time of the Franks around 750 A.D. The name of this vineyard refers to a former owner which either bore the name Villinger or came from the place of the same name in the eastern part of Baden.

SOMMERHALDE

Bombach | Baden
VDP.GROSSE LAGE®

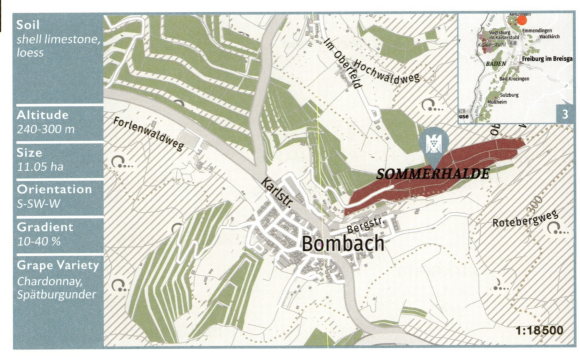

Soil
shell limestone, loess

Altitude
240-300 m

Size
11.05 ha

Orientation
S-SW-W

Gradient
10-40 %

Grape Variety
Chardonnay, Spätburgunder

VDP.Estates: **Bernhard Huber**

The VDP.GROSSE LAGE® SOMMERHALDE lies above the wine village Bombach in the Breisgau area of Baden. The south to west facing vineyard is moderately steep and rises at a 40 percent gradient from 240 to 300 metres above sea level. Calcareous shell limestone with a covering of loess determines a soil composition that is ideal for grape varieties like Spätburgunder and Chardonnay. The relatively cool microclimate preserves acidity in the grapes.

SONNENSTÜCK

Schliengen | Baden
VDP.GROSSE LAGE®

Soil
medium to deep, gritty-rocky calcarous loam, loess, tertiary marl

Altitude
260-400 m

Size
2.74 ha

Orientation
SW

Gradient
30-50 %

Grape Variety
Grauburgunder, Spätburgunder, Chardonnay

VDP.Estates: **Blankenhorn**

The sun and warm climate of the southern Rhine Valley near Schliengen pamper the VDP.GROSSE LAGE® SONNENSTÜCK. The vineyard is sloped with a 30 to 50 percent gradient that extends from 260 to 400 metres above sea level facing southwest. The soils are medium to deep, gritty-rocky calcarous loam, loess and tertiary marl.

SPIEGELBERG

Tiefenbach | Baden
VDP.GROSSE LAGE®

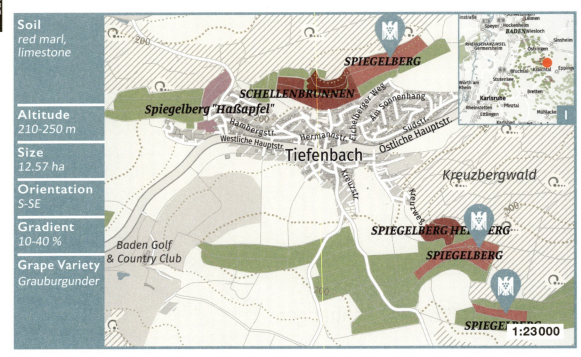

Soil
red marl, limestone

Altitude
210-250 m

Size
12.57 ha

Orientation
S-SE

Gradient
10-40 %

Grape Variety
Grauburgunder

VDP.Estates: Heitlinger

The VDP.GROSSE LAGE® SPIEGELBERG lies protected behind the forested peak of the Heinberg mountain. With a 40 percent slope gradient, this vineyard is one of the steepest in the vicinity. The soil is comprised primarily of red marl and limestone. The site has a south to southeast aspect and benefits from the very first rays of morning sunshine. The 13-hectare vineyard lies at 210 to 250 metres above sea level.

VORDERER WINKLERBERG

Ihringen | Baden
VDP.GROSSE LAGE®

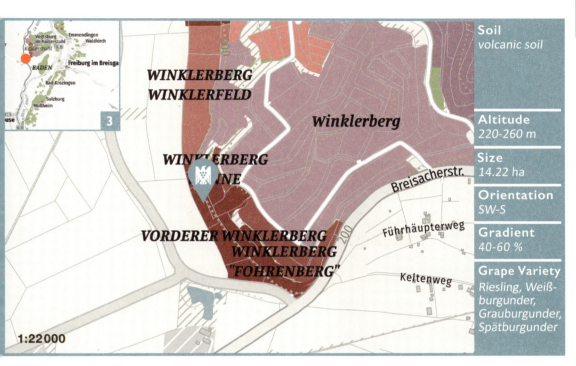

Soil
volcanic soil

Altitude
220-260 m

Size
14.22 ha

Orientation
SW-S

Gradient
40-60 %

Grape Variety
Riesling, Weißburgunder, Grauburgunder, Spätburgunder

VDP.Estates: Dr. Heger, Stigler

The VDP.GROSSE LAGE® VORDERER WINKLERBERG forms the southwest border of the Winklerberg vineyard (117 ha). It is the warmest vineyard in Germany and has a nearly mediterranean climate. The terraced GL VORDERER WINKLERBERG has numerous dry stone walls and together with the rocky soils and meagre rock faces of red tephrite, the warmth stored in them intensifies the microclimate. The soils are predominantly well-drained weathered volcanic rock with limestone. The GL VORDERER WINKLERBERG lies between 220 and 260 metres above sea level

History: The VORDERER WINKLERBERG vineyard was planted in a dolerite quarry at the beginning of the 19th century.

WIGOLDESBERG

Eichelberg | Baden
VDP.GROSSE LAGE®

Soil
red limestone, marl

Altitude
250-300 m

Size
4.5 ha

Orientation
S

Gradient
30-50 %

Grape Variety
Pinot Noir

VDP.Estates: Heitlinger

The VDP.GROSSE LAGE® WIGOLDESBERG is essentially the extension of the GL KAPELLENBERG. This 4.5-hectare vineyard is moderately steep with an up to 50 percent gradient that faces south and rises from 250 to 300 metres above sea level. The soils are dominated by red limestone and marl. This pale soil reflects the sunlight back into the vines.

History: The Romans were the first to discover the potential of this vineyard site for wine cultivation. The name goes back on the celtic "Berg des Wigold" ("hill of wigold"). In the 10th century the Benedictine monastery "Wigoldesberg" was built above the vineyard and the monchs recultivated the Wigoldesberg.

WINGERTE

Laufen | Baden
VDP.GROSSE LAGE®

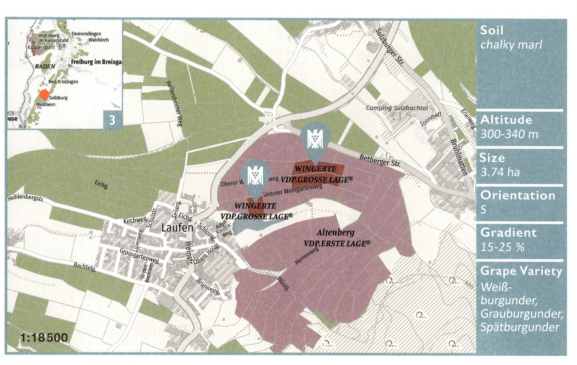

Soil
chalky marl

Altitude
300-340 m

Size
3.74 ha

Orientation
S

Gradient
15-25 %

Grape Variety
Weißburgunder, Grauburgunder, Spätburgunder

VDP.Estates: H. Schlumberger

The VDP.GROSSE LAGE® WINGERTE is in a protected convex slope within the Altenberg vineyard above the city of Laufen in Markgräflerland. The steep to very steep vineyards descend from 340 to 300 metres above sea level Calcareous marl with a share of loam comprises the soil of the GL WINGERTE. The main grape variety is Weißburgunder, Grauburgunder and Spätburgunder. The convex slope traps the warmth that determines the climate of the GL WINGERTE. This is further enhanced by warm Mediterranean winds that travel from the Rhône through the so-called "Burgundian gates".

WINKLEN

Ihringen | Baden
VDP.GROSSE LAGE®

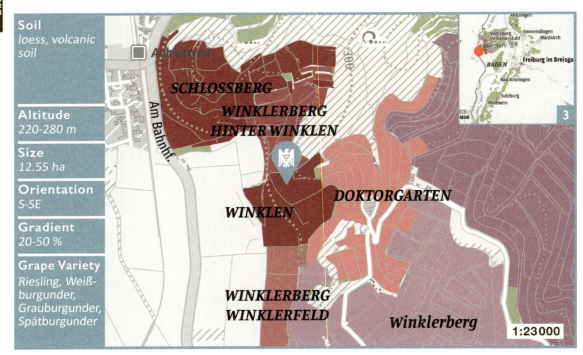

Soil
loess, volcanic soil

Altitude
220-280 m

Size
12.55 ha

Orientation
S-SE

Gradient
20-50 %

Grape Variety
Riesling, Weißburgunder, Grauburgunder, Spätburgunder

VDP.Estates: Stigler

VDP GROSSE LAGE® WINKLEN is part of the Ihringer Winklerberg, sitting in the town of Ihringen on a foothill running south from the Kaiserstuhl. It is among the warmest sites in all of Germany. The individual parcels of the Winklerberg enjoy an almost sub-tropical climate, as the Kaiserstuhl shields against cold north winds. The nearby Burgundian gate between the Rhine and Sâone valleys funnels warm Mediterranean air toward the Rhine. The GL WINKLEN faces toward the south and southeast, with black volcanic soils that store solar energy during the day and then return it to the vines at night. The hills are steep, with gradients up to 50 percent, and are terraced in some places.

WINKLERBERG "FOHRENBERG"

Ihringen | Baden
VDP.GROSSE LAGE®

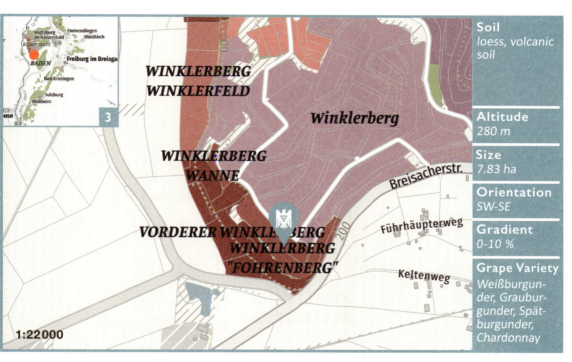

Soil	loess, volcanic soil
Altitude	280 m
Size	7.83 ha
Orientation	SW-SE
Gradient	0-10 %
Grape Variety	Weißburgunder, Grauburgunder, Spätburgunder, Chardonnay

VDP.Estates: Stigler

The VDP.GROSSE LAGE® WINKLERBERG "FOHRENBERG" surrounds the small, Asian-like pagoda in the middle of the southern tongue of the Winklerberg vineyard. It is located in the warmest vineyard area in Germany and has a Mediterranean climate. Warm air masses from the Rhône travel through the so-called Burgundian gates (through the Saône Valley and the plains between Jura and the Vosges Mountains) and over the Upper Rhine Plain. The dark and porous weathered volcanic rock also stores the warmth and radiates gradually to the vines. The GL lies on 280 metres above sea level and is 7,8 hectares in size. In this vineyard you find Chardonnay as well as Spätburgunder, Weissburgunder and Grauburgunder.

WINKLERBERG HINTER WINKLEN

Ihringen | Baden
VDP.GROSSE LAGE®

Soil
volcanic soil, loess

Altitude
220-260 m

Size
10.89 ha

Orientation
W-SW

Gradient
30-40 %

Grape Variety
Grauburgunder

VDP.Estates: Dr. Heger

While the rest of the Winklerberg classified site is typically very warm in summer, VDP GROSSE LAGE® WINKLERBERG HINTER WINKLEN tends to remain somewhat cooler. Little wonder, given that it sits at a hefty 220 to 260 meters in elevation and has a more open topography. A mountain spur – the Rappenecker – stretches out in front of the site, providing shade until mid-day, after which the vines and grapes enjoy full exposure to the sun. This west and southwest-facing site sees up to 1 700 hours of sunshine per year on average. The soils of this steep vineyard (inclines between 30 and 40 percent) are composed of dark volcanic rock and loess that store the sun's warmth.

WINKLERBERG WANNE

Ihringen | Baden
VDP.GROSSE LAGE®

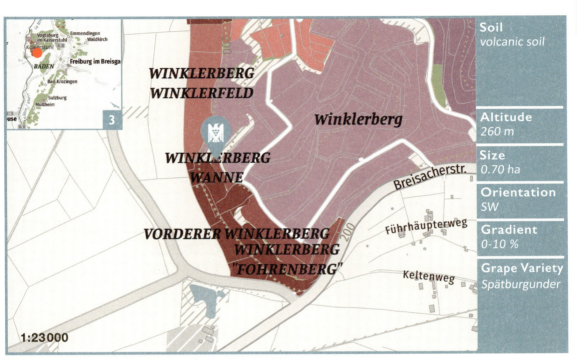

Soil
volcanic soil

Altitude
260 m

Size
0.70 ha

Orientation
SW

Gradient
0-10 %

Grape Variety
Spätburgunder

VDP.Estates: **Dr. Heger**

The VDP.GROSSE LAGE® WINKLERBERG WANNE is located in the village of Ihringen, just a few kilometres away from the Rhine River. At the southern tip of the Kaiserstuhl, this is the sunniest and warmest wine region in Germany. Spätburgunder grows on southwest-facing terraces that are braced with stone walls. The soil is weathered tephrit, a volcanic rock that stores warmth well. An extinct volcano protects the vineyard from the north wind.

History: The physician Ernst Georg Lydtin from Ihringen was responsible for the initial preparation of the Winklerberg parcel for vine cultivation. With the purchase of this parcel in 1813, he acquired a part of the former dolorite quarry in which he planted vines. The land was later braced with walls.

WINKLERBERG WINKLERFELD

Ihringen | Baden
VDP.GROSSE LAGE®

Soil
gravel, volcanic soil

Altitude
200 m

Size
9.32 ha

Orientation
SW

Gradient
0-10 %

Grape Variety
Spätburgunder, Weißburgunder, Chardonnay

VDP.Estates: Stigler

VDP.GROSSE LAGE® WINKLERBERG WINKLERFELD is the westernmost parcel within the Winklerberg classified site. It, like all other VDP.GROSSE LAGE® and VDP.ERSTE LAGE® sites here, benefits from the Winklerberg's special microclimate. After all, this little corner of the winemaking world is among the warmest anywhere in Germany. The climate ranges at times from Mediterranean to sub-tropical: it is protected to the north by the Kaiserstuhl, with warm Mediterranean air flowing in from France. The soils of the GL WINKLERBERG WINKLERFELD are rugged, craggy and composed primarily of dark volcanic soil – with that dark coloration lending it excellent warmth retention characteristics. Sitting at 200 meters in elevation, the GL looks out to the southwest over the Rhine. With inclines measuring up to 10 percent, it is among the flatter vineyards in the Winklerberg.

WORMSBERG

Tiefenbach | Baden
VDP.GROSSE LAGE®

Soil	red marl, limestone
Altitude	230-255 m
Size	1,2 ha
Orientation	S-SW
Gradient	40-70 %
Grape Variety	Spätburgunder / Pinot Noir

VDP.Estates: Heitlinger

The VDP.GROSSE LAGE® WORMSBERG thrones above the wine village Tiefenbach and carpets the flank of the Wormsberg Mountain. With a 70 percent slope gradient, the south to southwest facing site is quite steep and craggy. The red marl with white and blue layers of limestone reflects the light of the day back into the vines. This high light intensity benefits photosynthesis and ripening of the grapes so that abundant aroma and flavour compounds develop. The site lies at 230 to 255 metres above sea level and the nights are relatively cool.

Franken

Region:	VDP.GROSSE LAGE®:
6000 ha	376 ha
VDP.Wineries:	VDP.GROSSE LAGE® Sites:
28	23

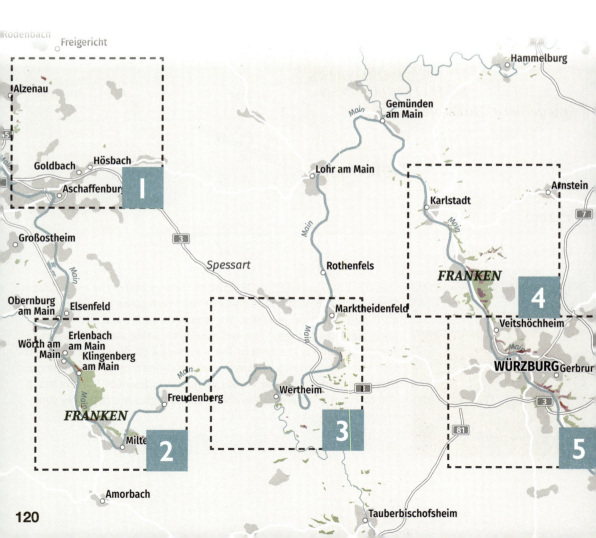

FRANKEN

Franken stands out among the ranks of the VDP.Regions in many ways. For one thing, the Silvaner grape variety dominates this wine-growing region that spreads from Hörstein near Aschaffenburg to Iphofen between Würzburg and Nuremburg along the Main River. Cultivation of the variety in Franken (Franconia) can be traced back 350 years. A second peculiarity is that many of the wines are sold in flattened ellipsoid Bocksbeutel bottles. Yet another unique feature is that hardly another region is so clearly divided geologically. Coloured sandstone dominates the Mainviereck district in the upper reaches of the river; this is where the great red wine villages of Franken (like Klingenberg and Bürgstadt) are found. In the Maindreieck district surrounding Würzburg, shell limestone determines the soils. Vines root in Keuper marl in the Steiger Forest district in the vicinity of Iphofen. All of theses geological formations stem from the Germanic Trias. Due to its long stretch—it is nearly 100 kilometres between Hörstein and Iphofen as the crow flies—Franken generally has a continental climate, but microclimates vary according to the locations of individual vineyards.

ALTTENBERG 1172[1]

Sommerhausen | Franken
VDP.GROSSE LAGE®

Soil
triassic shell limestone (Middle Muschelkalk)

Altitude
230 m

Size
6.38 ha

Orientation
SW

Gradient
45-75 %

Grape Variety
Silvaner, Riesling

VDP.Estates: Schloss Sommerhausen

The VDP.GROSSE LAGE® ALTTENBERG 1172[1] is a long strip of vineyard that follows the Main River between Sommerhausen and Eibelstadt in Franken. It lies at 230 metres above sea level and has a moderate to steep slope gradient of 45 to 75 percent that faces southwest. The mineral-rich shell limestone soils stem from the Quaderkalk Formation of the Germanic Trias. It contains marine fossils from the primordial ocean that was here 220 million years ago. The vineyard is classified for Silvaner and Riesling.

History: "Alttenberg" was first mentioned in a donation document in 1172! Since that, always been a vineyard, it's famous as the best spot for top-wine.

AM LUMPEN 1655®

Escherndorf | Franken
VDP.GROSSE LAGE®

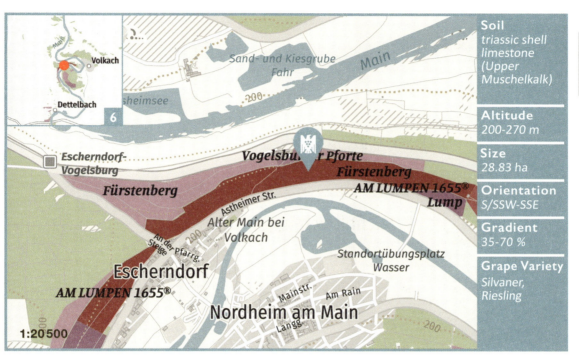

Soil
triassic shell limestone (Upper Muschelkalk)

Altitude
200-270 m

Size
28.83 ha

Orientation
S/SSW-SSE

Gradient
35-70 %

Grape Variety
Silvaner, Riesling

VDP.Estates: Michael Fröhlich, Horst Sauer, Rainer Sauer, Egon Schäffer, Zur Schwane

The VDP.GROSSE LAGE® AM LUMPEN 1655® is the prime parcel of the Eschendorfer Lump vineyard. The Lump opens toward the broad Main Valley like an amphitheatre. The GL within this vineyard is a steep slope with a 35 to 70 percent gradient and a mainly south exposition. This position protects the site from cold north winds in the winter and captures the warmth and light in the summer. The Main River also serves to mirror additional light into the vines. The soil is predominantly shell limestone. The slow moving river and the deep moist soils contribute to air humidity and promote the development of noble rot. These are ideal conditions for botrytized sweet wines.

History: "Am Lumpen" was first mentioned in a goods and regulations description dating 1655. This lends today's demarcated VDP.GROSSE LAGE® its name.

APOSTELGARTEN

Michelbach | Franken
VDP.GROSSE LAGE®

Soil
metamorphic rock (mica schist, gneiss, quartzite)

Altitude
200-280 m

Size
10,6 ha

Orientation
S

Gradient
40-50 %

Grape Variety
Riesling, Silvaner, Grauburgunder, Spätburgunder

VDP.Estates: Bernhard Höfler

The steep VDP.GROSSE LAGE® APOSTELGARTEN has a 40 to 50 percent gradient and faces south toward the sun. It is located in the Franconian community Michelbach and is bordered by a forest to the north and east. On clear days, one can look over the Main Plain all the way to the Taunus Mountains in Hessen. Stone walls in the vineyard store the warmth of the day. Where mica schist is present, the metamorphic rock soils shimmer silver to bronze.

History: Up until the 1950s, only Riesling was cultivated here. The Franconian author and lyric poet (1892-1973) Anton Schnack referred to the vineyard as "the ember for a Riesling for the gods". The vineyard became a protected historic monument in 1985.

BISCHOFSBERG

Großheubach | Franken
VDP.GROSSE LAGE®

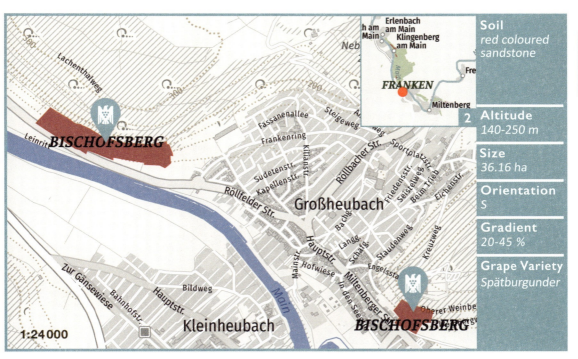

Soil
red coloured sandstone

Altitude
140-250 m

Size
36.16 ha

Orientation
S

Gradient
20-45 %

Grape Variety
Spätburgunder

VDP.Estates: Benedikt Baltes, Staatlicher Hofkeller Würzburg

The VDP.GROSSE LAGE® BISCHOFSBERG in the Grossheubach community in Franken has a slope gradient of 20 to 45 percent. Spätburgunder grows here near the Main River on rocky red coloured sandstone with loess deposits. The vineyard faces south and is partially terraced with dry stacked stone walls that influence the microclimate advantageously by storing the heat of the day. The GL BISCHOFSBERG lies at 140 to 250 metres above sea level.

History: The name of this vineyard can be connected to the Engelberg Monastery that is located above the village and other ecclesiastic influences.

CENTGRAFENBERG

Bürgstadt | Franken
VDP.GROSSE LAGE®

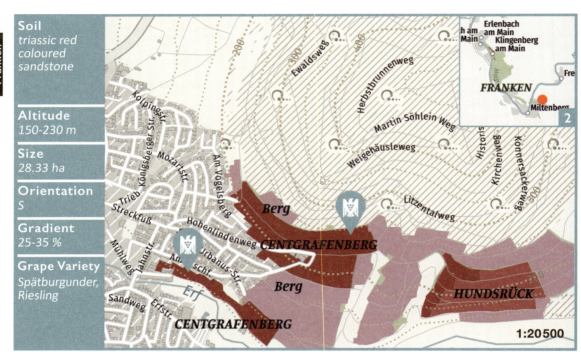

Soil
triassic red coloured sandstone

Altitude
150-230 m

Size
28.33 ha

Orientation
S

Gradient
25-35 %

Grape Variety
Spätburgunder, Riesling

VDP.Estates: **Rudolf Fürst**

The VDP.GROSSE LAGE® CENTGRAFENBERG lies well protected in the convex valley of the Miltenberg mountain. Over a long time the Main has digged a deep, narrow bed here. The GL CENTGRAFENBERG lies on the south side of a basin at a sharp south-western bend of river Main. Due to the Odenwald and Spessart mountains further protection, a warm microclimate develops. The CENTGRAFENBERG GL is gently sloped to steep with a 25 to 35 percent gradient. It lies at 150 to 230 metres a.s.l. The soil is shaped by the oldest stone in the typical Franconian Trias formation, the coloured sandstone – in different degrees of weathering. This ferreous sandstone with its red colour is particularly advantageous for Spätburgunder. The best plots for Riesling are located, where the hill bends to the West.

History: Before Churfranken, the western part of Franconia, became Bavarian, it was once mandated to the prince-bishops of Mainz.

FÜRSTLICHER KALLMUTH®

Homburg | Franken
VDP.GROSSE LAGE®

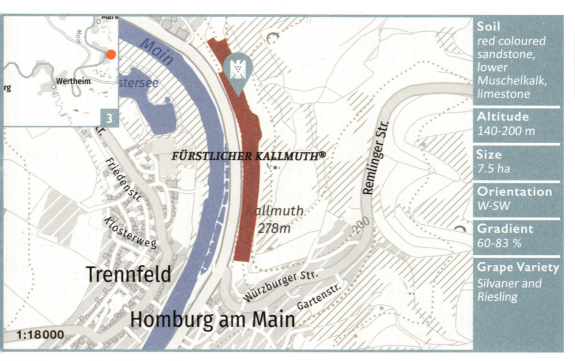

Soil
red coloured sandstone, lower Muschelkalk, limestone

Altitude
140-200 m

Size
7.5 ha

Orientation
W-SW

Gradient
60-83 %

Grape Variety
Silvaner and Riesling

Franken

VDP.Estates: Fürst Löwenstein

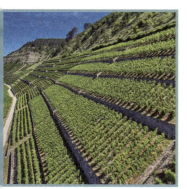

The VDP.GROSSE LAGE® FÜRSTLICHER KALLMUTH® is one of the steepest sites in Germany. Its steep to very steep slopes open towards the Main River in the west like an amphitheatre. The steep parts have a 60 to 83 percent gradient and face west. Twelve kilometres of dry stone walls that are up to five meters high run through the vineyard. The climate within the FÜRSTLICHER KALLMUTH GL can be described as sub-Mediterranean. Even in cooler summers, temperatures of up to 50 or even 60 °C (120-140 °F) can be measured. With 280-350 mm average precipitation during the vegetative period, the site is dry, but five natural mountain springs and aquifers provide the vines with sufficient water. The soils are quite skeletal with coloured sandstone in deeper horizons and shell limestone in shallower areas. Riesling and Silvaner are planted on the slopes.

HIMMELSPFAD

Retzstadt | Franken
VDP.GROSSE LAGE®

Soil
triassic shell limestone (Lower Muschelkalk)

Altitude
250 m

Size
2.19 ha

Orientation
S

Gradient
50-70 %

Grape Variety
Silvaner, Riesling

VDP.Estates: **Rudolf May**

The VDP.GROSSE LAGE HIMMELSPFAD is a historic open-field system parcel in the Langenberg vineyard in Retzstadt. This is the steepest parcel in the vineyard with a 65 percent gradient and it also has the highest solar radiation. The 2.2-hectare HIMMELSPFAD GL faces due south and is the warmest parcel. The soil is meagre, finely pored shell limestone; its white colour reflects the light into the vines. The HIMMELSPFAD GL lies at 250 metres above sea level The main variety is Silvaner (mainly planted in 1963).
History: The site is named after an old vineyard path.

HOHELEITE

Rödelsee | Franken
VDP.GROSSE LAGE®

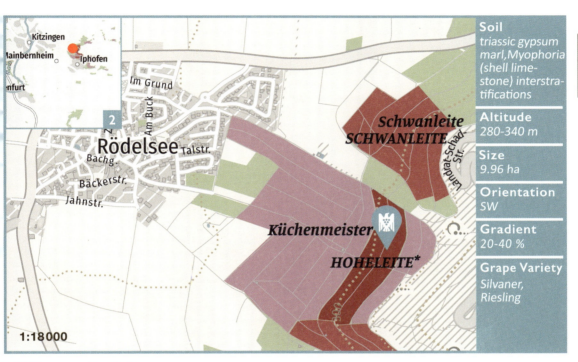

Soil
triassic gypsum marl, Myophoria (shell limestone) interstratifications

Altitude
280-340 m

Size
9.96 ha

Orientation
SW

Gradient
20-40 %

Grape Variety
Silvaner, Riesling

VDP.Estates: Paul Weltner

The VDP.GROSSE LAGE® HOHELEITE lies at 280 to 340 metres above sea level and extends as a continuation of the GL JULIUS-ECHTER-BERG along the Schwanberg below the Schwanberg Castle. It faces west to southwest and the hilltop protects it from the east wind. It is considered the prime parcel within the Küchenmeister vineyard. The soil of the 10-hectare GL HOHELEITE is quite diverse and includes triassic gypsum marl stemming from marine sediment (myophoria layers) that is interspersed with sandstone layers from the Benker, Stuttgart, and Hassberg formations.

History: The name stems from an earlier path, the "Hohen Weg" that crossed the mountain just below the forest. The "Hoheleit" was first documented in 1317 as property of the Ebrach Monastery.

HUNDSRÜCK

Bürgstadt | Franken
VDP.GROSSE LAGE®

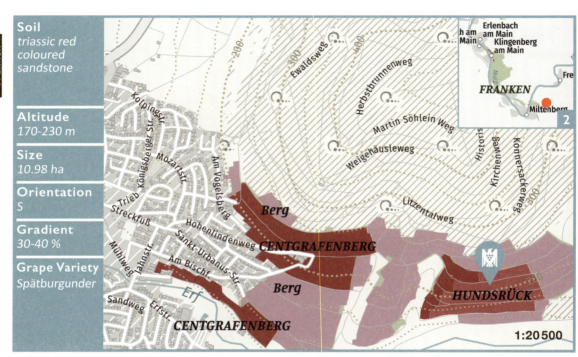

Soil
triassic red coloured sandstone

Altitude
170-230 m

Size
10.98 ha

Orientation
S

Gradient
30-40 %

Grape Variety
Spätburgunder

VDP.Estates: Benedikt Baltes, Rudolf Fürst

The VDP.GROSSE LAGE® HUNDSRÜCK is located in the Miltenberg valley basin where the Main River has carved a deep, tight gorge. Here at the most south-westerly bend of the Main River, one finds the south facing Bürgstadt vineyards Centgrafenberg and Hundsrück. This topography offers the protection of the Odenwald and Spessart Mountains, thus creating a warm microclimate. The GL HUNDSRÜCK encompasses the most eastern parcels of the Bürgstadter Mountain. It is a south-facing slope with an ideal 30 to 40 percent gradient. In the subsoil of the GL HUNDSRÜCK is a layer of weathered coloured sandstone that is red to orange in colour. This iron-rich soil warms easily, is well-aerated and also drains well. The very meagre soil allows no mistakes in cultivation, but when managed with thought and skill, it yields extraordinary Spätburgunder with finesse, elegance and impressive character.

JULIUS-ECHTER-BERG

Iphofen | Franken
VDP.GROSSE LAGE®

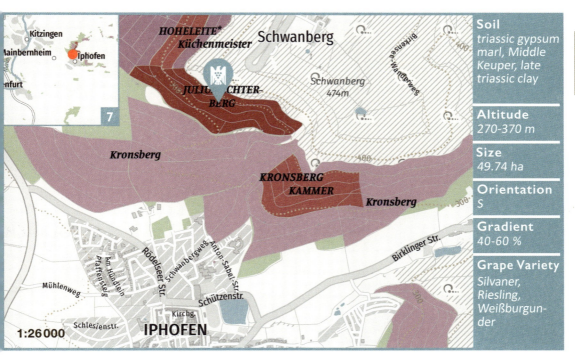

Soil
triassic gypsum marl, Middle Keuper, late triassic clay

Altitude
270-370 m

Size
49.74 ha

Orientation
S

Gradient
40-60 %

Grape Variety
Silvaner, Riesling, Weißburgunder

VDP.Estates: Juliusspital Würzburg, Johann Ruck, Paul Weltner, Hans Wirsching

The VDP.GROSSE LAGE® JULIUS-ECHTER-BERG lies on the slope of the Schwanberg, the western extension of the Steigerwald hills, and faces south. The forested hill top protects the very steep slope from north and east winds, thus allowing the GL to heat up in summer. The grey-brown Keuper marl stores the warmth of the day and releases it slowly in the evening. The soil in the upper area of the GL JULIUS-ECHTER-BERG is particularly skeletal. The coloured marl stems from layers of late triassic clay and 200-million-year-old marine fossil sediments. The GL JULIUS-ECHTER-BERG climbs from 270 to 370 metres a.s.l. at up to a steep 60 percent gradient.

History: The VDP.vintner Hans Wirsching urged that the site be named after the founder of Juliusspital, the Prinz-Bishop of Würzburg Julius Echter von Mespelbrunn (1545-1617). The Julius-Echter-Berg gained world fame through the 1950 Riesling Auslese from the VDP.winery Juliusspital at the coronation celebration of Queen Elizabeth II in London in the year 1953.

KARTHÄUSER

Volkach | Franken
VDP.GROSSE LAGE®

Soil
shell limestone, loam

Altitude
190-220 m

Size
11.55 ha

Orientation
S

Gradient
15-30 %

Grape Variety
Silvaner, Weißburgunder

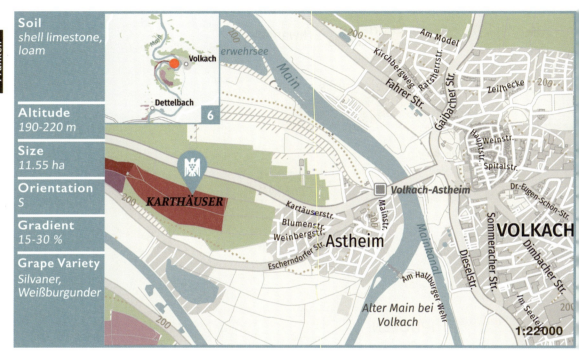

VDP.Estates: Rudolf Fürst, Juliusspital Würzburg

The VDP.GROSSE LAGE® KARTHÄUSER is located in the middle of the Main River bend at the Franconian community Volkach-Astheim. It lies at 190 to 220 metres above sea level and faces south with a slope gradient of up to 30 percent. The microclimate is warm and the shell limestone marl and alluvial soils are loose and have the ability to store moisture. Silvaner and Weissburgunder are cultivated here.

History: The name of this vineyard stems from the former Carthusian (Karthäuser) Cloister Marienbrück that is located in Volkach-Astheim. It was donated 1409 by Knight Erkinger von Seinsheim. Today it houses a museum of Christian image worship.

KRONSBERG KAMMER

Iphofen | Franken
VDP.GROSSE LAGE®

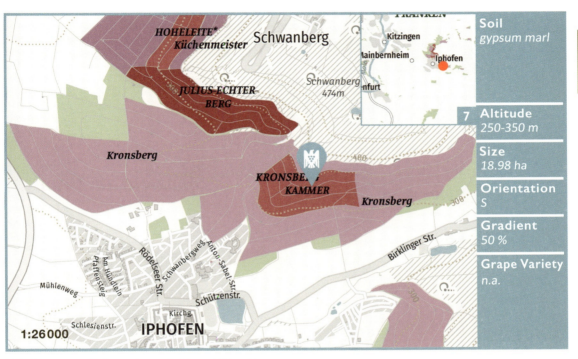

Soil	gypsum marl
Altitude	250-350 m
Size	18.98 ha
Orientation	S
Gradient	50 %
Grape Variety	n.a.

VDP.Estates: Johann Arnold, Hans Wirsching

The VDP.GROSSE LAGE® KRONSBERG KAMMER is a swale within the VDP.ERSTE LAGE® Iphofer Kronsberg. The vineyard rises steeply from 250 to 350 metres above sea level and a slope gradient of 50 percent. The soils are gypsum marl with high skeleton content and clayey loam with high calcium carbonate content. Because it is located in a swale, the GL KRONSBERG KAMMER is protected from the wind in the otherwise dry Kronsberg. The GL KRONSBERG KAMMER faces south, which brings sunlight and warmth that is stored well in the swale.

MAUSTAL

Sulzfeld | Franken
VDP.GROSSE LAGE®

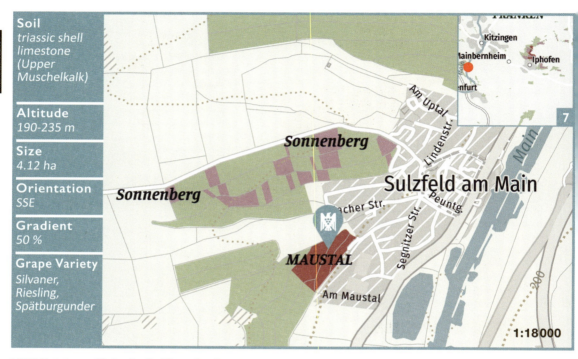

Soil
triassic shell limestone (Upper Muschelkalk)

Altitude
190-235 m

Size
4.12 ha

Orientation
SSE

Gradient
50 %

Grape Variety
Silvaner, Riesling, Spätburgunder

VDP.Estates: Zehnthof - Theo Luckert

The VDP.GROSSE LAGE® MAUSTAL lies within the Maustal vineyard, a large amphitheatre formed by the Main River south of Sulzfeld. The slope falls toward the south-southeast at a steep 50 percent gradient. The soil of the four-hectare GL is meagre, skeletal shell limestone that forces vines to thrust their roots deep. The slope is planted mostly with Silvaner, Riesling and Spätburgunder.

MÖNCHSHOF

Frickenhausen | Franken
VDP.GROSSE LAGE®

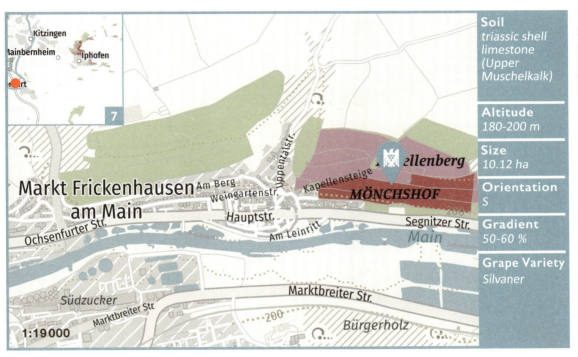

Soil
triassic shell limestone (Upper Muschelkalk)

Altitude
180-200 m

Size
10.12 ha

Orientation
S

Gradient
50-60 %

Grape Variety
Silvaner

VDP.Estates: Bickel-Stumpf

The VDP.GROSSE LAGE® MÖNCHSHOF is situated directly on the river in the narrow Main Valley in the lower corner of the Main triangle and is surrounded by the VDP.ERSTE LAGE® Kapellenberg. Between a south facing exposition with a 50-60 percent slope gradient and proximity to the water, solar radiation is high in the GL MÖNCHSHOF. The vine rows extend from 180 to 200 metres above sea level

PFÜLBEN

Randersacker | Franken
VDP.GROSSE LAGE®

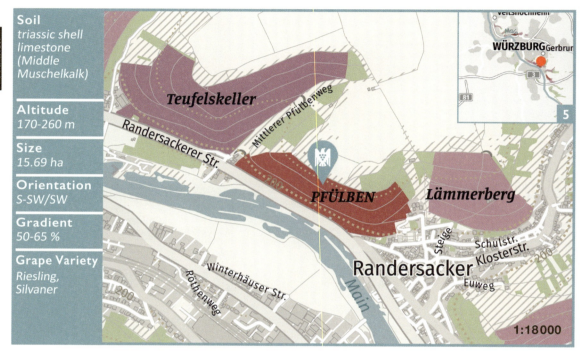

Soil
triassic shell limestone (Middle Muschelkalk)

Altitude
170-260 m

Size
15.69 ha

Orientation
S-SW/SW

Gradient
50-65 %

Grape Variety
Riesling, Silvaner

VDP.Estates: Wilhelm Arnold, Bürgerspital zum Hl. Geist, Juliusspital Würzburg, Schmitt's Kinder, Staatlicher Hofkeller Würzburg, Am Stein - Ludwig Knoll

Located west of Randersacker in the Maindreieck, the VDP.GROSSE LAGE® PFÜLBEN is reminiscent of a large bulging pillow ("phulwen" in Middle High German) that is pushed between the two side valleys bordering it. The steep slope drops toward the south and southwest from 170 to 260 metres above sea level at an incline of up to 65 percent. It is planted primarily with Riesling and Silvaner. The climate and ripening in the GL PFÜLBEN benefit from light and warmth reflected by the Main River. The medium to deep humus-rich soils of shell limestone marl warm easily and also store warmth well.

RATSHERR

Volkach | Franken
VDP.GROSSE LAGE®

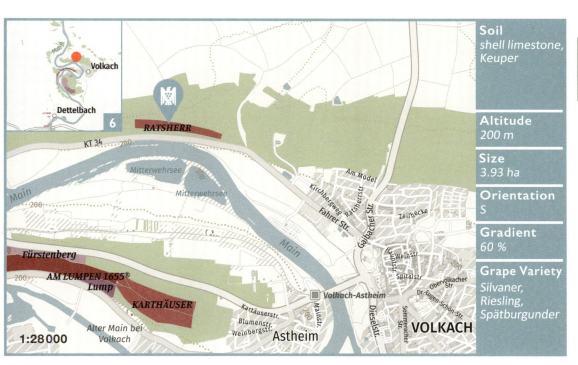

Soil
shell limestone, Keuper

Altitude
200 m

Size
3.93 ha

Orientation
S

Gradient
60 %

Grape Variety
Silvaner, Riesling, Spätburgunder

Franken

VDP.Estates: Zur Schwane

The VDP.GROSSE LAGE® RATSHERR is located on the bend of the Main River at Volkach in Franconia. It lies at 200 metres above sea level and faces south with a steep 60 percent slope gradient. The soils are the typical Franconian shell limestone with a meager covering of loam. Because it is protected by the Spessart Mountains, precipitation remains low. The GL RATSHERR is classified for Silvaner, Riesling and Spätburgunder.

History: There is a legend about the name of this vineyard that stems from the Thirty Years' War. The Swedes that held Volkach siege had settled where the vineyard is now located. They promised the town councilman (Ratsherr) that they would spare Volkach on a bet. He should enter a drinking contest with the leader of the Swedes and then please himself with the leader's lover. The councilman went to the local inn "Zum Schwane", chose the hardest drinking citizen and dressed him in his official clothing. The bet with the Swedes was won.

ROTHLAUF

Thüngersheim | Franken
VDP.GROSSE LAGE®

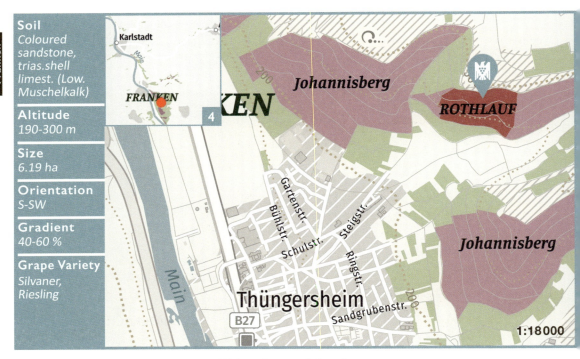

Soil
Coloured sandstone, trias.shell limest. (Low. Muschelkalk)

Altitude
190-300 m

Size
6.19 ha

Orientation
S-SW

Gradient
40-60 %

Grape Variety
Silvaner, Riesling

VDP.Estates: Bickel-Stumpf, Rudolf May, Gregor Schwab

The VDP.GROSSE LAGE® ROTHLAUF is the old historic parcel within the Johannisberg vineyard. It is not only the hottest part of the Johannisberg, it also has a unique soil structure. The 6.2 hectare vineyard plot drops toward the south and southwest. This area belongs to the so-called Thüngersheimer Sattel, a tectonic fault, where the coloured sandstone layer breaks through the shell limestone layer above it. The soil thus exhibits two representatives of the so-called Franconian geological trio (the third is Gipskeuper). The soils are meagre and skeletal. The vineyard climbs from 190 to 300 metres above sea level at a steep 40 to 60 percent gradient.

SCHLOSSBERG

Klingenberg | Franken
VDP.GROSSE LAGE®

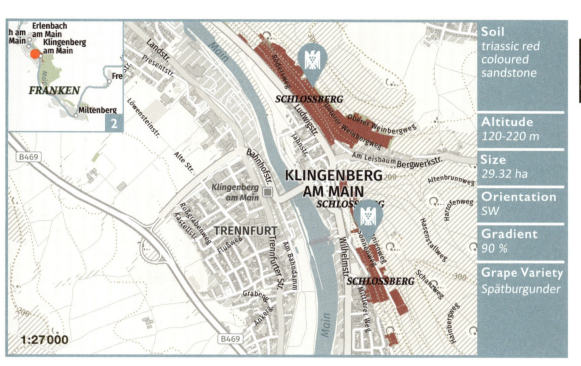

Soil
triassic red coloured sandstone

Altitude
120-220 m

Size
29.32 ha

Orientation
SW

Gradient
90 %

Grape Variety
Spätburgunder

VDP.Estates: **Benedikt Baltes, Rudolf Fürst**

Dry stone wall terraces climb one after the other up the dizzyingly steep 90 percent slope of the VDP.GROSSE LAGE® SCHLOSSBERG. Vines are planted on the terraces from 120 to 220 metres above sea level and benefit from the warmth stored in the southwest facing site long into the night. The SCHLOSSBERG GL has historically been considered the "great Burgundian vineyard of Germany". It is only possible to work the vineyard and harvest the grapes by hand. The soil is meagre and is comprised of rocky coloured sandstone. Despite the sandy fine earth, the soil has good available water capacity. Loess at the top of the hill provides the vineyard with necessary extra moisture. The site is protected as a historic monument.

History: Matthäus Merian the Elder wrote about Klingenberg in 1646: "A tiny little city that has achieved fame for wine cultivation – and what delicious wine it is."

SCHLOSSBERG

Castell | Franken
VDP.GROSSE LAGE®

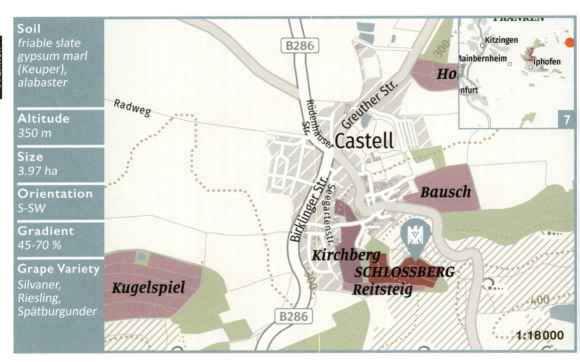

Soil
friable slate gypsum marl (Keuper), alabaster

Altitude
350 m

Size
3.97 ha

Orientation
S-SW

Gradient
45-70 %

Grape Variety
Silvaner, Riesling, Spätburgunder

VDP.Estates: Fürstlich Castell'sches Domänenamt

The VDP.GROSSE LAGE® SCHLOSSBERG is a very steep slope on the Burgberg above Castell. The slope falls from 350 metres above sea level at a 45 to 70 percent gradient and faces south and south-west. It is protected in the north and east by a forest, which is further enhanced in the convex south facing section of the slope. The 4 hectares of vines root in skeletal soils of Gipskeuper marl with high gypsum and alabaster content and blue slate clay layers. The humus-rich top layer is shallow and forces vines to thrust their roots directly into the rock below. Predominantly Silvaner and Riesling (particularly in the convex slope section) are planted here.

History: The two main fortresses of the Dukes of Castell once stood here. Duke Heinrich II and Herman II divided their family estate around the year 1266.

(SONNENSTUHL) HOHENROTH [1]

Randersacker | Franken
VDP.GROSSE LAGE®

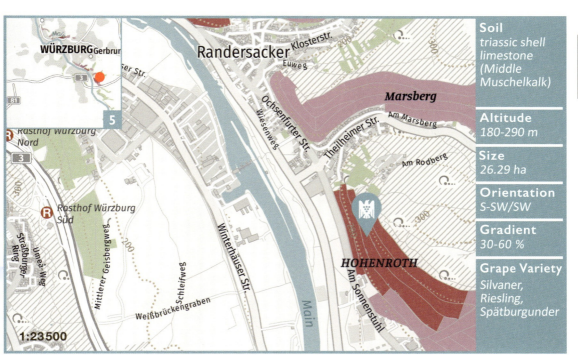

Soil
triassic shell limestone (Middle Muschelkalk)

Altitude
180-290 m

Size
26.29 ha

Orientation
S-SW/SW

Gradient
30-60 %

Grape Variety
Silvaner, Riesling, Spätburgunder

Franken

VDP.Estates: Wilhelm Arnold, Schmitt's Kinder, Am Stein - Ludwig Knoll, Störrlein Krenig

The VDP.GROSSE LAGE® HOHENROTH[1] (formerly named SONNENSTUHL HOHENROTH) is a dome-shaped mountain south of Randersacker in Franken. It lies at 180 to 290 metres above sea level and faces south-southwest toward the sun and the Main River at a steep up to 60 percent slope gradient. The soil is shell limestone from the Germanic Trias. The vineyard is classified for Silvaner, Riesling and Spätburgunder. The VDP.ERSTE LAGE® Sonnenstuhl is located directly behind this site. Both vineyards are braced with terrace walls that store the warmth of the sun.

History: The site was mentioned in a document dating 1240 as "monte Rode aput Randersacker", which translates to "on Mont Rode near Randersacker".

STEIN

Stetten | Franken
VDP.GROSSE LAGE®

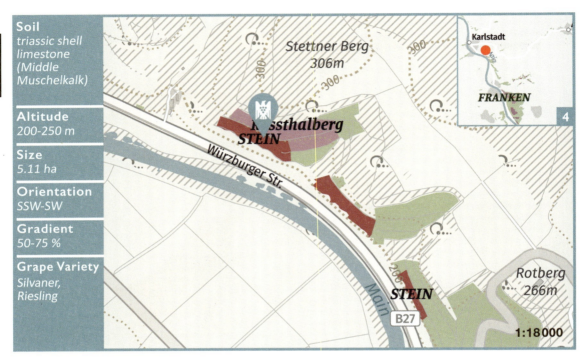

Soil
triassic shell limestone (Middle Muschelkalk)

Altitude
200-250 m

Size
5.11 ha

Orientation
SSW-SW

Gradient
50-75 %

Grape Variety
Silvaner, Riesling

VDP.Estates: Am Stein - Ludwig Knoll

Right where the VDP.GROSSE LAGE® STEIN (Stetten) is located, the Main valley is bordered by vertical shell lime river banks. Above these steep slope, around 80 metres beyond the river Main the vineyards begin and rise to 130 metres (250 m. above sea level) at a very steep 50 to 75 percent gradient. The micro climate of the 5-hectare GL STEIN is marked by the warm air masses that rise up the rocky slope by a natural thermal lift, bringing the warm air from the rocks into the vineyards and spreading it even to the upmost vines. The soil is dominated by weathered shallow shell limestone. The skeletal layer below, makes it hard for the vines to build deep roots. It takes years for them to grow into the rock and reach the precious minerals and nutrients.

STEIN-BERG[1]

Würzburg | Franken
VDP.GROSSE LAGE®

Franken

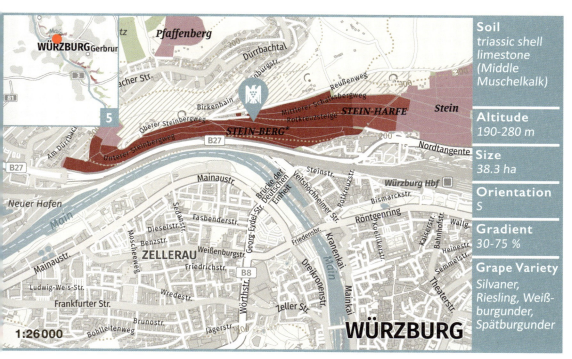

Soil
triassic shell limestone (Middle Muschelkalk)

Altitude
190-280 m

Size
38.3 ha

Orientation
S

Gradient
30-75 %

Grape Variety
Silvaner, Riesling, Weißburgunder, Spätburgunder

VDP.Estates: Bürgerspital zum Hl. Geist, Juliusspital Würzburg, Staatlicher Hofkeller Würzburg

The VDP.GROSSE LAGE® STEIN-BERG (Würzburg) is famous. The curved vineyard that thrones above Würzburg has a nearly Mediterranean climate. Not only do the slopes lie between 190 and 280 metres above sea level with a south exposition that is advantageous for collecting light and warmth, the yellow-grey weathered shell limestone with clayey loam and humus-rich fine earth also reflects light. In addition, the Main as well stores the heat. The slopes are mostly terraced and have up to a 75 percent gradient.

History: Wines from the Stein site have been known for many years as „Steinwein". This was Johann Wolfgang von Goethe's favourite wine. He wrote that he "never wants to taste other wine" and that it makes him "morose" when his "favourite beverage is missing". The wines have an extraordinary capacity for aging. A Stein wine from the year 1540 was possibly the oldest wine opened that was still enjoyable.

STEIN-HARFE

Würzburg | Franken
VDP.GROSSE LAGE®

Soil
triassic shell limestone (Middle Muschelkalk)

Altitude
190-280 m

Size
8.39 ha

Orientation
S

Gradient
25-45 %

Grape Variety
Silvaner, Riesling

VDP.Estates: Bürgerspital zum Hl. Geist

The VDP.GROSSE LAGE® STEIN-HARFE is among the best parcels of the famous Stein vineyard located above Würzburg. Its 8 hectares face south and are located in the centre of the Stein amphitheatre in its warmest and most sun-pampered position. The light reflected by the white shell limestone increases solar radiation. The soil is quite skeletal and contains various fine earths ranging from clayey loam to humus. The GL STEIN-HARFE rises from 190 to 280 metres above sea level at a 25 to 45 percent gradient. The main grape varieties are Silvaner and Riesling.

History: The Rotkreuzstiege path that separates this parcel from Würzburg leaves a vineyard in the shape of a "harfe" or "harp". This image is further enhanced by vine rows reminiscent of strings on a harp. The "Harpfe" parcel was first mentioned in documents in the second half of the 17th century.

Your art collection will get jealous.

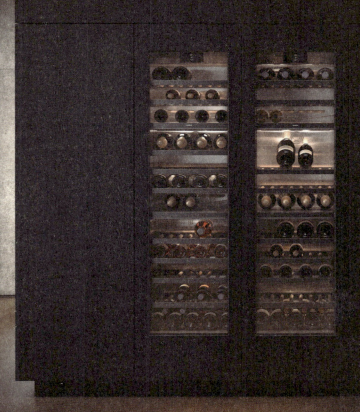

The difference is Gaggenau.

Grand architecture demands grand interior pieces. Your wine climate cabinet, much like your collection, speaks to who you are. Every Gaggenau piece is distinctively designed, crafted from exceptional materials, offers professional performance, and has done so since 1683.

Make a statement: gaggenau.com

Product displayed is the RW 466 364 | Energy efficiency class: A | at a range of energy efficiency classes from A+++ to G.

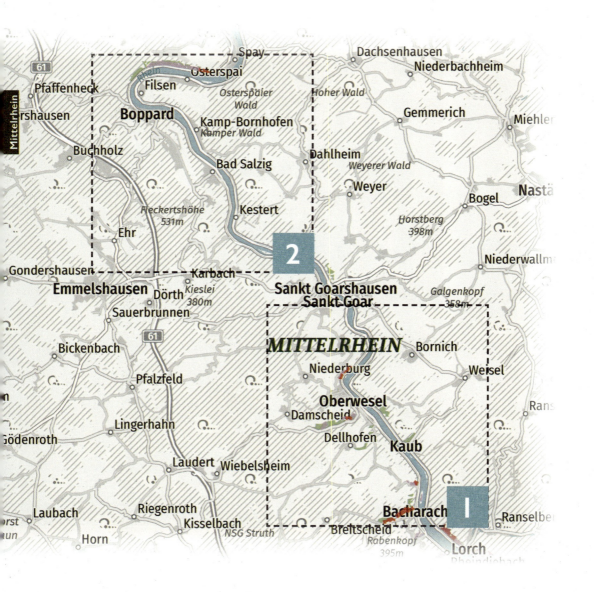

MITTELRHEIN

The comparatively small wine region Mittelrhein is among the warmest in Germany. The thermometer rises above 25 °C (77 °F) for up to 50 days in the vineyards on this 120 kilometre stretch along the Rhine River. The VDP.GROSSE LAGE® vineyards located between Oberdiebach und Spay are all on the left side of the Rhine and face south. The vineyards are extremely steep and terraced and demand hard labour. Slate and greywacke dominate the soils.

Region:	VDP.GROSSE LAGE®:
470 ha	33 ha
VDP.Wineries:	VDP.GROSSE LAGE® Sites:
5	8

AN DER RABENLEI

Boppard | Mittelrhein
VDP.GROSSE LAGE®

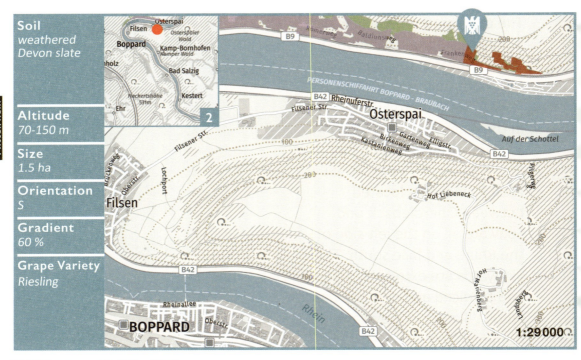

Soil weathered Devon slate

Altitude 70-150 m

Size 1.5 ha

Orientation S

Gradient 60 %

Grape Variety Riesling

Mittelrhein

VDP.Estates: Matthias Müller

The VDP.GROSSE LAGE® AN DER RABENLEI is located near the village Boppard in the Mittelrhein region, directly on a bend of the river Rhein. The steep slope has an incline of up to 60 percent. The exposition directly toward the south guarantees Riesling abundant hours of sunshine. The surface of the Rhine River serves as a source of warmth and inhibits frost. The soil of this small 1.5-hectare parcel is weathered Devon slate with a reddish hue due to high iron content.
History: The Roman military camp Bodobrica was built here in the 4th century. Because wine belonged to the military's standard nourishment, it is assumed that grapes were cultivated in Bopparder Hamm at that time. Written documents confirming wine cultivation in Boppard date from 643.

BERNSTEIN - AM LAUERBAUM

Engehöll | Mittelrhein
VDP.GROSSE LAGE®

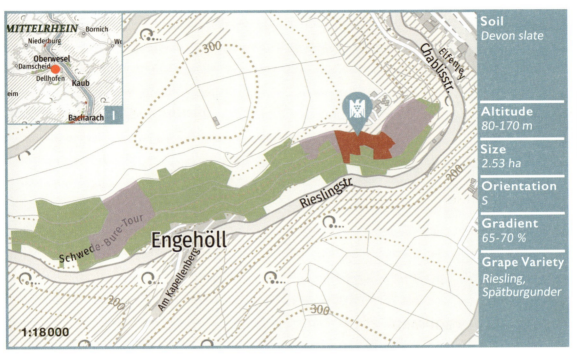

Soil
Devon slate

Altitude
80-170 m

Size
2.53 ha

Orientation
S

Gradient
65-70 %

Grape Variety
Riesling, Spätburgunder

VDP.Estates: Lanius-Knab

Brown-grey Devon slate dominates the soil of the VDP.GROSSE LAGE® BERNSTEIN – AM LAUERBAUM and because it drains so rapidly, it doesn't make it easy for vines to source water. This is further intenified by an extremely steep slope gradient of 65 to 70 percent. On the other side, this soil is rich in minerals and warms easily. Because the vineyard faces south, it gets plenty of sunshine and it is also protected from cold winds by the forest at the top of the hill – the GL BERNSTEIN – AM LAUERBAUM is thus often quite warm during the summer months. The vineyard lies between 80 and 170 metres above sea level.

History: The name of this site probably stems from the fact that berries (Beeren) grew on this slope. In 1416 the site was called "Berhelde", which translates to "berry heath". The name was later documented in 1484 as "Bernstejn".

ENGELSTEIN

Boppard | Mittelrhein
VDP.GROSSE LAGE®

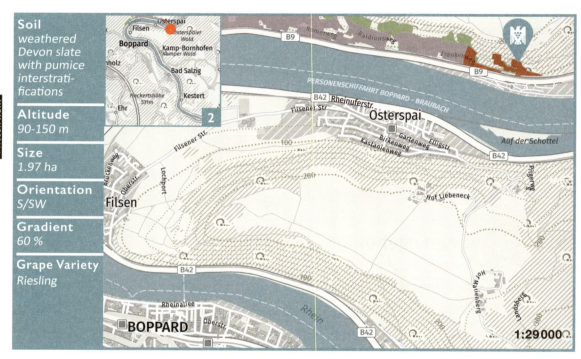

Soil
weathered Devon slate with pumice interstratifications

Altitude
90-150 m

Size
1.97 ha

Orientation
S/SW

Gradient
60 %

Grape Variety
Riesling

VDP.Estates: Matthias Müller

The VDP.GROSSE LAGE® ENGELSTEIN is situated on a steep slope with a 60 percent gradient in Boppard in the Mittelrhein valley. It forms the eastern border of the Bopparder Hamm vineyard that is named after the adjacent district of Boppard, Hamm. The GL ENGLSTEIN is located directly on the Rhine River between 90 and 150 metres above sea level. The southern exposition provides the Riesling that grows here with sunshine into the evening hours. The abundant European green lizards that live between the vines bask in the sunny microclimate. The soil is Devon slate, which shimmers reddish due to its iron content. The pumice interstratifications are of volcanic origin and stem from the Eifel maar.

History: The Roman military camp Bodobrica was built in Boppard in the 4th century. Because wine belonged to the military's standard nourishment, it is assumed that grapes were cultivated in Bopparder Hamm at that time.

IM HAHN

Bacharach | Mittelrhein
VDP.GROSSE LAGE®

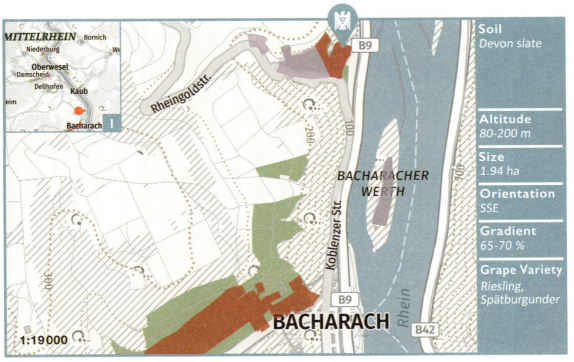

Soil
Devon slate

Altitude
80-200 m

Size
1.94 ha

Orientation
SSE

Gradient
65-70 %

Grape Variety
Riesling, Spätburgunder

VDP.Estates: **Toni Jost**

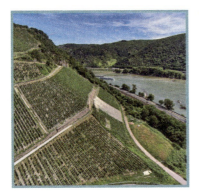

With a slope grade of 65 to 70 percent, the VDP.GROSSE LAGE® IM HAHN is a typical representative of the steep vineyards of the narrow Mittelrhein Valley. Located next to the Loreley on the Rhine River, this south to southeast facing site rises from 80 to 200 metres above sea level. The soil of the approximately two-hectare GL is comprised of dark weathered Devon slate. It warms easily and releases warmth to the vines on summer evenings and nights, thus prolonging the daily ripening phase. In addition to this, the reflection of sunshine from the Rhine River intensifies the solar radiation on the slope. Riesling is the predominant variety that grows in the higher reaches, while Spätburgunder grows at the foot of the slope.

OELSBERG

Oberwesel | Mittelrhein
VDP.GROSSE LAGE®

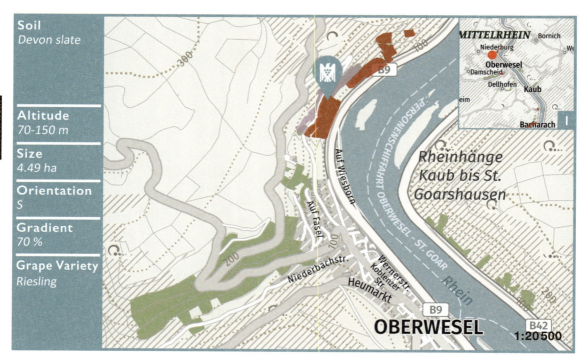

Soil
Devon slate

Altitude
70-150 m

Size
4.49 ha

Orientation
S

Gradient
70 %

Grape Variety
Riesling

VDP.Estates: Lanius-Knab

The VDP.GROSSE LAGE® OELSBERG is an extremely steep site with up to 70 percent gradient. It is located in Oberwesel in the Mittelrhein valley between 70 and 150 metres above sea level. Dry stone walls brace the vineyard terraces. The weathered slate soil exhibits loess loam deposits, which make the soil unusually rich for the region. A rift that runs across Europe ends here and has also thrust Triassic coloured sandstone to the surface in this site. The GL OELSBERG faces south to southeast directly above a bend of the Rhine River. The river flows directly towards the site and the sunshine reflected on the water's surface contributes to a particularly warm microclimate. Riesling is cultivated here.

History: The "Oelsbergsteig", a hiking path that belongs to the Rhine Castle Trail, leads through this vineyard.

POSTEN

Bacharach | Mittelrhein
VDP.GROSSE LAGE®

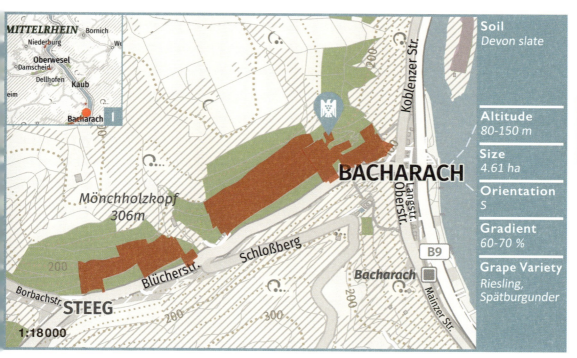

Soil
Devon slate

Altitude
80-150 m

Size
4.61 ha

Orientation
S

Gradient
60-70 %

Grape Variety
Riesling, Spätburgunder

VDP.Estates: Bastian, Ratzenberger

The VDP.GROSSE LAGE® POSTEN stretches along a sun-pampered south-facing slope in a protected side valley of the Rhine up to the city wall of Bacharach. The slope rises from 80 to 150 metres above sea level at an extremely steep 60 to 70 percent gradient. The weathered Devon slate that dominates here provides abundant minerals and warms easily. Water drains quickly here and vines must thrust their roots deep to find the moisture they need.

History: This site presumably gets its name from the watch tower, the so-called "Postenturm", that is built into the old city walls of Bacharach at the foot of the vineyard.

ST. JOST

Bacharach-Steeg | Mittelrhein
VDP.GROSSE LAGE®

Soil
Devon slate

Altitude
170-200 m

Size
6.02 ha

Orientation
S

Gradient
60 %

Grape Variety
Riesling

VDP.Estates: **Bastian, Toni Jost, Ratzenberger**

The VDP.GROSSE LAGE® ST. JOST is located at 170 to 200 metres above sea level above Bacharach-Steeg in the Mittelrhein valley. The 60 percent slope drops south toward the Münzbach creek. Riesling is cultivated here and enjoys optimal solar radiation. The Devon slate that dominates here is covered with a layer of wind deposited sand that stems from volcanic eruptions in the Neuwied Basin more than 10,000 years ago.

History: The GL ST. JOST is named after Saint Jodocus (Judoc), who was known as a pilgrim and a hermit. A chapel was dedicated to him that stood between Bacharach and Steeg until the Reformation.

WOLFSHÖHLE

Bacharach | Mittelrhein
VDP.GROSSE LAGE®

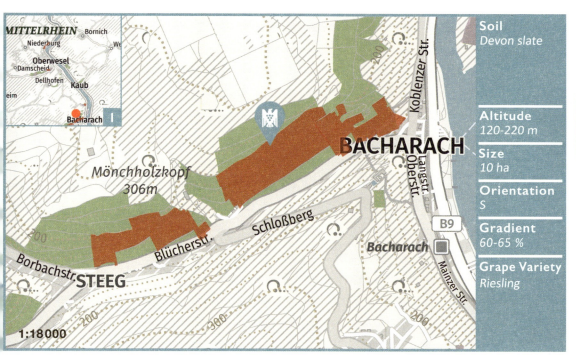

Soil
Devon slate

Altitude
120-220 m

Size
10 ha

Orientation
S

Gradient
60-65 %

Grape Variety
Riesling

VDP.Estates: **Bastian, Toni Jost, Ratzenberger**

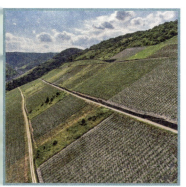

The south facing VDP.GROSSE LAGE® WOLFSHÖHLE lies well protected in the Steegertal, a side valley of the river Rhein. Mostly Riesling grows on the steep 60 to 65 percent slope. The vineyard drops from 220 down to 120 metres above sea level. The soil is medium heavy clay slate and crystalline schist, which warms well. The GL WOLFSHÖHLE comprises approximately 10 hectares.

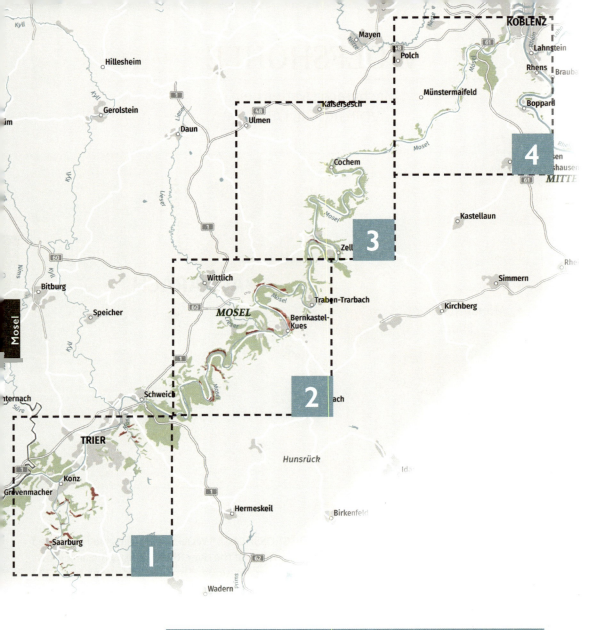

Region:	VDP.GROSSE LAGE®:
8800 ha	1258 ha
VDP.Wineries:	VDP.GROSSE LAGE® Sites:
31	74

MOSEL – SAAR – RUWER

A cool climate dominates the Mosel, Saar and Ruwer that is exemplary throughout the wine world. Hang time for the region's predominant variety, Riesling, is longer in most years than it is in other German wine regions. Riesling often remains on the vine here for 160 days, compared to the 100 days that are considered the classic benchmark elsewhere. This allows grapes plenty of time to accumulate aroma intensity. The three rivers, in particular the Mosel, provide a passive source of warmth to ensure a moderate and stable climate. The rivers also provide good air circulation, sweeping warm air away and allowing cool air to refresh grapes on the slopes at night.

The landscape here at the 50th degree of latitude is stunning. Extremely steep vineyard sites bank the sharply winding Mosel River. The south-exposed vineyard slopes accumulate heat on hot summer days and dark slate soils accentuate this by functioning like a solar panel. Vines climb the steep slopes to dizzying heights, some with stone terraces, others straight up the fall line trained on individual posts. Vineyard labour is demanding and in some places only possible by hand.

It is somewhat cooler on the Saar and Ruwer. The vineyards are on average more highly elevated and because many of the vineyard sites are located in side valleys, the influence of both rivers is less. Germany's most famous wine comes from the VDP.GROSSE LAGE® SCHARZHOFBERG. The 2003 SCHARZHOFBERG Riesling Trockenbeerenauslese from the VDP.Estate Egon Müller achieved worldwide the highest price ever for a bottle of wine – 14 566 Euros at the VDP.Mosel Auction of 2015.

ABTSBERG

Mertesdorf | Ruwer
VDP.GROSSE LAGE®

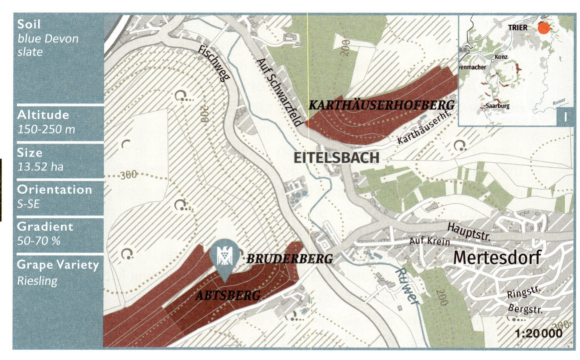

Soil
blue Devon slate

Altitude
150-250 m

Size
13.52 ha

Orientation
S-SE

Gradient
50-70 %

Grape Variety
Riesling

Mosel

VDP.Estates: Maximin Grünhaus

The VDP.GROSSE LAGE® ABTSBERG lies at the entrance to a side valley of the Ruwer. It turns from its southeast exposition above the Ruwer into a due south exposition in the side valley. The very steep 50 to 70 percent gradient rises from 150 to 250 metres above sea level and is comprised of blue Devon slate. The GL ABTSBERG is 13.5 hectares in size and planted with Riesling.

History: The Abtsberg was documented as a property of the Sankt Maximin Abbey in 966. Wine was probably grown here since the 4th century. The GL ABTSBERG is a monopole vineyard that belongs to the VDP.Estate Maximin Grünhaus.

ALTENBERG

Kanzem | Saar
VDP.GROSSE LAGE®

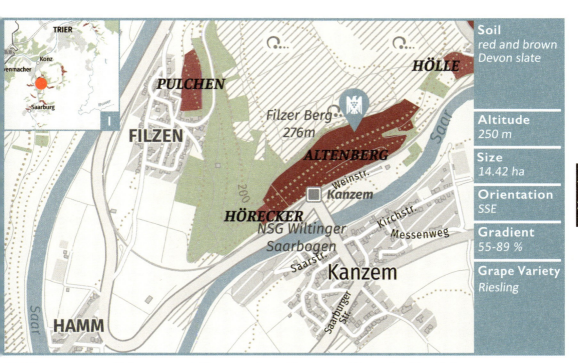

Soil
red and brown Devon slate

Altitude
250 m

Size
14.42 ha

Orientation
SSE

Gradient
55-89 %

Grape Variety
Riesling

Mosel

VDP.Estates: von Othegraven, Stiftungsweingut Vereinigte Hospitien, Van Volxem

The VDP.GROSSE LAGE® ALTENBERG stretches majestically along the Saar overlooking a bend in the river. The south-southeast exposition collects plenty of sunlight, which is enhanced by warm summer thermals and the forested hilltop that shields from north and west winds. The soil is predominantly red and brown slate and weathered Rotliegend soil. The GL ALTENBERG lies at 250 metres above sea level at a very steep 55 to 89 percent gradient. Predominantly Riesling grows here.

APOTHEKE

Trittenheim | Mosel
VDP.GROSSE LAGE®

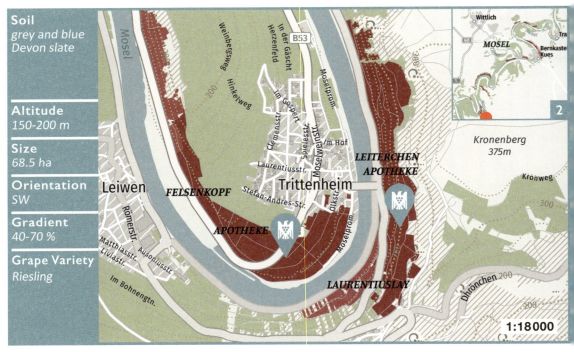

Soil
grey and blue Devon slate

Altitude
150-200 m

Size
68.5 ha

Orientation
SW

Gradient
40-70 %

Grape Variety
Riesling

VDP.Estates: Grans-Fassian, Josef Milz

The VDP.GROSSE LAGE® APOTHEKE is located across from the wine village Trittenheim on the right bank of the Mosel. The world-famous site is extremely steep and has a 40 to 70 percent gradient and southwest exposition. The soil is rocky and comprised of grey-blue slate, which stores warmth from the sun during the day and radiates it in the vineyard in the night. This provides the predominant Riesling grape variety plenty of time to fully ripen. The site covers 68.5 hectares at 150 to 200 metres above sea level.

History: Contrary to what the name suggests, the site name does not refer to the healing properties of the wine. It is a variation of the name Abteiberg, which belonged to the Trier Abbey. Up until the year 1909, vintners had to use a ferry to get to the vineyard. The large rock on which the ferry was tied can still be seen in the centre of the vineyard's base.

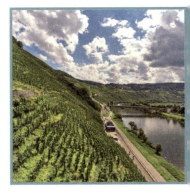

AUGENSCHEINER

Trier | Mosel
VDP.GROSSE LAGE®

Soil	coloured sandstone
Altitude	120 m
Size	2.17 ha
Orientation	SW
Gradient	35-50 %
Grape Variety	Riesling

Mosel

VDP.Estates: Stiftungsweingut Vereinigte Hospitien

The vines in the VDP.GROSSE LAGE® AUGENSCHEINER in Trier does not grow in the slate that is so typical for the Mosel, but in coloured sandstone. The narrow 2-hectare strip of vineyard follows the bank of the Mosel and benefits from the warmth and light reflection from the river, which is further enhanced by its southwest aspect. The vineyard slope rises up to 120 metres above sea level at a 35 to 50 percent gradient.

History: It is said that Margrave Alfred from Brandenburg, who plundered Trier as he passed in 1552, could successfully be placated with a goblet of Augenscheiner wine and kept from setting fire to the St. Martin Monastery. He continued on his way with four barrels of Augenscheiner wine. The GL AUGENSCHEINER is a monopole vineyard of the VDP.Estate Vereinigte Hospitien.

BADSTUBE

Bernkastel | Mosel
VDP.GROSSE LAGE®

Soil
grey-blue Devonian slate

Altitude
110-250 m

Size
27.2 ha

Orientation
SW-S

Gradient
40-65 %

Grape Variety
Riesling

VDP.Estates: Joh. Jos. Prüm, S. A. Prüm, Wwe. Dr. H. Thanisch, Erben Thanisch

The soil of the VDP.GROSSE LAGE® BADSTUBE consists of grey-blue slate with clay content. Loam is partly also present and the soil texture varies from rocky and coarse to fine grained. The GL BADSTUBE covers the middle of the slope along the Mosel. The vineyard rises from 110 to 250 metres above sea level at a steep 40-65 percent incline and faces southwest to south. Many of the vines were planted around 1950 and are over 70 years old

History: The name Badstube probably stems from the Middle Ages when there was likely a hot spring here that was used for recreation.

BOCKSTEIN

Ockfen | Saar
VDP.GROSSE LAGE®

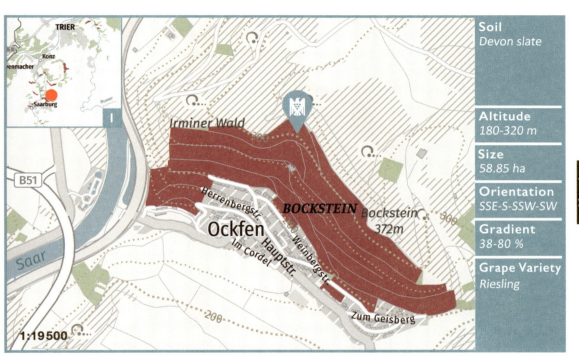

Soil
Devon slate

Altitude
180-320 m

Size
58.85 ha

Orientation
SSE-S-SSW-SW

Gradient
38-80 %

Grape Variety
Riesling

VDP.Estates: Dr. Fischer - Hofstätter Weis, Forstmeister Geltz-Zilliken, Reichsgraf von Kesselstatt, Nik Weis - St. Urbans-Hof, von Othegraven, Van Volxem, Dr. Wagner

The VDP.GROSSE LAGE® BOCKSTEIN drops at a 38 to 80 percent gradient in a side valley of the Saar. It forms an amphitheatre around the village of Ockfen. Its rocky, craggy soil is marked with skeletal Devon slate and weathered greywacke. The soil's dark colour stores the warmth well in this south-southeast to southwest facing site. In some areas one also finds quartzite sandstone and yellowish fine earth. The forested mountain ridge protects the site from fall winds. **History:** There is evidence that the Romans once grew wine here, but exactly where the name Bockstein originates remains a mystery. The most fanciful interpretation points to a goat bock (Geißbock), and claims that goats had become destructive in the vineyard and were thus ceremonially sacrificed. A second, more realistic theory is traced to a hunter named "Freiherr von Bock". On his lands there was a group of bare rocks on the ridge above the vineyard. In any case, the site was once the property of the Kings of Prussia.

BRAUNE KUPP

Wiltingen | Saar
VDP.GROSSE LAGE®

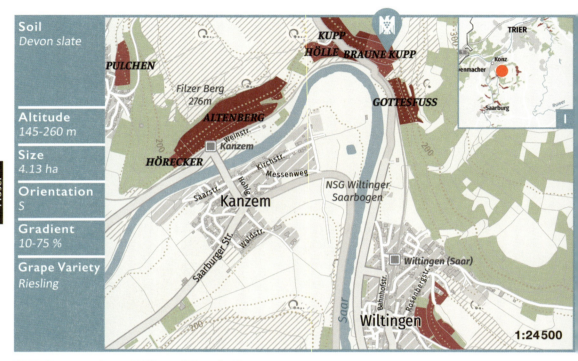

Soil
Devon slate

Altitude
145-260 m

Size
4.13 ha

Orientation
S

Gradient
10-75 %

Grape Variety
Riesling

Mosel

VDP.Estates: Egon Müller - Scharzhof

The VDP.GROSSE LAGE® BRAUNE KUPP thrones majestically over a bend of the Saar River near Wiltingen. The slope faces directly south and falls toward the river from 260 to 145 metres above sea level at a 10 to an extremely steep 75 percent gradient. The reflection from the river intensifies the light in the vineyard. The soil is comprised of weathered Devon slate with clayey loam that contributes positively to water storage capacity.
Information: The GL BRAUNE KUPP is a monopole vineyard of the VDP.Estate Egon Müller-Scharzhof.

BRAUNFELS

Wiltingen | Saar
VDP.GROSSE LAGE®

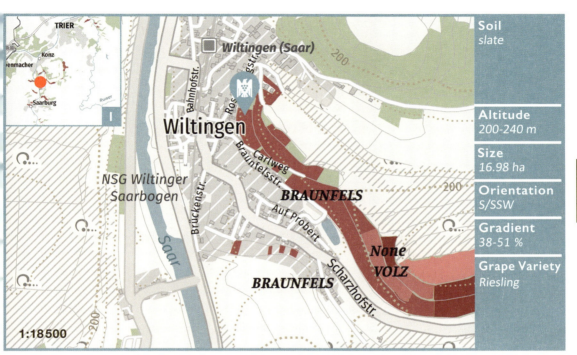

Soil
slate

Altitude
200-240 m

Size
16.98 ha

Orientation
S/SSW

Gradient
38-51 %

Grape Variety
Riesling

VDP.Estates: Reichsgraf von Kesselstatt, Stiftungsweingut Vereinigte Hospitien, Van Volxem

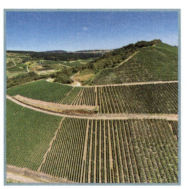

The 17-hectare VDP.GROSSE LAGE® BRAUNFELS is located above the village of Wiltingen and below the GL VOLZ and GL SCHARZHOFBERGER PERGENTSKNOPP. It curves around the foot of the Scharzberg and faces south to south-southwest. It borders the famous GL SCHARZHOFBERGER on its east side. The site is quite steep with a slope gradient of 38 to 51 percent. The grey slate soil warms easily and drains well, which encourages vines to thrust their roots deep in search of water.

BRUDERBERG

Mertesdorf | Ruwer
VDP.GROSSE LAGE®

Soil
blue Devon slate

Altitude
140-150 m

Size
1 ha

Orientation
E-SE

Gradient
60-75 %

Grape Variety
Riesling

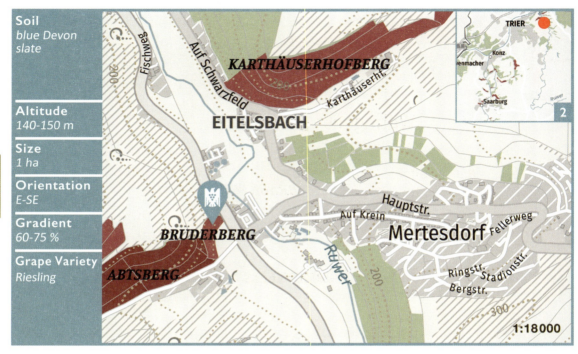

VDP.Estates: Maximin Grünhaus

The 1-hectare VDP.GROSSE LAGE® BRUDERBERG is located at the end of a side valley of the Ruwer in the lower part of the VDP.Estate Maximin Grünhaus vineyards where it borders a protective forest. The site faces east and southeast and rises from 140 to 150 metres above sea level at a very steep 60 to 75 percent gradient. The vines root in weathered blue Devon slate with a share of sandy loam. The soil's well-balanced water availability provides vines with enough moisture, even in dry vintages.

Information: The GL BRUDERBERG is a monopole vineyard that belongs to the VDP. Estate Maximin Grünhaus. The estate's vineyards BRUDERBERG, HERRENBERG and ABTSBERG were cultivated by the Benedictine Sankt Maximin Abbey in Trier from the 7th century until the end of the 18th century.

DOCTOR

Bernkastel-Kues | Mosel
VDP.GROSSE LAGE®

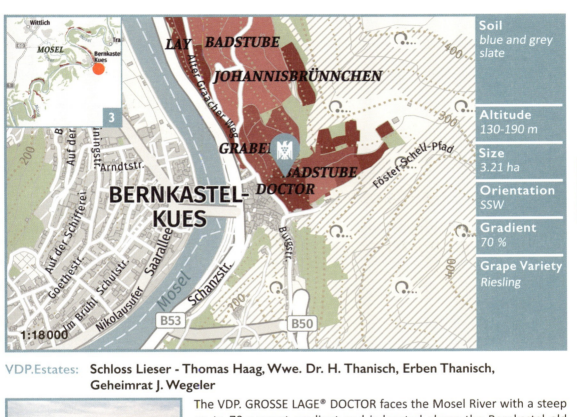

Soil
blue and grey slate

Altitude
130-190 m

Size
3.21 ha

Orientation
SSW

Gradient
70 %

Grape Variety
Riesling

VDP.Estates: Schloss Lieser - Thomas Haag, Wwe. Dr. H. Thanisch, Erben Thanisch, Geheimrat J. Wegeler

The VDP. GROSSE LAGE® DOCTOR faces the Mosel River with a steep up to 70 percent gradient and is located above the Bernkastel old town. It orients to the south-southwest and due to its exposition and steepness, it enjoys many hours of intense sunshine. The dark, rocky soil comprised of weathered Devon slate with high fine earth content stores warmth and moisture well. The 3.2-hectare GL DOCTOR lays wind exposed at 130 to 190 metres above sea level. It is planted with ungrafted Riesling vines.

History: The Doctor vineyard once was the most expensive vineyard in the world. According to legend, Archbishop of Trier Boemund II became severely ill in 1360 and no medication proved effective. Drinking two bottles of Bernkastel wine finally healed him. There is though confirmed documentation of King Edward VII of Great Britain drinking this wine as medicine. Other fans were Kaiser Wilhelm II., US President Dwight D. Eisenhower, and the German Chancellor Konrad Adenauer.

DOMHERR

Piesport | Mosel
VDP.GROSSE LAGE®

Soil
deep Devon slate with clay content

Altitude
110-160 m

Size
4.33 ha

Orientation
S-SE

Gradient
30-70 %

Grape Variety
Riesling

VDP.Estates: Haart, Reichsgraf von Kesselstatt, Stiftungsweingut Vereinigte Hospitien

The VDP.GROSSE LAGE® DOMHERR lies in the centre of the GL GOLD-TRÖPFCHEN in a protected bend of the Mosel River between the communities of Alt-Piesport and Ferres. The vineyard faces south to southeast and rises from 110 to 160 metres above sea level. The slope gradient is 30 to 70 percent. The deep weathered Devon slate soils have a high share of clay content and thus good water storage capacity. The forested area on the ridge above the vineyard slope also provides the vines with moisture.

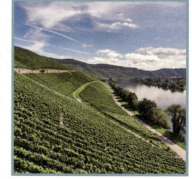

DOMPROBST

Graach an der Mosel | Mosel
VDP.GROSSE LAGE®

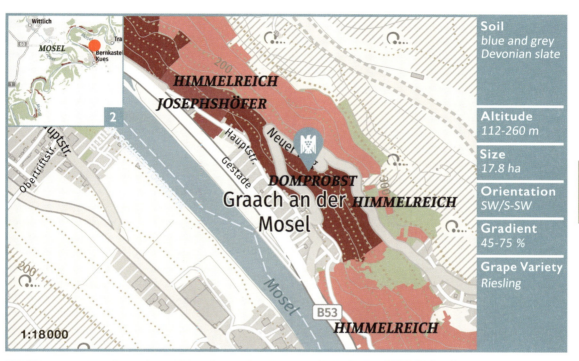

Soil
blue and grey Devonian slate

Altitude
112-260 m

Size
17.8 ha

Orientation
SW/S-SW

Gradient
45-75 %

Grape Variety
Riesling

VDP.Estates: Reichsgraf von Kesselstatt, Dr. Loosen, S. A. Prüm, Willi Schaefer

The VDP.GROSSE LAGE® DOMPROBST is located above the village Graach on the Mosel River. This steep vineyard rises from 110 to 260 metres above sea level at a 45 to 70 percent slope. The soils of this southwest to south-southwest facing GL are grey-blue Devonian slate with a share of clay that lends the subsoil good water storage capacity. The site is well protected from the wind and can get hot in the summer months. Many of the vines in the VDP.GROSSE LAGE® DOMPROBST are very old and ungrafted, trained in the old traditional method on individual stakes and up to a 100 years old.

History: In the 18th century, vintners of this vineyard were required to pay a tithe to the Trier cathedral provost in the form of 10 percent of their harvest. A document from 1731 appraises the value of the vineyard at 200 Florin (gold coin).

FEILS

Biebelhausen, Schoden | Saar
VDP.GROSSE LAGE®

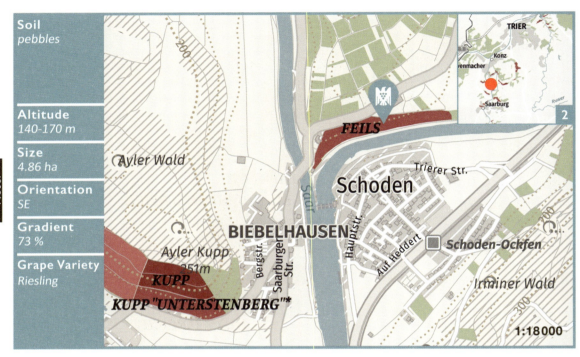

Soil
pebbles

Altitude
140-170 m

Size
4.86 ha

Orientation
SE

Gradient
73 %

Grape Variety
Riesling

VDP.Estates: Peter Lauer, Nik Weis - St. Urbans-Hof

The VDP.GROSSE LAGE® FEILS rises at a steep 73 percent gradient on the bank of the peninsula at the fork of the Saar and the Saar Channel and is planted with Riesling. Between the due south exposition and its proximity to the water, the GL FEILS is one of the warmest sites in the Saar Valley. The site's high solar radiation is further intensified by light reflected from the river. Further determining the microclimate is the temperature regulating effect of the Saar. The soils are rubble with a mixture of river sediments, sand, and pebbles. The GL FEILS encompasses 4.8 hectares.

FELSENKOPF

Trittenheim | Mosel
VDP.GROSSE LAGE®

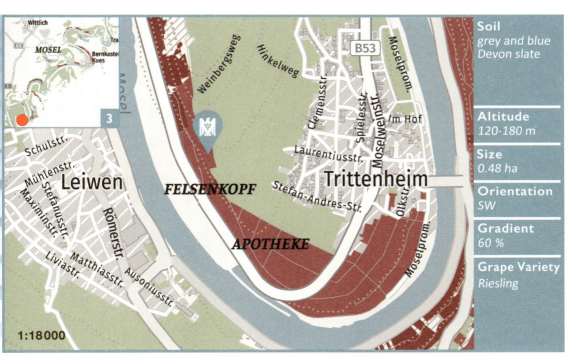

Soil
grey and blue Devon slate

Altitude
120-180 m

Size
0.48 ha

Orientation
SW

Gradient
60 %

Grape Variety
Riesling

VDP.Estates: Josef Milz

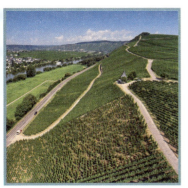

The 0.5-hectare VDP.GROSSE LAGE® FELSENKOPF is located at the beginning of the riverbend near Trittenheim. It rises from the bank of the Mosel River at 120 metres to 180 metres above sea level at a solid 60 percent incline. The vines were planted in the year 1972 and are trained in the typical Mosel fashion on individual stakes. The soil is rocky grey and blue Devon slate.
Information: The GL FELSENKOPF is a monopole vineyard that belongs to the VDP.Estate Josef Milz.

FÖRSTERLAY

Lösnich | Mosel
VDP.GROSSE LAGE®

Soil
rocky, weathered clayey slate

Altitude
110-260 m

Size
10.33 ha

Orientation
n.a.

Gradient
10-60 %

Grape Variety
Riesling

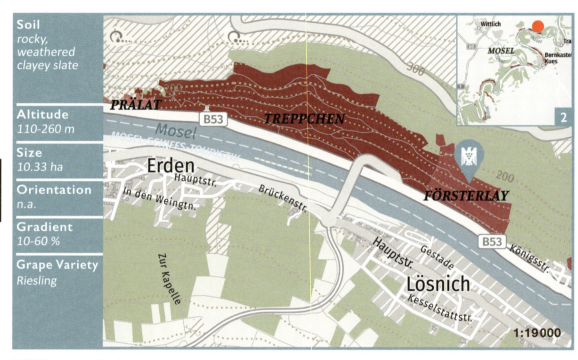

VDP.Estates: Dr. Loosen

The VDP.GROSSE LAGE® FÖRSTERLAY borders the somewhat more famous GL TREPPCHEN to the east. It rises from the bank of the Mosel River from 110 to 260 metres above sea level at a slope gradient of 10 to 60 %. Due to its proximity to the river, the vineyard benefits from increased solar radiation and a well-regulated microclimate. The soils are rocky, weathered clayey slate.

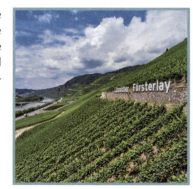

GOLDBERG

Wawern | Saar
VDP.GROSSE LAGE®

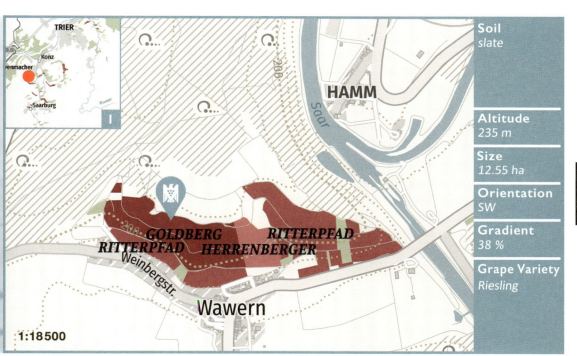

Soil
slate

Altitude
235 m

Size
12.55 ha

Orientation
SW

Gradient
38 %

Grape Variety
Riesling

Mosel

VDP.Estates: Van Volxem

The VDP.GROSSE LAGE® GOLDBERG is a southwest facing vineyard in a side valley of the Saar. It extends along a slope above the village Wawern. The GL GOLDBERG climbs up to 235 metres above sea level at an incline of 38 percent. The typical slate of the region dominates the soil.

GOLDTRÖPFCHEN

Neumagen-Dhron, Piesport | Mosel
VDP.GROSSE LAGE®

Soil: grey Devon slate
Altitude: 120-200 m
Size: 69.77 ha
Orientation: SSW-S-SE
Gradient: 40-90 %
Grape Variety: Riesling

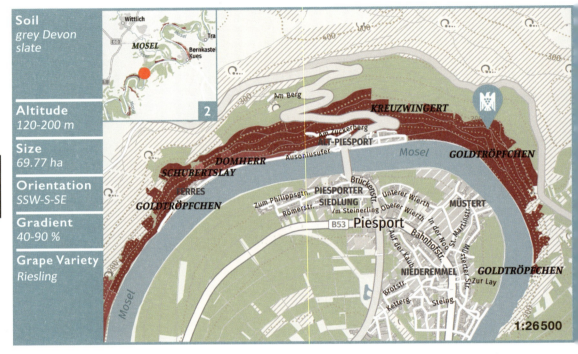

VDP.Estates: Grans-Fassian, Willi Haag, Haart, Reichsgraf von Kesselstatt, Schloss Lieser - Thomas Haag, Stiftungsweingut Vereinigte Hospitien, Nik Weis - St. Urbans-Hof

The VDP.GROSSE LAGE® GOLDTRÖPFCHEN resembles a huge amphitheatre that surrounds Piesport on the outer bend of the Mosel. The exposition turns from southeast to south to south-southwest. The sunshine duration in the vineyard is long and the east and west slopes shield the sides opposite from wind. The vineyard is extremely steep in some places and rises from 120 to 200 metres above sea level at a slope gradient of 40 to 90 percent. The easily warmed soil is comprised of deep, very weathered, dark Devon slate that contains quartz and minerals. In some places there is a high share of fine earth. The site generally has good available water capacity.

History: The name "Goldtröpfchen" means "gold droplet". It could possible come from the Celtic word for hill or mountain, "col". Another hypothesis points to the glittery soil or golden drops of liquid that form on the ripe or botrytized grapes.

GOTTESFUSS

Wiltingen | Saar
VDP.GROSSE LAGE®

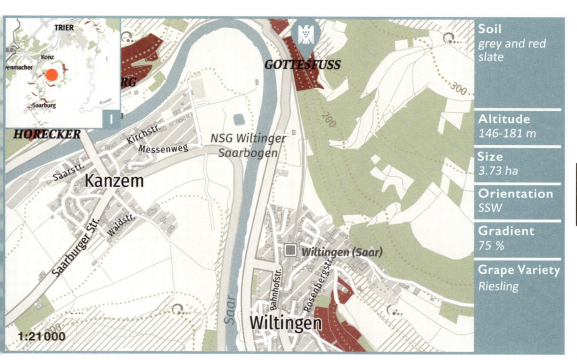

Soil
grey and red slate

Altitude
146-181 m

Size
3.73 ha

Orientation
SSW

Gradient
75 %

Grape Variety
Riesling

Mosel

VDP.Estates: Reichsgraf von Kesselstatt, Van Volxem

The VDP.GROSSE LAGE® GOTTESFUSS borders the GL BRAUNE KUPP on its south side directly on the Saar River. The site is very steep with a 75 percent slope gradient. It faces south-southwest and benefits particularly from the midday and evening sunshine. The Saar also reflects additional light into the vineyard. The soil is comprised of grey and red slate and because it is so rocky, it can't store much moisture and force vines to thrust their roots deep to source the nutrients they need. The GL GOTTESFUSS lies between 146 and 181 metres above sea level.

GRABEN

Bernkastel-Kues | Mosel
VDP.GROSSE LAGE®

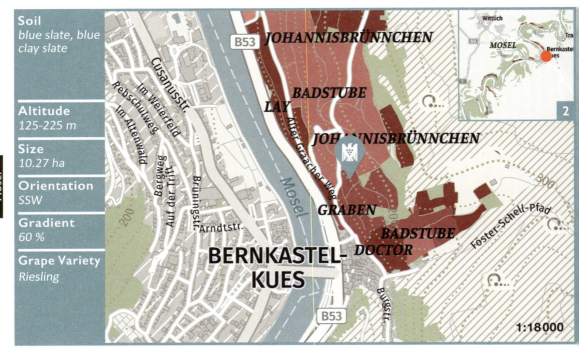

Soil
blue slate, blue clay slate

Altitude
125-225 m

Size
10.27 ha

Orientation
SSW

Gradient
60 %

Grape Variety
Riesling

VDP.Estates: S. A. Prüm, Wwe. Dr. H. Thanisch, Erben Thanisch, Geheimrat J. Wegeler

The VDP.GROSSE LAGE® GRABEN is located above Bernkastel to the north and surrounds the famous VDP.GROSSE LAGE® DOCTOR. The vineyard rises from 125 to 225 metres above sea level at a steep 60 percent gradient. The GL GRABEN faces south-southwest. Vines root in grey-blue slate and blue clay slate. The clay content in this soil ensures vines a good source of moisture.

GRAFENBERG

Piesport | Mosel
VDP.GROSSE LAGE®

Soil
red Devon slate

Altitude
120-200 m

Size
7.72 ha

Orientation
S-SE

Gradient
50-75 %

Grape Variety
Riesling

VDP.Estates: Haart, Reichsgraf von Kesselstatt

A distinguishing trait of the VDP.GROSSE LAGE® GRAFENBERG is the high share of fine earth in its red Devon slate soils. The small earth particles translate to a large surface area that allows water to be stored over a prolonged time period. Located in a bend of the Mosel River across from Neumagen-Dhron, the site captures the full strength of the morning sun with its south to southeast aspect. One can climb approximately 600 red sandstone stairsteps in this vineyard from 120 metres to 200 metres above sea level. At a 50 to 75 percent slope gradient, this is steep viticulture at its best.

HERRENBERG

Mertesdorf | Ruwer
VDP.GROSSE LAGE®

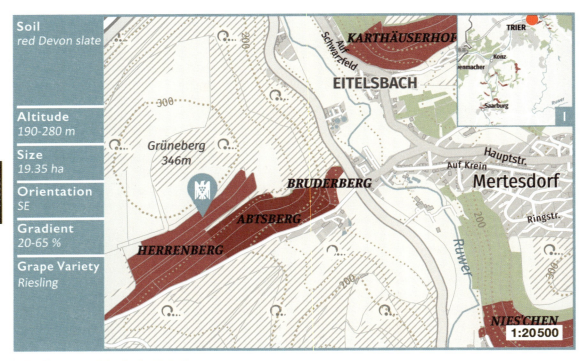

Soil
red Devon slate

Altitude
190-280 m

Size
19.35 ha

Orientation
SE

Gradient
20-65 %

Grape Variety
Riesling

Mosel

VDP.Estates: **Maximin Grünhaus**

The VDP.GROSSE LAGE® HERRENBERG is a southeast facing site located in a side valley of the Ruwer that borders the GL ABTSBERG to the west. The forested cap of the hill provides vines protection from cold north winds. The weathered red Devon slate soil is deep and provides vines with good water availability even in dry years. The GL HERRENBERG rises from 190 to 280 metres above sea level at a moderate 20 to steep 65 percent slope gradient.

Information: The GL HERRENBERG is a monopole vineyard that belongs to the VDP.Estate Maximin Grünhaus. The estate's vineyards BRUDERBERG, HERRENBERG and ABTSBERG were cultivated by the Benedictine Sankt Maximin Abbey in Trier from the 7th century until the end of the 18th century. The Maximin Grünhaus estate house was originally a monastery building and was first mentioned in a document dating February 6 in the year 966.

HERRENBERG

Serrig | Saar
VDP.GROSSE LAGE®

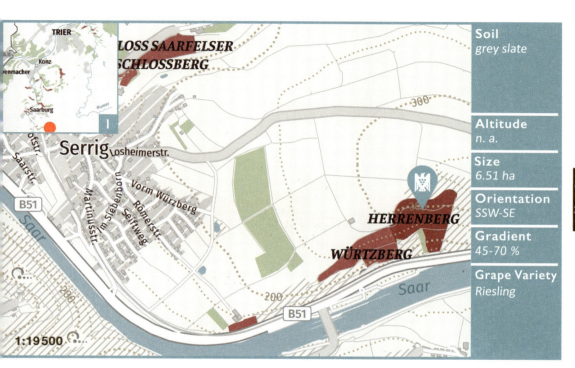

Soil
grey slate

Altitude
n. a.

Size
6.51 ha

Orientation
SSW-SE

Gradient
45-70 %

Grape Variety
Riesling

Mosel

The VDP.GROSSE LAGE® HERRENBERG south of Serrig rises above a bend in the Saar River at a steep 70 percent slope gradient. The vineyard turns from south-southwest to southeast and captures the sunlight in its vine rows throughout the day. The soils are skeletal grey slate.

HERRENBERGER

Wawern | Saar
VDP.GROSSE LAGE®

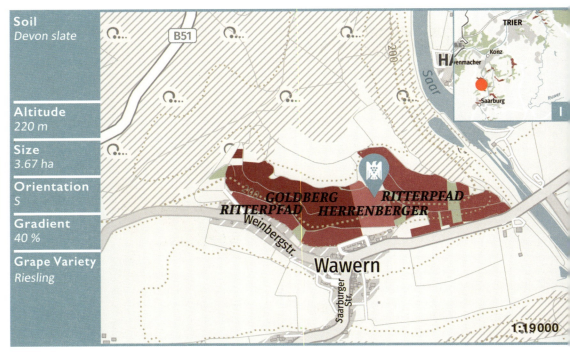

Soil
Devon slate

Altitude
220 m

Size
3.67 ha

Orientation
S

Gradient
40 %

Grape Variety
Riesling

VDP.Estates: von Othegraven

The VDP.GROSSE LAGE® HERRENBERGER is located in a side valley of the Saar above the village Wawern. The vines root in highly weathered Devon slate with a high share of loam. The loam allows the soil to store moisture well. The site has an optimal south-facing aspect that allows vines to benefit fully from the day's sunshine. The vineyards of Wawern enjoy the highest number of sunshine hours on the Saar. The vineyard slope has a homogenous 40 percent gradient and is located at around 220 metres above sea level.

Information: The GL HERRENBERGER is a monopole vineyard that belongs to the VDP.Estate von Othegraven.

HIMMELREICH

Graach | Mosel
VDP.GROSSE LAGE®

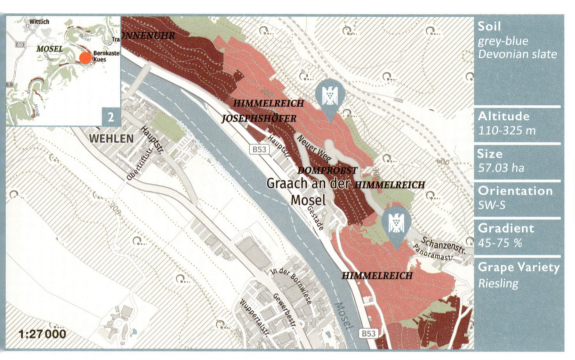

Soil
grey-blue Devonian slate

Altitude
110-325 m

Size
57.03 ha

Orientation
SW-S

Gradient
45-75 %

Grape Variety
Riesling

VDP.Estates: Schloss Lieser - Thomas Haag, Dr. Loosen, Joh. Jos. Prüm, S. A. Prüm, Willi Schaefer, Geheimrat J. Wegeler,

Many of the vines in the VDP.GROSSE LAGE® HIMMELREICH are very old and ungrafted and trained in the old traditional method on individual stakes. The vineyard faces southwest to south toward the light-reflecting, temperature-regulating Mosel River, which helps protect it from frost. Its position in the Mosel Valley also protects it from wind. The soils are easily warmed grey-blue Devonian slate. Aquifers cross through the slope and provide vines with very good moisture throughout the year. The vineyard lies between 110 and 325 metres above sea level and with a 45 to 75 percent it is fairly steep.

HOFBERGER

Neumagen-Dhron, Piesport | Mosel
VDP.GROSSE LAGE®

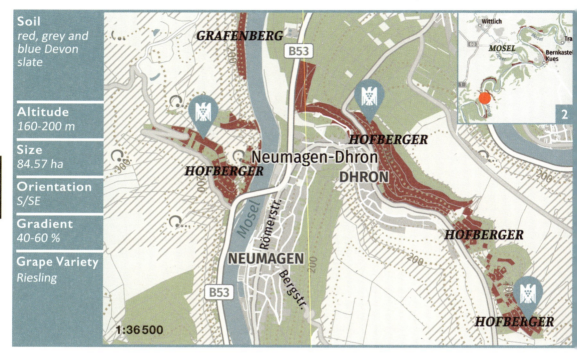

Soil
red, grey and blue Devon slate

Altitude
160-200 m

Size
84.57 ha

Orientation
S/SE

Gradient
40-60 %

Grape Variety
Riesling

Mosel

1:36 500

VDP.Estates: Grans-Fassian, Josef Milz

The VDP.GROSSE LAGE® HOFBERGER winds around Dhron and Neumagen-Dhron. The vineyard slope has a south to southeast aspect and the best parcels benefit from extra warmth due to the sun's reflection from the Mosel River. The vines of the two VDP. Wine Estates Josef Milz and Grans-Fassian were planted between 1967 and 1974—now quite a respectable age. The vineyard climbs from 160 to 200 metres above sea level at a 40 to 60 percent slope gradient. The soils are red, grey and blue Devon slate.

History: The Prussian vineyard classification recognized the Hofberger vineyard as one of the best in the Mittelmosel region. The monks of the Benedictine Tholey Abbey in Saarland were great fans of the wines from the Hofberger vineyard.

HÖLLE

Wiltingen | Saar
VDP.GROSSE LAGE®

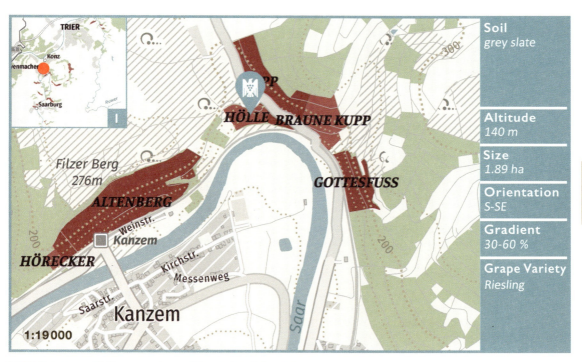

Soil
grey slate

Altitude
140 m

Size
1.89 ha

Orientation
S-SE

Gradient
30-60 %

Grape Variety
Riesling

VDP.Estates: Stiftungsweingut Vereinigte Hospitien

The VDP.GROSSE LAGE® HÖLLE is situated on a bend of the Saar River between Kanzem and Wiltingen. Shaped like a concave mirror and facing south-southeast, the site captures and intensifies the sunlight. These attributes are further enhanced by the proximity to the Saar River, a source of warmth and light reflection. Located in a slope similar to the GL BRAUNE KUPP, this 1.9-hectare vineyard also has the same soil structure as its more famous neighbour: grey slate with a share of loam. Loam provides vines with good water availability. The vineyard rises up to 140 metres above sea level at a steep 30 to 60 percent gradient.

Information: The name "Hölle" stems from "Helde", the historic term for a steep slope. The GL Hölle in Wiltingen is a monopole vineyard of the VDP.Estate Vereinigte Hospitien.

HÖRECKER

Kanzem | Saar
VDP.GROSSE LAGE®

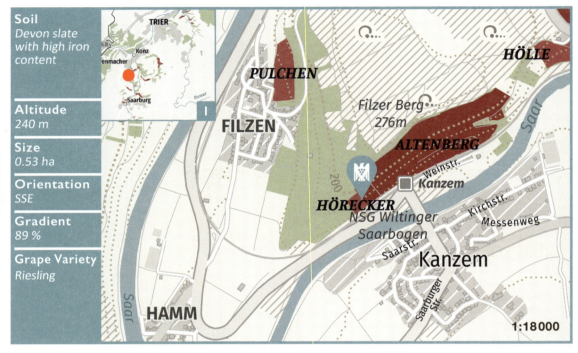

Soil
Devon slate with high iron content

Altitude
240 m

Size
0.53 ha

Orientation
SSE

Gradient
89 %

Grape Variety
Riesling

Mosel

VDP.Estates: von Hövel

The VDP.GROSSE LAGE® HÖRECKER is a small extension of the GL ALTENBERG toward the southwest. The site faces south-southeast, exposing the vines and grapes to plenty of sunshine. The soils are rocky green-grey slate with a share of fine earth that supports water availability. The half-hectare GL HÖRECKER has an extremely steep 89 percent slope gradient and together with the GL ALTENBERG is one of the steepest sites on the Saar.

HÜTTE

Oberemmel | Saar
VDP.GROSSE LAGE®

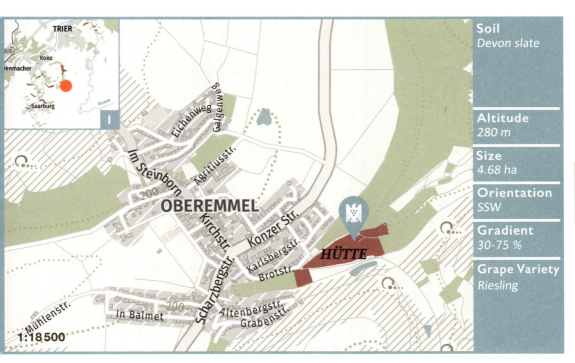

Soil
Devon slate

Altitude
280 m

Size
4.68 ha

Orientation
SSW

Gradient
30-75 %

Grape Variety
Riesling

Mosel

VDP.Estates: von Hövel

The VDP.GROSSE LAGE® HÜTTE is located above the little tributary Langwiesbach in the same side valley in which the famous Scharzhofberg is found. The vineyard lies at 280 metres above sea level at a slope gradient of 30 to 75 percent. The elevated, rather unprotected position is quite windy. The GL HÜTTE faces south-southwest. The soil of the 5-hectare vineyard is rocky-gritty, highly weathered slate.

JOHANNISBRÜNNCHEN

Bernkastel-Kues | Mosel
VDP.GROSSE LAGE®

Soil
grey-blue Devonian slate

Altitude
150-325 m

Size
12 ha

Orientation
W-SW

Gradient
40-60 %

Grape Variety
Riesling

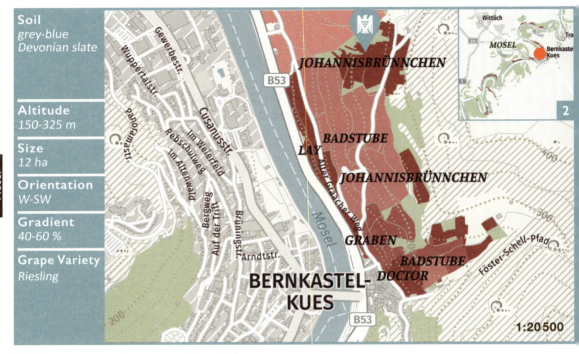

VDP.Estates: Dr. Loosen, Joh. Jos. Prüm

Grey-blue Devonian slate with a share of clay determines the soils of the 12-hectare VDP.GROSSE LAGE® JOHANNISBRÜNNCHEN. It rises above the Mosel River from 150 to 325 metres above sea level at a 40 to 60 percent incline and turns from west to southwest. An adjacent forest at the top of the hill offers protection.

JOSEPHSHÖFER

Graach | Mosel
VDP.GROSSE LAGE®

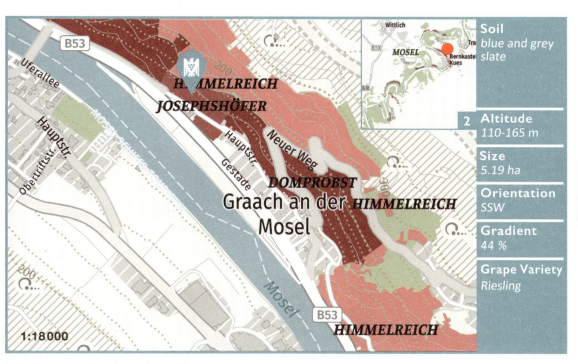

Soil
blue and grey slate

Altitude
110-165 m

Size
5.19 ha

Orientation
SSW

Gradient
44 %

Grape Variety
Riesling

VDP.Estates: **Reichsgraf von Kesselstatt**

The south facing 5-hectare VDP.GROSSE LAGE® JOSEPHSHÖFER lies between the two GL DOMPROBST and SONNENUHR (Wehlen). The very steep site climbs from 110 to 165 metres above sea level at a 44 percent gradient. The soil is comprised of deep, weathered Devon slate debris and abundant rocks, particularly in the higher areas. At the foot of the slope, more fine earth is present. The site has good available water capacity. The microclimate of the GL JOSEPHSHÖFER is determined by the rapid warming properties of the soil and the wind-protected position.

History: The site is named after the monastery that once owned it. This is also now the name of the hamlet Hofsiedlung Josephshof, previously called Merteshof. The site was documented as the monastery vineyard in 1100.

JUFFER SONNENUHR

Brauneberg | Mosel
VDP.GROSSE LAGE®

Soil
grey and blue Devon slate with iron inclusions

Altitude
110-185 m

Size
2.17 ha

Orientation
SSE-S-SSW

Gradient
70-85 %

Grape Variety
Riesling

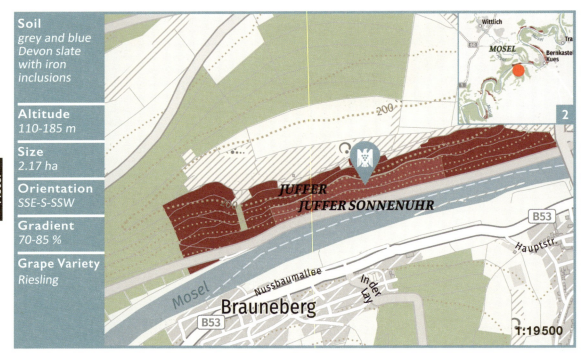

VDP.Estates: Fritz Haag, Willi Haag, Reichsgraf von Kesselstatt, Schloss Lieser - Thomas Haag, Wwe. Dr. H. Thanisch, Erben Thanisch,

The VDP.GROSSE LAGE® JUFFER SONNENUHR lies nestled in the heart of the GL JUFFER, well protected from the wind. Vines benefit from the sunlight, which is amplified in the concave slope. With a slope gradient of 70 to 85 percent, it is together with the encompassing GL JUFFER, one of the steepest vineyard locations at the Mittelmosel. As in the GL JUFFER, weatherd blue and grey Devon slate with iron interstratifications dominate the soil and provide well-balanced water availability. The GL JUFFER SONNENUHR rises from the bank of the Mosel River at 110 metres to 185 metres above sea level.

History: Several theories exist about the name "Juffer". The word means a virgin, a pious woman or a bigot in old Rhine dialect. This could stem from the fact that the vineyard once belonged to a Franciscan nunnery or it could refer to the three unmarried daughters of a former owner of the site.

JUFFER

Brauneberg | Mosel
VDP.GROSSE LAGE®

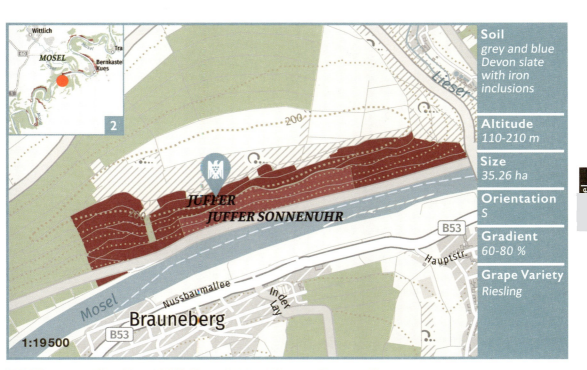

Soil
grey and blue Devon slate with iron inclusions

Altitude
110-210 m

Size
35.26 ha

Orientation
S

Gradient
60-80 %

Grape Variety
Riesling

VDP.Estates: Fritz Haag, Willi Haag, Schloss Lieser - Thomas Haag, Wwe. Dr. H. Thanisch, Erben Thanisch

With a slope gradient of up to 80 percent, the VDP.GROSSE LAGE® JUFFER in Brauneberg is one of the steepest sites of the Mittelmosel. The site encircles the famous JUFFER SONNENUHR and is protected by a forest belt on the ridge. The south-facing site benefits fully from the sun's energy during the day, which provides vines ideal conditions for ripening fruit. The soils are comprised of grey and blue Devon slate with iron interstratifications. This soil is quite weathered and provides good water storage capacity while simultaneously preventing waterlogging. The GL JUFFER rises from the bank of the Mosel River at 110 up to 210 metres above sea level.

History: Several theories exist about the name "Juffer". The word means a virgin, a pious woman or a bigot in old Rhine dialect. This could stem from the fact that the vineyard once belonged to a Franciscan nunnery or it could refer to the three unmarried daughters of a former owner of the site.

KARTHÄUSERHOFBERG

Trier | Ruwer
VDP.GROSSE LAGE®

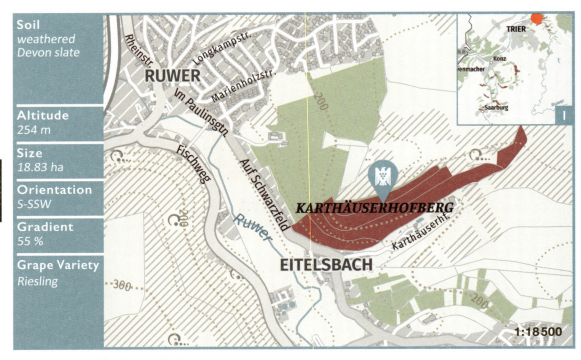

Soil
weathered Devon slate

Altitude
254 m

Size
18.83 ha

Orientation
S-SSW

Gradient
55 %

Grape Variety
Riesling

Mosel

VDP.Estates: Karthäuserhof

The VDP.GROSSE LAGE® KARTHÄUSERHOFBERG extends into a side valley of the Ruwer River, a short distance from the mouth of the Mosel River. The rounded, convex slope has an approximately 55 percent gradient. Forests to the east and above on the hilltop protect the vines in this south to south-southwest facing site. The 18.8-hectare vineyard has weathered Devon slate soils.
History: The GL KARTHÄUSERHOFBERG is a monopole vineyard of the VDP.Estate Kartäuserhof. The vineyard was already classified in the top vineyard category in Mosel-Saar-Ruwer in 1868. It once belonged to the monks of Karthäuser who received the vineyard from Archbishop Baldwin of Luxembourg in 1335.

KEHRNAGEL

Kasel | Ruwer
VDP.GROSSE LAGE®

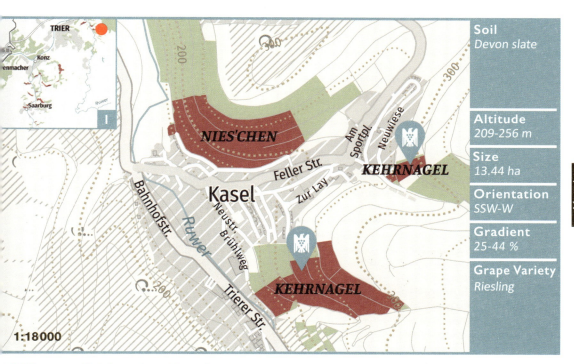

Soil
Devon slate

Altitude
209-256 m

Size
13.44 ha

Orientation
SSW-W

Gradient
25-44 %

Grape Variety
Riesling

Mosel

VDP.Estates: Reichsgraf von Kesselstatt

The VDP.GROSSE LAGE® KEHRNAGEL is located directly on the Ruwer River south of the little town Kasel. It faces south-southwest to west and is nestled in a forest that protects it from wind. The soil is weathered brown Devon slate with good water storage capacity. The GL KEHRNAGEL is fairly elevated at 209 to 256 metres above sea level and the vineyard slope has a 25 to 44 percent gradient.

KIRCHBERG

Hatzenport | Mosel
VDP.GROSSE LAGE®

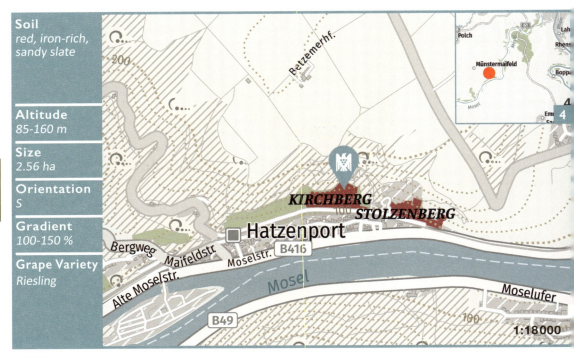

Soil
red, iron-rich, sandy slate

Altitude
85-160 m

Size
2.56 ha

Orientation
S

Gradient
100-150 %

Grape Variety
Riesling

VDP.Estates: **Heymann-Löwenstein**

Due to its steepness, the VDP.GROSSE LAGE® KIRCHBERG above Hatzenport is braced with walls. Corresponding to its wine village, which is the warmest and driest in the Mosel, the GL KIRCHBERG is hot in the summer. The south-facing vineyard has a slope gradient between 100 and 150 percent (45-56°) and has red, iron-rich sandy slate. The site lies between 85 and 160 metres above sea level.

History: The Kirchberg vineyard is named after the Hatzenport St. Johannis church (Kirche), that is located on a terrace that borders the vineyard to the east and overlooks the Mosel River.

KREUZWINGERT

Piesport | Mosel
VDP.GROSSE LAGE®

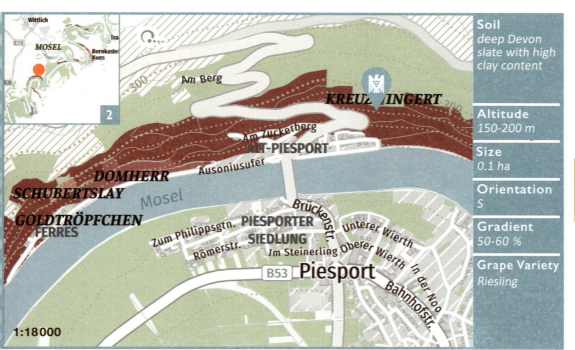

Soil
deep Devon slate with high clay content

Altitude
150-200 m

Size
0.1 ha

Orientation
S

Gradient
50-60 %

Grape Variety
Riesling

Mosel

VDP.Estates: **Haart**

The VDP.GROSSE LAGE® KREUZWINGERT faces directly south on a steep hill above the GL GOLDTRÖPFCHEN. The VDP.Estate Haart's monopole vineyard is not only the smallest GL in the Mosel with 0.1-hectare, it is also the smallest in all of Germany. The vineyard's exposition and the high share of clay in the deep Devon slate soils provide ideal conditions for the vines. The GL KREUZWINGERT has a slope gradient of 50 to 60 percent and rises from 150 to 200 metres above sea level.

History: The Kreuzwingert vineyard was already included in the Prussian vineyard classifications of 1868. The word "Kreuz" means cross and "Wingert" is a vineyard. This name stems from the ancestors of family Haart who sponsored a station for the Way of the Cross on the path to the old church in the GL GOLDTRÖPFCHEN.

193

Kupp "Neuenberg"[1]

Ayl | Saar
VDP.GROSSE LAGE®

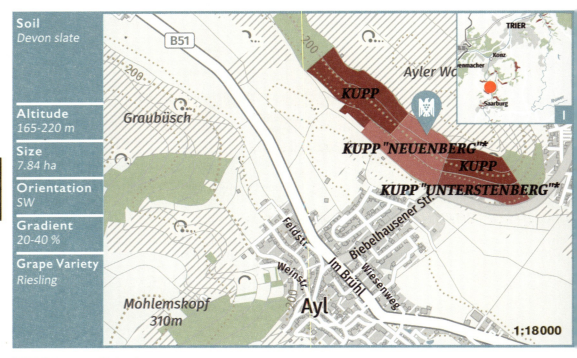

Soil
Devon slate

Altitude
165-220 m

Size
7.84 ha

Orientation
SW

Gradient
20-40 %

Grape Variety
Riesling

VDP.Estates: Peter Lauer

The VDP.GROSSE LAGE® KUPP "NEUENBERG"[1] is located in a protected position below a forest on the south-west-facing slope of the Ayler Kupp Mountain. It rises from 165 to 220 metres above sea level at a slope gradient of 20 to 40 percent. The soils are rocky with a high share of Devon slate and skeletal fragments.

History: The wines from the Ayler Kupp were among the most expensive on the Saar River at the beginning of the last century. The 1904 vintage achieved a price of 15,030 gold marks, the highest price to have ever been paid for a wine from the Saar at that time. A vineyard named Kupp was first mentioned in 1304 in documentation of its ownership by Wilhelmus, the mayor of Trier.

Kupp "Unterstenberg"[1]

Ayl | Saar
VDP.GROSSE LAGE®

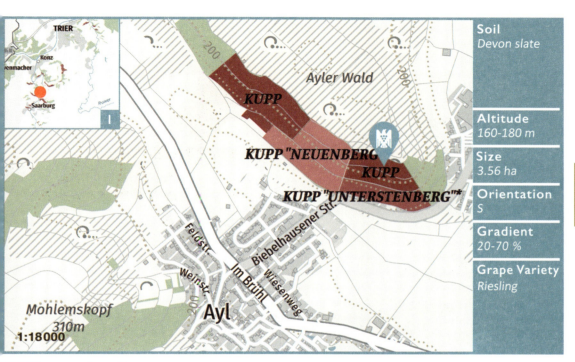

Soil
Devon slate

Altitude
160-180 m

Size
3.56 ha

Orientation
S

Gradient
20-70 %

Grape Variety
Riesling

Mosel

VDP.Estates: Peter Lauer

The sun-exposed south facing slope of the VDP.GROSSE LAGE® KUPP "UNTERSTENBERG"[1] lies in the eastern third of the Kupp vineyard close to the river on the bottom of the Ayler Kupp Mountain. Its slope gradient is a very steep 70 percent. The soil is rocky, grey weathered Devon slate debris with skeletal content. The parcel is planted with Riesling.

History: The first documentation of a site named Kupp stems from the year 1304. In 1906 a Fuder barrel (960 litres) of "1904 Ayler Kupp" was sold for 15,030 gold marks, the highest price ever achieved for a wine from the Saar.

KUPP, Ayl

Ayl | Saar
VDP.GROSSE LAGE®

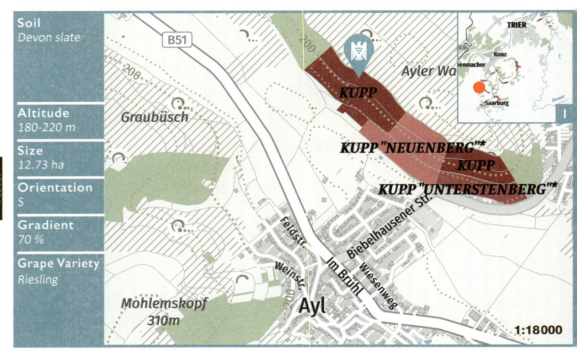

Soil
Devon slate

Altitude
180-220 m

Size
12.73 ha

Orientation
S

Gradient
70 %

Grape Variety
Riesling

VDP.Estates: **Peter Lauer**

The VDP.GROSSE LAGE® KUPP is essentially the peak of the Kupp vineyard, the prime parcel with an ideal exposure to the sun. Half-moon-shaped, it stretches around from an east through a southwest exposition, from the warming Saar into the cooler Saargau at a slope gradient of 70 percent. As a result, two contrasting microclimates with differing wine styles are found within one vineyard. The soil is rocky and comprised mostly of weathered blue-grey Devon slate with skeletal portions. Primarily Riesling grows here.

History: The first documentation of a site named Kupp stems from the year 1304. The wines from this sight have been highly sought since 1850. In 1904, a bottler of Ayler Kupp cost 10 gold marks, while a Château d'Yquem cost only nine.

KUPP, Saarburg

Saarburg | Saar
VDP.GROSSE LAGE®

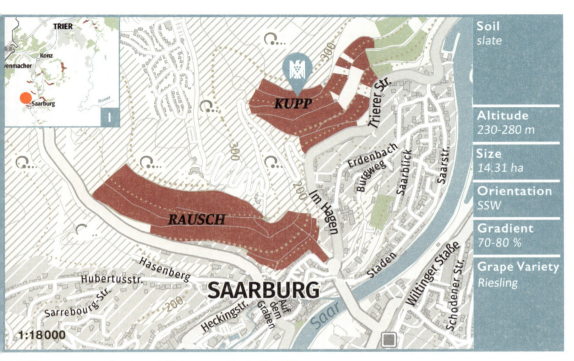

Soil
slate

Altitude
230-280 m

Size
14.31 ha

Orientation
SSW

Gradient
70-80 %

Grape Variety
Riesling

VDP.Estates: Dr. Fischer - Hofstätter Weis, Dr. Wagner

The VDP.GROSSE LAGE® KUPP rises above the outskirts of Saarburg at an extremely steep 70 to 80 percent gradient. A forest at the top of the hill protects the site from cold winds. The vines are often trained on individual stakes. Vines thrust their roots deep into the well-drained slate soil in search of water reserves. The 14-hectare vineyard faces south-southwest.

KUPP, WILTINGEN

Wiltingen | Saar
VDP.GROSSE LAGE®

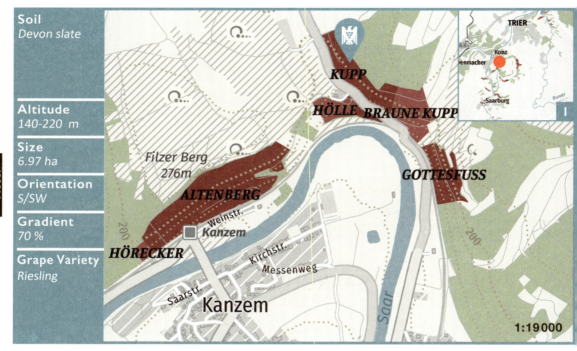

Soil
Devon slate

Altitude
140-220 m

Size
6.97 ha

Orientation
S/SW

Gradient
70 %

Grape Variety
Riesling

VDP.Estates: Egon Müller - Scharzhof, Stiftungsweingut Vereinigte Hospitien, von Othegraven, Van Volxem

The steep 70 percent gradient of the VDP.GROSSE LAGE® KUPP faces south and southwest and captures plenty of sunshine. The vineyard lies between 140 and 220 metres above sea level. The soil is fine-grained, pale, weathered Devon slate with reddish interstratifications.

LAURENTIUSLAY

Leiwen | Mosel
VDP.GROSSE LAGE®

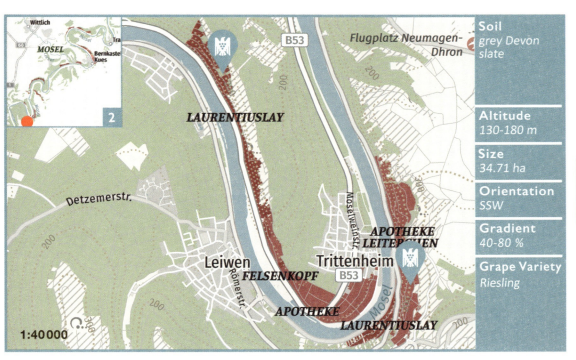

Soil
grey Devon slate

Altitude
130-180 m

Size
34.71 ha

Orientation
SSW

Gradient
40-80 %

Grape Variety
Riesling

VDP.Estates: Grans-Fassian, Nik Weis - St. Urbans-Hof

The rocky, 34-hectare VDP.GROSSE LAGE® LAURENTUSLAY rises from 130 to 180 metres above sea level at a steep 40 percent to very steep 80 percent slope gradient and is visibly prominent from quite a distance as one travels down the Mosel. The vines are not shaded and benefit from a south-southwest aspect with intense sunshine nearly the entire day. The grey Devon slate stores the warmth of the day and radiates it into the vines during the night. The climate is hot, yet due to its exposition this GL is well aerated.

LAY

Bernkastel-Kues | Mosel
VDP.GROSSE LAGE®

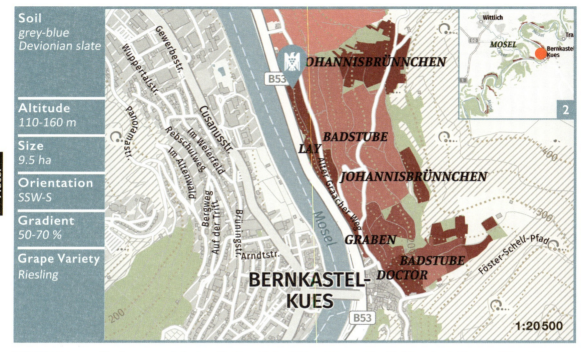

Soil
grey-blue Devonian slate

Altitude
110-160 m

Size
9.5 ha

Orientation
SSW-S

Gradient
50-70 %

Grape Variety
Riesling

VDP.Estates: Dr. Loosen, Joh. Jos. Prüm, S. A. Prüm, Wwe. Dr. H. Thanisch, Erben Thanisch, Geheimrat J. Wegeler

The VDP.GROSSE LAGE ® LAY is located right next to the town of Bernkastel on the Mosel River. The site faces southsouthwest to south and the vines, partly very old and ungrafted, are often still trained in the traditional Mosel fashion on individual stakes. This makes it easier to tend the vines in the steep 50 to 70 percent slope gradient that rises from 110 to 160 metres above sea level. The solar radiation in this slope is further intensified by its proximity to the reflecting surface of the river making the site warm. The soil is grey-blue Devonian slate with some clay content, which guarantees good water storativity.

History: The word "Lay" has a Celtic origin and means slate rock.

LAYET

Mehring | Mosel
VDP.GROSSE LAGE®

Soil
slate

Altitude
140-180 m

Size
2.52 ha

Orientation
S

Gradient
60-75 %

Grape Variety
Riesling

VDP.Estates: Nik Weis - St. Urbans-Hof

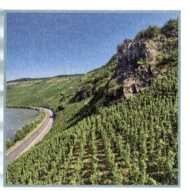

The VDP.GROSSE LAGE® LAYET is situated on a bend of the Mosel River bordering the Blattenberg vineyard across from Mehring. Due to its advantageous position on a broader section of the river, it enjoys a moderate climate and stores warmth while being pampered by the sun and wind. Additional sunlight is also reflected from the water's surface. The soils are blue slate with quartzite interstratifications.
Information: The vineyard's name "Layet" is the Old German word for slate.

LEITERCHEN

Trittenheim | Mosel
VDP.GROSSE LAGE®

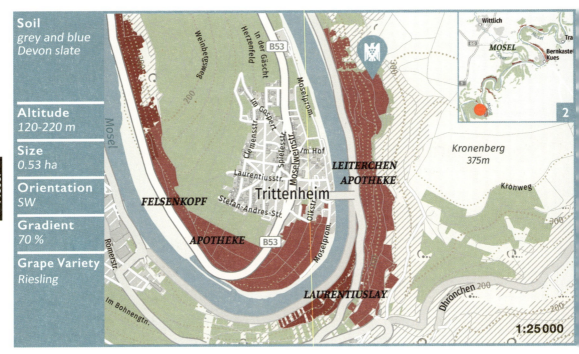

Soil
grey and blue Devon slate

Altitude
120-220 m

Size
0.53 ha

Orientation
SW

Gradient
70 %

Grape Variety
Riesling

VDP.Estates: **Josef Milz**

"Leiterchen" translates to "little ladder" and with a breathtaking slope gradient of up to 70 percent, this 0.5-hectare vineyard aptly demonstrates that definition. The vines in the VDP.GROSSE LAGE® LEITERCHEN cling to individual stakes on the southwest facing slope that is braced with walls that provide not only stability, but also contribute to the microclimate by storing the sun's warmth. The soil is weathered grey and blue Devon slate, which drains very well and encourages vines to thrust their roots deep in search of moisture. The vineyard is located directly across from the wine village Trittenheim and is surrounded by the VDP.GROSSE LAGE® APOTHEKE.
Information: The GL LEITERCHEN is a monopole vineyard that belongs to the VDP.Estate Josef Milz.

MARIENBURG

Pünderich | Mosel
VDP.GROSSE LAGE®

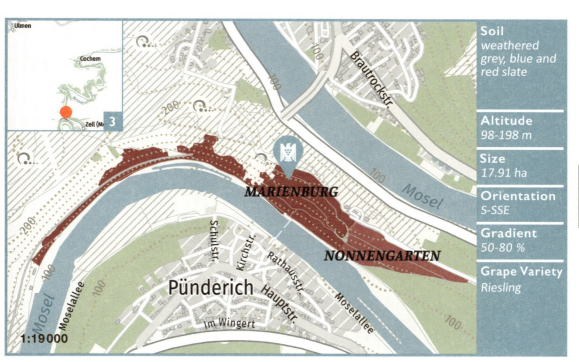

Soil
weathered grey, blue and red slate

Altitude
98-198 m

Size
17.91 ha

Orientation
S-SSE

Gradient
50-80 %

Grape Variety
Riesling

VDP.Estates: Clemens Busch

Great diversity distinguishes the VDP.GROSSE LAGE® MARIENBURG. Due to its position on a sharp bend of the Mosel River, the microclimate of this south to south-southeast facing vineyard varies greatly within a small area, which lends the wines complexity. The vineyard falls from 198 to 98 metres above sea level toward the river at a steep 50 to 80 percent gradient. As in very few other vineyards, the soils in the GL MARIENBURG vary from weathered grey or blue slate to the more seldom red slate. Red slate is found in the Rothenpfad parcel nearby the railroad viaduct. The Fahrlay parcel located directly next to the Pünderich ferry dock is the only part of the GL MARIENBURG in which blue slate dominates. The rock content is very high and goes very deep. The Falkenlay parcel between Fahrlay and Rothenpfad has deeper soil and is marked by grey slate.

NIEDERBERG HELDEN

Lieser | Mosel
VDP.GROSSE LAGE®

Soil
blue Devon slate

Altitude
110-190 m

Size
33.42 ha

Orientation
S-SW

Gradient
80 %

Grape Variety
Riesling

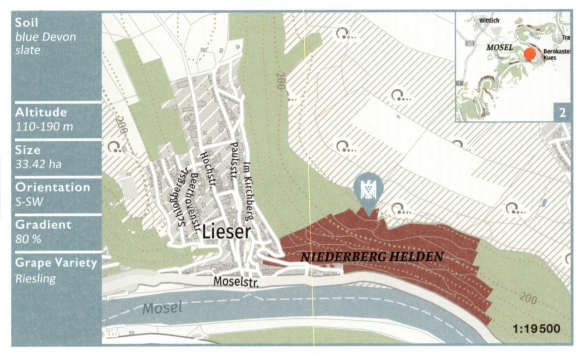

VDP.Estates: Schloss Lieser - Thomas Haag, Wwe. Dr. H. Thanisch, Erben Thanisch

A special feature of the VDP.GROSSE LAGE® NIEDERBERG HELDEN is its protected, warm microclimate. The site faces south and southwest and forms a gentle, warm basin in the centre. This is advantageous for high ripeness of fruit and makes it predestined for the production of noble sweet wines. A plateau on the ridge of the hill provides sufficient water availability. The loose, weathered Devon slate soil promotes water drainage, while the high share of fine earth supplies nutrients. The name NIEDERBERG HELDEN resulted from the connexion of two individual parcels. The vineyard is located between 110 and 190 metres above sea level and the slope has a steep 80 percent incline.

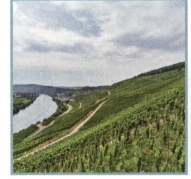

NIES'CHEN

Kasel | Ruwer
VDP.GROSSE LAGE®

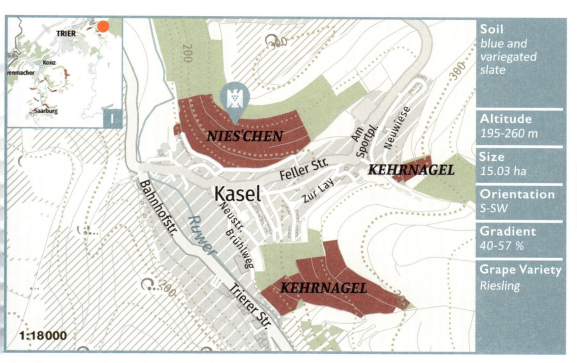

Soil
blue and variegated slate

Altitude
195-260 m

Size
15.03 ha

Orientation
S-SW

Gradient
40-57 %

Grape Variety
Riesling

Mosel

VDP.Estates: Reichsgraf von Kesselstatt

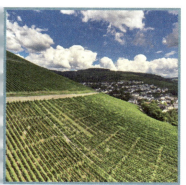

The VDP.GROSSE LAGE® NIES'CHEN is a knoll that extends toward the south and southwest to the edge of the wine village Kasel. The vineyard climbs from 195 to 260 metres above sea level at a slope of 40 to 57 percent. The cool character of the Ruwer dominates the upper parcels of the GL NIES'CHEN, which are simultaneously exposed to cool winds and intense sunshine. The climate is warmer towards the foot of the hill, where vines benefit from the proximity to the moderating Mosel River. Blue slate and variegated slate determine the soils and are particularly well drained in the upper reaches.

History: The name of the site is the diminutive form of the name Agnes, possibly referring to the Abbess Agnes of the Cloister St. Irminen.

NONNENGARTEN

Pünderich | Mosel
VDP.GROSSE LAGE®

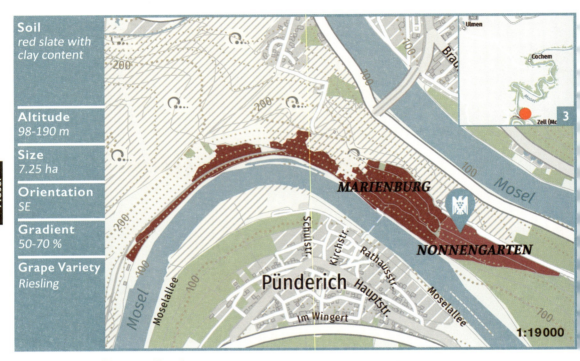

Soil
red slate with clay content

Altitude
98-190 m

Size
7.25 ha

Orientation
SE

Gradient
50-70 %

Grape Variety
Riesling

VDP.Estates: **Clemens Busch**

The VDP.GROSSE LAGE ® NONNENGARTEN borders the GL MARIENBURG just downriver. The soils here are deeper and heavier. Red slate with clay content comprises the unique soil that is found only here in the "Garden of the Nuns" and lends the site its reddish appearance. The slope faces southeast and benefits from the midday and evening sunshine. It rises up to 190 metres above sea level at a steep 50 to 70 percent incline.

History: The name stems from the Augustine Cloister Marienburg that is located on the ridge above the Pünderich vineyards Marienburg and Nonnengarten.

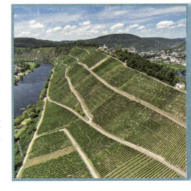

OHLIGSBERG

Wintrich | Mosel
VDP.GROSSE LAGE®

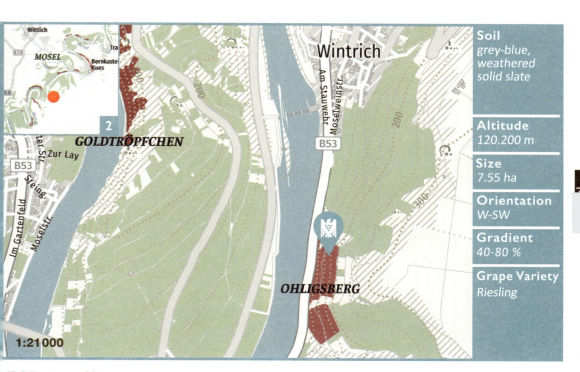

Soil
grey-blue, weathered solid slate

Altitude
120.200 m

Size
7.55 ha

Orientation
W-SW

Gradient
40-80 %

Grape Variety
Riesling

VDP.Estates: **Haart**

The VDP.GROSSE LAGE® OHLIGSBERG is located directly on the Mosel and faces mostly toward the west, but small sections have a southwest or even south exposition. With a 40 to 80 percent gradient, the site is extremely steep in some parts and all labour must be executed manually. The soil is grey-blue weathered Devon slate with bands of quartzite. The seven vineyard hectares lie at 120 to 200 metres above sea level. Because the Mosel is dammed quite broadly here, the reflection of light is quite high and the dark soil stores the warmth well.

History: The name originates from the "zum Oelberg" Chapel. The wines from the Ohligsberg chapel were very highly esteemed in the 19th and beginning of the 20th century. They were among the most famous and valuable wines in Germany. In 1922, wine from the 1913 vintage was served at the Nobel Prize ceremony.

PRÄLAT

Erden | Mosel
VDP.GROSSE LAGE®

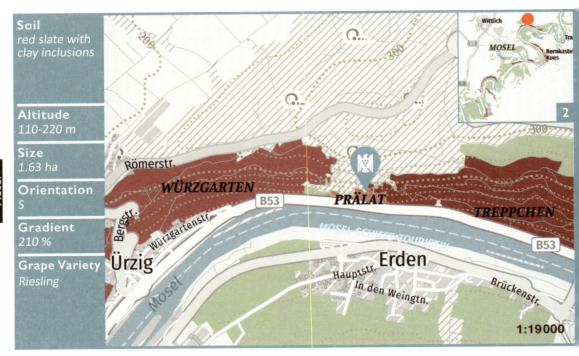

Soil
red slate with clay inclusions

Altitude
110-220 m

Size
1.63 ha

Orientation
S

Gradient
210 %

Grape Variety
Riesling

VDP.Estates: **Dr. Loosen**

The VDP.GROSSE LAGE® PRÄLAT rises rocky, steep, and rugged across river from the Mosel village Erden. Bare red rock frequently protrudes between the vines that cling to the exceedingly steep slope in this little vineyard. The slope rises at 210 percent (65°); rarely are German vineyards any steeper. The soil is comprised of iron-rich red slate with clay content. Due to its position on a bend of the Mosel and protection provided from the surrounding vineyards, the microclimate of the GL PRÄLAT is warm. It benefits from the intense solar radiation of a south-facing site and the warmth-storing capacity of massive rock. The vines grow between 110 and 220 metres above sea level.

History: The Prälat parcel once belonged to the Treppchen vineyard, but was demarcated separately at the end of the 19th century. The new name honours the Ürzig vintner's son Prelate Professor Dr. Franz Steffens (1853-1930).

PULCHEN

Filzen | Saar
VDP.GROSSE LAGE®

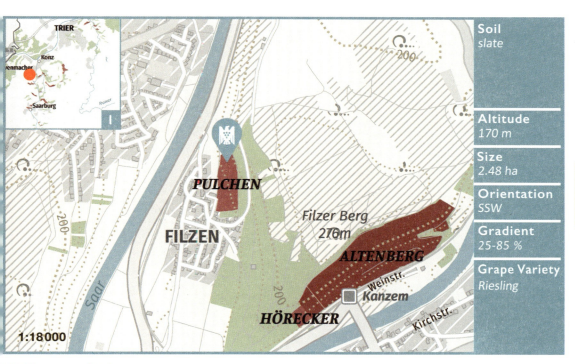

Soil
slate

Altitude
170 m

Size
2.48 ha

Orientation
SSW

Gradient
25-85 %

Grape Variety
Riesling

Mosel

VDP.Estates: Piedmont

The VDP.GROSSE LAGE® PULCHEN is located above the little wine town Filzen. The vineyard drops toward the Saar River at a moderate 25 percent to an extremely steep 85 percent slope gradient. Because it faces south-southwest, it enjoys plenty of sunshine during the day. The GL PULCHEN lies at 170 metres above sea level.

RAUSCH

Saarburg | Saar
VDP.GROSSE LAGE®

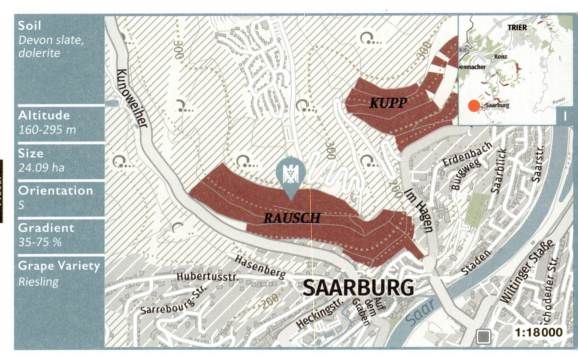

Soil
Devon slate, dolerite

Altitude
160-295 m

Size
24.09 ha

Orientation
S

Gradient
35-75 %

Grape Variety
Riesling

Mosel

VDP.Estates: Forstmeister Geltz-Zilliken, Dr. Wagner

The VDP.GROSSE LAGE® RAUSCH lies in the middle of the Rausch vineyard slope in about the very same place as the historic "Franzens Knüppchen". It is located below the forested peak of the hill and looks over the little town of Saarburg toward the Saar River. It has a south exposition and turns lightly inwards toward a side valley of the Saar. The vineyards climb from 160 to 295 metres above sea level at a gradient of 35 to 75 percent. The GL RAUSCH is well protected from the wind and gets sunshine the entire day. Greywacke, soft, finely foliated Devon slate, and reddish fine earth dominate the soil. A volcanic layer also broke the surface and some basalt (diabase) can be found.

History: The name comes from "Rusche", an old dialect term for rubble.

RITTERPFAD

Wawern | Saar
VDP.GROSSE LAGE®

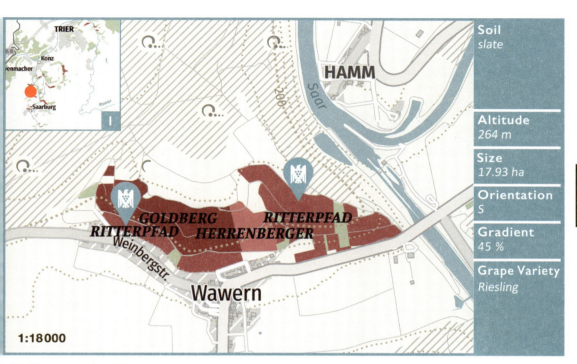

Soil
slate

Altitude
264 m

Size
17.93 ha

Orientation
S

Gradient
45 %

Grape Variety
Riesling

Mosel

VDP.Estates: **Van Volxem**

The VDP.GROSSE LAGE® RITTERPFAD is the final vineyard of Wawern at the foot of the slope close to the Saar River. The vineyard faces south and benefits from the full strength of the sun's light. The vineyards of Wawern enjoy the highest number of sunshine hours on the Saar. The GL RITTERPFAD has a steep slope gradient of 45 percent and is located at 264 metres above sea level.

ROSENBERG

Kinheim | Mosel
VDP.GROSSE LAGE®

Soil
slate

Altitude
n.a.

Size
47.98 ha

Orientation
SE

Gradient
n.a.

Grape Variety
Riesling

Mosel

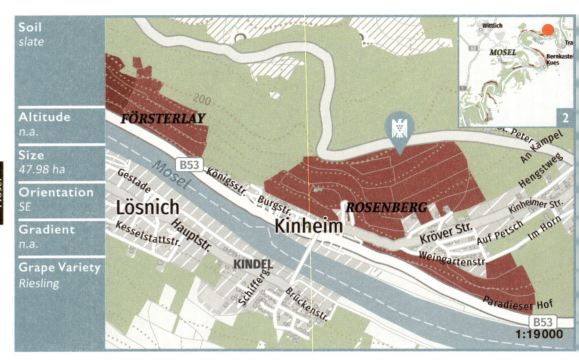

VDP.Estates: **Dr. Loosen**

The VDP.GROSSEN LAGE® ROSENBERG surrounds the city centre of Kinheim on a slope overlooking the Mosel River. It faces south and southeast and collects increased solar radiation and warmth due to its proximity to the river and light reflection from the water's surface. The soils are well-drained slate that encourage vines to root deep in search of sufficient moisture.

RÖTTGEN

Winningen | Mosel
VDP.GROSSE LAGE®

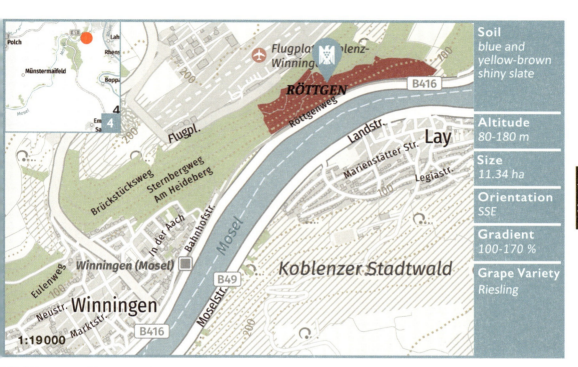

Soil
blue and yellow-brown shiny slate

Altitude
80-180 m

Size
11.34 ha

Orientation
SSE

Gradient
100-170 %

Grape Variety
Riesling

VDP.Estates: **Heymann-Löwenstein, Knebel**

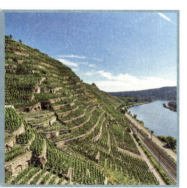

The vineyard terraces of the VDP.GROSSE LAGE® RÖTTGEN climb miraculously up the steep slope from the banks of the Mosel at a 100 to 170 percent incline (45-60°), making it one of the steepest vineyards in Germany. The soil is blue and yellow-brown slate, which also lends the dry stone terrace walls (built without mortar) a warm colour. The microclimate of this protected little vineyard can get hot occasionally. The summer sun heats the south-southeast facing vineyard and its massive walls throughout the day. Because the slate continues to radiate warmth, the night coolness does not set in until quite late. The vineyard comprises a little biotope; numerous beneficial insects and lizards find a habitat in the artistically stacked vineyard walls.
History: The name stems from the word "Rödchen", which refers to a small fallow land parcel. Indeed, the site on this cliff near Winningen was first planted in 1822.

SCHARZHOFBERGER PERGENTSKNOPP

Wiltingen | Saar
VDP.GROSSE LAGE®

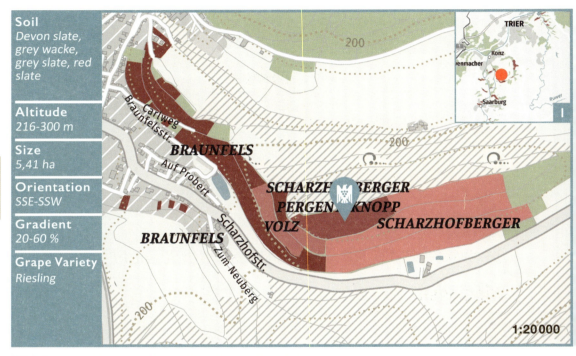

Soil
Devon slate, grey wacke, grey slate, red slate

Altitude
216-300 m

Size
5,41 ha

Orientation
SSE-SSW

Gradient
20-60 %

Grape Variety
Riesling

Mosel

VDP.Estates: Reichsgraf von Kesselstatt, Van Volxem

The VDP.GROSSE LAGE® SCHARZHOFBERGER PERGENTSKNOPP is located directly above one of the most famous vineyards in Germany, the GL SCHARZHOFBERGER. The conditions of the two vineyards are indeed quite similar. The soils of the GL SCHARZHOFBERGER PERGENTSKNOPP is a mix of different types of slate ranging from grey and red Devon slate to greywacke. Because the soils are quite weathered, they are also well drained. The GL SCHARZHOFBERGER PERGENTSKNOPP rises from 216 to 300 metres above sea level at a slope gradient of around 60 percent. The top of the hill is only lightly forested and the vineyard is thus always well-aerated. The aspect turns from south-southeast to south to south-southwest and enjoys sunshine throughout the day.

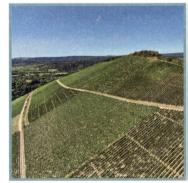

SCHARZHOFBERGER

Wiltingen | Saar
VDP.GROSSE LAGE®

Soil
Devon slate, grey wacke, grey slate, red slate

Altitude
216-300 m

Size
23.45 ha

Orientation
SSE-SSW

Gradient
20-60 %

Grape Variety
Riesling

Mosel

VDP.Estates: von Hövel, Reichsgraf von Kesselstatt, Egon Müller - Scharzhof, Stiftungsweingut Vereinigte Hospitien, Van Volxem

The famous VDP.GROSSE LAGE® SCHARZHOFBERGER is quite unique, particularly due to its soil. Nowhere alongside the Mosel, Saar or Ruwer is the red and grey slate so extremely weathered as it is here. The rock content is a high 70 percent. The fine earth is clayey-silty and friable, and in places it contains iron-oxide and is red. The GL SCHARZHOFBERGER lies east of Wiltingen in a wind-exposed side valley of the Saar. It faces mostly south, south-southeast and south-southwest. The slope climbs from 216 to 300 metres above sea level at a 20 to steeper 60 percent gradient. The vineyard is 23 hectares in size. The wind makes the microclimate fairly cool and is responsible for high temperature fluctuations. The forested ridge top provides vines with sufficient water.

Information: The Scharzhofberg is one of the internationally most highly esteemed white wine vineyards. Its wines achieve high prices at auctions regularly.

SCHLOSS SAARFELSER SCHLOSSBERG

Serrig | Saar
VDP.GROSSE LAGE®

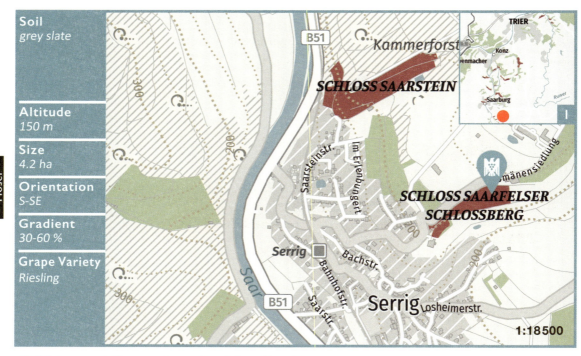

Soil
grey slate

Altitude
150 m

Size
4.2 ha

Orientation
S-SE

Gradient
30-60 %

Grape Variety
Riesling

Mosel

VDP.Estates: Stiftungsweingut Vereinigte Hospitien

The VDP.GROSSE LAGE® SCHLOSS SAARFELSER SCHLOSSBERG follows a side valley of the Saar toward the east from Schloss Saarfels. The slope has a 30 to 60 percent gradient and benefits from its protected location in the valley and its south to southeast aspect. An additional advantageous factor for grape ripening is the well-drained grey slate soil that stores the warmth of the sun and releases it into the vines. This 4-hectare site is a monopole vineyard of the VDP.Estate Vereinigte Hospitien.

History: The sparkling wine producer Adolf Wagner planted the Schloss Saarfels vineyard next to the newly build Schloss Saarfels between 1912 and 1914.

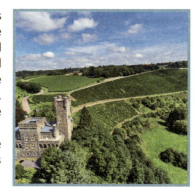

SCHLOSS SAARSTEIN

Serrig | Saar
VDP.GROSSE LAGE®

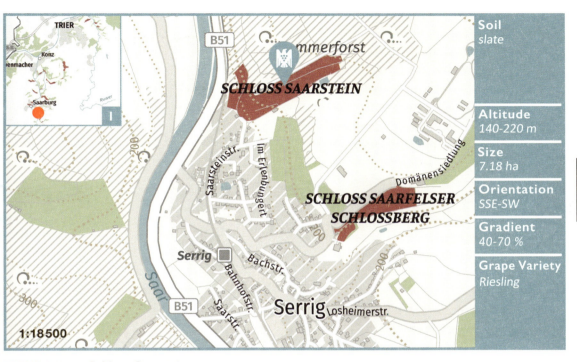

Soil
slate

Altitude
140-220 m

Size
7.18 ha

Orientation
SSE-SW

Gradient
40-70 %

Grape Variety
Riesling

Mosel

VDP.Estates: Schloss Saarstein

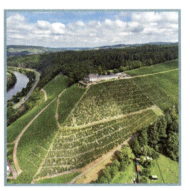

The VDP.GROSSE LAGE® SCHLOSS SAARSTEINER faces south-southeast and makes a small turn toward the west just north of the village Serrig. The vineyard climbs from 140 to 220 metres above sea level at a steep 40 to very steep 70 percent slope gradient. The steeps part of the GL is on the west end and looks toward the Saar River. The east side lies protected in a flatter convex swale. The soil and the microclimate of the 7.2-hectare vineyard is quite heterogeneous. The main variety, Riesling, is planted on greywacke, slate, and brown earth. Reddish bands are found in the western parts of the vineyard, while in the east there is oil shale and very weathered slate. The neighbouring municipal forest provides the site with sufficient water.

SCHONFELS

Ayl | Saar
VDP.GROSSE LAGE®

Soil
Devon slate

Altitude
200-250 m

Size
1.98 ha

Orientation
SSE-SE

Gradient
74 %

Grape Variety
Riesling

Mosel

VDP.Estates: Peter Lauer

The VDP.GROSSE LAGE® SCHONFELS is extremely steep with up to a 74 percent gradient. It is located south of Ayl on the Saar River and its terraces face south-southeast to southeast. The river moderates the climate and reflects the sunlight, which intensifies solar radiation in this well-exposed vineyard. There is no forrest line on top of the slope. Therefore intense winds fall down the slope, cooling down the temperature of the grapes. The 2-hectare GL SCHONFELS lies at 200 to 250 metres above sea level. The very rocky soil is comprised of Devon slate. The Riesling vines here are around 100 years old.

SCHUBERTSLAY

Piesport | Mosel
VDP.GROSSE LAGE®

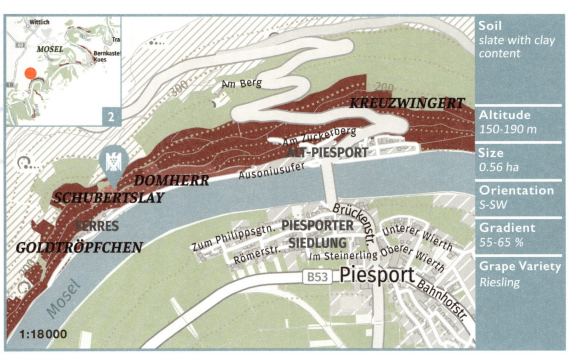

Soil
slate with clay content

Altitude
150-190 m

Size
0.56 ha

Orientation
S-SW

Gradient
55-65 %

Grape Variety
Riesling

VDP.Estates: Stiftungsweingut Vereinigte Hospitien

The rugged, rocky stone terraces of the VDP.GROSSE LAGE® SCHUBERTSLAY are home to some of the oldest vines in the Mosel. They date back to the year 1902 when they were planted by the VDP.Estate Vereinigte Hospitien. Some of the Riesling vines are even ungrafted. This vineyard, encompassed by the GL GOLDTRÖPFCHEN, faces south to southwest and combined with the warmth-storing capacity of the dry-stone walls that brace the slope, the temperatures can get quite hot. The soils are comprised of slate with high clay content, which provides good water availability for the vines. The vineyard rises from 150 to 190 metres above sea level at a slope gradient of 55 to 65 percent.

CUSTOMISED
ELEGANT
SECURE
Tradition and Quality from Austria since 1892

Partner of
VDP.German Prädikat Wine Estates

BT-Watzke GmbH
Griesstraße 25, 8243 Pinggau, Austria
Tel.: +43 3339 22201-0
E-Mail: office@bt-watzke.at

www.bt-watzke.com

SONNENUHR, Wehlen

Wehlen | Mosel
VDP.GROSSE LAGE®

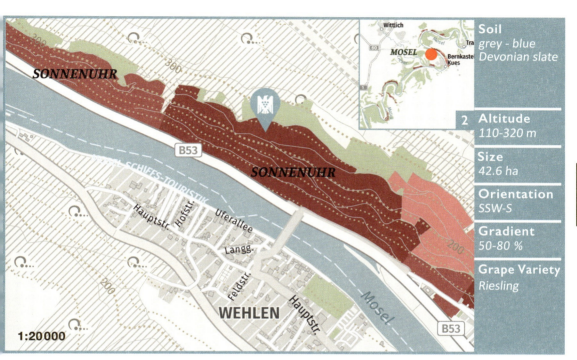

Soil
grey - blue Devonian slate

Altitude
110-320 m

Size
42.6 ha

Orientation
SSW-S

Gradient
50-80 %

Grape Variety
Riesling

VDP.Estates: Reichsgraf von Kesselstatt, Schloss Lieser - Thomas Haag, Dr. Loosen, Joh. Jos. Prüm, S. A. Prüm, Willi Schaefer, Geheimrat J. Wegeler

The southsouthwest to south facing VDP.GROSSE LAGE® (Wehlen) SONNENUHR is located across the Mosel river from the village of Wehlen. The site climbs at a very steep slope gradient of 50 to 80 percent. The vines grow on weathered Devonian slate debris soil. The rock content is high. The long sunshine duration, the intense heat radiation of the soil, and the proximity of the Mosel determine the microclimate of this GL. In these steep sites a high amount of the vines of the main grape variety Riesling (99 percent) are ungrafted and trained on individual posts.

History: The Sonnenuhr vineyard is named after the sundial built by the vintner Jodocus Prüm of Wehlen in 1842 for charity to offer local inhabitants the ability to determine the time of day. In the early 20th century, the monument's name was also used to name the wines of the parcels surrounding the sundial—before, it was common to use just the village name Wehlen.

SONNENUHR, ZELTINGEN

Zeltingen | Mosel
VDP.GROSSE LAGE®

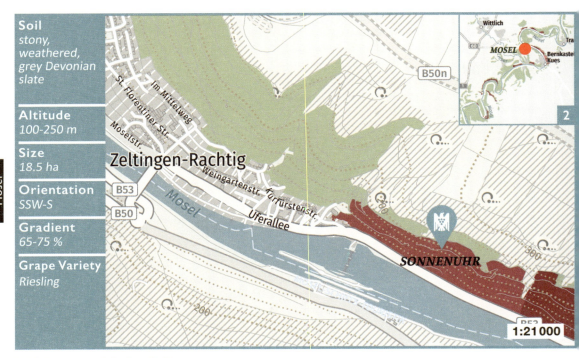

Soil
stony, weathered, grey Devonian slate

Altitude
100-250 m

Size
18.5 ha

Orientation
SSW-S

Gradient
65-75 %

Grape Variety
Riesling

VDP.Estates: Joh. Jos. Prüm

The VDP.GROSSE LAGE® SONNENUHR (Zeltingen) is directly adjacent to the eponymous vineyard that belongs to the village Wehlen. The vineyard faces southsouthwest to south and drops at an incline of 65 to 75 % toward the Mosel. Reflection from the river intensifies the light and solar radiation in the GL SONNENUHR. The soils are rocky, grey Devonian slate with some clay. The partly up to 100 year-old, and often ungrafted vines grow between 110 and 250 metres a.s.l.

History: The Wehlen vintner Jodocus Prüm built a sundial (Sonnenuhr) in this vineyard, as he did in the neighboured Wehlen vineyard. The wines produced here at that time were named for their villages: Zeltingen. It was not until the beginning of the 20th century that single-vineyard labelling prevailed. By then, the "Zeltinger Sonnenuhr" only encompassed the parcel surrounding the sundial, had a size of about 0.3 ha and was a monopoly of Joh. Jos. Prüm. This part is still owned by the VDP.Estate Prüm.

STOLZENBERG

Hatzenport | Mosel
VDP.GROSSE LAGE®

Soil
grey-brown sandy slate

Altitude
85-180 m

Size
1.78 ha

Orientation
S

Gradient
100-150 %

Grape Variety
Riesling

VDP.Estates: Heymann-Löwenstein

With only 1.7 hectares, the VDP.GROSSE LAGE® STOLZENBERG is not only small, but also very steep. With a 100 to 150 percent (45-56°) slope gradient, the cultivation of vines requires terraces (in local dialect called "Chöre" instead of "Terrassen"). The GL STOLZENBERG belongs to Hatzenport, one of the warmest and driest villages in the Mosel and the character of this south-facing site is correspondingly hot and meagre. The soil is grey-brown sandy slate. Vines are planted between 85 and 180 metres above sea level.

TREPPCHEN

Erden | Mosel
VDP.GROSSE LAGE®

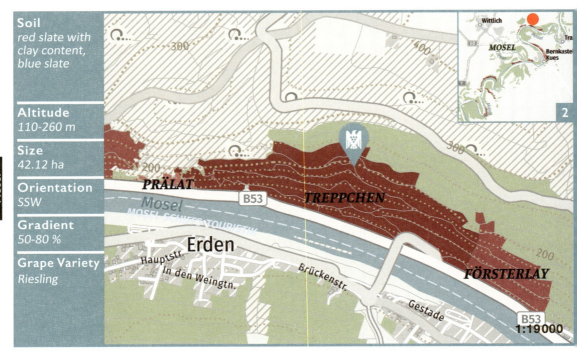

Soil
red slate with clay content, blue slate

Altitude
110-260 m

Size
42.12 ha

Orientation
SSW

Gradient
50-80 %

Grape Variety
Riesling

VDP.Estates: Dr. Loosen, S. A. Prüm

The VDP.GROSSE LAGE® TREPPCHEN climbs from 110 to 260 metres above sea level at a slope incline of 50 to 80 percent. It is located across from Erden on the Mosel and faces southwest. Dry stone vineyard walls cross the slope and store warmth. Riesling vines are trained on individual posts. The soil of the GL TREPPCHEN is red clay slate debris and the share of rock is quite high.

History: There is evidences, that already the Romans produced wines from the vineyard site Treppchen. In 1992 the remains of an ancient Roman pressing house were found here dating back to the 3. century.

UHLEN "BLAUFÜSSER LAY"[1]

Winningen | Mosel
VDP.GROSSE LAGE®

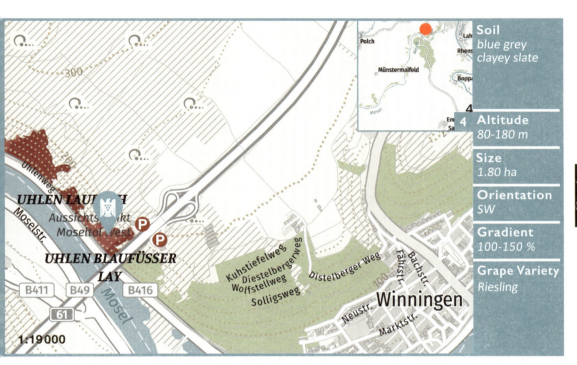

Soil
blue grey clayey slate

Altitude
80-180 m

Size
1.80 ha

Orientation
SW

Gradient
100-150 %

Grape Variety
Riesling

VDP.Estates: **Heymann-Löwenstein, Knebel**

Because differing types of slate distinguish the parcels of the Uhlen vineyard, the VDP decided to classify them into four different VDP.GROSSE LAGE® vineyards. One of these is the VDP.GROSSE LAGE® UHLEN "BLAUFÜSSER LAY"[1]. The slate here is blue-grey and clayey and lends wines a unique character. The dark slate and terrace walls of this southwest-facing parcel store the warmth of the day and radiate it into the vines at night. Cultivation of this extremely steep 100 to 150 percent (45 to 56°) slope would not be possible without small terraces. The dry stone walls were built and continue to be maintained without the use of mortar. Vintners are proud that these vineyard terrace walls provide a habitat for rare animals like European green lizards and Apollo butterflies.

UHLEN "LAUBACH"[1]

Winningen | Mosel
VDP.GROSSE LAGE®

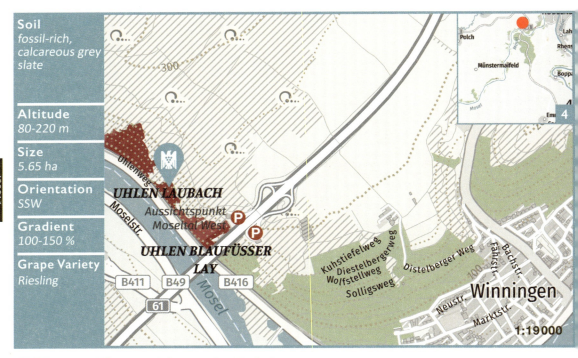

Soil
fossil-rich, calcareous grey slate

Altitude
80-220 m

Size
5.65 ha

Orientation
SSW

Gradient
100-150 %

Grape Variety
Riesling

VDP.Estates: Heymann-Löwenstein, Knebel

One vineyard, three geologies. Because four different slate types are found in the breathtakingly steep Uhlen vineyard, it has been classified into four different vineyard parcels. Like the GL UHLEN, the soil of VDP.GROSSE LAGE® UHLEN "LAUBACH"[1] is grey slate with calcareous, fossil-rich interstratifications. The slate in this south to southwest facing site collects warmth well. It would be impossible to cultivate this extremely steep 100 to 150 percent (45 to 56 °) slope without terraces. The dry stone walls were built and continue to be maintained without the use of mortar, which allows them to provide a habitat for rare animals like European green lizards. Vintners are also quite proud of the Apollo butterflies that thrive here.

UHLEN "ROTH LAY"[1]

Winningen | Mosel
VDP.GROSSE LAGE®

Soil
grey to dark red, iron-rich slate

Altitude
80-200 m

Size
5.09 ha

Orientation
S

Gradient
100-150 %

Grape Variety
Riesling

Mosel

VDP.Estates: **Heymann-Löwenstein, Knebel**

"Roth" is the Old German word for the colour red, which is descriptive of the typical Mosel slate in the steep terraces of the VDP.GROSSE LAGE® UHLEN "ROTH LAY"[1]. High iron oxide content lends this rock its colour, which is also mixed with grey slate. This rocky slope rises from 80 to 200 metres above sea level at an extremely steep 100 to 150 % gradient. The Mosel River reflects the sunshine into this due south-facing site. The warmth is stored in the dry stone walls of the terraces and radiated into the vines at night. Worthy of note are the rare fauna that find a habitat in the non-mortared terrace walls of the GL UHLEN "ROTH LAY"[1] and the neighbouring VDP.GROSSE LAGE® vineyards. The European green lizards and numerous types of beetle help keep the soils loose. The rare Apollo butterflies that are native here highlight the beauty of this vineyard.

UHLEN

Kobern-Gondorf, Winningen | Mosel
VDP.GROSSE LAGE®

Soil
fossil-rich, calcareous grey slate and red iron-rich slate

Altitude
80-200 m

Size
1.47 ha

Orientation
S-SW

Gradient
100-150 %

Grape Variety
Riesling

Mosel

VDP.Estates: **Heymann-Löwenstein, Knebel**

The extremely steep VDP.GROSSE LAGE® UHLEN virtually clings to a south to southwest facing cliff west of Winningen; the slope drops at 100 to 150 percent (45 to 56 °) toward the Mosel River. Grey slate with a high content of calcareous fossils and reddish, iron-rich sandy slate comprise the meagre, rocky foundation of this slope that hugs a bend of the Mosel. The vines climb from 80 to 200 metres above sea level and benefit from a warm microclimate in vineyard terraces. Because the dry stone walls of the terraces are not built or repaired with mortar, they are a habitat for diverse flora and fauna including the rare European green lizards and Apollo butterflies.

History: The name Uhlen stems from the German word for owl.

VOLZ

Wiltingen | Saar
VDP.GROSSE LAGE®

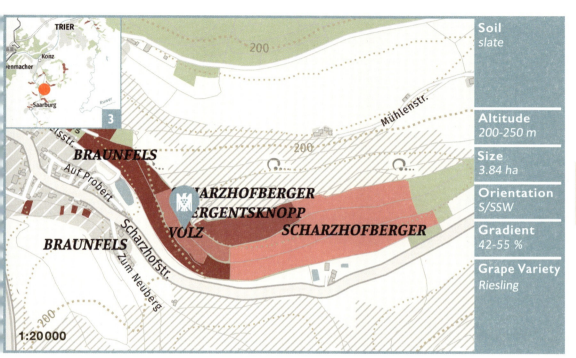

Soil
slate

Altitude
200-250 m

Size
3.84 ha

Orientation
S/SSW

Gradient
42-55 %

Grape Variety
Riesling

Mosel

VDP.Estates: Reichsgraf von Kesselstatt, Van Volxem

The VDP.GROSSE LAGE® VOLZ thrives in a famous neighbourhood. The GL SCHARZHOFBERGER borders this GL to the west, while the GL SCHARZHOFBERGER PERGENTSKNOPP borders it to the north. The vineyard curves around the Scharzberg and faces south to south-southwest. The well-drained slate soil encourages vines to root deep. The 3.8-hectare vineyard is quite steep with a 42 to 55 percent slope gradient.

WÜRTZBERG

Serrig | Saar
VDP.GROSSE LAGE®

Soil
grey slate

Altitude
200 m

Size
4.98 ha

Orientation
SSE

Gradient
30-60 %

Grape Variety
Riesling

Mosel

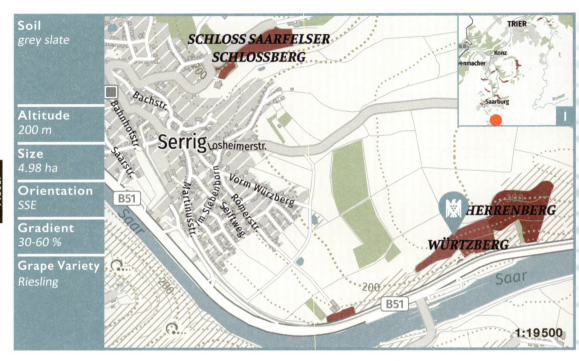

The VDP.GROSSE LAGE® WÜRTZBERG rises above a bend in the Saar River south of Serrig at around 200 metres above sea level. The site benefits from a south-southeast aspect and is surrounded by a forest that protects it. The Saar intensifies the sunlight and simultaneously moderates the climate. The soils are comprised of red slate, quartzite and humus.

WÜRZGARTEN

Ürzig | Mosel
VDP.GROSSE LAGE®

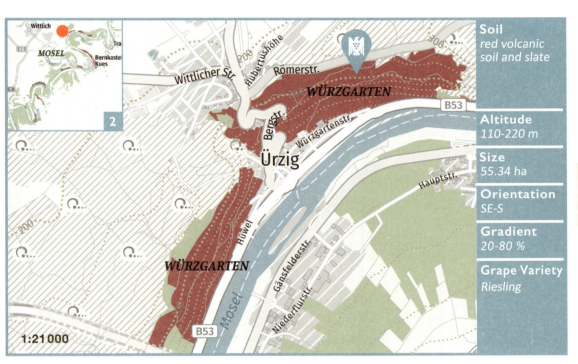

Soil
red volcanic soil and slate

Altitude
110-220 m

Size
55.34 ha

Orientation
SE-S

Gradient
20-80 %

Grape Variety
Riesling

VDP.Estates: Dr. Loosen

The VDP.GROSSE LAGE® WÜRZGARTEN opens like a bright red, very steep, south to southeast facing amphitheatre across from the village Erden directly on the Mosel River. The soil is weathered red slate debris with high rock content. High iron oxide concentrations in the soil lend the vineyard its lively colour. The site climbs from 110 to 220 metres above sea level at an up to 80 percent gradient and Riesling vines are planted and trained on individual posts.

History: The name stems from the medieval wine village tradition of making "Würzweine" or "spiced wines". To this end, herb gardens were planted in vineyards like Würzgarten. A document from the 13th century states the name of the fief vintner as Godefridus Th. Wurzegard. Today, a show herb garden exists in the steep slope of the vineyard.

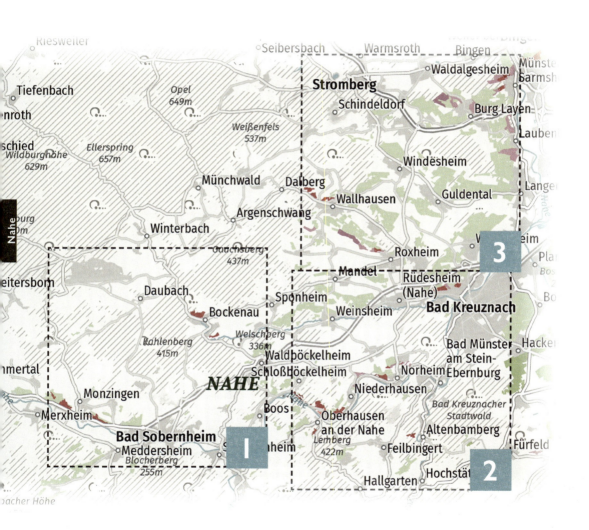

NAHE

Although the 550 hectares of the small wine region Nahe make up only a small share of the VDP.Classified vineyards, they propose a broad geological spectrum. The vineyards spread from the southern edge of the Rhenish Massif to the Alsenz and Glan side valleys of the Nahe River. In the lower Nahe between Wallhausen and Bingerbrück, Devon rocks like phyllite, green schist and quartzite are found. Upper Rotliegend sandstone comprises the subsoil of the great part of the Nahe region. Blue and red slate determine the soils around Monzingen. Between Bad Münster and Schloßböckelheim weathered volcanic soils dominate. The region is relatively cool, but many vineyards have a significantly warmer microclimate due to their aspect, protected locations or proximity to the Nahe River.

A vineyard classification existed on the Nahe over one hundred years ago in the form of land parcel categories for property taxes. The results are illustrated in the Nahe Vineyard Map for the Administrative District Coblenz dating 1901.

Region:	VDP.GROSSE LAGE®:
4 200 ha	302 ha
VDP.Wineries:	VDP.GROSSE LAGE® Sites:
9	19

AUF DER LEY

Monzingen | Nahe
VDP.GROSSE LAGE®

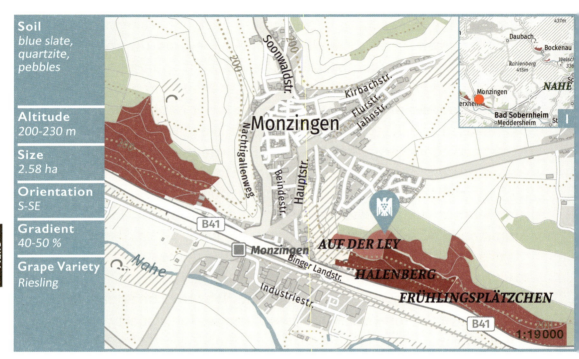

Soil
blue slate, quartzite, pebbles

Altitude
200-230 m

Size
2.58 ha

Orientation
S-SE

Gradient
40-50 %

Grape Variety
Riesling

VDP.Estates: Emrich-Schönleber

The VDP.GROSSE LAGE® AUF DER LEY originates from a historic cadastre and is a south to southeast facing site located above the GL HALENBERG. The soils are comprised of blue slate, quartzite and pebbles. The slope of the GL AUF DER LEY has a gradient of 40-50 percent. Despite its elevated position above 200-230 metres, the vineyard is quite warm, due to thermals that carry the warm air upwards.

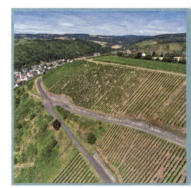

BASTEI

Traisen | Nahe
VDP.GROSSE LAGE®

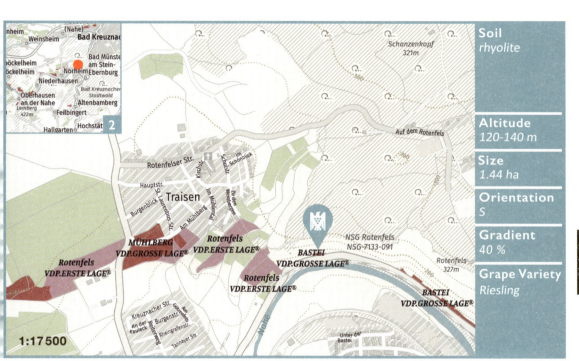

Soil	rhyolite
Altitude	120-140 m
Size	1.44 ha
Orientation	S
Gradient	40 %
Grape Variety	Riesling

Nahe

VDP.Estates: Dr. Crusius, Gut Hermannsberg

The VDP.GROSSE LAGE® BASTEI sits like a parabolic reflector at the foot of the breath-taking, steep and rocky Rotenfels Mountain directly above the Nahe. The white rock and the surface of the Nahe River reflect the sunlight into this vineyard strip, contributing to the high solar radiation and collection of summer warmth in the south-facing GL BASTEI. The small 1.44-hectare vineyard site lies at 120-140 metres above sea level with a steep slope gradient of 40 percent. The soils contains 20-60 percent rock and comprised of porphyry and rocky-gravely loam.

BRÜCKE

Oberhausen | Nahe
VDP.GROSSE LAGE®

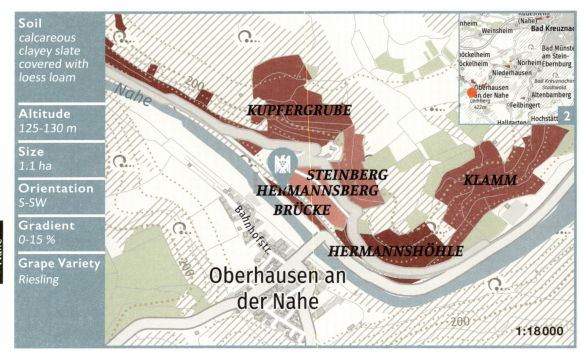

Soil
calcareous clayey slate covered with loess loam

Altitude
125-130 m

Size
1.1 ha

Orientation
S-SW

Gradient
0-15 %

Grape Variety
Riesling

VDP.Estates: H. Dönnhoff

The parcels of the VDP.GROSSE LAGE® BRÜCKE lie in a protected, south-facing place in the Nahe. The particularly mild climate is regulated by its proximity to the river. Vines flower here early and the vegetation period is long. The soil is weathered grey slate and has a layer of loess loam. The GL BRÜCKE lies at 125 to 130 metres above sea level and has an up to 15 percent incline toward the Nahe River. **History:** The VDP.GROSSE LAGE® BRÜCKE takes its mane for the neighbouring Luitpold Bridge that connects the vineyard on the Niederhäuser side with the village Oberhausen. This was the former border between Bavaria (Oberhausen) and Prussia (Niederhausen). The vintner Hermann Dönnhoff purchased this small one-hectare vineyard in 1931. Due to this site's special attributes, it became registered and protected despite its small size. It is a monopole vineyard that belongs to the VDP.Estate Dönnhoff.

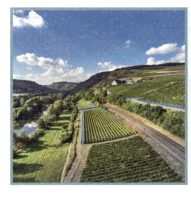

BURGBERG

Dorsheim | Nahe
VDP.GROSSE LAGE®

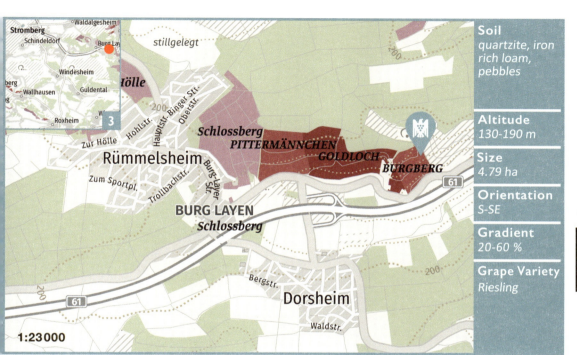

Soil
quartzite, iron rich loam, pebbles

Altitude
130-190 m

Size
4.79 ha

Orientation
S-SE

Gradient
20-60 %

Grape Variety
Riesling

VDP.Estates: Schlossgut Diel, Kruger-Rumpf

The VDP.GROSSE LAGE® BURGBERG is a steep slope with a 20 to 60 percent gradient that faces south and southeast. It lies between 130 and 190 metres above sea level just below the Burg Layen fortress ruin. Its convex form is surrounded by rock faces that protect it from winds coming from the north, west and east thus capturing the warmth of the day in the vineyard. The soil of this four-hectare GL is comprised of iron-rich loam with a high share of quartzite and pebbles. Because cold air is trapped here on frosty winter nights, the foot of the slope is ideally suited for the production of ice wine. The GL BURGBERG is planted entirely with Riesling.

History: The name, which gives reference to the Burg Layen fortress, has existed since the 14th century and appeared for the first time in the land cadastre in 1819.

DAUTENPFLÄNZER

Münster-Sarmsheim | Nahe
VDP.GROSSE LAGE®

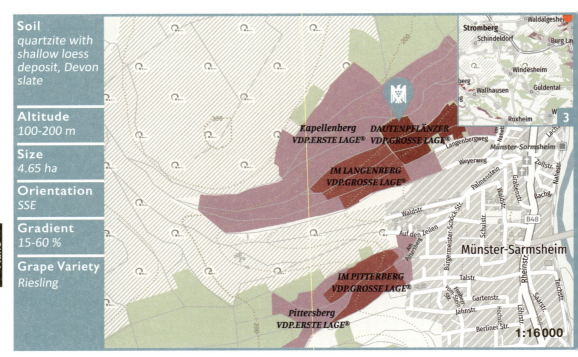

Soil
quartzite with shallow loess deposit, Devon slate

Altitude
100-200 m

Size
4.65 ha

Orientation
SSE

Gradient
15-60 %

Grape Variety
Riesling

VDP.Estates: Kruger-Rumpf

The VDP.GROSSE LAGE® DAUTENPFLÄNZER is at the heart of the Kapellenberg vineyard. The 15 to 60 percent slope between 100 and 200 metres above sea level faces south-southeast in a side valley of the Nahe that is protected from the west wind. The soils are quartzite and Devon slate covered with a layer of loess-loam with good water storage capacity. The main variety cultivated is Riesling.

Name origin: The word "Daute" means young seedling and "Pflänzer" means planter. This leads to the assumption that young vines were once bred here.

DELLCHEN

Norheim | Nahe
VDP.GROSSE LAGE®

Soil
grey slate with a top layer of porphyry

Altitude
140-200 m

Size
3.19 ha

Orientation
S

Gradient
50-70 %

Grape Variety
Riesling

VDP.Estates: H. Dönnhoff

The VDP.GROSSE LAGE® DELLCHEN is a natural beauty. The steep dry stone terraces of this GL cling to an extremely steep south-facing slope with up to 70 percent gradient. The soils are predominantly porphyry and slate, but also gravelly loam, which provides good water availability. The abundance of rock and the dry stone walls store warmth and energy during the day and release it into the vines at night. This provides grapes a longer ripening period in which they achieve high physiological ripeness. The site lies at 140 to 200 metres above sea level.

History: The site was long neglected due to its steepness. The name stems from a small convex trough in the meagre cliff face, which is called a "Dellchen" in colloquial German.

FELSENBERG

Schloßböckelheim | Nahe
VDP.GROSSE LAGE®

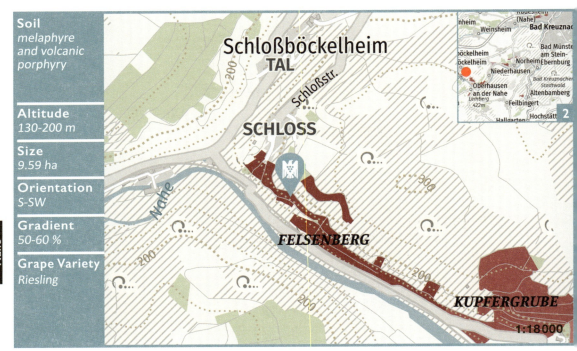

Soil
melaphyre and volcanic porphyry

Altitude
130-200 m

Size
9.59 ha

Orientation
S-SW

Gradient
50-60 %

Grape Variety
Riesling

VDP.Estates: Dr. Crusius, H. Dönnhoff, Gut Hermannsberg, Schäfer-Fröhlich

The VDP.GROSSE LAGE® FELSENBERG lies in one of the most spectacular parts of the Nahe. The south-facing slope is nearly black with melaphyre volcanic rock (rhyolite) and rises with a 50 to 60 percent gradient up to a belt of rock that protects the GL FELSENBERG from fall winds. The soil contains abundant rubble from the eroding rock belt and is loose and well-aerated. The soil's rapid warming properties work together with its well-protected location to promote early vegetation and to prolong the ripening period. The high rock content ensures good drainage. The vineyard soil also includes porphyry, stony-gritty loam, and fine earth. The GL FELSENBERG is 10 hectares in size and lies between 130 and 200 metres above sea level.

FELSENECK

Bockenau | Nahe
VDP.GROSSE LAGE®

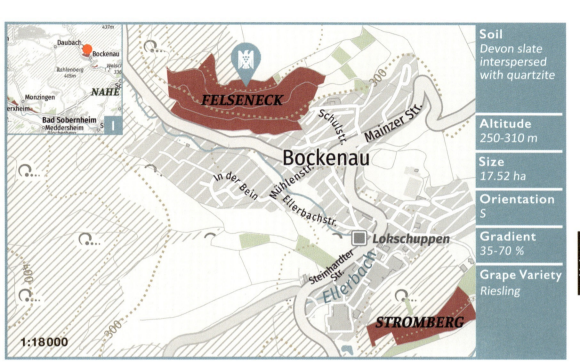

Soil
Devon slate interspersed with quartzite

Altitude
250-310 m

Size
17.52 ha

Orientation
S

Gradient
35-70 %

Grape Variety
Riesling

VDP.Estates: **Schäfer-Fröhlich**

The VDP.GROSSE LAGE® FELSENECK is located in the Ellerbach River basin, a side valley of the upper Nahe. The vineyard faces due south and it rises a steep slope with 35 to 70 percent gradient from 250 to 310 metres above sea level up to a high forested plateau that protects it from cold fall winds. The soil is weathered Waderner Schichten, a conglomerate of blue-grey Devon slate. The rocky soils are easily warmed and well-drained. The slope has easy access to light and warmth from the sun, which is advantageous for its microclimate.

FELSENECK

Wallhausen | Nahe
VDP.GROSSE LAGE®

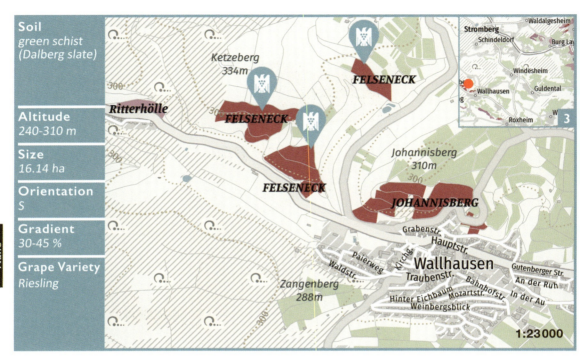

Soil
green schist (Dalberg slate)

Altitude
240-310 m

Size
16.14 ha

Orientation
S

Gradient
30-45 %

Grape Variety
Riesling

VDP.Estates: **Prinz Salm**

The VDP.GROSSE LAGE® FELSENECK in Wallhausen can boast quite a unique treasure: green Dalberg slate. This special kind of green slate is unique and can only be found in Wallhausen and Dalberg. It is a true geological rarity in Germany. This is accompanied with loamy clay and sandy loam. The slopes of the GL FELSENECK have a south to southeast exposition and are classified as very steep with an up to 45 percent gradient. The vineyard area encompasses 16 hectares.
History: The vineyard site was firstly mentioned in 1219.

FRÜHLINGSPLÄTZCHEN

Monzingen | Nahe
VDP.GROSSE LAGE®

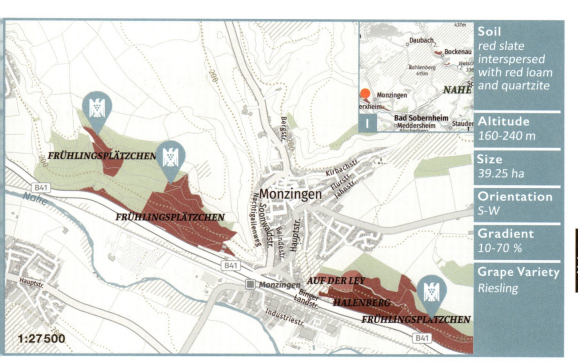

Soil
red slate interspersed with red loam and quartzite

Altitude
160-240 m

Size
39.25 ha

Orientation
S-W

Gradient
10-70 %

Grape Variety
Riesling

VDP.Estates: Emrich-Schönleber, Schäfer-Fröhlich

The VDP.GROSSE LAGE® FRÜHLINGSPLÄTZCHEN is just what the name implies in German, a "special place in spring". Its partly steep with a 70 percent gradient and south facing aspect allows the site to thaw early and the first messages of spring appear as the snow melts. The intense solar radiation and exposition of this GL allow early and persistent warming. Soils are predominantly red slate and gravel, often interspersed with red loam from the Rotliegend lithostratigraphic unit. The vineyard lies between 160 and 240 metres above sea level.

GOLDLOCH

Dorsheim | Nahe
VDP.GROSSE LAGE®

Soil
gravel in shallow loam

Altitude
140-210 m

Size
11.83 ha

Orientation
S-SW

Gradient
15-55 %

Grape Variety
Riesling

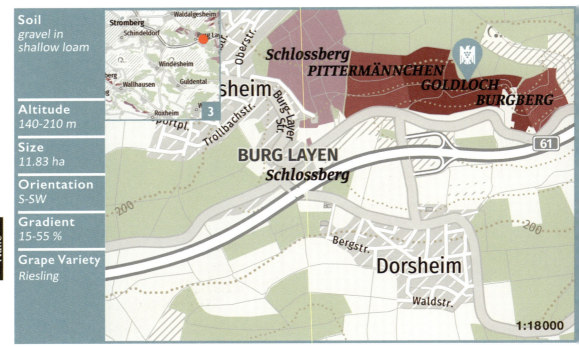

VDP.Estates: Schlossgut Diel, Kruger-Rumpf, Joh. Bapt. Schäfer

The south facing VDP.GROSSE LAGE® GOLDLOCH lies well protected in the Trollbach Valley directly next to the GL PITTERMÄNNCHEN. Long sunshine duration and good availability of water provide ideal growth conditions. The steep slopes have a 15 to 55 percent gradient and are for the most part terraced. The GL GOLDLOCH covers 12 hectares between 140 and 210 metres above sea level The soil is rocky-gritty loam slope wash over rocky Upper Rotliegend conglomerate that is covered with a thin loam layer with abundant pebbles. Primarily Riesling grows in this GL.

History: The Goldloch vineyard appears for the first time in the land cadastre in 1819, but was documented as "Am Loch" in 1756. There is only speculation about the addition "Gold" to the name. Discovery of gold, that the quality of the wine brought vintners gold, or the colour of the vineyard in the evening sun are all considered possibilities.

HALENBERG

Monzingen | Nahe
VDP.GROSSE LAGE®

Soil
Devon slate interspersed with quartzite

Altitude
160-220 m

Size
7.76 ha

Orientation
S-SW

Gradient
20-70 %

Grape Variety
Riesling

VDP.Estates: Emrich-Schönleber, Schäfer-Fröhlich

The VDP.GROSSE LAGE® HALENBERG is one of the smallest vineyards in Monzingen, but it has the best reputation. It lies to the east of town between 160 and 220 metres above sea level. The 20 to 70 percent slope with a south to southwest exposition is warmed in summer by thermal air. The soil is weathered Waderner Schichten, a conglomerate of blue-grey slate and quartzite, that makes the steep vineyard easily warmed. The site is prone to dryness in summer. The difficult, arid growing conditions cause vines to compensate with small, highly aromatic grapes.

HERMANNSBERG

Niederhausen | Nahe
VDP.GROSSE LAGE®

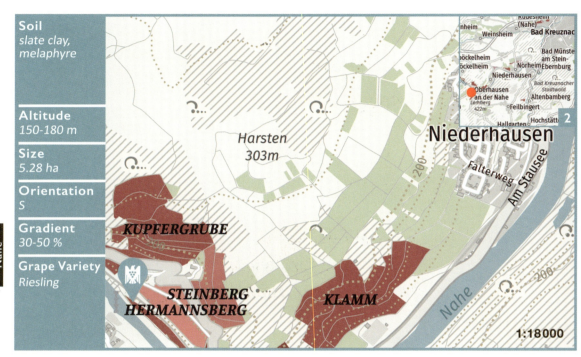

Soil
slate clay, melaphyre

Altitude
150-180 m

Size
5.28 ha

Orientation
S

Gradient
30-50 %

Grape Variety
Riesling

VDP.Estates: Gut Hermannsberg

Extreme variations between soils – from volcanic to clay slate – in sites less than 200 metres apart is what characterizes the vineyards of Niederhausen. Clay slate determines the foundation of the VDP.GROSSE LAGE® HERMANNSBERG, but melaphyre is also present, which stems from gravelling that took place there 100 years ago. This vineyard has a 30 to 50 percent slope gradient that faces south and is directly adjacent to the VDP.Estate Gut Hermannsberg. It is well protected in the Nahe Valley and enjoys cool air circulation at 130 to 160 metres above sea level. The proximity of the Nahe River intensifies the site's solar radiation through reflection of sunlight. The site is predestined for the production of ice wine.

History: The name of this site could come from Hermes, the patron of all messengers and travellers. It is a monopole vineyard that belongs to the VDP.Estate Gut Hermannsberg.

HERMANNSHÖHLE

Niederhausen | Nahe
VDP.GROSSE LAGE®

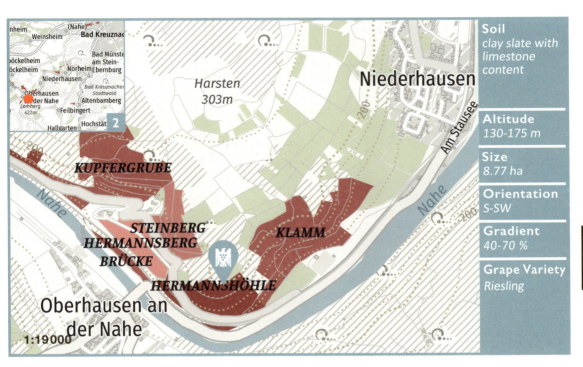

Soil
clay slate with limestone content

Altitude
130-175 m

Size
8.77 ha

Orientation
S-SW

Gradient
40-70 %

Grape Variety
Riesling

VDP.Estates: H. Dönnhoff

The south facing VDP.GROSSE LAGE® HERMANNSHÖHLE lies directly on a bend of the Nahe River with perfect exposition to the sun. The vineyard slopes stretch between 130 and 175 metres above sea level. The slope gradient is between 40 and 70 percent. The main soil is black-grey weathered slate with optimal capacity for storing warmth. This is mixed with extrusive igneous rock, limestone and porphyry with abundant fine earth. The share of rock is 15 percent and provides good soil drainage. It is prone to erosion in some areas. Primarily Riesling is cultivated in the GL Hermannshöhle.

Info: The Hermannshöhle vineyard has been the most highly reputed site in the Nahe region for over a century. It is the benchmark for the classification of other vineyards in the region.

IM KAHLENBERG

Bad Kreuznach | Nahe
VDP.GROSSE LAGE®

Soil
gravelly loam

Altitude
135-160 m

Size
11.85 ha

Orientation
S

Gradient
10-40 %

Grape Variety
Riesling

VDP.Estates: H. Dönnhoff

The VDP.GROSSE LAGE® IM KAHLENBERG is located within the Kahlenberg vineyard northwest of Bad Kreuznach at 135 to 160 metres above sea level. It is the filet piece in the Kahlenberg slope that faces south at a 10 to 40 percent gradient. The soil is gravelly loam that provides warmth and good water availability. Rotliegend red sandstone is also present in some places. The main variety grown here is Riesling.

IM LANGENBERG

Münster-Sarmsheim | Nahe
VDP.GROSSE LAGE®

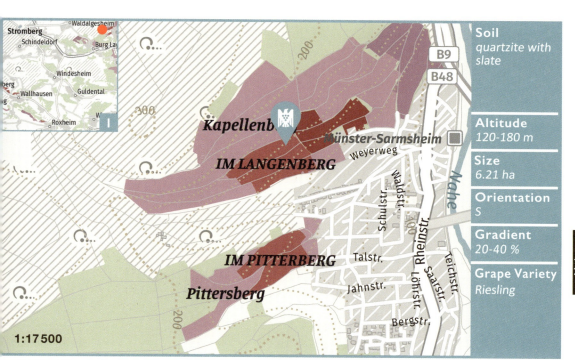

Soil
quartzite with slate

Altitude
120-180 m

Size
6.21 ha

Orientation
S

Gradient
20-40 %

Grape Variety
Riesling

VDP.Estates: **Kruger-Rumpf**

The VDP.GROSSE LAGE® IM LANGENBERG is located in the middle of the Kapellenberg vineyard slope between 120 and 180 metres above sea level. The six-hectare site faces south-southeast with a 20 to 40 percent slope. The GL borders the VDP.GROSSE LAGE® DAUTENPFLÄNZER to the east. The soil is quartzite and Devon slate covered with loam, which contributes to good water storage capacity. The GL IM LANGENBERG is well protected from the wind due to its location in a side valley of the Nahe below the Münster forest.

IM MÜHLBERG

Roxheim | Nahe
VDP.GROSSE LAGE®

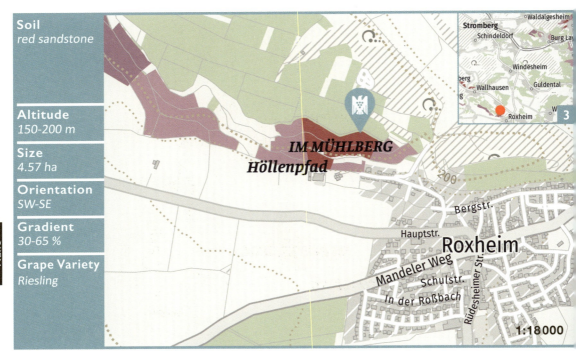

Soil
red sandstone

Altitude
150-200 m

Size
4.57 ha

Orientation
SW-SE

Gradient
30-65 %

Grape Variety
Riesling

VDP.Estates: H. Dönnhoff

The 4.5-hectare VDP.GROSSE LAGE® IM MÜHLENBERG is located in the middle of the Höllenpfad vineyard and rises at a 30 to 65 percent slope above the village of Roxheim. The site has a southwest to southeast aspect. The soils radiate the warm red colour of the weathered Rotliegend red sandstone on which it is based.

IM PITTERBERG

Münster-Sarmsheim | Nahe
VDP.GROSSE LAGE®

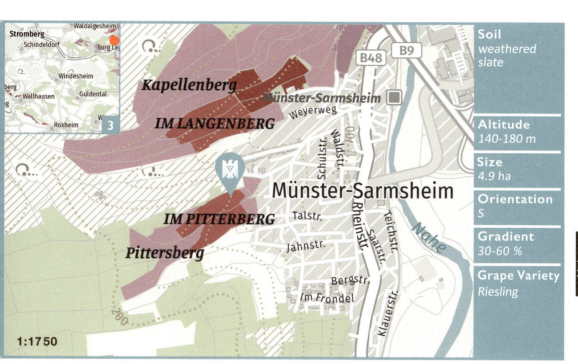

Soil
weathered slate

Altitude
140-180 m

Size
4.9 ha

Orientation
S

Gradient
30-60 %

Grape Variety
Riesling

VDP.Estates: **Kruger-Rumpf**

The VDP.GROSSE LAGE® IM PITTERBERG lies in a small convex slope in the upper Nahe Valley in the middle of the Pittersberg vineyard. The south-facing site is ensured sufficient sunshine that warms the grey Devon slate and its weathered debris. The soil is highly mineral. Very fine loam covers the slate. The soil is well-drained and holds little moisture, which can lead to dryness in summer. Nighty fall winds are diverted by hills. Primarily Riesling grows in this site.

JOHANNISBERG

Wallhausen | Nahe
VDP.GROSSE LAGE®

Soil
red slate
(Rotliegend)

Altitude
210-300 m

Size
12.08 ha

Orientation
S

Gradient
40-55 %

Grape Variety
Riesling &
Spätburgunder

VDP.Estates: **Prinz Salm**

The VDP.GROSSE LAGE® JOHANNISBERG rises impressively above Wallhausen with a slope gradient of up to 55 percent. The terraced vineyard lies at 210 to 300 metres above sea level in the well-protected Gräfenbachtal, a side valley of the Nahe. Due to its steepness and south-facing aspect, solar radiation is extremely high in the GL JOHANNISBERG and the resulting wines are powerful. The soils are predominantly Rotliegend sandstone and slate from the Permian period that are covered with a layer of gravelly sand and gravelly loam. The vines are up to 65 years old with roots reaching 20 metres deep.

History: The Johannisberg was mentioned quite early, in the 12th century, in a land registry of the Barons von Dalberg. It is among the oldest documented vineyards in Europe. There are also findings from older dates that reach back to the Romans.

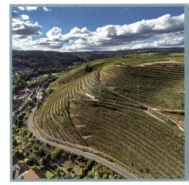

KIRSCHHECK

Norheim | Nahe
VDP.GROSSE LAGE®

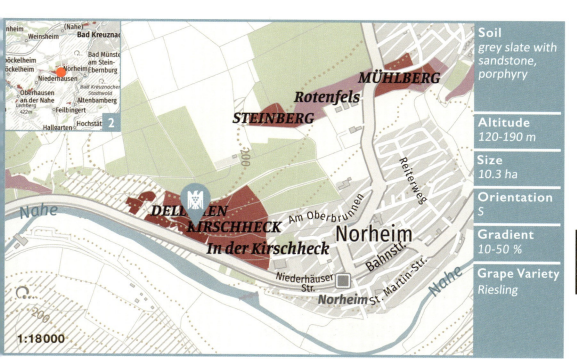

Soil	grey slate with sandstone, porphyry
Altitude	120-190 m
Size	10.3 ha
Orientation	S
Gradient	10-50 %
Grape Variety	Riesling

VDP.Estates: Dr. Crusius, H. Dönnhoff

The VDP.GROSSE LAGE® KIRSCHHECK is a south-facing slope on the undulating bank of the Nahe near Norheim. The 10-hectare site has a moderate 10 to a steep 50 percent slope gradient and sits at 120 to 190 metres above sea level. The soils are comprised of grey slate and sandstone from the Permian period, but in some areas also of loess and loess loam banks. The soils, in particular the slate parts, are easily warmed and provide grapes with an extended ripening period along with good water availability.

KLAMM

Niederhausen | Nahe
VDP.GROSSE LAGE®

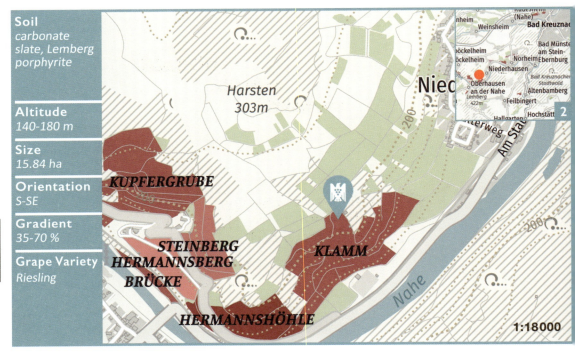

Soil
carbonate slate, Lemberg porphyrite

Altitude
140-180 m

Size
15.84 ha

Orientation
S-SE

Gradient
35-70 %

Grape Variety
Riesling

VDP.Estates: H. Dönnhoff, Gut Hermannsberg

With a slope gradient of 70 percent, the VDP.GROSSE LAGE® KLAMM is the steepest site in the Nahe region. Its slope is situated between 140 and 180 metres above sea level and is partially terraced. The terrace walls and the rocky, porous soils store the warmth well. Contributing to high solar radiation is the south to southeast aspect of the GL KLAMM. The soils are weathered volcanic rock with porphyrite content and black slate.

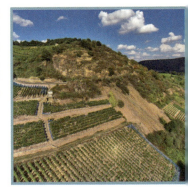

KRÖTENPFUHL

Bad Kreuznach | Nahe
VDP.GROSSE LAGE®

Soil
loess loam with quartzite, pebbles

Altitude
135-153 m

Size
6.96 ha

Orientation
S

Gradient
10-40 %

Grape Variety
Riesling

VDP.Estates: **H. Dönnhoff**

The VDP.GROSSE LAGE® KRÖTENPFUHL is located directly on the periphery of Bad Kreuznach at 135 to 153 metres above sea level. Due to the abundance of small pebbles in the loamy gravel soils, this south-facing slope warms easily and stores the energy into the evening allowing grapes more time to ripen. There are aquifers deep under the surface of the GL KRÖTENPFUHL that provide sufficient moisture even in periods of drought. During rainy weather, water collects at the foot of the slope. The site has a 10 to 40 percent gradient and encompasses seven hectares.

History: The KRÖTENPFUHL has historically been the top site of Bad Kreuznach and is known under this name since 1832.

KUPFERGRUBE

Schloßböckelheim | Nahe
VDP.GROSSE LAGE®

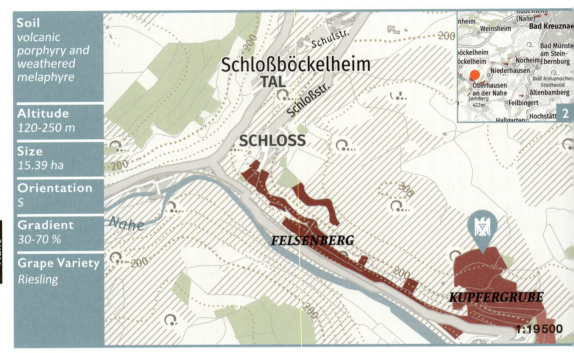

Soil
volcanic porphyry and weathered melaphyre

Altitude
120-250 m

Size
15.39 ha

Orientation
S

Gradient
30-70 %

Grape Variety
Riesling

VDP.Estates: Dr. Crusius, Gut Hermannsberg, Schäfer-Fröhlich

The terraced vineyard slopes of the VDP.GROSSE LAGE® KUPFERGRUBE are in a spectacular location directly next to a volcanic cliff. The site has a south to southwest exposition and a 30 to 70 percent slope gradient. The dark, mineral-rich, weathered volcanic soils with a high share of fine earth and rock warm rapidly. The soil is loose and very well-drained, which can lead to dryness in summer. The vineyard lies at 120 to 250 metres. Riesling grows here.

LEISTENBERG

Oberhausen | Nahe
VDP.GROSSE LAGE®

Soil
grey, weathered shale with carbonate content

Altitude
140-180 m

Size
3.42 ha

Orientation
S-E

Gradient
30-40 %

Grape Variety
Riesling

VDP.Estates: H. Dönnhoff

The VDP.GROSSE LAGE® LEISTENBERG is located on the Lemberg in a side valley of the Nahe River. At 400 metres above sea level, the Lemberg is the highest mountain in the Nahe region. The vineyard faces southeast with a 30 to 40 percent slope gradient. It encompasses three vineyard hectares and is planted exclusively with Riesling. The soil is weathered, grey clay slate.

MÜHLBERG

Traisen | Nahe
VDP.GROSSE LAGE®

Soil
porphyry

Altitude
200-250 m

Size
3.05 ha

Orientation
S

Gradient
30-50 %

Grape Variety
Riesling

VDP.Estates: Dr. Crusius

The 3-hectare VDP.GROSSE LAGE® MÜHLBERG is south-facing slope with up to a 50 percent gradient. It is located on the shoulder of the impressive, steep Rotenfels Mountain, where it is protected from rain and wind. The soil is mainly porphyry covered with a layer of loess and loam that is easily warmed and provides good water availability for advantageous vegetation.

PITTERMÄNNCHEN

Dorsheim | Nahe
VDP.GROSSE LAGE®

Soil
clay slate and gravel, weathered grey slate

Altitude
150-210 m

Size
7.68 ha

Orientation
S

Gradient
20-50 %

Grape Variety
Riesling

VDP.Estates: Schlossgut Diel, Joh. Bapt. Schäfer

The VDP.GROSSE LAGE® PITTERMÄNNCHEN is a south-facing vineyard slope with a 20 to 50 percent gradient that is located above the Trollbach tributary in the Trollbach Valley. The direct exposition to the sun warms the vineyard quickly. In the rockiest areas, temperatures can reach up to 50 °C (122 °F). The vineyard cools down at night, providing for exciting aroma development and preservation of good acid structure. The soils of the GL PITTERMÄNNCHEN, situated between 150 and 210 metres above sea level, are predominantly weathered grey Devon slate and clay slate with pebbles. A covering layer of loam provides good available water for the vines.

History: The name Pittermänchen comes from a silver coin that was called a "Petermännchen". This signified the high value of the vine yards. In the 16th century 32 Petermännchen equalled one guilder.

ROTENBERG

Altenbamberg | Nahe
VDP.GROSSE LAGE®

Soil
weathered rhyolite and clay slate

Altitude
250-350 m

Size
5.64 ha

Orientation
S

Gradient
50-75 %

Grape Variety
Riesling

VDP.Estates: **Gut Hermannsberg**

The VDP.GROSSE LAGE® ROTENBERG is a south facing site with a 50 to 75 percent slope located in the Alsenz Valley, a side valley of the Nahe. It rises from 250 metres to the edge of the forest on the peak of the hill at 350 metres above sea level. The foundation is comprised weathered rhyolite and clay slate. The reddish colour of the soil is due to its high iron content and gives this site its name, which can be translated to "Red Mountain". The top soil is rocky and meagre. The adjacent forest protects the vines from the cold air, but cold air drafts still slow vegetation and grapes can and do hang on the vine longer here to ripen.

STEINBERG

Niederhausen | Nahe
VDP.GROSSE LAGE®

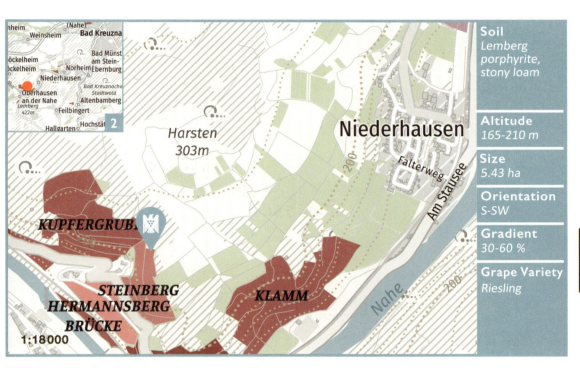

Soil
Lemberg porphyrite, stony loam

Altitude
165-210 m

Size
5.43 ha

Orientation
S-SW

Gradient
30-60 %

Grape Variety
Riesling

VDP.Estates: **Gut Hermannsberg**

The VDP.GROSSE LAGE® STEINBERG is exactly what its name says: a rock mountain. The soil is hard and meagre, comprised of yellowish to white volcanic rock – porphyrite with high fossil content. The GL STEINBERG lies on a bend in the river that faces south to southwest with a 30 to 60 percent slope gradient. The Nahe Valley protects this site from west winds and it benefits from the sun's reflection from the surface of the river just below it.

STEINBERG

Traisen | Nahe
VDP.GROSSE LAGE®

Soil
porphyry

Altitude
250-300 m

Size
1.85 ha

Orientation
S

Gradient
50 %

Grape Variety
Riesling

VDP.Estates: Dr. Crusius

The VDP.GROSSE LAGE® STEINBERG is the hilltop that caps the Rotenfels vineyard in Traisen on the west side. The south-facing slope has a steep gradient of 50 percent gradient between 250 and 300 metres above sea level. The soils of the small 1.85-hectare GL are comprised of volcanic rock—well drained, loamy, weathered porphyry and quartz porphyry.

STROMBERG

Bockenau | Nahe
VDP.GROSSE LAGE®

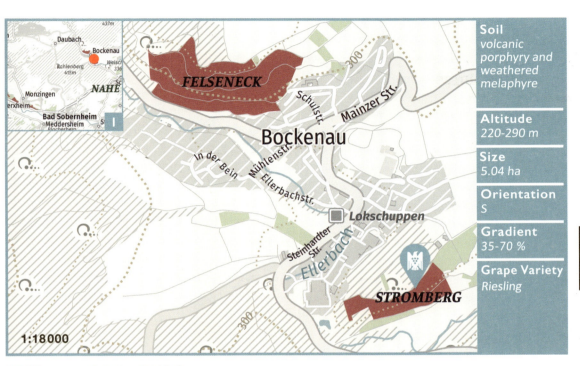

Soil
volcanic porphyry and weathered melaphyre

Altitude
220-290 m

Size
5.04 ha

Orientation
S

Gradient
35-70 %

Grape Variety
Riesling

VDP.Estates: **Schäfer-Fröhlich**

Steep and interspersed with rocky faces, the VDP.GROSSE LAGE® STROMBERG is located above the Ellerbach River south of Bockenau. The vineyard faces due south and warms well. Despite its elevation at 220 to 290 metres above sea level, it is well protected from cold winds by the forested peak of the Stromberg Mountain and the narrow Ellerbach Valley also holds the warmth well. The volcanic porphyry and weathered melaphyre soils also warm quickly. Mostly Riesling is cultivated in this GL and the vines are up to 60 years old.

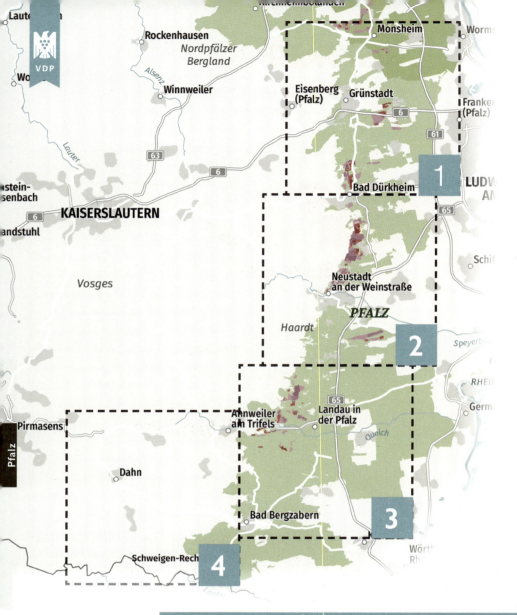

Region:	VDP.GROSSE LAGE®:
23 600 ha	589 ha
VDP.Wineries:	VDP.GROSSE LAGE® Sites:
25	51

PFALZ

The Pfalz is among the largest of the VDP.Regions. Its numerous vineyards are distributed along 85 kilometres of the German Wine Road. Situated between the Haardt Mountains and Palatinate Forest in the east and the Rhine River in the west, the Pfalz borders the most southern vineyards of Rheinhessen to the north and reaches Schweigen in the south on the border to Alsace. The Pfalz is pampered with an average of 1 800 hours of sunshine annually. Warm air masses from the Rhine Plain also contribute significantly to making the Pfalz one of the warmest regions in Germany. The region is geologically determined by the formation of the Rhine Rift Valley and rift flank uplifts—numerous different soils exist including limestone, clay, basalt and loam. From Kallstadt to Ungstein to Bad Dürkheim, the top sites are located on a limestone reef, while weathered Bunter (variegated) sandstone determines the soils between Wachenheim and Gimmeldingen. The main focus of the Mittelhaardt wines is traditionally Riesling.

In the area south of Neustadt, many of the wineries are praised for their wines from Pinot varieties as well as their Rieslings. One often finds shell limestone with superb conditions for the production of Weißburgunder, Grauburgunder and Spätburgunder. There are also superb terroirs to be found in the south for Riesling, for example the VDP.GROSSE LAGE® KASTANIENBUSCH in Birkweiler where Upper Rotliegend red slate is found.

AUF DER HOHL

Burrweiler | Pfalz
VDP.GROSSE LAGE®

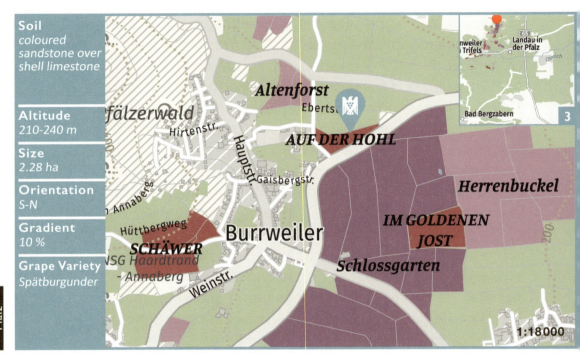

Soil
coloured sandstone over shell limestone

Altitude
210-240 m

Size
2.28 ha

Orientation
S-N

Gradient
10 %

Grape Variety
Spätburgunder

VDP.Estates: Herbert Meßmer

The VDP.GROSSE LAGE® AUF DER HOHL lies east of the little wine city Burrweiler at the foot of the Haardt Mountains in the Palatinate forest. The vineyards turn from the south toward the north and rise gently from 210 to 240 metres at a 10 percent slope gradient. Shielded by the Haardt Mountains and influenced by the warm foehn winds that sweep down the slopes toward the Rhine River, the climate here is Mediterranean-like in the summer. Coloured sandstone over shell limestone dominates the geology of the GL AUF DER HOHL.

BÜRGERGARTEN IM BREUMEL

Haardt | Pfalz
VDP.GROSSE LAGE®

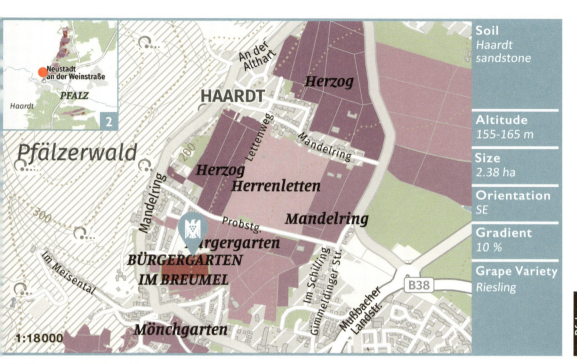

Soil
Haardt sandstone

Altitude
155-165 m

Size
2.38 ha

Orientation
SE

Gradient
10 %

Grape Variety
Riesling

VDP.Estates: **Müller-Catoir**

The VDP.GROSSE LAGE® BÜRGERGARTEN IM BREUMEL is surrounded by a protective wall and is located within the Bürgergarten vineyard at the foot of the Haardt hills within walking distance of the little city Haardt. The 2.4-hectar plateau-like site lies at 155 to 165 metres above sea level and is slightly tilted at a 10 percent gradient toward the south and east. The high sandstone wall protects the GL BÜRGERGARTEN IM BREUMEL from cold air influences and helps create a unique microclimate. The site warms rapidly in the morning, but due to the proximity of the forest, it also cools more quickly than the rest of the Bürgergarten in the evening. The soil is deep and is comprised of variegated sandstone gravel with a high degree of weathering. The main grape variety is Riesling.

FELSENBERG

Leistadt | Pfalz
VDP.GROSSE LAGE®

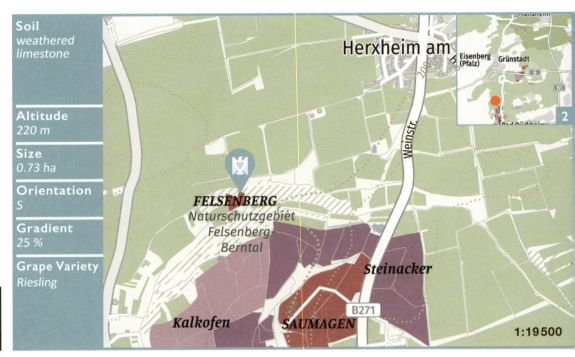

Soil: weathered limestone
Altitude: 220 m
Size: 0.73 ha
Orientation: S
Gradient: 25 %
Grape Variety: Riesling

VDP.Estates: **Rings**

The VDP.GROSSE LAGE® FELSENBERG lies north of Bad Dürkheim on the edge of the Haardt Mountains in the middle of the Felsenberg-Berntal Nature Reserve. The vineyard faces south. Weathered, porous limestone dominates the soil. The site lies at 220 metres above sea level and has a slope gradient of 25 percent.

FREUNDSTÜCK

Forst | Pfalz
VDP.GROSSE LAGE®

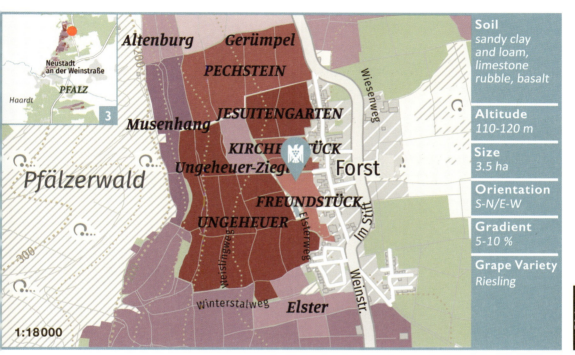

Soil
sandy clay and loam, limestone rubble, basalt

Altitude
110-120 m

Size
3.5 ha

Orientation
S-N/E-W

Gradient
5-10 %

Grape Variety
Riesling

VDP.Estates: Geh. Rat Dr. von Bassermann-Jordan, Reichsrat von Buhl, Georg Mosbacher

At just 3.5 hectares, the VDP.GROSSE LAGE® FREUNDSTÜCK is the smallest of the vineyards in Forst and is located directly adjacent to GL KIRCHENSTÜCK and GL UNGEHEUER. The GL FREUNDSTÜCK also benefits from the warmth radiated from the surrounding buildings and although the microclimate is relatively warm, it cools down more during the night than the GL KIRCHENSTÜCK. Bunter sandstone rubble with clay particles comprises the soils found over a limestone plate. The site is relatively flat with a 5 to 10 percent slope that is oriented toward the south. The site lies at 110 to 120 metres above sea level.

History: The classification of this site is based on the Royal Bavarian Land Classification of 1828, which places the Freundstück at the pinnacle of Pfalz vineyards.

GAISBÖHL

Ruppertsberg | Pfalz
VDP.GROSSE LAGE®

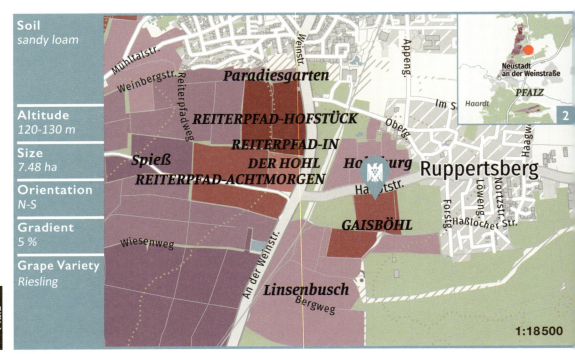

Soil
sandy loam

Altitude
120-130 m

Size
7.48 ha

Orientation
N-S

Gradient
5 %

Grape Variety
Riesling

VDP.Estates: Dr. Bürklin-Wolf

Warm fall winds from the central Haardt hills and the due south exposition provide the VDP.GROSSE LAGE® GAISBÖHL in Ruppertsberg with an exceptionally warm climate. The average summer temperature of 20 °C is quite high for a flat vineyard with up to 5 percent gradient. The soil is comprised of sandy loam, sedimentary clay layers, and weathered variegated sandstone. It is well drained and warms quickly. The GL GAISBÖHL encompasses 7.5 hectares at 120 tp 130 metres above sea level. Predominantly Riesling grows in this site.

History: The site was first mentioned in the 14th century as "Geizebuhel", which indicates that goats once grazed here. "Buhel" means "Hill" and "Geize" are "goats". In the imperial Bavarian land parcel classification of 1828, the Gaisböhl was considered the prime vineyard in Ruppertsberg.

GRAINHÜBEL

Deidesheim | Pfalz
VDP.GROSSE LAGE®

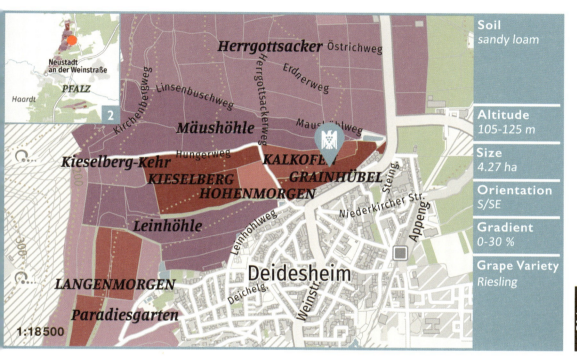

Soil sandy loam
Altitude 105-125 m
Size 4.27 ha
Orientation S/SE
Gradient 0-30 %
Grape Variety Riesling

VDP.Estates: Geh. Rat Dr. von Bassermann-Jordan, Georg Siben Erben, Von Winning,

The VDP.GROSSE LAGE® GRAINHÜBEL lies relatively flat (up to 30 percent slope) at the edge of Deidesheim in the direction of Forst. Sandy loam dominates the soils. A share of marl clay is also present. The soils are friable and possess good water availability. The 4.2-hectare vineyard faces south and rises from 105 to 125 metres above sea level.

History: The site was first mentioned as "an der Gryne" in documents dating 1412. The name either stems from "Grain", which indicates washed away ground, or from "Grien" which points to soil with pebbles and gravel. "Hübel" is a synonym for "Hügel", which is a hill. According to the viticultural expert Johann Philipp Bronner (1792 – 1864), the site was considered to be the best in Deidesheim in the 19th century. At that time it comprised several parcels: Oberer Grain, Crain Chausse, Grainhübel and Unterer Grain.

HERRENBERG

Ungstein | Pfalz
VDP.GROSSE LAGE®

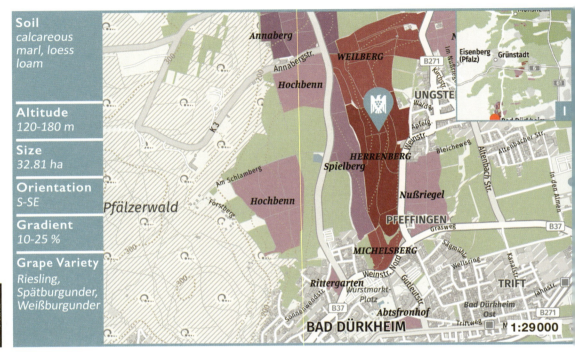

Soil
calcareous marl, loess loam

Altitude
120-180 m

Size
32.81 ha

Orientation
S-SE

Gradient
10-25 %

Grape Variety
Riesling, Spätburgunder, Weißburgunder

VDP.Estates: Fitz-Ritter, Pfeffingen, Karl Schaefer

A special feature of the VDP.GROSSEN LAGE® HERRENBERG is its soils. While coloured sandstone dominates the wine village Ungstein, this vineyard is based on highly calcareous loess-loam with good available water capacity. The south to southeast facing 33-hectare vineyard is protected from cold air influences on a foothill of the Haardt hills at 120 to 180 metres. Its slope is moderately steep with a 10 to 25 percent gradient.

History: In 1828 the Herrenberg vineyard was classified by the Royal-Bavarian Land Taxation laws as a first class vineyard. The name originates from the dukes ("Herren") of Leiningen. It was their favourite vineyard in the Pfalz.

HEYDENREICH[3]

Schweigen | Pfalz
VDP.GROSSE LAGE®

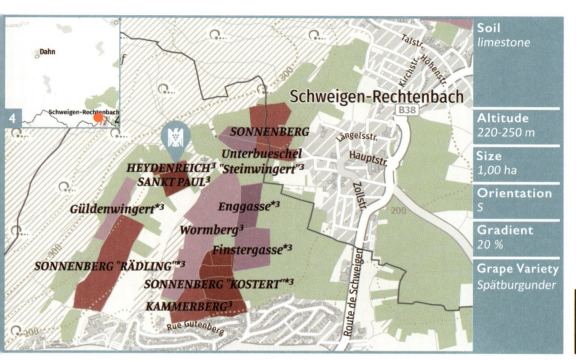

Soil
limestone

Altitude
220-250 m

Size
1,00 ha

Orientation
S

Gradient
20 %

Grape Variety
Spätburgunder

VDP.Estates: Friedrich Becker

Quite a unique soil structure distinguishes the VDP.GROSSE LAGE® HEYDENREICH. Like the somewhat more well-known VDP.GROSSE LAGE® SANKT PAUL that lies below it, the soil is comprised of pure limestone that is covered with a 20 to 50 centimetre deep layer of loose soil. The water storage capacity is very good. The steep south-facing slope is also protected in a valley that allows it to store plenty of warmth during the day that continues to radiate in the evening hours. Cool breezes from the forest and the neighbouring Lauer Valley provide refreshing aeration. Also unusual for the GL HEYDENREICH is that it is not located in Germany, but rather in France. It is part of the Sonnenberg vineyard that straddles the border of the two countries.

History: The vineyards on the border between Schweigen in Germany and Wissembourg in France were once called "Wechsellagen" (alternating sites) because they altered their nationality repeatedly throughout history.

HOHENMORGEN

Deidesheim | Pfalz
VDP.GROSSE LAGE®

Soil
loam, loamy sand, sandstone rubble

Altitude
n.a.

Size
2.72 ha

Orientation
N-S

Gradient
4-12 %

Grape Variety
Riesling

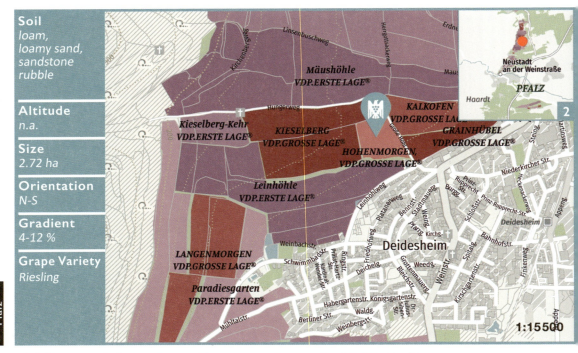

VDP.Estates: Geh. Rat Dr. von Bassermann-Jordan, Dr. Bürklin-Wolf

The VDP.GROSSE LAGE® HOHENMORGEN is situated on a 140 metre elevated plateau in a protected amphitheatre in the foothills of the Haardt hills on the edge of Deidesheim. Typical weathered coloured sandstone and limestone rubble, loam and sand comprise the soils. The top soil is rather rocky and warms quickly. The calcareous content of the soil provides good water storage capacity. The site is around 3 hectares in size and has a 4 to 12 percent incline that faces north to south. It is bordered to the east with a sandstone wall that stores warmth.

History: The name stems from the old measurement of area called a "morgen" as well as its exposed position on a plateau. It was first mentioned in 1828 when it was classified as one of the best sites in Deidesheim.

HÖLLE - UNTERER FAULENBERG

Gleisweiler | Pfalz
VDP.GROSSE LAGE®

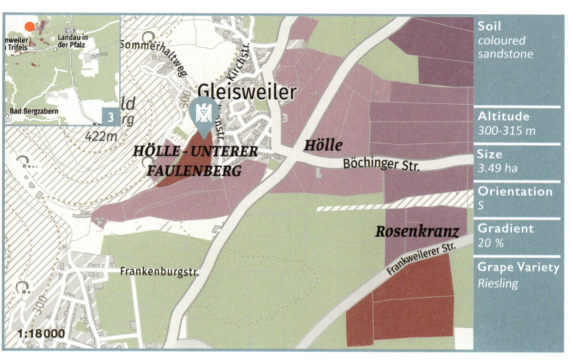

Soil
coloured sandstone

Altitude
300-315 m

Size
3.49 ha

Orientation
S

Gradient
20 %

Grape Variety
Riesling

VDP.Estates: **Theo Minges**

The VDP.GROSSE LAGE® HÖLLE – UNTERER FAULENBERG is a small 3.5-hectare parcel of the Hölle vineyard. The town Burrweiler borders it on the east side and the parcel nearly reaches the forest of the 600-metre Teufelsberg. The southeast-facing incline has a 20 percent gradient. Typical weathered coloured sandstone with significant limestone deposits comprises the soils. The limestone warms well and has good water storage capacity. An underground spring also provides vines with nourishment.

IDIG

Königsbach | Pfalz
VDP.GROSSE LAGE®

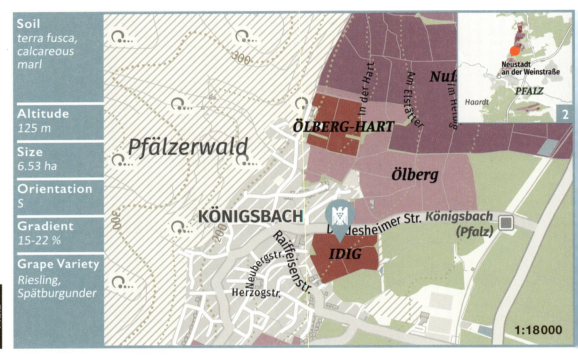

Soil
terra fusca, calcareous marl

Altitude
125 m

Size
6.53 ha

Orientation
S

Gradient
15-22 %

Grape Variety
Riesling, Spätburgunder

VDP.Estates: A. Christmann

The VDP.GROSSE LAGE® IDIG rests majestically on an impressive limestone massif. The slope drops at a 15 to 22 percent gradient toward the south – relatively steep for the Pfalz. The Haardt hills and the Rolandsberg are close enough to protect the site from cold west winds, but far enough not to throw a shadow over the site. The 6.5-hectare vineyard lies at 125 metres above sea level and enjoys long summer days with sunshine long into the evening. Gentle winds fall from the neighbouring Stabenberg and keep grapes dry and healthy. The top soil of the GL IDIG is Terra fusca, which unites limestone and clay with variegated sandstone rubble and sometimes even with basalt. Riesling and Spätburgunder grow here.

IM GOLDENEN JOST

Burrweiler | Pfalz
VDP.GROSSE LAGE®

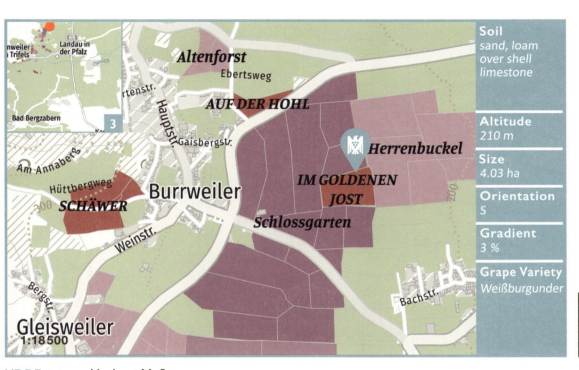

Soil
sand, loam over shell limestone

Altitude
210 m

Size
4.03 ha

Orientation
S

Gradient
3 %

Grape Variety
Weißburgunder

VDP.Estates: **Herbert Meßmer**

The small 4-hectare VDP.GROSSE LAGE® IM GOLDENEN JOST lies at 210 metres above sea level in the eastern corner of the Schlossgarten vineyard. The parcel faces south and is well exposed to the sun during the day. The soils are deep, sandy loach with high shell limestone content and optimal water availability.

IM GROSSEN GARTEN

Großkarlbach | Pfalz
VDP.GROSSE LAGE®

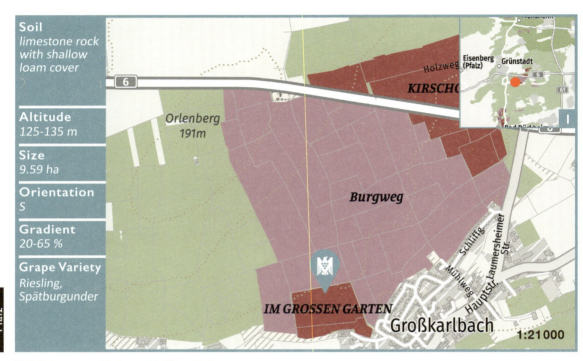

Soil
limestone rock with shallow loam cover

Altitude
125-135 m

Size
9.59 ha

Orientation
S

Gradient
20-65 %

Grape Variety
Riesling, Spätburgunder

VDP.Estates: Knipser, Philipp Kuhn

The wind-protected, steep south slope and versatile lime-dominated soil structure distinguish the VDP.GROSSE LAGE® IM GROSSEN GARTEN. This filet parcel of the VDP.ERSTE LAGE® Grosskarlbacher Burgweg is situated in an ancient, intact river valley in which the Eckbach tributary has deposited diverse sediments like pebbles, sand and loess over a limestone basement. The soils vary between softer and more solid limestone, massive limestone rock and various sediments.

(IM SONNENSCHEIN) "GANZ HORN"[1]

Siebeldingen | Pfalz
VDP.GROSSE LAGE®

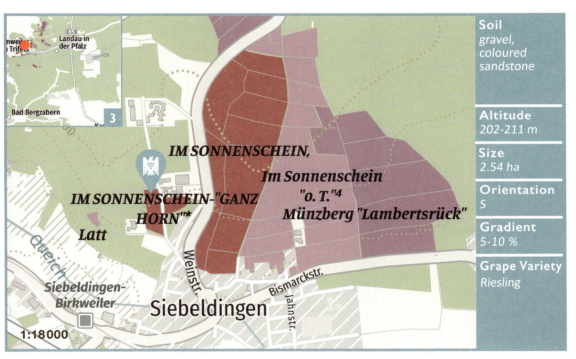

Soil
gravel, coloured sandstone

Altitude
202-211 m

Size
2.54 ha

Orientation
S

Gradient
5-10 %

Grape Variety
Riesling

VDP.Estates: Ökonomierat Rebholz

The VDP.GROSSE LAGE® "GANZ HORN"[1] (formerly known as IM SONNENSCHEIN-"GANZ HORN"[1]) is located within the Sonnenschein vineyard and can be differentiated through its geologically young soil. While the Sonnenschein exhibits soil that stems from the Germanic Trias 220 million years ago (which the Rhine has brought from the depths to the surface), the soil of the GL "GANZ HORN"[1] is 1 million years old and is gravel with variegated sandstone, pebbles, loam, and sand. This was transported here during and after the ice ages and deposited on the slopes of the Queich Valley. These well-drained soils are well suited for Riesling, the predominant grape planted here. The vineyard lies between 202 and 211 metres above sea level and has a slope gradient of 5 to 10 percent.

History: All vineyard parcel names from the old "Siebeldinger Ganshorn" became obsolete with the wine laws of 1971 when the entire site became named "Im Sonnenschein".

IM SONNENSCHEIN

Siebeldingen | Pfalz
VDP.GROSSE LAGE®

Soil
shell limestone

Altitude
160-180 m

Size
31.96 ha

Orientation
S-SW

Gradient
5-20 %

Grape Variety
Riesling, Weiß-burgunder, Spätburgunder

VDP.Estates: Ökonomierat Rebholz, Dr. Wehrheim

The name of the VDP.GROSSE LAGE® IM SONNENSCHEIN translates to "in the sunshine", which indeed this directly south to south-west facing site is. It rises from 160 to 180 metres above sea level at a 5 to 20 percent grade on a slope in the Quiechtal. This valley stretches in south to south-west direction in the foothills of the Palatinate Forest. This GL encompasses the original sites called "Berg" and "Im Sonnenschein". Due to the subsidence and faulting of the Rhine Graben and the significant uplift of the Palatinate Forest, very old and deep-lying geological formations have been pushed to the surface in the vicinity of Siebeldingen. Limestone from the Triassic period 220 million years ago dominates the soil of the GL IM SONNENSCHEIN.

JESUITENGARTEN

Forst | Pfalz
VDP.GROSSE LAGE®

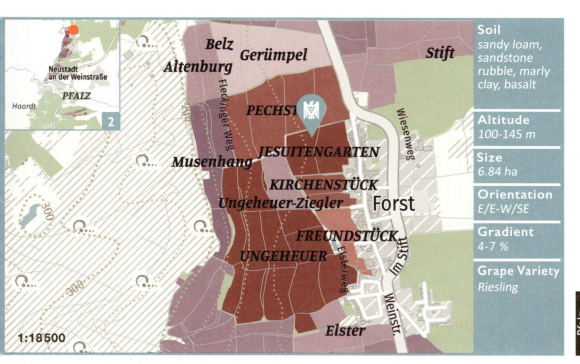

Soil
sandy loam, sandstone rubble, marly clay, basalt

Altitude
100-145 m

Size
6.84 ha

Orientation
E/E-W/SE

Gradient
4-7 %

Grape Variety
Riesling

VDP.Estates: Acham-Magin, Geh. Rat Dr. von Bassermann-Jordan, Reichsrat von Buhl, Dr. Bürklin-Wolf, Georg Mosbacher, Von Winning

The VDP.GROSSE LAGE® JESUITENGARTEN is located on the outskirts of Forst directly in the neighbourhood of four other prime vineyards: GL KIRCHENSTÜCK, GL UNGEHEUER and GL PECHSTEIN. Due to its high mineral content, optimal available water capacity, and diverse soils of calcareous and clay, sandy loam with sandstone rubble, and in some places a high concentration of weathered basalt or humus, this is considered one of the very best vineyards in the Pfalz. The basalt components help warm the east facing site quickly in the morning sun. A west to east breeze cools and dries the grapes in the evening and helps to ensure that even highly ripe grapes remain healthy. The vineyard slopes at 4 to 7 percent and spreads between 100 and 145 metres above sea level. Exclusively Riesling grows here.

History: The site was placed in the second highest category in the Bavarian vineyard classification of 1828. The Jesuit Monastery of Neustadt an der Weinstraße was the former owner of the site.

KALKBERG

Duttweiler | Pfalz
VDP.GROSSE LAGE®

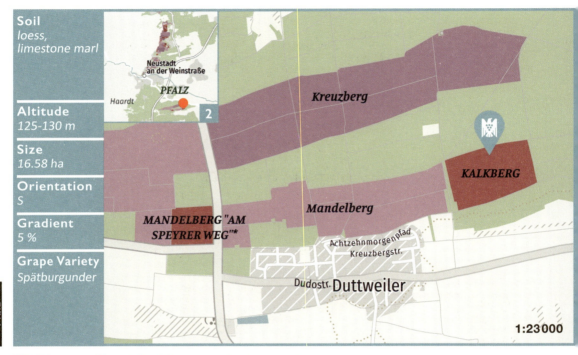

Soil
loess, limestone marl

Altitude
125-130 m

Size
16.58 ha

Orientation
S

Gradient
5 %

Grape Variety
Spätburgunder

VDP.Estates: Bergdolt - Klostergut St. Lamprecht

The VDP.GROSSE LAGE® KALKBERG gets its name from its soil: "Kalk" is "limestone", while "berg" is "mountain". The pararendzina soil comprised of loess over loose limestone marl is highly calcareous and has excellent available water capacity. This makes it ideal for Spätburgunder, which is the main variety planted. The 5 percent incline makes it a flat site and it is located on the south side of a loess bank (its ridge follows west to east and little stream glens border each side). The site is approximately 16 hectares in size and lies between 125 and 130 metres above sea level.

KALKOFEN

Deidesheim | Pfalz
VDP.GROSSE LAGE®

Soil
sand, loam with limestone marl

Altitude
185-200 m

Size
4.91 ha

Orientation
N-S/S/E-W

Gradient
2-10 %

Grape Variety
Riesling

VDP.Estates: Geh. Rat Dr. von Bassermann-Jordan, Reichsrat von Buhl, Dr. Bürklin-Wolf, Georg Mosbacher, Georg Siben Erben, Von Winning

It is not surprising that limestone dominates the geology of the VDP.GROSSE LAGE® KALKOFEN. Abundant limestone intersperses loam and limestone marl and appears occasionally as gravel in this 5-hectare site. The soil of this south-facing vineyard is heavy and has a medium water storage capacity. The GL KALKOFEN rises from 185 to 200 metres above sea level at 2 to 10 percent slope. The slight elevation allows the vine rows good aeration and a sandstone wall on the north side protects them. The site is located in a narrow, warm belt along the foothills of the Haardt hills. The average temperatures are high and precipitation is low.

History: The name points not only to the abundance of limestone in this vineyard, but also that there was indeed a Kalkofen (limestone oven) located in this site in the 15th century. The Kalkofen has long been known for the high quality of its wines and was already classified in 1828.

KALMIT

Ilbesheim | Pfalz
VDP.GROSSE LAGE®

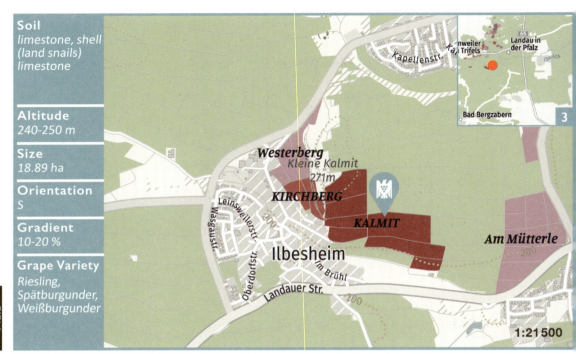

Soil
limestone, shell (land snails) limestone

Altitude
240-250 m

Size
18.89 ha

Orientation
S

Gradient
10-20 %

Grape Variety
Riesling, Spätburgunder, Weißburgunder

VDP.Estates: **Kranz, Siegrist**

The VDP.GROSSE LAGE® KALMIT is located on the south facing slope of the 127-metre high Kleine Kalmit. The old name for Kalmit was "mons calvus" which means "bald mountain". The GL KALMIT lies within the 112-hectare Kalmit vineyard. The soil is tertiary limestone and shell limestone covered with a rather shallow layer of humus. The parcel drops from the peak of the Kleine Kalmit at nearly 250 meters above sea level down to 240 metres. The site is planted predominantly with Riesling, Weißburgunder and Spätburgunder.

KAMMERBERG³

Schweigen | Pfalz
VDP.GROSSE LAGE®

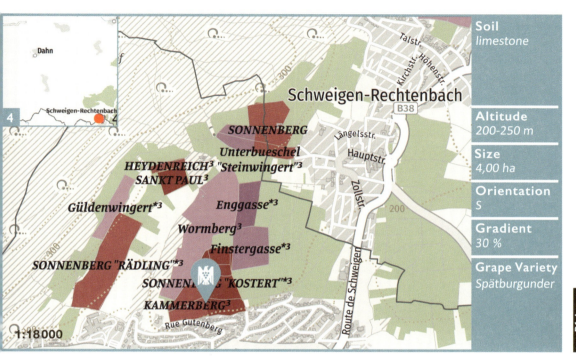

Soil
limestone

Altitude
200-250 m

Size
4,00 ha

Orientation
S

Gradient
30 %

Grape Variety
Spätburgunder

VDP.Estates: Friedrich Becker

The VDP.GROSSE LAGE® KAMMERBERG is located in the French part of the Sonnenberg vineyard. Its slope drops at a 30 percent gradient toward Weißenburg (Wissembourg) in the south. The soil is weathered limestone, loam, and clay over pure limestone subsoil. This soil is predestined for Spätburgunder. Due to intense solar radiation, the site warms quickly, and grapes ripen well. The proximity to the Lauter Valley simultaneously provides the side with cool winds in the night, which help preserve fresh acidity.

History: The wines of the Kammerberg already enjoyed great popularity among the monks at the Benedictine monastery in Weißenburg hundreds of years ago in the early Middle Ages. They stored the "Kammer" (chamber) wines in their monastery cellar. Despite this, the site was forgotten until Friedrich Becker rediscovered it in 1965. As this plot is located in France, German wine estates are not allowed to use the vineyards name on the label.

KASTANIENBUSCH "KÖPPEL"[1]

Birkweiler | Pfalz
VDP.GROSSE LAGE®

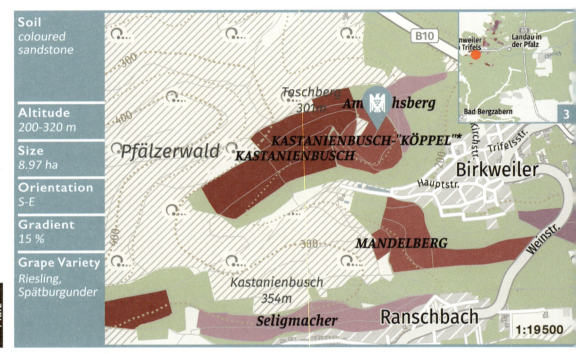

Soil
coloured sandstone

Altitude
200-320 m

Size
8.97 ha

Orientation
S-E

Gradient
15 %

Grape Variety
Riesling, Spätburgunder

VDP.Estates: Ökonomierat Rebholz, Dr. Wehrheim

The VDP.GROSSE LAGE® KASTANIENBUSCH "KÖPPEL"[1] is a circular cone-shaped rise planted with vines at the eastern foot of the Hohenberg in the Palatinate Forest. The vineyard faces south to east and is bordered by the GL KASTANIENBUSCH to the west. The coloured sandstone of the GL KASTANIENBUSCH "KÖPPEL"[1] differs from the soil of its neighbour, where iron-rich Rotliegend slate dominates. The 9-hectare vineyard extends from 200 to 320 metres above sea level at a gentle 15 percent gradient.

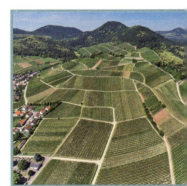

KASTANIENBUSCH

Birkweiler | Pfalz
VDP.GROSSE LAGE®

Soil
Rotliegend, sandstone

Altitude
200-320 m

Size
29.26 ha

Orientation
S

Gradient
10-40 %

Grape Variety
Riesling

VDP.Estates: Ökonomierat Rebholz, Dr. Wehrheim

The VDP.GROSSE LAGE® KASTANIENBUSCH lies well protected from the wind in a convex swale at the foot of the Hohenberg between 200 and 320 metres above sea level. Numerous chestnut (Kastanien) trees grow on the hill. The site is quite steep in places and due to the south exposition high temperatures can be reached during the day. The fairly high altitude brings much cooler temperatures in the night. The high diurnal fluctuation leads to early budbreak and a long ripening period, which is advantageous for aroma development. The diversity of the soil also makes the site quite unique. Rotliegend, a skeletal, very iron-rich slate is found in the GL KASTANIENBUSCH, just as is variegated sandstone debris and limestone with limestone marl stratifications and a bit of fine earth. Vintners have planted various grape varieties according to soil type. The slope gradient is between 10 and 40 percent.

KIESELBERG

Deidesheim | Pfalz
VDP.GROSSE LAGE®

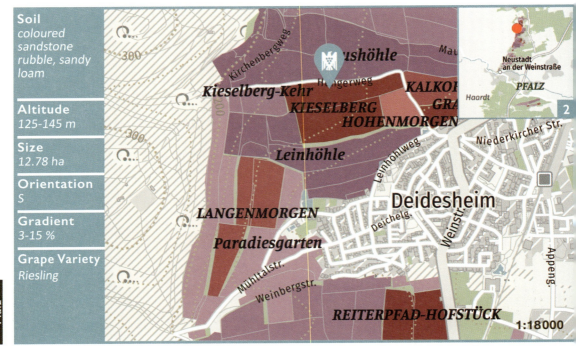

Soil
coloured sandstone rubble, sandy loam

Altitude
125-145 m

Size
12.78 ha

Orientation
S

Gradient
3-15 %

Grape Variety
Riesling

VDP.Estates: Geh. Rat Dr. von Bassermann-Jordan, Reichsrat von Buhl, Georg Mosbacher, Georg Siben Erben, Von Winning

The VDP.GROSSE LAGE® KIESELBERG is located on a flat, high plateau above Deidesheim in the wind shadow of the Haardt hills. The 12.7-hectare south-facing site rises from 125 to 145 metres at a slope of 3 to 15 percent. Well-exposed, yet protected it usually yields highly ripe grapes. The soils of the GL KIESELBERG are diversely structured. The typical regional weathered coloured sandstone includes fist-sized sandstones as well as loamy sand and rubble.

History: The Royal Bavarian Land Classification of 1828 categorized the Kieselberg as one of the best in the Pfalz.

KIRCHBERG

Ilbesheim | Pfalz
VDP.GROSSE LAGE®

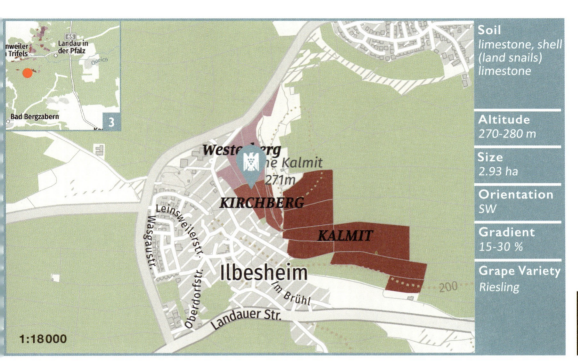

Soil
limestone, shell (land snails) limestone

Altitude
270-280 m

Size
2.93 ha

Orientation
SW

Gradient
15-30 %

Grape Variety
Riesling

VDP.Estates: Kranz

The VDP.GROSSE LAGE® KIRCHBERG is a small 3-hectare parcel in the Kalmit vineyard located directly under its highest peak, the 280 metres high Kleine Kalmit mountain, directly on the outskirts of Ilbesheim. Loess and shell limestone dominate the soils with the lime, in particular, providing good water availability. The 15 to 30 percent slope of this parcel faces southwest and collects the warmth of the evening sun. This warmth is stored in the soils and released into the vines late into the evening.

KIRCHENSTÜCK

Forst | Pfalz
VDP.GROSSE LAGE®

Soil: sandy clay, clay marl, loam, limestone rubble, basalt

Altitude: 120-140 m

Size: 3.41 ha

Orientation: NE-SW / E/SE

Gradient: 5-10 %

Grape Variety: Riesling

VDP.Estates: Acham-Magin, Geh. Rat Dr. von Bassermann-Jordan, Reichsrat von Buhl, Dr. Bürklin-Wolf, Von Winning

A particularly unique microclimate distinguishes the VDP.GROSSE LAGE® KIRCHENSTÜCK. The site is directly adjacent to the Forster Church (Kirche is German for church) and is surrounded by a knee-high sandstone wall. The warmth radiated from these constructions benefits the vines. They also direct airflow into the vineyard creating a warm, dry air current that drives out moisture and cold in the evening. The east to southeast-facing vineyard is located at 120 to 140 metres above sea level and has a gentle 5 to 10 percent slope gradient. The soils of the GL KIRCHENSTÜCK are diverse and vary from basalt and sandstone to limestone rubble and clay with a layer of clay in the middle section and a water-storing limestone plate two metres under the surface.

History: The Kirchenstück was included in the Royal Bavarian Land Classification of 1828 with the highest rating of alle vineyards in the Pfalz.

KIRSCHGARTEN

Laumersheim | Pfalz
VDP.GROSSE LAGE®

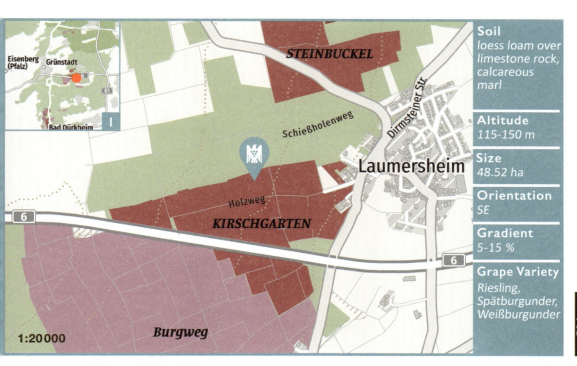

Soil
loess loam over limestone rock, calcareous marl

Altitude
115-150 m

Size
48.52 ha

Orientation
SE

Gradient
5-15 %

Grape Variety
Riesling, Spätburgunder, Weißburgunder

VDP.Estates: Knipser, Philipp Kuhn

The southeast facing VDP.GROSSE LAGE® KIRSCHGARTEN begins directly at the city limits of Laumersheim and stretches up the side of the mountain to cooler, higher elevations. The soils also become increasingly powerful and the limestone becomes more dominant. The parts of the vineyard closest to the city are protected from the wind and also benefit from the warmth radiated by the houses. A nearby embankment also benefits the microclimate. The Orlenberg Mountain helps shield the GL KIRSCHGARTEN from cool west winds. Loess loam mixed with limestone forms the top soil, which has good water storage capacity. The site lies at around 115 to 150 metres above sea level and has a slope gradient of around 15 percent.

History: The parcel was originally the property of a nunnery that belonged to the Kirschgarten Monastery in Worms. The site was first mentioned in documents dating 1654 as "Im Kirschgarthen".

LANGENMORGEN

Deidesheim | Pfalz
VDP.GROSSE LAGE®

Soil
weathered coloured sandstone, limestone, loamy sand

Altitude
150-160 m

Size
10.39 ha

Orientation
SE/E-W

Gradient
14-20 %

Grape Variety
Riesling, Weißburgunder

VDP.Estates: Geh. Rat Dr. von Bassermann-Jordan, Dr. Bürklin-Wolf, A. Christmann, Georg Mosbacher, Georg Siben Erben, Von Winning

The VDP.GROSSE LAGE® LANGENMORGEN is located on a southeast slope of the Haardt hills west of Deidesheim. It rises from 150 to 160 metres above sea level at a slope of 14 to 20 percent and opens towards the Rhine Plain. The 10-hectare site enjoys long sun exposure and the mountains also contribute to a special microclimate by providing protection from precipitation, cold winds, and frost. The soils are loess loam with high lime content with the typical regional red and white coloured sandstone in the rocky subsoil. Loess deposits provide good water availability and nutrition for vines. The statue "Steinerne Eva" is positioned at the upper border of the GL LANGENMORGEN.

History: The Langenmorgen vineyard was mentioned in written documents for the first time in 1491. A "Morgen" was a measurement of area and the name derives from the long shape of this site.

MANDELBERG "AM SPEYRER WEG" *

Kirrweiler | Pfalz
VDP.GROSSE LAGE®

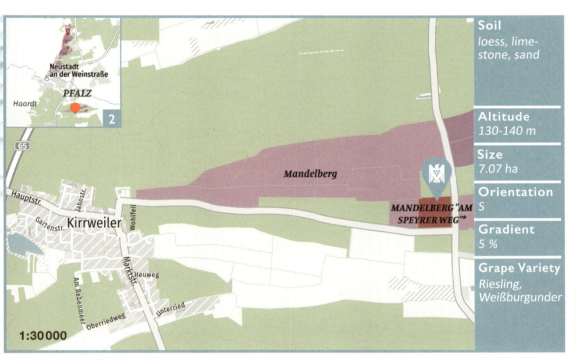

Soil
loess, limestone, sand

Altitude
130-140 m

Size
7.07 ha

Orientation
S

Gradient
5 %

Grape Variety
Riesling, Weißburgunder

VDP.Estates: Bergdolt - Klostergut St. Lamprecht

The VDP.GROSSE LAGE® MANDELBERG "AM SPEYRER WEG" lies between 130 and 140 metres above sea level and faces south at a flat 5 percent incline. Loess, limestone and sand are all present in the soils. The wines from this vineyard benefit from the advantageous conditions at the foot of the Haardt Mountains. The Palatinate Forest shields vines from bad weather that comes from the north and the west.

MANDELBERG

Birkweiler | Pfalz
VDP.GROSSE LAGE®

Soil
shell limestone

Altitude
260-320 m

Size
14.04 ha

Orientation
S-E

Gradient
5-10 %

Grape Variety
Weißburgunder

VDP.Estates: Ökonomierat Rebholz, Dr. Wehrheim

The VDP.GROSSE LAGE® MANDELBERG lies southwest of Birkweiler in the wind and rain protected south-east slope at 260 to 320 metres above sea level on the edge of the Palatinate Forest. The slope has a 5 to 10 percent gradient. Vines root in shell limestone with loam and clay marl with white limestone pebbles. The pebbles store the day's warmth and release it into the vines at night, thus prolonging the ripening period for grapes.

MANDELPFAD

Dirmstein | Pfalz
VDP.GROSSE LAGE®

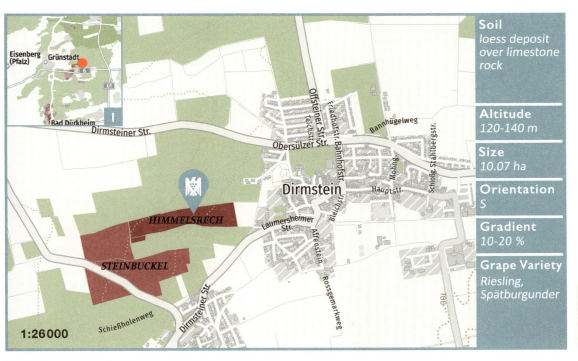

Soil
loess deposit over limestone rock

Altitude
120-140 m

Size
10.07 ha

Orientation
S

Gradient
10-20 %

Grape Variety
Riesling, Spätburgunder

VDP.Estates: Knipser

The VDP.GROSSE LAGE® MANDELPFAD is the filet piece of the Mandelpfad vineyard. It lies at 120 to 140 metres above sea level with a 10 to 20 percent south-facing slope. A bordering valley basin protects the site from west winds and allows the vineyard to warm easily in summer. Limestone and porous loess comprise the soils of the GL MANDELPFAD. These soils and the massive limestone plate below, provide good water availability even in dry years. The predominant grape variety is Riesling.

MEERSPINNE-IM MANDELGARTEN

Gimmeldingen | Pfalz
VDP.GROSSE LAGE®

Soil
coloured sandstone over limestone

Altitude
150-170 m

Size
7.24 ha

Orientation
SE

Gradient
5-10 %

Grape Variety
Riesling

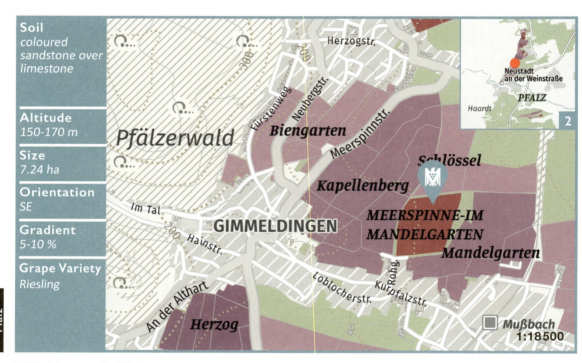

VDP.Estates: A. Christmann

The VDP.GROSSE LAGE® MEERSPINNE-IM MANDELGARTEN is situated between 150 and 170 metres in the middle section of a foothill of the Haardt Mountains, which are a part of the Palatinate Forest. The slope falls southeast toward the Rhine River and is bathed in early morning sunshine. Cold evening air steams from the Gimmeldinger Valley and Palatinate Forest cool the vines and preserve valuable acidity in the grapes. The 7-hectare GL MEERSPINNE sits on a massive limestone basement that over time was successively covered with eroding coloured sandstone rubble and wind-deposited calcareous loess. The soil's available water capacity is good.

History: The Meerspinne is legendary, but it was not revived again until the year 2015. The "Mersbin" was mentioned in the ledgers kept by the monks of the Wissembourg Monastery in Alsace as the origin of outstanding wines.

MICHELSBERG

Bad Dürkheim | Pfalz
VDP.GROSSE LAGE®

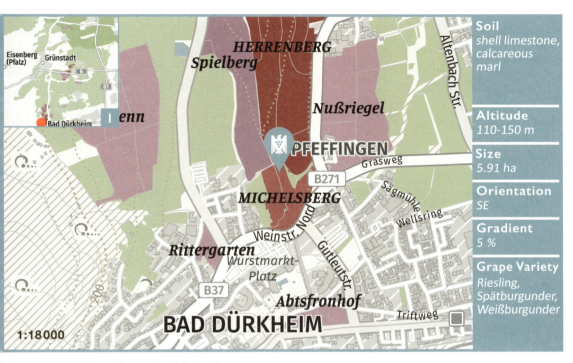

Soil
shell limestone, calcareous marl

Altitude
110-150 m

Size
5.91 ha

Orientation
SE

Gradient
5 %

Grape Variety
Riesling, Spätburgunder, Weißburgunder

VDP.Estates: Fitz-Ritter, Karl Schaefer

The VDP.GROSSE LAGE® MICHELSBERG terraces are built on a former mussel bank—dense calcareous marl, shell limestone and sandy loam determine the soils. The south-east-facing vineyard slopes at 5 percent from 110 to 150 metres above sea level. The sandstone walls of the terraces store warmth and protect the GL MICHELSBERG from frost and during summer release heat into the vines until late in the night, extending the ripening season. The slope also enjoys good aeration and allows moisture to evaporate quickly.

History: The Michelsberg is the oldest site to be mentioned in documents dating 1155. The name stems from the pilgrimage chapel St. Michael that stood in the site until the year 1601.

MÜNZBERG

Godramstein | Pfalz
VDP.GROSSE LAGE®

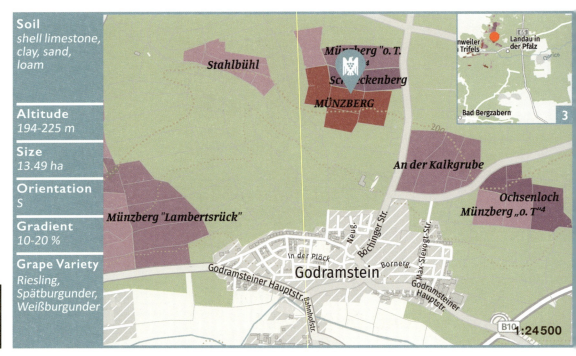

Soil
shell limestone, clay, sand, loam

Altitude
194-225 m

Size
13.49 ha

Orientation
S

Gradient
10-20 %

Grape Variety
Riesling, Spätburgunder, Weißburgunder

VDP.Estates: Münzberg - Gunter Keßler

The VDP.GROSSE LAGE® MÜNZBERG is situated on a gentle 10 to 20 percent incline facing south. Shell limestone, sand and loam dominates the soils of this 13.5-hectare GL. It includes the Schlangenpfiff, which is considered the best parcel of the Münzberg vineyard. Its warm soils evidently attract snakes (Schlangen) and lizards.
History: The Münzberg site was included in the Royal Bavarian Land Classification of 1828 with very high ratings.

ÖLBERG-HART

Königsbach | Pfalz
VDP.GROSSE LAGE®

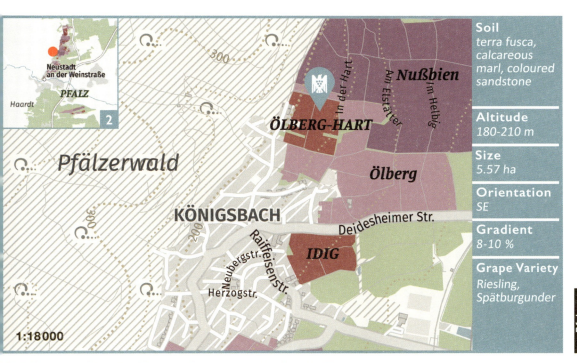

Soil
terra fusca, calcareous marl, coloured sandstone

Altitude
180-210 m

Size
5.57 ha

Orientation
SE

Gradient
8-10 %

Grape Variety
Riesling, Spätburgunder

VDP.Estates: Geh. Rat Dr. von Bassermann-Jordan, A. Christmann

The VDP.GROSSE LAGE® ÖLBERG-HART is the choice parcel of the Ölberg vineyard. It is located directly on the edge of the Palatinate Forest on the crest of the Haardt hills and rises from 180 to 210 metres above sea level at a 8 to 10 percent slope. The south-east exposition opens toward the Rhine Plain and bathes vines in sunshine from the early morning hours. The forest provides cool air and a shadow on hot afternoons. Refreshing breezes from the valley also reach the vines. The soils are Terra fusca, a tertiary calcareous marl, which is mixed with coloured sandstone rubble in the upper surface. The clay content in the soil provides vines with good water availability.

History: The ÖLBERG-HART was categorized in the Royal Bavarian Land Classification of 1828 as the best parcel of the Ölberg.

PECHSTEIN

Forst | Pfalz
VDP.GROSSE LAGE®

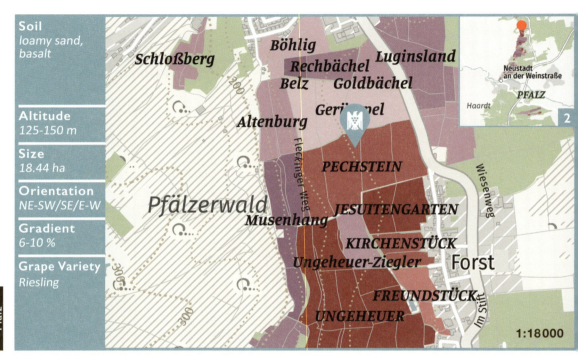

Soil
loamy sand, basalt

Altitude
125-150 m

Size
18.44 ha

Orientation
NE-SW/SE/E-W

Gradient
6-10 %

Grape Variety
Riesling

VDP.Estates: Acham-Magin, Geh. Rat Dr. von Bassermann-Jordan, Reichsrat von Buhl, Dr. Bürklin-Wolf, Georg Mosbacher, Karl Schaefer, Von Winning

The name of the VDP.GROSSE LAGE® PECHSTEIN stems from the black basalt rubble that is found here together with weathered red sandstone, sandy loam and friable clay. The extinct volcano, Pechsteinkopf, which is seen above the forest, distributed large quantities of volcanic rock over the area in ancient times. The basalt rubble that contributes to easy warming of this site actually does not stem from the site's subsoil, but rather from an old stone quarry just a couple hundred metres away. The 18 hectare GL PECHSTEIN is located at 120 to 150 metres above sea level and has a gentle 6 to 10 percent slope gradient. The share of clay and loam in the Pechstein contributes to its excellent water storage capacity.

History: The Pechstein site was included in the Royal Bavarian Land Classification of 1828 with very high ratings.

REITERPFAD-ACHTMORGEN

Ruppertsberg | Pfalz
VDP.GROSSE LAGE®

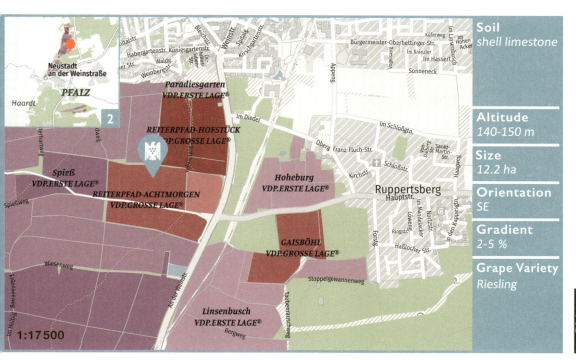

Soil
shell limestone

Altitude
140-150 m

Size
12.2 ha

Orientation
SE

Gradient
2-5 %

Grape Variety
Riesling

VDP.Estates: Bergdolt - Klostergut St. Lamprecht

The 12-hectare VDP.GROSSE LAGE® REITERPFAD-ACHTMORGEN is situated in the lower, southeast facing slope of the VDP.ERSTE LAGE® Reiterpfad and borders the road from Deidesheim to Ruppertsberg. The flat 2 to 5 percent slope has a nearly Mediterranean climate. The Haardt hills protect it from cold west winds and rain, allowing it to benefit from the warm Rhine Plain weather. Stone walls that cross the lower Reiterpfad also store the warmth of the day and release it into the vines in the night. The soils have a high limestone content that stems from an ancient mussel bank that has been thrust to the surface by a tectonic shift. This weathered shell limestone mixes with sand, sandy loam, and coloured sandstone rubble. Although the soils are very rocky, they have high water storage capacity.

REITERPFAD-HOFSTÜCK

Ruppertsberg | Pfalz
VDP.GROSSE LAGE®

Soil
coloured sandstone

Altitude
150-180 m

Size
10.98 ha

Orientation
SE

Gradient
5-15 %

Grape Variety
Riesling

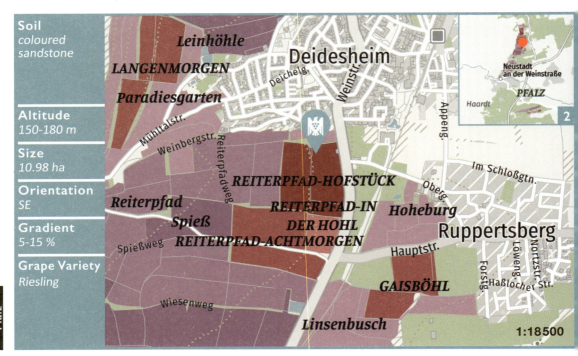

VDP.Estates: Reichsrat von Buhl, A. Christmann

Stone walls partially surround and cross through the VDP.GROSSE LAGE® REITERPFAD–HOFSTÜCK. They store heat and radiate warmth in the vineyard. The site lies at 130 to 150 metres above sea level and comprises ten hectares within the 77-hectare Reiterpfad. The climate in the south-east facing vineyard slope is protected from cold weather influences. The GL is one of the warmest sites in the Pfalz and its climate can be described as Mediterranean. The GL REITERPFAD-HOFSTÜCK sits on a limestone pedestal. The top soil is mixed with variegated sandstone, loess, and occasionally basalt. Nearly exclusively Riesling is planted here.

REITERPFAD-IN DER HOHL

Ruppertsberg | Pfalz
VDP.GROSSE LAGE®

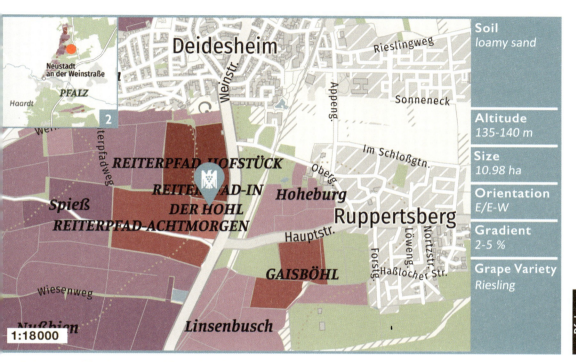

Soil
loamy sand

Altitude
135-140 m

Size
10.98 ha

Orientation
E/E-W

Gradient
2-5 %

Grape Variety
Riesling

VDP.Estates: Reichsrat von Buhl, Dr. Bürklin-Wolf

The VDP. GROSSE LAGE® REITERPFAD–IN DER HOHL is a prime parcel within the 77-hectare Reiterpfad vineyard. The soils here are somewhat lighter with a high share of loamy sand. Limestone is also occasionally found in the soil mix. The relatively flat site tilts gently toward the south at a 5 percent gradient. Despite this, it is well protected and benefits from both the morning and evening sunshine. The vineyard is one of the warmest in the Pfalz. It is planted mostly with Riesling.

ROSENKRANZ-IM UNTERN KREUZ

Böchingen | Pfalz
VDP.GROSSE LAGE®

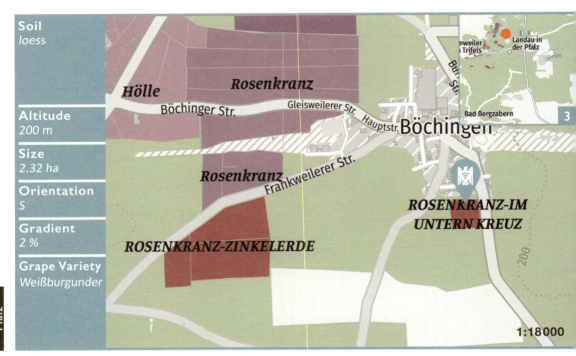

Soil
loess

Altitude
200 m

Size
2.32 ha

Orientation
S

Gradient
2 %

Grape Variety
Weißburgunder

VDP.Estates: Theo Minges

The VDP.GROSSE LAGE® ROSENKRANZ – IM UNTERN KREUZ is located south of the little wine village Böchingen at around 200 metres above sea level at the foot of the 600-metre Teufelsberg in the Palatinate Forest hills. Loess with high silt content dominates the soils, which provide vines with sufficient water and nutrients.

ROSENKRANZ-ZINKELERDE

Böchingen | Pfalz
VDP.GROSSE LAGE®

Soil
calcareous marl

Altitude
200 m

Size
16.39 ha

Orientation
S

Gradient
15 %

Grape Variety
Spätburgunder

VDP.Estates: Theo Minges

The lime-rich marl soil of the VDP.GROSSE LAGE® ROSENKRANZ – ZINKELERDE makes it predestined for red wine production. While this soil is well-aerated and warms quickly, the high share of calcium carbonate enhances the preservation of acidity in grapes and wine. The GL ROSENKRANZ-ZINKELERDE has a sunny, south-facing aspect and is shielded from bad weather by the Haardt Mountains and the Palatinate Forest. The Mediterranean-like climate is influenced by a type of warm foehn wind that occurs here on the edge of the Palatinate Forest. The GL ROSENKRANZ-ZINKELERDE lies at 200 metres above sea level and has a slope gradient of 15 percent.

SANKT PAUL

Schweigen | Pfalz
VDP.GROSSE LAGE®

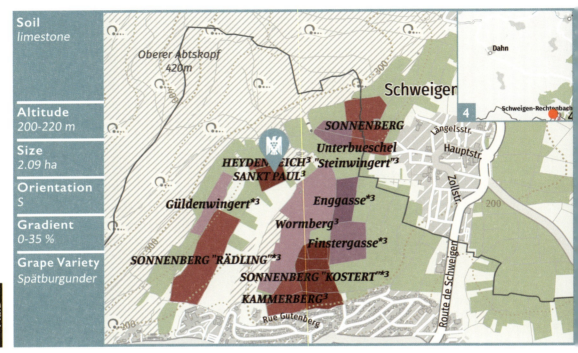

Soil
limestone

Altitude
200-220 m

Size
2.09 ha

Orientation
S

Gradient
0-35 %

Grape Variety
Spätburgunder

VDP.Estates: Friedrich Becker

The 2-hectare VDP.GROSSE LAGE® SANKT PAUL lies in the French section of the Sonnenberg vineyard at 200 to 220 metres above sea level. The steep south-facing slope is protected in a valley basin and collects plenty of warmth during the day. The nearby Palatinate forest causes a significant sink in temperatures each night. After only 25-50 cm of loose soil, vine roots meet pure limestone—perfect pre-conditions for Pinot varieties.

Information: The GL SANKT PAUL is named after the eponymous castle in the immediate vicinity. As this plot is located in France, German wine estates are not allowed to use the vineyards name on the label.

SAUMAGEN

Kallstadt | Pfalz
VDP.GROSSE LAGE®

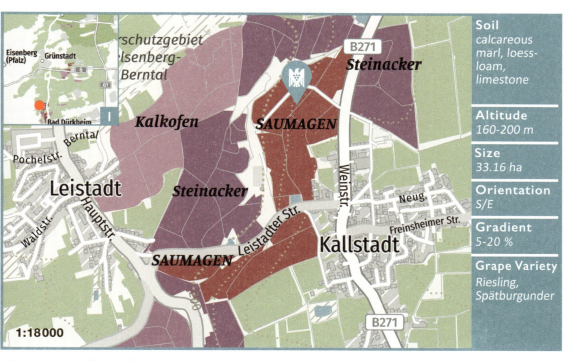

Soil
calcareous marl, loess-loam, limestone

Altitude
160-200 m

Size
33.16 ha

Orientation
S/E

Gradient
5-20 %

Grape Variety
Riesling, Spätburgunder

VDP.Estates: Philipp Kuhn, Rings

The vines of the 33-hectare VDP.GROSSE LAGE® SAUMAGEN root in deep, well-drained loess-loam and calcareous marl with abundant small limestones. It is located at the foot of the Haardt, the mountain range that runs parallel to the Rhine River on the eastern edge of the Palatinate Forest. The vineyard lies between 160 and 200 metres above sea level. 30 percent of the slope is moderately steep with a 20 percent gradient. The remaining part is flat with only 5 percent gradient.

SCHÄWER

Burrweiler | Pfalz
VDP.GROSSE LAGE®

Soil
schist (Devon slate), coloured sandstone

Altitude
270-295 m

Size
7.2 ha

Orientation
S

Gradient
20-30 %

Grape Variety
Riesling

VDP.Estates: Herbert Meßmer, Theo Minges

A very unusual geology for the region is found in the VDP.GROSSE LAGE® SCHÄWER. A tectonic shift of the Upper Rhine Rift has pushed grey Devon slate (schist) to the surface. The typical weathered coloured sandstone, loam and eroded slope rubble is also present. The southeast-facing slope rises at a 20 to 30 percent gradient, which is relatively steep for this area. The dark slate captures the suns warmth and releases it in the night. The Haardt Mountains protect the site from cool west winds.

SCHWARZER HERRGOTT

Zellertal | Pfalz
VDP.GROSSE LAGE®

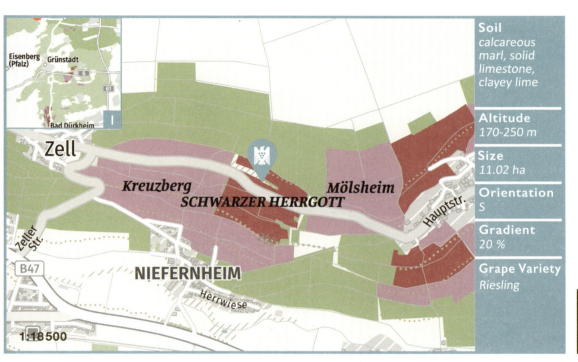

Soil
calcareous marl, solid limestone, clayey lime

Altitude
170-250 m

Size
11.02 ha

Orientation
S

Gradient
20 %

Grape Variety
Riesling

VDP.Estates: **Philipp Kuhn**

The approximately 11-hectare, south-facing VDP.GROSSE LAGE® SCHWARZER HERRGOTT is located on a limestone plateau. Rocky, pale porous limestone and heavy, loamy layers of marl comprise the steep terraced slope – by no means easy soils to work. The name of this site stems from a huge black crucifix that can be seen from a distance. The Donnersberg Mountain in the west protects the SCHWARZER HERRGOTT (Black Lord) from rain and storms, which can also lead to very dry summers and a low annual precipitation of only 400 mm. The slope warms quickly, often promoting early flowering and a long ripening period for grapes. Valley fog and late frost rarely reach the SCHWARZER HERRGOTT at its 170 to 250 metres above sea level.

History: The English Monk Philipp and his brothers produced wine for the Eucharist here as early as 700 A.C. His monastery was located on the Way of St. James between Speyer and Worms and was one of the most important pilgrimage monasteries in the Middle Ages.

SONNENBERG "KOSTERT"[1,3]

Schweigen | Pfalz
VDP.GROSSE LAGE®

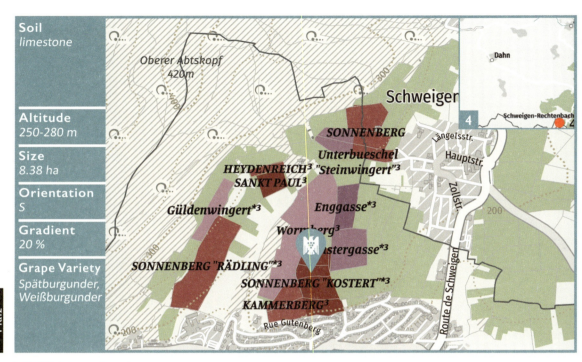

Soil
limestone

Altitude
250-280 m

Size
8.38 ha

Orientation
S

Gradient
20 %

Grape Variety
Spätburgunder, Weißburgunder

VDP.Estates: **Bernhart**

The vines of the VDP.GROSSE LAGE® SONNENBERG "KOSTERT"[1,3] root in a respectable slope of up to 20 percent directly above the French city Wissembourg. The vineyard faces directly south and benefits from direct sun radiation the entire day. Limestone dominates the soils, but there is also some clay and calcareous marl present. The 9-hectare GL KOSTERT lies between 250 and 280 metres above sea level.

History: The name Kostert could possibly stem from "köstlich", which means "tasty". It is claimed that the monks of the neighbouring Cistercian monastery St. Paulin praised the wines of the Kostert vineyard as being very tasty. As this vineyard is located in France, German wine estates are not allowed to use the vineyards name on the label.

SONNENBERG "RÄDLING" [1,3]

Schweigen | Pfalz
VDP.GROSSE LAGE®

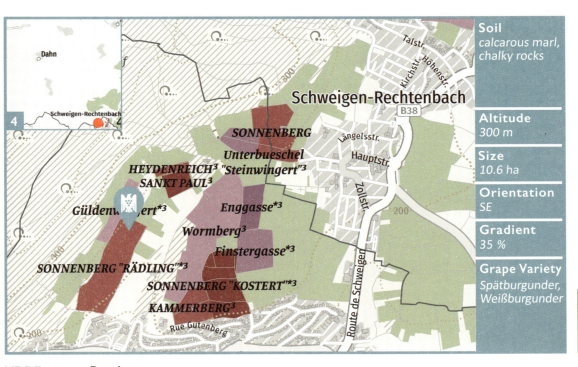

Soil
calcareous marl, chalky rocks

Altitude
300 m

Size
10.6 ha

Orientation
SE

Gradient
35 %

Grape Variety
Spätburgunder, Weißburgunder

VDP.Estates: **Bernhart**

The soils of the VDP.GROSSE LAGE® SONNENBERG "RÄDLING"[1,3] are quite meagre: calcareous marl with limestone, sometimes even with pure rock with a scant layer of earth towards the top of the site. Available water in the upper reaches is low, but is quite sufficient down lower. This steep southeast-facing GL rises at a 35 percent gradient to 300 metres above sea level and is situated in a wind-protected side valley of Lauter. As this vineyard is located in France, German wine estates are not allowed to use the vineyards name on the label.

SONNENBERG

Leinsweiler | Pfalz
VDP.GROSSE LAGE®

Soil
shell limestone, marl

Altitude
170 m

Size
9.48 ha

Orientation
S

Gradient
15-30 %

Grape Variety
Riesling, Spätburgunder

VDP.Estates: Siegrist

The well exposed VDP.GROSSE LAGE® SONNENBERG faces south on the lower slope of the Fohrenberg in the Palatinate Forest where it is well protected from rain and cold weather fronts from the west. With a 30 percent slope, the site is relatively steep compared to the other rather flat sites of the Pfalz. This intensifies the solar radiation. Marl and limestone with abundant fossilized mussels and even shark teeth distinguish this 9.5-hectare GL. The soils have good water storage capacity.

SONNENBERG

Schweigen | Pfalz
VDP.GROSSE LAGE®

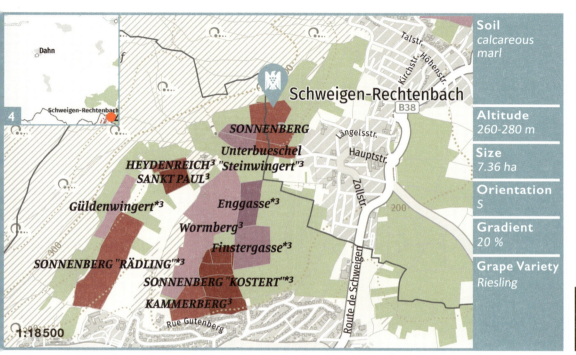

Soil
calcareous marl

Altitude
260-280 m

Size
7.36 ha

Orientation
S

Gradient
20 %

Grape Variety
Riesling

VDP.Estates: Friedrich Becker, Bernhart

The VDP.GROSSE LAGE® SONNENBERG in Schweigen is a true border crosser. It is the only German vineyard that is located in two countries. While the eastern part lies on German terrain in the Pfalz, the western part is located in the Alsace region of France. The vineyard faces south at a gentle slope incline of 20 percent. This corner of the Pfalz is one of the warmest areas in Germany. 2000 hours of sunshine annually, warm foehn winds and protection from the deep pressure regions through proximity to the Palatinate forest result in a Mediterranean-like climate. The GL SONNENBERG rises from 260 to 280 metres above sea level at a 20 percent slope incline. The soils are light, easily warmed and well-aerated lime-rich marl.

History: Because the border region between the Alsace and southern Pfalz changed its nationality often in the course of history, the Sonnenberg vineyard is also sometimes called "Wechsellage".

STEINBUCKEL

Laumersheim | Pfalz
VDP.GROSSE LAGE®

Soil
loess, loess loam over limestone rock, calcarous marl

Altitude
120-150 m

Size
25 ha

Orientation
SE

Gradient
5-10 %

Grape Variety
Riesling, Spätburgunder

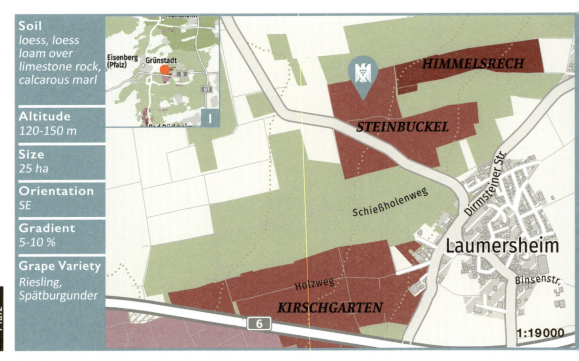

VDP.Estates: Knipser, Philipp Kuhn

The VDP GROSSE LAGE® STEINBUCKEL is a qualitatively very valuable parcel within the Mandelberg vineyard. Particularly noteworthy is the soil structure, which is calcareous marl with abundant limestone over a massive block of limestone. It is southeast-facing, most protected, convex section of the Mandelberg with a 5 to 10 percent gradient. Cool winds from the neighbouring Leininger Valley allow grapes to ripen slowly and preserve acidity. STEINBUCKEL wines are considered particularly long-lived. Mostly Riesling is cultivated here.

UNGEHEUER

Forst | Pfalz
VDP.GROSSE LAGE®

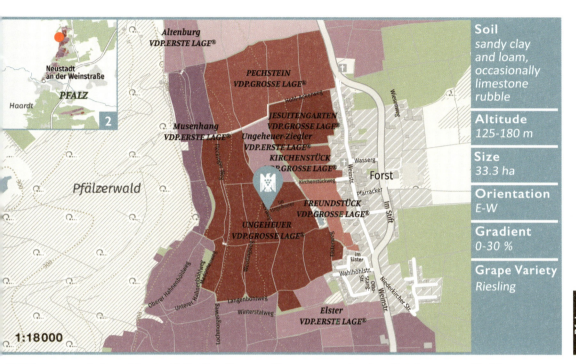

Soil
sandy clay and loam, occasionally limestone rubble

Altitude
125-180 m

Size
33.3 ha

Orientation
E-W

Gradient
0-30 %

Grape Variety
Riesling

VDP.Estates: Acham-Magin, Geh. Rat Dr. von Bassermann-Jordan, Reichsrat von Buhl, Dr. Bürklin-Wolf, Georg Mosbacher, Georg Siben Erben, Von Winning

The famous VDP.GROSSE LAGE® UNGEHEUER is located above the city of Forst in the middle of the slope that rises from 125 to 180 metres above sea level toward the Haardt hills. The gentle slope incline of 30 percent faces east and west providing optimal warming. The soil is quite diverse and heterogeneous and includes a bit of volcanic basalt rock in some areas. The soil is otherwise dominated by sandy clay from weathered coloured sandstone, loam and limestone rubble. Good available water capacity provides vines with optimal moisture and minerals. Riesling is the sole variety planted here.

History: The Bavarian land parcel classification of 1828 categorized this site as a top vineyard. The Chancellor of the German Empire Otto von Bismarck (1815-1898) commented on the wine: "Dieses Ungeheuer schmeckt mir ungeheuer," which can be translated to "This colossal tastes colossally good". The name "Forster Ungeheuer" stems from a government scribe named Johann Adam Ungeheuer in Deideshem in 1699.

WEILBERG

Ungstein | Pfalz
VDP.GROSSE LAGE®

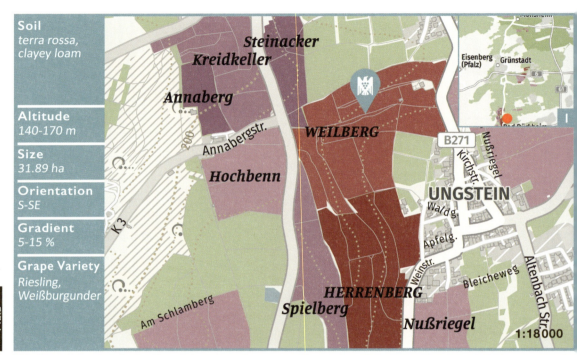

Soil
terra rossa, clayey loam

Altitude
140-170 m

Size
31.89 ha

Orientation
S-SE

Gradient
5-15 %

Grape Variety
Riesling, Weißburgunder

VDP.Estates: **Pfeffingen, Rings, Karl Schaefer**

The VDP.GROSSE LAGE® WEILBERG lies in a south to southeast exposition surrounding a 2000-year-old Roman winery. The vineyard slopes are 140 to 170 metres above sea level and have a 5 to 15 percent gradient. An advantageous microclimate and soil structure distinguish this site. In local dialect one speaks of "Roterde", a red-coloured clayey loam with a share of limestone and silt. This type of soil is normally only found on the Mediterranean and is known there as "Terra Rossa". The red colour is an indication of the high iron content. The GL WEILBERG is around 32 hectares in size and planted mostly with Riesling.

History: The Weilberg is essentially the origin of viticulture in the Pfalz. Roman settlers planted vines and established a winery at this location, initiating viticulture to the region 2000 years ago.

Region:	VDP.GROSSE LAGE®:
3 200 ha	620 ha
VDP.Wineries:	VDP.GROSSE LAGE® Sites:
35	50

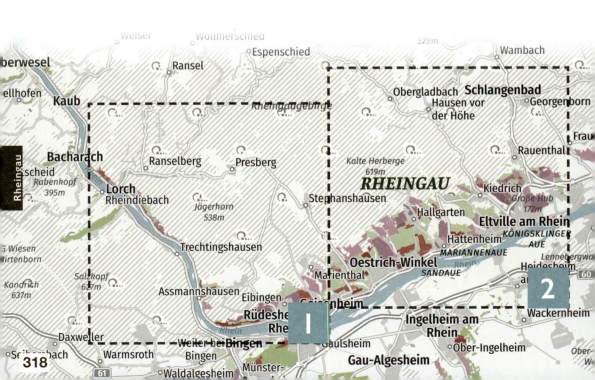

RHEINGAU

Rheingau is the place where the Rhine River suddenly changes direction to flow from east to west for nearly 30 kilometres. It begins in Hochheim above the Main River, which flows directly into the eastern bend of the Rhine. The Rhine Valley opens broadly beginning in Wiesbaden and the vineyards that fall gently southward from the protective, forested ridge of the Taunus foothills toward the Rhine enjoy abundant sunshine.

The river is broad here and stores warmth, providing a mild and stable climate. From Rüdesheim downstream, the Rhine acts increasingly as a reflective surface for light. The Rhine becomes significantly narrower here as it changes direction to flow north; the vineyards become steeper and more meagre. In this part of the Rheingau down to Lorchhausen, particularly in the vicinity of Assmannshausen, the predominant grape variety changes from Riesling to Spätburgunder. Quartzite and shale distinguish the steep sites of the lower Rheingau, while loess, loam, sand, gravel and marl are found in the middle and upper Rheingau.

BAIKENKOPF

Rauenthal | Rheingau
VDP.GROSSE LAGE®

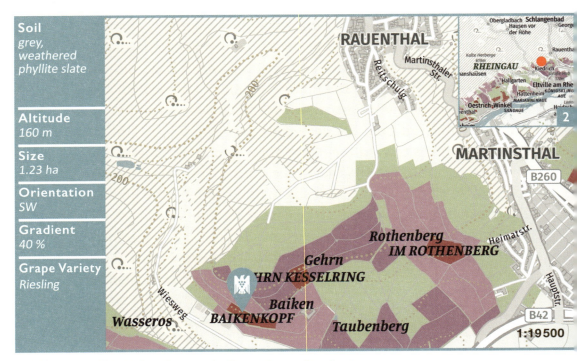

Soil
grey, weathered phyllite slate

Altitude
160 m

Size
1.23 ha

Orientation
SW

Gradient
40 %

Grape Variety
Riesling

VDP.Estates: Hessische Staatsweingüter Kloster Eberbach

The VDP.GROSSE LAGE® BAIKENKOPF belongs to the Rheingau village Rauenthal and is located in a crook at the base of the Rauenthal mountain near the Sulzbach tributary. Riesling is cultivated on this 40 slope that faces southwest. Vines benefit from optimal sun exposure and cool, fresh air from the Taunus forest. The GL BAIKENKOPF lies at 160 metres above sea level. Weathered phyllite slate and quartzite determine the soils. Underground aquifers provide the vineyard with good water availability.

History: By the end of the 19th century, the Rauenthal wines already enjoyed an excellent international reputation. This inspired the Royal Prussian estate administration to use the proceeds from the sale of property on the Neroberg in Wiesbaden to purchase the Wilhelmy Wine Estate in Rauenthal. This explains why Hessische Staatsweingüter buildings are found today in the Baiken vineyard surrounding the BAIKENKOPF.

BERG KAISERSTEINFELS

Rüdesheim am Rhein | Rheingau
VDP.GROSSE LAGE®

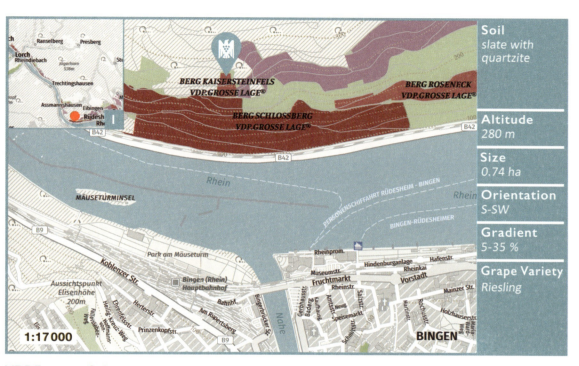

Soil
slate with quartzite

Altitude
280 m

Size
0.74 ha

Orientation
S-SW

Gradient
5-35 %

Grape Variety
Riesling

VDP.Estates: **Leitz**

The impressive and sun pampered, south facing slope of the VDP. GROSSE LAGE® BERG KAISERSTEINFELS rises prominently above the bend in the Rhine at Rüdesheim. The Nahe empties into the Rhine directly opposite this partially terraced vineyard. At 5 to 35 percent gradient, the GL is steep to very steep. The soil of the 0.7 hectares is meagre and rocky; one finds quartzite slate rubble and in some areas there is a small share of red slate interstratification. The well drained soil is prone to dryness. The GL BERG KAISERSTEINFELS lies at 280 metres above sea level. Predominantly Riesling grows here.
History: The name stems from the bare, rocky soil structure (Steinfels) and from Emperor Charles the Great (Kaiser der Große) who had the grape variety Orléans planted here.

BERG ROSENECK

Rüdesheim am Rhein | Rheingau
VDP.GROSSE LAGE®

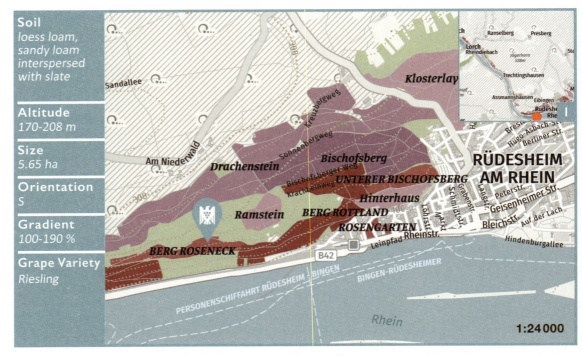

Soil
loess loam, sandy loam interspersed with slate

Altitude
170-208 m

Size
5.65 ha

Orientation
S

Gradient
100-190 %

Grape Variety
Riesling

VDP.Estates: Fritz Allendorf, Friedrich Fendel, August Kesseler, Leitz, Hessische Staatsweingüter Kloster Eberbach, Geheimrat J. Wegeler

The VDP.GROSSE LAGE® BERG ROSENECK is situated beneath the Niederwald Monument in Rüdesheim in the Rheingau. The name of the vineyard comes from "Rosenhecke" which means "rose hedge" and refers to the protruding granite cliff within the vineyard where wild rose, rose hip and sloe grow. The south-facing vineyard rises from 170 to 208 metres above sea level at an impressive 100 to 190 percent (45-62°) gradient. The Taunus Mountains shield the site from the wind. The section in the western part of the vineyard, where the soil is very rocky, is among the steepest parcels in Germany. The eastern part of the site is flatter and deep loess loam soil dominates.
History: Wine was first cultivated here around the year 1200. At that time the vines wandered up the mountain in small terraces. In the course of land consolidation, the paths were paved and the terraced vineyard areas were thus rescued.

BERG ROTTLAND

Rüdesheim am Rhein | Rheingau
VDP.GROSSE LAGE®

Soil
red slate, quartzite

Altitude
100-150 m

Size
17.85 ha

Orientation
S

Gradient
15-50 %

Grape Variety
Riesling

VDP.Estates: Fritz Allendorf, Friedrich Fendel, Johannishof, Künstler, Leitz, Balthasar Ress, Hessische Staatsweingüter Kloster Eberbach, Geheimrat J. Wegeler

The numerous walls that cross the VDP.GROSSE LAGE® BERG ROTTLAND store warmth. The site lies above Rüdesheim at the foot of the Niederwalddenkmal monument on the majestic Rüdesheimer Berg at 100 to 150 metres above sea level. Facing completely south, the 15 to 50 percent grade slope is fully exposed to the abundant sunlight of the broad Rhine Valley. The rocky, skeletal soil has a high share of red slate and occasional appearance of grey slate, quartzite, and pebbles and partial covering with a shallow layer of loess. The soil warms easily and gradually releases these temperatures to the vines. The good drainage and low water storage capacity of the rocky subsoil makes it prone to drying. The fog banks that form in the Rhine Valley promote noble rot. Even in average years, Spätlese and Auslese of high quality are harvested.

BERG SCHLOSSBERG

Rüdesheim am Rhein | Rheingau
VDP.GROSSE LAGE®

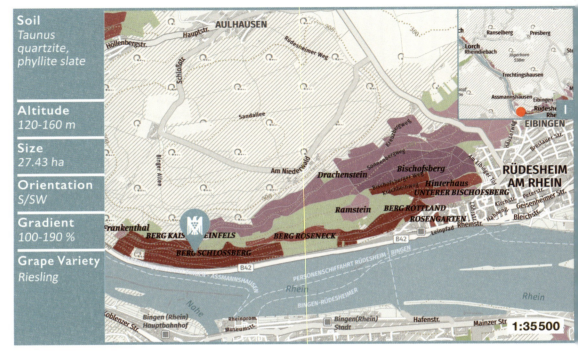

Soil
Taunus quartzite, phyllite slate

Altitude
120-160 m

Size
27.43 ha

Orientation
S/SW

Gradient
100-190 %

Grape Variety
Riesling

VDP.Estates: Friedrich Fendel, August Kesseler, Künstler, Leitz, Balthasar Ress, Hessische Staatsweingüter Kloster Eberbach, Geheimrat J. Wegeler

The impressive VDP.GROSSE LAGE® BERG SCHLOSSBERG lies in the bend of the Rhine River called the "Binger Loch", which is west of Rüdesheim opposite Bingen and the Mouse Tower. The Rhine changes course here and travels north again after its east-west intermezzo in Rheingau. Steeper than anywhere else in Rheingau, the vine rows climb a 100 to 190 percent (45-62°) gradient from 120 to 160 metres above sea level and are braced by mighty vineyard walls. Because the slope bulges toward the sun and the Rhine River reflection also makes its contribution, solar radiation in this south to southwest facing GL is high. Taunus quartzite and phyllite slate dominate the soil of this steep 27-hectare vineyard, which is quite well drained and stores warmth well.

Information: The name of this GL stems from Schloss Ehrenfels, now a castle in the vineyard.

DOMDECHANEY

Hochheim am Main | Rheingau
VDP.GROSSE LAGE®

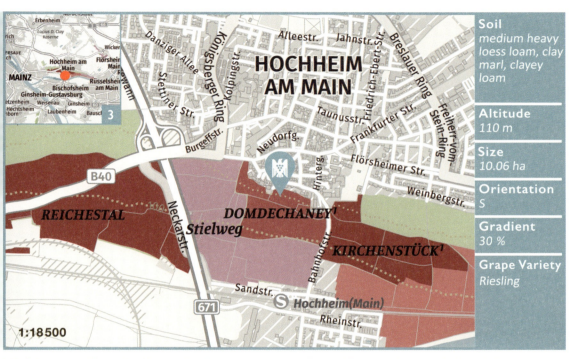

Soil
medium heavy loess loam, clay marl, clayey loam

Altitude
110 m

Size
10.06 ha

Orientation
S

Gradient
30 %

Grape Variety
Riesling

VDP.Estates: Künstler, Hessische Staatsweingüter Kloster Eberbach, Domdechant Werner

The VDP.GROSSE LAGE® DOMDECHANEY lies in the wind shadow of Hochheim's city wall and faces south toward the Main River, well protected from the north wind. Hochheim's St. Peter and Paul Church towers over the northeast corner of the 10.5-hectare vineyard. The site has a 30 percent gradient and lies at 110 meters of elevation. The soil is quite homogenous and consists of heavy loam. It retains water very well, which benefits the vines in dry vintages. The protected microclimate minimizes the threat of frost in this GL. Riesling is the primary variety.

History: The Domdechaney was once the property of the Chapter of the Cathedral of Mainz. The summer residence of the deacon of Mainz Cathedral was located directly in the vineyard next to the church.

DOOSBERG

Oestrich | Rheingau
VDP.GROSSE LAGE®

Soil
clayey loess loam, gravelly loess loam

Altitude
110-130 m

Size
61.35 ha

Orientation
S/SSW

Gradient
5-10 %

Grape Variety
Riesling

VDP.Estates: F. Allendorf, A. Eser, Prinz von Hessen, P. J. Kühn, Prinz, B. Ress, F. B. Schönleber, Josef Spreitzer, Hess. Staatsweing. Kl. Eberbach, Geheimrat J. Wegeler

The VDP.GROSSE LAGE® DOOSBERG is located on the eastern outskirts of the Rheingau village Oestrich. The persistent wind in this site is particularly advantageous in the autumn, because it dries rain and fog from the grapes and protects them from fungal infection. The GL DOOSBERG has a 5 to 10 percent incline that faces south to southwest at 110 to 130 metres above sea level. Gravel and loess loam comprise the soils. The bands of gravel and the gentle slope permit water reserves to be stored. The GL DOOSBERG is a Riesling vineyard.

History: The name stems from the word "Dachsberg", which means "badger mountain". Badgers once built their dens here in the loamy humus-rich soil.

GEHRN KESSELRING

Rauenthal | Rheingau
VDP.GROSSE LAGE®

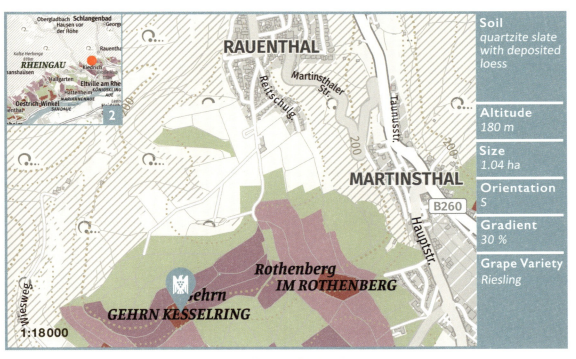

Soil
quartzite slate with deposited loess

Altitude
180 m

Size
1.04 ha

Orientation
S

Gradient
30 %

Grape Variety
Riesling

VDP.Estates: Hessische Staatsweingüter Kloster Eberbach

The VDP.GROSSE LAGE® GEHRN KESSELRING is a 1-hectare parcel of the VDP.ERSTE LAGE® GEHRN in the Rheingau village Rauenthal. The site faces south and has a slope gradient of 30 percent. It is located 180 metres above sea level. Riesling is cultivated here on quartzite and slate with wind deposited loess.

History: The vineyard "ufm Giren" was mentioned in documents dating 1688. The Old High German word "Ger" means "spear" and refers to the wedge shape of the site that is reminiscent of the tip of a spear.

GRÄFENBERG

Kiedrich | Rheingau
VDP.GROSSE LAGE®

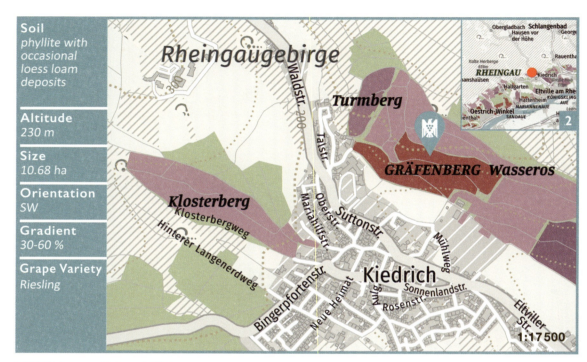

Soil
phyllite with occasional loess loam deposits

Altitude
230 m

Size
10.68 ha

Orientation
SW

Gradient
30-60 %

Grape Variety
Riesling

VDP.Estates: **Robert Weil**

With up to 60 percent gradient, the VDP.GROSSE LAGE® GRÄFENBERG is a rather steep site in the Rheingau. The close to 11-hectare southwest facing slope lies in the protected Kiedrich Valley, but is well-aerated by fall winds from the Taunus Mountains, which helps prolong the hanging period. The soil is medium to deep stony-gritty phyllite and a share of loess loam is advantageous to water storage capacity. The vines root deeply in the stony soil. The site lies at 230 metres above sea level and is planted with Riesling.

History: "Graf" translates to "duke" and "Berg" to "mountain". The Gräfenberg was mentioned as early as the 12th century as the "Mons Rhingravii". The wine from this site achieved its first international fame when Robert Weil delivered a Riesling Auslese from the legendary 1893 vintage to numerous kings and imperial courts.

GREIFFENBERG

Schloss Vollrads | Rheingau
VDP.GROSSE LAGE®

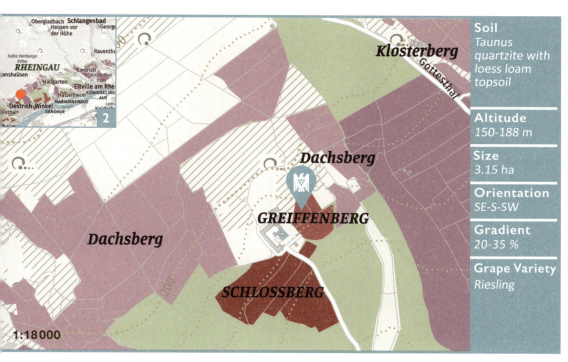

Soil
Taunus quartzite with loess loam topsoil

Altitude
150-188 m

Size
3.15 ha

Orientation
SE-S-SW

Gradient
20-35 %

Grape Variety
Riesling

VDP.Estates: Schloss Vollrads

The 3-hectare VDP.GROSSE LAGE® GREIFFENBERG is a monopole vineyard of Schloss Vollrads and lies just west of the estate in a somewhat cooler part of the Rheingau. The southeast to southwest facing slope climbs from 150 to 188 metres above sea level at a moderate 20 percent to fairly steep 35 percent gradient. The soils are Taunus quartzite with loess loam topsoil.

Information: The name of the vineyard traces back to the former owner family of Schloss Vollrads Estate—the noble family von Greiffenclau.

HASENSPRUNG

Winkel | Rheingau
VDP.GROSSE LAGE®

Soil
loess loam

Altitude
110-160 m

Size
26.84 ha

Orientation
S-SW

Gradient
3-15 %

Grape Variety
Riesling

VDP.Estates: Fritz Allendorf, August Eser, Hamm, Prinz von Hessen, F. B. Schönleber, Schloss Vollrads Geheimrat J. Wegeler

The VDP.GROSSE LAGE® HASENSPRUNG is located near Schloss Johannisberg in the village Winkel in the Rheingau. Riesling is cultivated here on fertile loess loam soils. The GL HASENSPRUNG vineyard has a 3 to 15 percent slope gradient that rises from 110 to 160 metres above sea level and faces south to southwest.

History: There are two possible explanations for the origin of the name of this vineyard. One is that wild hares (Hasen), which are also a symbol for fertility, inhabited the field and vineyard. Some of the vintners in Winkel project the theory that the parcels in this vineyard were once so narrow that a hare could have jumped over them. There also exists a folk legend that the 1811 vintage wine from this vineyard inspired the author Johann Wolfgang von Goethe to write his poem collection "West-Eastern Diwan".

HASSEL

Hattenheim | Rheingau
VDP.GROSSE LAGE®

Soil
loess loam

Altitude
120 m

Size
11.87 ha

Orientation
S

Gradient
20-25 %

Grape Variety
Riesling

VDP.Estates: Barth, August Eser, Kaufmann, Georg Müller Stiftung

The soil of the VDP.GROSSE LAGE® HASSEL excels with good water storage capacity. The basement is loess loam that provides vines with enough moisture even in very dry summers. In addition to this, the soil warms well. The vineyard extends between Hattenheim and Eltville to the west and slopes south toward the Rhine at a gentle 20 to 25 percent gradient. The GL HASSEL lies at around 120 metres above sea level and encompasses 12 hectares.

Information: Like the neighbouring GL NUSSBRUNNEN, the name of the GL HASSEL stems from hazelnut (Haselnuss). The vineyard was already referred to as "Hasele" in the 14th century and probably refers to hazel shrubs growing in the vicinity.

HOHENRAIN

Erbach | Rheingau
VDP.GROSSE LAGE®

Soil
loess loam

Altitude
110 m

Size
6.64 ha

Orientation
SW

Gradient
15 %

Grape Variety
Riesling

VDP.Estates: Jakob Jung, Baron Knyphausen, von Oetinger

The VDP.GROSSE LAGE® HOHENRAIN is located above the heart of Erbach in the Rheingau. Its 15 percent slope gradient faces south-west at around 110 metres above sea level. Riesling grapes can bathe in the sunshine throughout the day. A three-metre high wall in the western part of the vineyard stores warmth and protects the site from wind. The word "Rain" means a slope on the edge of a corridor; "Hohen" translates to "high".

History: This site was mentioned as a single vineyard under the name "Wingart de Reyngen" in a document dating 1519. Beginning in 1543, the vineyard was then referred to as "Hohenreine".

HÖLLE

Johannisberg | Rheingau
VDP.GROSSE LAGE®

Soil
Taunus quartzite, stony-gravelly loam

Altitude
140-150 m

Size
5.4 ha

Orientation
SSW

Gradient
20-40 %

Grape Variety
Riesling

VDP.Estates: Johannishof, Geheimrat J. Wegeler

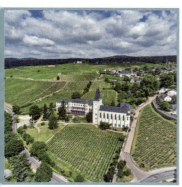

The VDP.GROSSE LAGE® HÖLLE lies at the edge of the village Johannisberg and slopes south-southwest toward the Elsterbach creek. On one side, the Rhine Valley protects this 5.4-hectare vineyard from the wine, yet it is broad and open here and also allows full exposition to the sun. The GL HÖLLE lies between 140 and 150 metres above sea level with a slope gradient of 20 to 40 percent. The vines root in easily warmed Taunus quartzite and pebbly-stony loam with good water storage capacity.

History: The name Hölle does not come from the hot temperatures, but rather from the name "Halde" (heap or pile). The site was first mentioned as "Helda in Monti Sanctis Johannis" in documents dating 1180.

HÖLLE

Hochheim am Main | Rheingau
VDP.GROSSE LAGE®

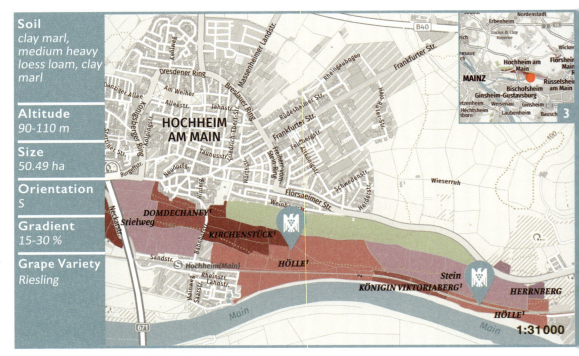

Soil
clay marl, medium heavy loess loam, clay marl

Altitude
90-110 m

Size
50.49 ha

Orientation
S

Gradient
15-30 %

Grape Variety
Riesling

VDP.Estates: Joachim Flick, Künstler, Hessische Staatsweingüter Kloster Eberbach, Domdechant Werner

The VDP. GROSSE LAGE® HÖLLE stretches southward down to the Main River. The slopy (up to 32% gradient) upper section of the 50-hectare vineyard gradually flattens to 6 percent toward the bank of the river. The GL HÖLLE lies at 90 to 110 meters of elevation. The Taunus Mountains, situated ten miles to the north, protect the site from wind and rain while the Main River soaks up heat during the day. The heavy loess, loess loam and clay marl soils store warmth and moderate any temperature fluctuations between day and night. The vineyard is interspersed with sandy-pebbly soil deposits from the Main terraces. The GL HÖLLE is also known for its unique source of water: aquifers bringing water from the Taunus Mountains happen to come to the surface here. The vineyard is primarily planted with Riesling.

History: Translated literally, the vineyard's name means "Hell." But in fact it does not stem from a religious or climatic context. "Hölle" instead simply derives from the term "halde" (hill).

HÖLLENBERG

Assmannshausen | Rheingau
VDP.GROSSE LAGE®

Soil
purple phyllite slate

Altitude
140-160 m

Size
20.98 ha

Orientation
S/SSW

Gradient
100-145 %

Grape Variety
Spätburgunder

VDP.Estates: Fritz Allendorf, Friedrich Fendel, August Kesseler, Krone Assmannshausen, Künstler, Balthasar Ress, Hessische Staatsweingüter Kloster Eberbach

Rising at a 100 to 145 percent (45-55°) slope gradient from 140 to 160 metres above sea level, the VDP.GROSSE LAGE® HÖLLENBERG is among the steepest vineyards in the Rheingau. The greater part of the vineyard is on south and south-southwest facing slopes of the Eichbachtal, a side valley of the Rhine near Assmannshausen in the lower Rheingau. Purple phyllite slate is a typical component of the GL HÖLLENBERG soils, which lends good capacity to store warmth. The Rhine River further enhances stable temperatures. The GL HÖLLENBERG is well known for its Spätburgunder.

History: Spätburgunder was cultivated in the parcels that today belong to the GL HÖLLENBERG already 500 years ago—presumably since 1470. Johann Wolfgang von Goethe, usually a white wine drinker, praised the red wine from this vineyard during his journey along the Rhine in 1814.

IM ROTHENBERG

Rauenthal | Rheingau
VDP.GROSSE LAGE®

Soil
Rotliegend clay slate

Altitude
190 m

Size
1.93 ha

Orientation
S-SW

Gradient
83-96 %

Grape Variety
Riesling

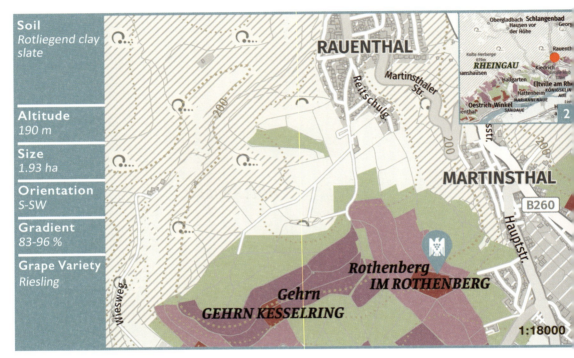

VDP.Estates: Diefenhardt

The VDP.GROSSE LAGE® IM ROTHENBERG is located in the upper, somewhat cooler part of the Rheingau. It is surrounded by the VDP.ERSTE LAGE® Rothenberg just below the edge of the forest. The vineyard rises to 190 metres above sea level at a very steep 83 to 96 percent (39-46 °) slope gradient. It faces south to southwest. Grape ripening benefits fully from sunshine throughout the day. The soils are eroded Taunus quartzite—a thin layer of loess over quartzite with slate intercalations.

JESUITENGARTEN

Winkel | Rheingau
VDP.GROSSE LAGE®

Soil
alluvial soil with shallow sand and pebble interstratifications

Altitude
90-97 m

Size
21.29 ha

Orientation
S/SW

Gradient
3 %

Grape Variety
Riesling

VDP.Estates: Fritz Allendorf, August Eser, Hamm, Prinz von Hessen, Johannishof, F. B. Schönleber, Josef Spreitzer, Schloss Vollrads, Geheimrat J. Wegeler

The VDP.GROSSE LAGE® JESUITENGARTEN is among the warmest vineyards in the Rheingau. This is due in part to the alluvial soils of sandy loam with gravel and sandy interstratifications. The proximity to the Rhine River also makes its contribution: the vineyard directly borders the riverbank path where the warmth-storing effect has its greatest influence. Budbreak and flowering occur early in this microclimate, which allows grapes a prolonged ripening period. The site lies at around 100 metres above sea level and with only a 3 percent slope toward the south and southwest, it is quite flat.

History: The origin of the name stems from the year 1606 when the Archbishop of Mainz bequeathed the St. Bartholomew Chapel and its vineyard to the Jesuit College in Mainz. The vineyard continued to be in the possession of the Jesuits until 1773.

JUNGFER

Hallgarten | Rheingau
VDP.GROSSE LAGE®

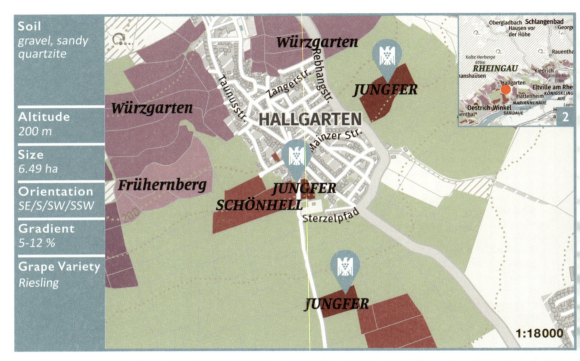

Soil
gravel, sandy quartzite

Altitude
200 m

Size
6.49 ha

Orientation
SE/S/SW/SSW

Gradient
5-12 %

Grape Variety
Riesling

VDP.Estates: Fritz Allendorf, August Eser, Prinz von Hessen, August Kesseler, Peter Jakob Kühn, Georg Müller Stiftung, Prinz, Balthasar Ress, Josef Spreitzer

The VDP.GROSSE LAGE® JUNGFER is located in a gentle swale east of the village Hallgarten. Wind-protected and facing southeast to southwest, the pebbly-sandy quartzite soil collects the warmth of the day and releases it into the vines at night, thus prolonging the daily ripening period. With only an up to 12 percent slope, the vineyard is fairly flat. It encompasses 6.5 hectares and lies at around 200 metres above sea level.

History: The Cistercian monks that settled in the Rheingau probably named this site after the Holy Virgin (Jungfrau) Mary.

KAPELLENBERG

Lorch | Rheingau
VDP.GROSSE LAGE®

Soil	slate, sand, loam
Altitude	110-180 m
Size	2.93 ha
Orientation	SSW
Gradient	10-45 %
Grape Variety	Spätburgunder, Riesling

VDP.Estates: **Graf von Kanitz**

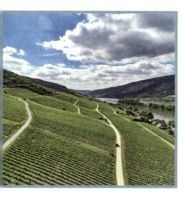

The VDP.GROSSE LAGE® KAPELLENBERG lies in a wind-protected narrow valley in the lower Rheingau. The slope faces south-southwest and climbs from 110 to 180 metres above sea level at a steep 45 % gradient. In contrast to the upper Rheingau where Taunus quartzite dominates, the soils here are defined by slate. Sand and loam also join the slate in the GL KAPELLENBERG. The vineyard is located in the heart of the UNESCO World Heritage Upper Middle Rhine Valley.
History: The GL KAPELLENBERG was first mentioned in documents dating 1480 as "hinter der Capelle", which means "behind the chapel". The name comes from the St. Markus Chapel from the 14th century, which no longer exists today.

KIRCHENPFAD

Rüdesheim | Rheingau
VDP.GROSSE LAGE®

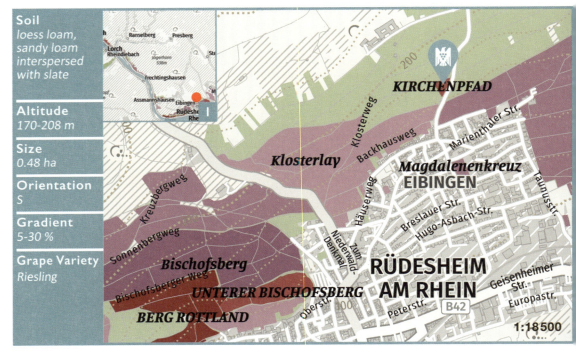

Soil
loess loam, sandy loam interspersed with slate

Altitude
170-208 m

Size
0.48 ha

Orientation
S

Gradient
5-30 %

Grape Variety
Riesling

VDP.Estates: Friedrich Fendel, Freimuth, Leitz, Geheimrat J. Wegeler

The VDP.GROSSE LAGE® KIRCHENPFAD is situated between the St. Hildegard Abbey and the Rüdesheim hamlet Eibingen. One has a good view here of the Rüdesheim centre and the Rhine River all the way to Bingen and the mouth of the Nahe River. This south-facing Riesling vineyard rises at a 5 to 30 percent gradient from 170 to 208 metres above sea level. The soils are loess loam and sandy loam with slate interstratifications. They have good water storage capacity.
History: The path through the vineyard that once led to the church in Eibingen lends this site its name: "Kirche" is church, while "Pfad" is path. Eibingen has belonged to the city of Rüdesheim in Rheingau since 1935.

KIRCHENSTÜCK

Hochheim am Main | Rheingau
VDP.GROSSE LAGE®

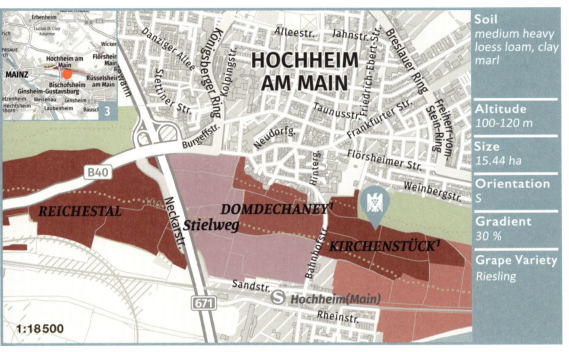

Soil
medium heavy loess loam, clay marl

Altitude
100-120 m

Size
15.44 ha

Orientation
S

Gradient
30 %

Grape Variety
Riesling

VDP.Estates: Künstler, Hessische Staatsweingüter Kloster Eberbach, Domdechant Werner

The VDP.GROSSE LAGE® KIRCHENSTÜCK is an elongated terrace that slopes from the southern border of the village of Hochheim down to the Main River. The southern exposition means that it enjoys the warmth of the sun all day long. The site is composed of medium-heavy loess loam and clay marl over deep subsoil, with a good water supply. The city of Hochheim protects the 15-hectare vineyard from kabatic winds, while the Taunus Mountains protect the vineyards from heavy rainfall and inclement weather. The GL slopes moderately at a 30 percent gradient from 100 to 120 meters of elevation. Hochheim's famous St. Peter and Paul parish church overlooks the GL KIRCHENSTÜCK from its west side. The vineyard was likely named for this church as the German word for church is Kirche.

KLAUS

Johannisberg | Rheingau
VDP.GROSSE LAGE®

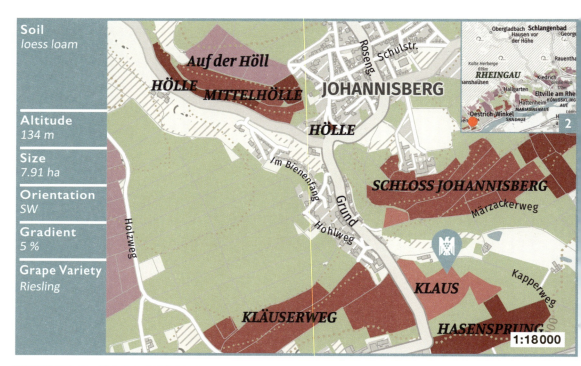

Soil
loess loam

Altitude
134 m

Size
7.91 ha

Orientation
SW

Gradient
5 %

Grape Variety
Riesling

VDP.Estates: Prinz von Hessen

The southwest-facing VDP.GROSSE LAGE® KLAUS lies at 134 metres above sea level in Johannisberg in the Rheingau. The calcareous loess with gravel content has a good capacity for storing water and warmth. The GL KLAUS is also well protected from the wind. Riesling is cultivated here.

History: This vineyard was first mentioned in documents dating 1248. The name stems from the former Benedictine Cloister Sankt Georgsklause. The cloister was dissolved in 1452 due to the claimed "immorality" of the nuns that dwelled there. The cloister's estate continues to exist today.

KLÄUSERWEG

Geisenheim | Rheingau
VDP.GROSSE LAGE®

Soil
deep, calcareous, stony loess loam a. tert. marl over quartzite with slate

Altitude
110-150 m

Size
20.61 ha

Orientation
SE/SW

Gradient
10-40 %

Grape Variety
Riesling

VDP.Estates: Fritz Allendorf, Freimuth, Hochschule Geisenheim University, Prinz von Hessen, Johannishof, Geheimrat J. Wegeler

The VDP.GROSSE LAGE® KLÄUSERWEG lies to the west of the Johannisberg Schlossberg vineyard. Riesling is cultivated here on deep, calcareous loess loam that is interspersed with rocks and quartzite. The proximity to the Taunus Mountains shields the vineyard from cold north winds. The GL KLÄUSERWEG has a 10 to 40 percent slope that inclines toward the south between 110 and 150 metres above sea level.

History: "Via Clusen" was first mentioned in documents dating 1292. Beginning in the 14th century, it was referred to as "Cluserweg". Like the GL KLAUS, the name of the GL KLÄUSERWEG stems from the former Benedictine Cloister Sankt Georgsklause. The cloister was dissolved in 1452 due to the claimed "immorality" of the nuns that dwelled there. The cloister's estate continues to exist today.

KÖNIGIN VIKTORIABERG

Hochheim am Main | Rheingau
VDP.GROSSE LAGE®

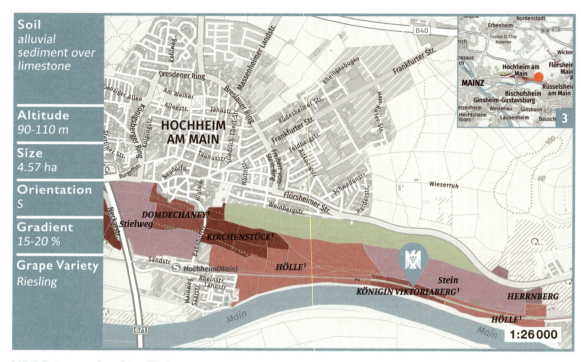

Soil
alluvial sediment over limestone

Altitude
90-110 m

Size
4.57 ha

Orientation
S

Gradient
15-20 %

Grape Variety
Riesling

VDP.Estates: Joachim Flick

The VDP.GROSSE LAGE® KÖNIGIN VIKTORIABERG lies alongside the Main river between Hochheim and Flörsheim in the Rheingau. The vineyard faces south and gently ascends from 100 to 110 meters of elevation at a 15 to 20 percent gradient. The vineyard is approximately 100 meters wide and rises to a sandy path above it. The soil is comprised of alluvial sediment over limestone. Sitting at the foot of an escarpment, the vineyard is shielded from the cold north wind. The microclimate on the Main River hinders the collection of cold air pockets.

History: England's Queen Victoria visited Hochheim in 1845. On the tour, she was invited to a wine tasting in the village's "best and most beautiful" vineyard. Five years later, the queen granted permission for the vineyard to be named after her. A monument dedicated to the queen was unveiled in 1854.

LANGENBERG

Martinsthal | Rheingau
VDP.GROSSE LAGE®

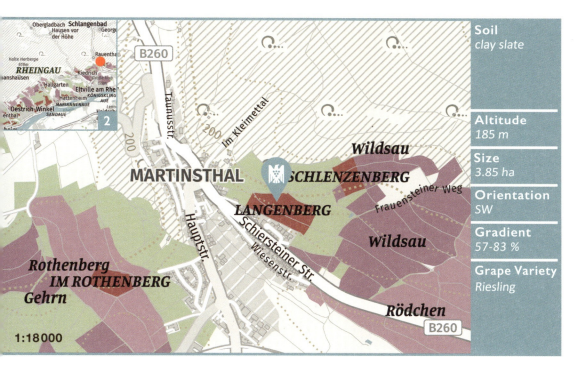

Soil
clay slate

Altitude
185 m

Size
3.85 ha

Orientation
SW

Gradient
57-83 %

Grape Variety
Riesling

VDP.Estates: Diefenhardt

The VDP.GROSSE LAGE® LANGENBERG is located above the village Martinsthal at 185 metres above sea level. The steep 57 to 83 percent slope gradient faces southwest. The unusually deep, nutrient-rich clay slate soils on the steep slope of the Martinsthal Mountain have good water storage capacity. The Riesling vines here also benefit from optimal solar radiation.

LENCHEN

Oestrich-Winkel | Rheingau
VDP.GROSSE LAGE®

Soil
loess loam interspersed w. gravel, heavy tertiary iron-rich cla±y marl, quartzite

Altitude
110-135 m

Size
33.46 ha

Orientation
S/SSW/SW

Gradient
5-20 %

Grape Variety
Riesling

1:19500

VDP.Estates: Fritz Allendorf, August Eser, Peter Jakob Kühn, Georg Müller Stiftung, F. B. Schönleber, Josef Spreitzer, Geheimrat J. Wegeler

The south to southeast facing VDP.GROSSE LAGE® LENCHEN has a gentle 5 to 20 percent slope and lies between 110 and 135 metres above sea level. The soil is predominantly loess loam with gravel. There are also heavier tertiary inclusions of iron-rich clay marl and quartzite. Due to underground aquifers, the GL LENCHEN has good available water capacity even in dry years. The walls that enclose the vineyard store warmth during the day and release it into the Riesling vines at night.

History: There is a few theories where the name of this vineyard originates. Three possibilities are considered. The name could come from "Berglehne", which means "mountain flank". Or it could be the diminutive form of the word "Lehen", which is a fiefdom. Yet another hypothesis is that is an abbreviation of "Landflechterbrunnen". In the year 1920, a Trockenbeerenauslese was harvested with an astounding 303° Oechsle (62 °Brix).

MARCOBRUNN

Erbach | Rheingau
VDP.GROSSE LAGE®

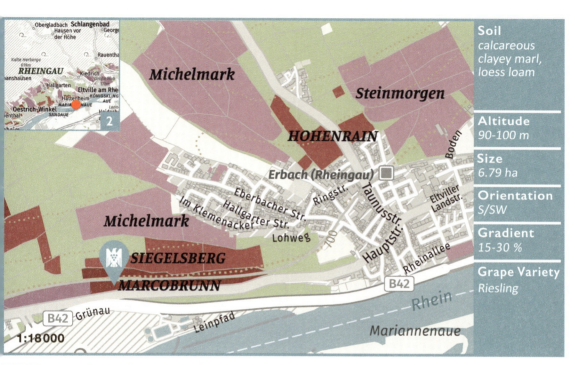

Soil
calcareous clayey marl, loess loam

Altitude
90-100 m

Size
6.79 ha

Orientation
S/SW

Gradient
15-30 %

Grape Variety
Riesling

VDP.Estates: Baron Knyphausen, Hessische Staatsweingüter Kloster Eberbach, von Oetinger

The VDP.GROSSE LAGE® MARCOBRUNN follows 700 metres of the old country road between Erbach and Hattenheim just a small distance away from the Rhine River. The 6.7 hectare vineyard is completely south facing and lies at 90 to 100 metres above sea level The soil is comprised of tertiary marl and deep loess loam with mica content. Parts of the soil are highly calcareous. Subterranean water availability is quite good and vines benefit from this, particularly in hot and dry years.

History: Before the year 1200, this site was referred to as "Markenburne" or "Markenborne". This likely comes from the word "Marka", which meant border. A spring ("Brunnen") is located on the border between Erbach and Hattenheim. When the people of Erbach encased the spring in 1810, they engraved it at the top with "Marcobrunnen Gemarkung Erbach". On the other side, the people of Hattenheim countered with the inscription "So is just and so shall it be. For Erbach the water and for Hattenheim the wine!"

MÄUERCHEN

Geisenheim | Rheingau
VDP.GROSSE LAGE®

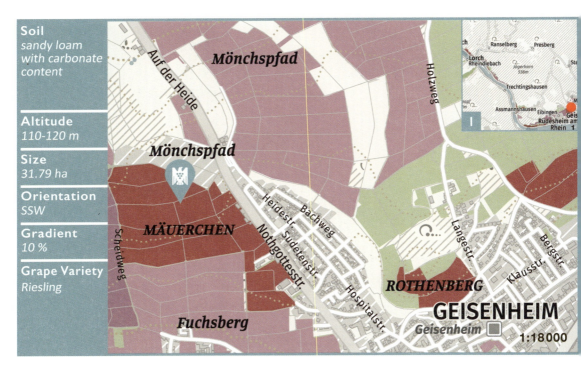

Soil
sandy loam with carbonate content

Altitude
110-120 m

Size
31.79 ha

Orientation
SSW

Gradient
10 %

Grape Variety
Riesling

VDP.Estates: Freimuth

The VDP.GROSSE LAGE® MÄUERCHEN belongs to Geisenheim in the Rheingau. "Mauer" means wall and, as one would assume, the vineyard is indeed surrounded by walls. These walls shield the site from wind and also store warmth. The vineyard has a 10 percent incline that faces southwest between 110 to 120 metres above sea level and is planted with Riesling. The soils are sandy loam with carbonate content and thus fertile and nutrition-rich.

MITTELHÖLLE

Johannisberg | Rheingau
VDP.GROSSE LAGE®

Soil
Taunus quartzite

Altitude
120-170 m

Size
5.75 ha

Orientation
SSW

Gradient
10-30 %

Grape Variety
Riesling

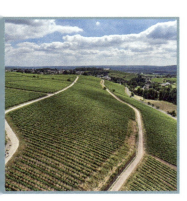

The south to southwest facing VDP.GROSSE LAGE® MITTELHÖLLE lies in a protected side valley of the Elsterbach below the Hansenberg Castle. The 5.75 hectare site is sloped to steep with 10 to 30 percent gradient. The vines, predominantly Riesling, grow on Taunus quartzite and stony-pebbly loess loam with quartzite in the subsoil.

History: Although "Hölle" means "hell" in German, this is probably not, where the name derives from. The name stems from the old German world "Helda", which refers to a steep slope.

NONNBERG FUSSHOL

Wicker | Rheingau
VDP.GROSSE LAGE®

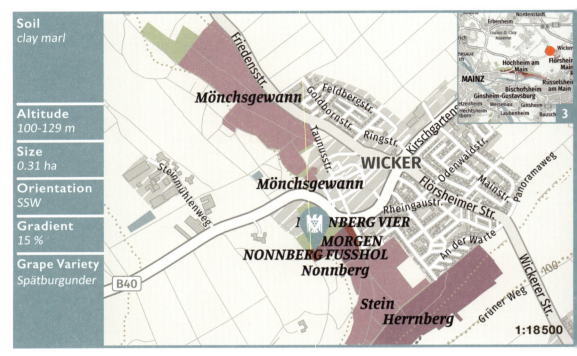

Soil
clay marl

Altitude
100-129 m

Size
0.31 ha

Orientation
SSW

Gradient
15 %

Grape Variety
Spätburgunder

VDP.Estates: **Joachim Flick**

The VDP.ERSTE LAGE® NONNBERG FUSSHOL is located beneath the village of Wicker in the Rheingau. The site has a 15 percent incline that faces south-southwest between 100 and 129 metres above sea level. The clay marl soil is partially interspersed with gravel and has good water availability. A historic quarrystone wall bordering the vineyard stores warmth and protects from winds. Spätburgunder is cultivated here. The GL NONNBERG FUSSHOL is a monopole vineyard that belongs to the VDP.Estate Joachim Flick.

History: The oldest documents that mention this vineyard Nonnberg stem from the year 1281. In these it is documented that the Retter Monastery and the Tiefenthal Cloister exchanged properties. A nun's vineyard (Nonnenweinberg) is described. At the beginning of the 19th century, earth-moving work was undertaken to change this vineyard's aspect toward the south.

NONNBERG VIER MORGEN

Wicker | Rheingau
VDP.GROSSE LAGE®

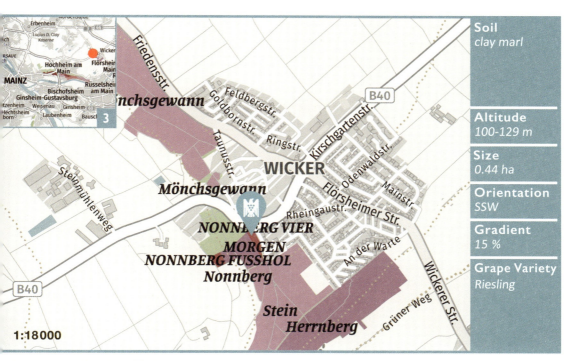

Soil
clay marl

Altitude
100-129 m

Size
0.44 ha

Orientation
SSW

Gradient
15 %

Grape Variety
Riesling

VDP.Estates: Joachim Flick

The VDP.GROSSE LAGE® NONNBERG VIER MORGEN is located beneath the village of Wicker in the Rheingau. The site has a 15 percent incline that faces south-southwest between 100 and 129 metres above sea level. The clay marl soil is partially interspersed with gravel and has good water availability. A historic quarrystone wall bordering the vineyard stores warmth and protects from winds. Riesling is cultivated here. The GL NONNBERG VIER MORGEN is a monopole vineyard that belongs to the VDP.Estate Joachim Flick.

History: The oldest documents that mention this vineyard stem from the year 1281. In these it is documented that the Retter Monastery and the Tiefenthal Cloister exchanged properties. A nun's vineyard (Nonnenweinberg) is described. At the beginning of the 9th century, earth-moving work was undertaken to change this vineyard's aspect toward the south.

NUSSBRUNNEN

Hattenheim | Rheingau
VDP.GROSSE LAGE®

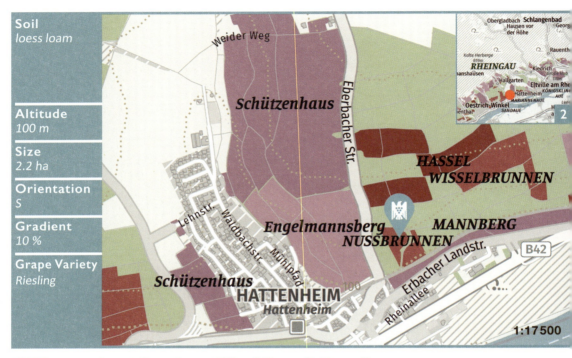

Soil
loess loam

Altitude
100 m

Size
2.2 ha

Orientation
S

Gradient
10 %

Grape Variety
Riesling

VDP.Estates: August Eser, Georg Müller Stiftung, Balthasar Ress

History: The VDP.GROSSE LAGE® NUSSBRUNNEN lies east of Hattenheim above the railroad track that runs through the Rheingau. The 2.2 hectare vineyard lies at around 100 metres above sea level on a gentle southeast facing slope of 10 percent gradient. As the lowest lying of the historic open-filed system parcels, this GL is well protected from the cold north wind and simultaneously benefits from the intensity of the Rhine Valley sun. The soils is sandy loam, light tertiary marl, and deep loess. An impermeable layer in the subsoil guarantees vines access to water, even in hot and dry years. Predominantly Riesling grows in the GL NUSSBRUNNEN.

PFAFFENWIES RÖDER

Lorch | Rheingau
VDP.GROSSE LAGE®

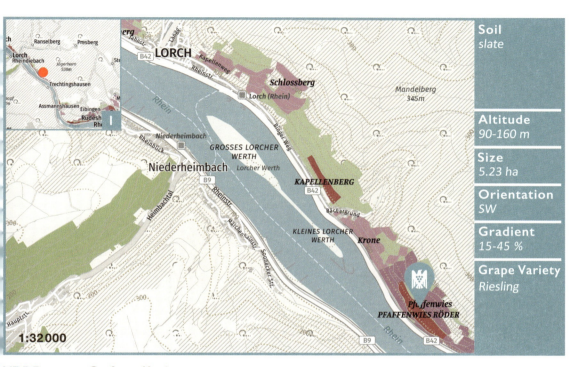

Soil
slate

Altitude
90-160 m

Size
5.23 ha

Orientation
SW

Gradient
15-45 %

Grape Variety
Riesling

VDP.Estates: **Graf von Kanitz**

The VDP.GROSSE LAGE® PFAFFENWIES RÖDER in Lorch enjoys a view of the Rhine River and the Rheinstein Fortress. Rocky slate and quartzite dominate the soil. Riesling is cultivated in this partially steep slope that has up to a 45 percent gradient. The vineyard lies at 90 to 160 metres above sea level. The nearby Rhine River has a temperature and humidity regulating effect on the microclimate of the GL PFAFFENWIES.

History: The vineyard was first mentioned as "Pafenwies" in documents dating 1211. In 1235 it was also referred to as "Paffenwissen". The site was named after Pfarrer (priest) Dydo, son of Knight Nikolaus von Scharfenstein.

REICHESTAL

Hochheim am Main | Rheingau
VDP.GROSSE LAGE®

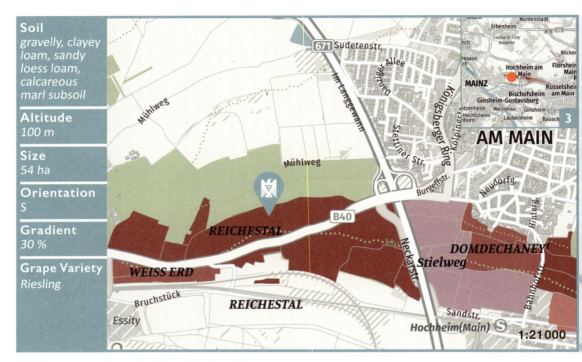

Soil
gravelly, clayey loam, sandy loess loam, calcareous marl subsoil

Altitude
100 m

Size
54 ha

Orientation
S

Gradient
30 %

Grape Variety
Riesling

VDP.Estates: Künstler, Domdechant Werner

The name of the VDP.GROSSE LAGE® REICHESTAL refers to the fertile soil of a valley floor site. The vineyard is situated in Hochheim in Rheingau near the Main River shortly before it empties into the Rhine. A warm microclimate forms here. The GL REICHESTAL has a slope gradient of 30 percent and lies at approximately 100 metres above sea level. Loess loam dominates the soil, which is sandy, gravelly and found over a basement of calcareous marl. Because the soils are quite loose, the vines can root deeply and find abundant minerals and nutrients. The soils have good moisture availability and warm quickly permitting Riesling to flower early ripen long into the autumn.

RÖDCHEN

Martinsthal | Rheingau
VDP.GROSSE LAGE®

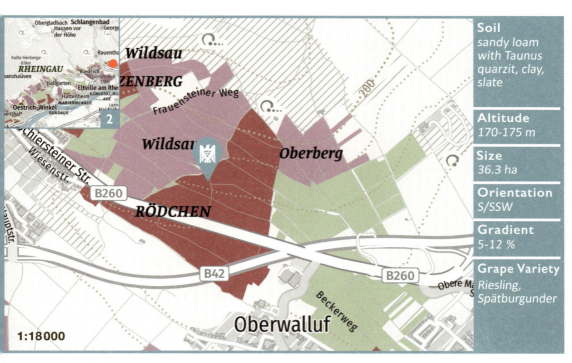

Soil
sandy loam with Taunus quarzit, clay, slate

Altitude
170-175 m

Size
36.3 ha

Orientation
S/SSW

Gradient
5-12 %

Grape Variety
Riesling, Spätburgunder

VDP.Estates: Diefenhardt

The VDP.GROSSE LAGE® RÖDCHEN is classified for Riesling and Spätburgunder. The clay slate and sandy loam with Taunus quartzite allow vines to thrust their roots deep and find abundant nutrition. The GL RÖDCHEN lies at 170 to 175 metres above sea level and has a slope gradient of 5 to 12 percent.

History: Two clues to the origin of this vineyard's name exist. To begin with, the site was created by clearing a fallow forest and overgrown field ("roden" means to clear). Secondly, its cadastre number belonged to the Rode Cloister and the eponymous village that was later renamed "Martinsthal".

ROSENGARTEN

Oestrich-Winkel | Rheingau
VDP.GROSSE LAGE®

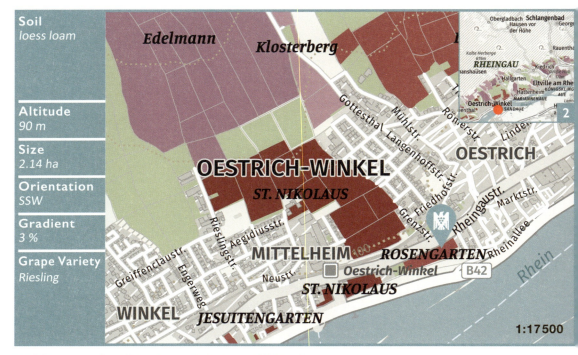

Soil
loess loam

Altitude
90 m

Size
2.14 ha

Orientation
SSW

Gradient
3 %

Grape Variety
Riesling

VDP.Estates: Josef Spreitzer, Geheimrat J. Wegeler

Numerous stone walls that retain warmth cross the VDP.GROSSE LAGE® ROSENGARTEN. The site borders Oestrich to the east, close to the Rhine River. The flat south slope is 2.1 hectares in size situated at 90 metres above sea level. The soils are comprised primarily of loess loam, pebbly and very sandy loam with a high share of carbon and terraced sediment.

History: As the name leads one to believe, there was once a rose garden here. In the German wine law reform of 1971, the historic open-field system land parcel called "Oestricher Rosengarten" disappeared and was changed to "Oestricher Lenchen". Since 2014, this prime vineyard once again carries its historic name ROSENGARTEN.

ROSENGARTEN

Rüdesheim | Rheingau
VDP.GROSSE LAGE®

Soil
very gravelly and sandy loam, terrace sediments

Altitude
93 m

Size
1.22 ha

Orientation
S

Gradient
0 %

Grape Variety
Riesling

VDP.Estates: Leitz

The small 1.22 hectare VDP.GROSSE LAGE® ROSENGARTEN is located in Rüdesheim in the Rheingau directly on the Rhine River at 93 metres above sea level. Riesling is cultivated on very gravelly, sandy loam and terrace sediment in a flat site. This soil formation is advantageous for water drainage. Historic quartzite walls enclose the GL ROSENGARTEN.

History: The GL ROSENGARTEN gets its name from the adjacent Brömserburg castle garden. Built in 1044, it is one of the oldest castles in the region.

ROTHENBERG

Geisenheim | Rheingau
VDP.GROSSE LAGE®

Soil
eroded Taunus quartzite with loess deposits

Altitude
135-145 m

Size
5.43 ha

Orientation
S/SE

Gradient
15-44 %

Grape Variety
Riesling

VDP.Estates: Hochschule Geisenheim University, Geheimrat J. Wegeler

The VDP.GROSSE LAGE® ROTHENBERG is a steeper site that drops at an up to 44 percent gradient down to the first buildings of Geisenheim. The 5 hectares face due south at 135 to 145 meters above sea level. The soils are eroded Taunus quartzite with loess deposits. The soil has good available water capacity.

History: "Roth" is an old German spelling for "red" and "berg" means "mountain". The vineyards was first mentioned in written documents in 1145. In the world's oldest vineyard classification map, which dates 1867, the site is given superior Class I status, equal to Rüdesheimer Berglagen, Schloss Johannisberg, Steinberg, Marcobrunn and Gräfenberg.

SCHLENZENBERG

Martinsthal | Rheingau
VDP.GROSSE LAGE®

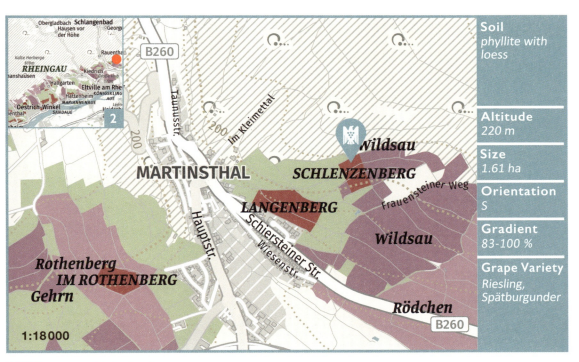

Soil
phyllite with loess

Altitude
220 m

Size
1.61 ha

Orientation
S

Gradient
83-100 %

Grape Variety
Riesling, Spätburgunder

VDP.Estates: Diefenhardt

The VDP.GROSSE LAGE® SCHLENZENBERG encompasses 1.6 hectares of classified area. It is located in the steep slope section of the Martinsthaler Wildsau vineyard and faces south. The slope has a gradient of up to 100 percent (45°). Mineral-rich phyllite slate and clay slate dominate the soil. Riesling and Spätburgunder are cultivated in the GL SCHLENZENBERG. It is a monopole vineyard of the VDP.Estate Diefenhardt.

SCHLOSS JOHANNISBERG

Johannisberg | Rheingau
VDP.GROSSE LAGE®

Soil
loess loam over quartzite

Altitude
110-180 m

Size
17.85 ha

Orientation
SE-S-SW

Gradient
0-40 %

Grape Variety
Riesling

VDP.Estates: Domäne Schloss Johannisberg

The VDP.GROSSE LAGE® SCHLOSS JOHANNISBERG surrounds the famous Schloss Johannisberg. A thick forest belt to the north protects the site from cold winds. The broad, lake-like Rhine to the south reflects and intensifies light in the 18-hectare south-west to south-east facing slope. With a yearly average of 1,700 hours of sunshine, the GL SCHLOSS JOHANNISBERG has the highest solar radiation of all vineyards in the Rheingau. The site has a steeper 40 percent gradient and lies between 110 and 180 metres above sea level. The soil is pure Taunus quartzite covered with a medium to deep layer of loess loam that has good warmth and water storage capacity.

History: The vineyard was already called "monte sancti Johannis" in documents dating 1143. Exclusively Riesling has been cultivated here since 1720, making it the world's first contiguous vineyard that is planted with this noble variety.

SCHLOSSBERG

Schloss Vollrads | Rheingau
VDP.GROSSE LAGE®

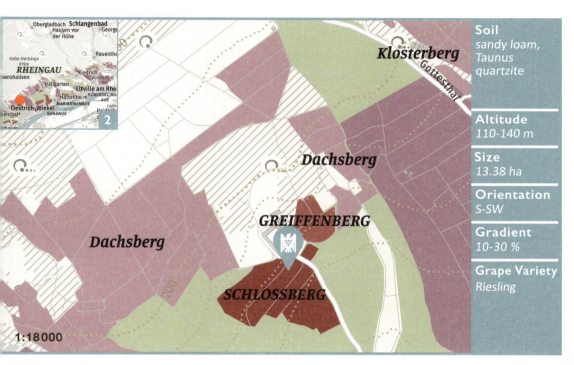

Soil
sandy loam, Taunus quartzite

Altitude
110-140 m

Size
13.38 ha

Orientation
S-SW

Gradient
10-30 %

Grape Variety
Riesling

VDP.Estates: Schloss Vollrads

The VDP.GROSSE LAGE SCHLOSSBERG is a parcel within the Schloss Vollrads vineyard and is a monopole site. It is located below the castle and above the Rhine River. The castle forests shield the site from cold north winds. The site faces south to southwest at 110 to 140 metres above sea level. Vines root in sandy loam and Taunus quartzite – soils that provide well-balanced water availability.
Information: Schloss Vollrads is one of the oldest wine estates in the world.

SCHÖNHELL

Hallgarten | Rheingau
VDP.GROSSE LAGE®

Soil
loess loam, sandy gravel

Altitude
170-200 m

Size
6.34 ha

Orientation
S-SSW

Gradient
10-20 %

Grape Variety
Riesling

VDP.Estates: Fritz Allendorf, Prinz, Barth, August Eser, Hamm, Kaufmann, Krone Assmannshausen, Peter Jakob Kühn, Fürst Löwenstein, Josef Spreitzer, Geheimrat J. Wegele

The VDP.GROSSE LAGE® SCHÖNHELL is located in Hallgarten in the Rheingau at 170 to 200 metres above sea level. The 10 to 20 percent slope faces south to south-southwest toward the Rhine River. Riesling is cultivated here on fertile soils with good available water capacity. The soils are comprised of loess loam, clay and sandy gravel. The forest of the Hallgarten Zange Mountain to the north shields the GL SCHÖNHELL from cold weather.

History: The name of the GL SCHÖNHELL stems from the 14th century. It means "schöne Halde", which translates to "beautiful slope".

SELIGMACHER

Lorchhausen | Rheingau
VDP.GROSSE LAGE®

Soil	slate
Altitude	160 m
Size	15.95 ha
Orientation	SSW
Gradient	100-145 %
Grape Variety	Riesling

VDP.Estates: August Kesseler

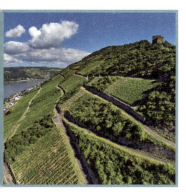

The VDP.GROSSE LAGE® SELIGMACHER is the most northern VDP. Vineyard in the Rheingau wine region. It is located shortly before Lorchhausen in a narrow valley of the lower Rheingau directly bordering the Mittelrhein wine region. The well-drained slate soils force vines to root deep to find sufficient water reserves. The 16-hectare site has a very steep 100 to 145 percent (45-55°) slope gradient, which makes it one of the steepest vineyards in the Rheingau. It faces south-southwest and collects abundant solar radiation during the day. The slate warms easily and the proximity to the Rhine River provides climate moderating influences. The GL SELIGMACHER lies at 160 metres above sea level.

SIEGELSBERG

Erbach | Rheingau
VDP.GROSSE LAGE®

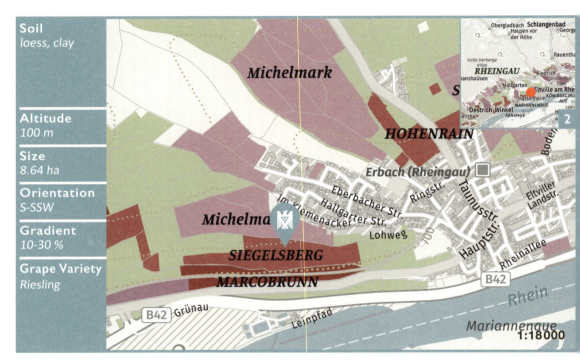

Soil
loess, clay

Altitude
100 m

Size
8.64 ha

Orientation
S-SSW

Gradient
10-30 %

Grape Variety
Riesling

VDP.Estates: August Eser, Jakob Jung, Baron Knyphausen, Georg Müller Stiftung, Hessische Staatsweingüter Kloster Eberbach, von Oetinger

The VDP.GROSSE LAGE® SIEGELSBERG is a south to south-southwest facing slope with a 10 to 30 percent gradient located in Erbach in the Rheingau. Riesling is cultivated here at 100 metres above sea level on clay covered with a layer of loess loam with a high share of fine-grained earth. The vineyard benefits from optimal solar radiation and is shielded from the wind, which leads to early flowering and ripening. The soil type makes both good water drainage and storage of moisture possible.

ST. NIKOLAUS

Oestrich-Winkel | Rheingau
VDP.GROSSE LAGE®

Soil
calcareous loess loam with gravel, sandy loess

Altitude
90-110 m

Size
28.51 ha

Orientation
ESE/S/SSW

Gradient
5-12 %

Grape Variety
Riesling, Spätburgunder

VDP.Estates: Fritz Allendorf, August Eser, Peter Jakob Kühn, F.B. Schönleber, Josef Spreitzer, Geheimrat J. Wegeler

The VDP.GROSSE LAGE® ST. NIKOLAUS runs right through the Rheingau village Mittelheim, from the bank of the Rhine River all the way up to the edge of the VDP.ERSTE LAGE® Mittelheimer Edelmann and the Oestricher Klosterberg. The vineyard turns from east-southeast to south to south-southwest with some parcels benefiting more from the morning sun and others from the sun in the afternoon. The proximity to the Rhine River provides warmth and inhibits harsh winter and spring frosts. The GL ST. NIKOLAUS is rather flat at a 5 to 12 percent gradient but climbs from 90 to 110 metres above sea level. Deep calcareous loess loam with gravel intercalations, sandy loess, alluvial sediments and quartz pebbles determine the soil composition.

Information: The name of this vineyard comes from the old sandstone statue of Saint Nikolaus that stands at the upper end of the site.

STEINBERGER

Hattenheim | Rheingau
VDP.GROSSE LAGE®

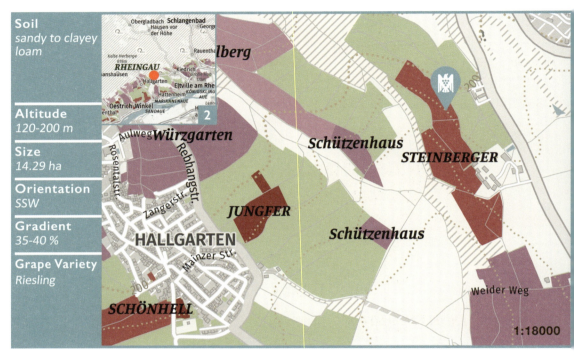

Soil
sandy to clayey loam

Altitude
120-200 m

Size
14.29 ha

Orientation
SSW

Gradient
35-40 %

Grape Variety
Riesling

VDP.Estates: Hessische Staatsweingüter Kloster Eberbach

The VDP.GROSSE LAGE® STEINBERGER is surrounded with stone walls that are up to five metres high and border Kloster Eberbach. The walls once served to protect the vineyard from grape thieves, but they also shield from cold air from the neighbouring forest. The vineyard lies at 120 to 200 metres above sea level and has a steepness of 35 to 40 percent. The soils are comprised of sandy and clayey loam. THE GL STEINBERGER is a monopole vineyard that belongs to the Hessische Staatsweingüter.

History: The vineyard can be traced back to the Cistercian monks that once dwelled in Kloster Eberbach. It was recorded in the estate records from 1211 as "Oculus Memorie". The wine laws of 1971 register "Steinberg" as a village of Hattenheim and thus Hattenheim does not additionally appear on the label.

UNTERER BISCHOFSBERG

Rüdesheim | Rheingau
VDP.GROSSE LAGE®

Soil
Taunus quartzite, loess loam topsoil

Altitude
135 m

Size
3.86 ha

Orientation
SE

Gradient
5-10 %

Grape Variety
Riesling

1:18000

VDP.Estates: Freimuth, Hessische Staatsweingüter Kloster Eberbach

The VDP.GROSSE LAGE® UNTERER BISCHOFSBERG continues the vine rows of the GL BERG ROTTLAND to the city limits of Rüdesheim. With only a 5 to 10 percent gradient, it is a rather flat site for Rüdesheimer Berg. Taunus quartzite with a layer of loess loam determines the soil of this gentle incline that faces southeast toward the Rhine River and Rüdesheim. The vineyard lies at 135 metres above sea level.

WALKENBERG

Walluf | Rheingau
VDP.GROSSE LAGE®

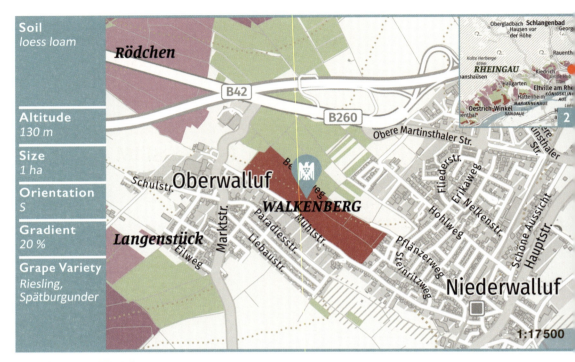

Soil
loess loam

Altitude
130 m

Size
1 ha

Orientation
S

Gradient
20 %

Grape Variety
Riesling, Spätburgunder

VDP.Estates: Toni Jost

The VDP.GROSSE LAGE® WALKENBERG is located in the village Walluf in the Rheingau. The vineyard lies on the south slope of a Taunus foothill at 130 metres above sea level where it is shielded from cold north winds. It has a gentle 20 percent slope gradient. Loess loam over and gravel with high fine-grained earth content dominates the soil. The southern exposure provides optimal solar radiation. Proximity to the Rhine River also contributes to an advantageous microclimate, because temperature extremes in summer and winter are moderated by the water's surface. The GL WALKENBERG is classified for Riesling and Spätburgunder.

History: At the foot of the vineyard is a historic textile mill where felt was produced by matting, condensing and pressing – a process that is called "walken" in German.

WEISS ERD

Kostheim | Rheingau
VDP.GROSSE LAGE®

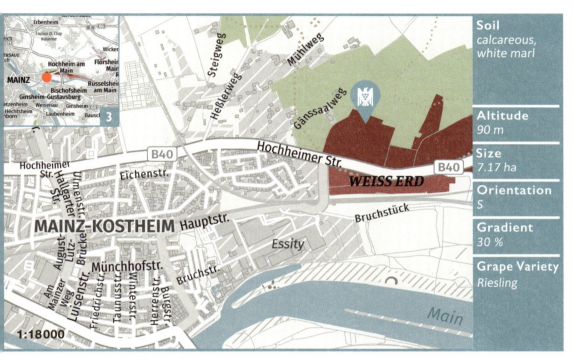

Soil
calcareous, white marl

Altitude
90 m

Size
7.17 ha

Orientation
S

Gradient
30 %

Grape Variety
Riesling

VDP.Estates: Künstler

The name of the VDP.GROSSE LAGE® WEISS ERD can be translated to "white earth", which is well suited because the soil indeed comprises calcareous, white marl that appears particularly white in the dry summer months. The GL is situated east of Kostheim above the Main River only a few kilometres from the mouth of the Rhine River. The vines thus enjoy the warm, moderate climate of the Rhine Plain. At the same time, cool air masses from the Taunus Mountain provide cool nights. The 7-hectare GL WEISS ERD stretches long and faces south at a 30 percent slope gradient.

WISSELBRUNNEN

Hattenheim | Rheingau
VDP.GROSSE LAGE®

Soil
loess loam, marl

Altitude
70-100 m

Size
5.91 ha

Orientation
S

Gradient
10 %

Grape Variety
Riesling

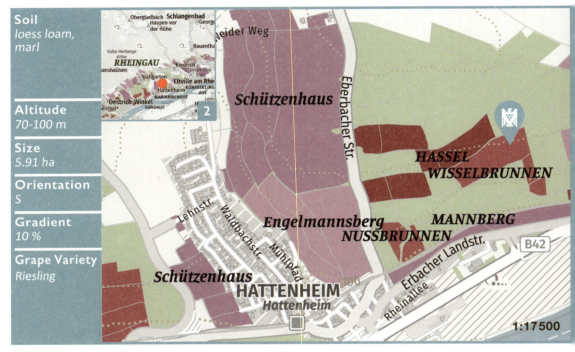

VDP.Estates: Barth, August Eser, Kaufmann, Baron Knyphausen, Georg Müller Stiftung, Balthasar Ress, Josef Spreitzer

The VDP.GROSSE LAGE® WISSELBRUNNEN lies along the train route between Eltville and Hattenheim and benefits from the sunlight reflected from the broad Rhine River just a few metres away. The almost 6-hectare southwest slope lies at 100 metres above sea level. Predominantly Riesling grows on the medium heavy, tertiary marl and deep calcareous loam. The soil is warm and well-drained, yet still retains enough moisture to nourish the vines. The site is quite flat at 10 percent gradient.

See You!

THE WORLD'S NO.1:

INTERNATIONAL TRADE FAIR
FOR WINES AND SPIRITS

Düsseldorf, Germany   www.prowein.com

Messe Düsseldorf GmbH
P.O. Box 10 10 06 _ 40001 Düsseldorf _ Germany
Tel. +49 211 4560-01 _ Fax +49 211 4560-668
www.messe-duesseldorf.de

Region:	VDP.GROSSE LAGE®:
26 600 ha	410 ha
VDP.Wineries:	VDP.GROSSE LAGE® Sites:
16	37

RHEINHESSEN

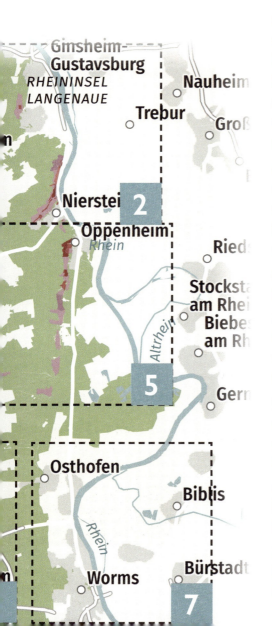

The Rheinhessen wine region covers a large triangle on the left side of the Rhine River between Bingen and Mainz in the north and Worms in the south. It is among the largest and most historic of the German wine regions. The Romans cultivated wine here and the oldest documentation of German vineyards mentions a site in Rheinhessen, the "Glöck" in Nierstein. Sources from 1402 mention "Rüssling" (Riesling) as the grape variety for the first time in Worms. Due to its geographic location, topography, the Donnersberg as a protective shield to the west, proximity to the Rhine River, and a geological mixture of rock and fertile loam and loess soils, Rheinhessen possesses abundant resources for high-quality viticulture. Often called "the land of one thousand hills", Rheinhessen has over 1600 hours of sunshine and only 550 mm precipitation annually, making it one of the driest regions in Germany.

AULERDE

Westhofen | Rheinhessen
VDP.GROSSE LAGE®

Soil
clay marl and weathered limestone loam, loess deposit over

Altitude
90-100 m

Size
8.38 ha

Orientation
S

Gradient
10-15 %

Grape Variety
Riesling

VDP.Estates: K. F. Groebe, Wittmann

The VDP.GROSSE LAGE® AULERDE is usually the warmest site in Westhofen where grapes ripen the earliest. It is protected in the west by the Kirchspiel slope. The three parcels that are classified as the GL AULERDE comprise four hectares. The vineyard rises at a 10 to 15 percent gradient from the Upper Rhine Plain to 100 metres above sea level. Clayey marl with a small share of loess-loam and limestone dominate the soils of the GL AULERDE. Yellow clayey sand and gravelly sand comprise the subsoil. Riesling is the predominant variety in the AULERDE vineyard.

History: First mentioned in documents dating 1380.

BRUDERSBERG

Nierstein | Rheinhessen
VDP.GROSSE LAGE®

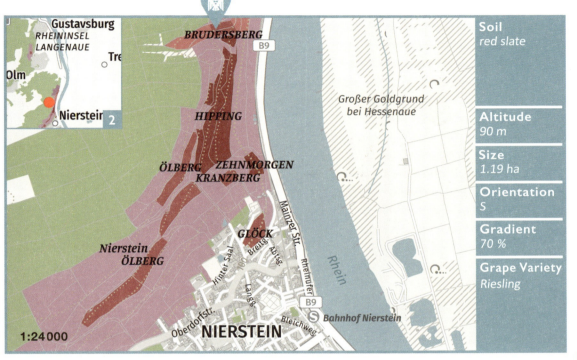

Soil
red slate

Altitude
90 m

Size
1.19 ha

Orientation
S

Gradient
70 %

Grape Variety
Riesling

VDP.Estates: St. Antony

The VDP.GROSSE LAGE® BRUDERSBERG is a small, special exception on the Roter Hang. Contrary to all of the other sites located directly on the Rhine River, this vineyard does not face toward the east, but toward the south. The 1.2-hectare BRUDERSBERG is protected from the north wind in a little side valley of the Roter Hang. The soil is red, clayey slate with iron oxide, the famous red soil that dominates the slope that faces east toward the Rhine River and stretches from Nackenheim in the north to Nierstein in the south and gives the Roter Hang its name. With a slope of 70 percent, the BRUDERSBERG GL is quite steep. The steep, south aspect of the slope and the light reflected from the Rhine amplify the solar radiation in this vineyard.

History: The name goes back to the family of the Court of Haxthäuser, whose four brothers shared ownership from 1804 to 1835.

BRUNNENHÄUSCHEN

Westhofen | Rheinhessen
VDP.GROSSE LAGE®

Soil
clay marl with abundant limest., soil part. red due to high iron content

Altitude
180-240 m

Size
13.05 ha

Orientation
S

Gradient
20 %

Grape Variety
Riesling, Spätburgunder

VDP.Estates: Gutzler, Keller, Wittmann

The greater share of vines of the VDP.GROSSE LAGE® BRUNNENHÄUSCHEN are located in the parcel historically called "Abtserde". The Abtserde was a separate vineyard, the very best parcel of the Brunnenhäuschen vineyard located on the lower border of the site, until the new wine laws of 1971. The BRUNNENHÄUSCHEN GL borders directly on the MORSTEIN GL and faces south. The climate is rather cool due to the west winds that waft through the site, contributing to a prolonged vegetation period with later ripening of fruit. Clayey marl with limestone pebbles and limestone rock comprise soils that provide good water availability even in dry periods. Due to high iron oxide content, the soils are reddish and often called "Terra Rossa". Riesling and Spätburgunder are the main varieties grown in the BRUNNENHÄUSCHEN GL.

History: The location was documented in 1721 by the name of "am brunnenhäuschen", which is based on a spring which is connected to a water reservoir.

BÜRGEL

Flörsheim-Dalsheim | Rheinhessen
VDP.GROSSE LAGE®

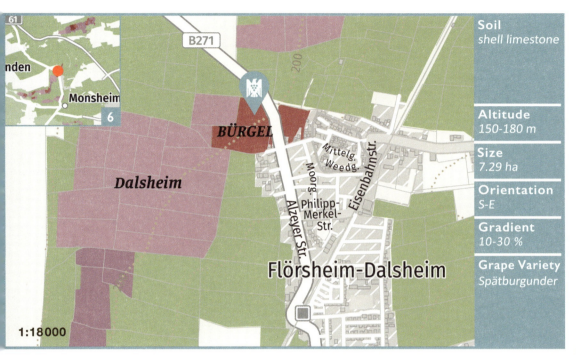

Soil
shell limestone

Altitude
150-180 m

Size
7.29 ha

Orientation
S-E

Gradient
10-30 %

Grape Variety
Spätburgunder

VDP.Estates: Keller

The soil of VDP.GROSSE LAGE® BÜRGEL is marked by the ochre yellow Terra Fusca limestone, but the parcel in question here is predominantly shell limestone. The BÜRGEL GL is only a small area of the eponymous vineyard located northwest of Flörsheim-Dalsheim. The VDP.GROSSE LAGE® has a south to east aspect and lies between 150 and 180 metres above sea level. The soil forms fissures as it dries, which aid aeration and drainage. The high lime content benefits the balance of acidity in the wines. The predominant variety cultivated is Spätburgunder.

History: The location was mentioned in 1286 with the name "retro montem" and 1358 with the name "uf dem berge". These layer names are a derivation to mountains.

BURGWEG

Bodenheim | Rheinhessen
VDP.GROSSE LAGE®

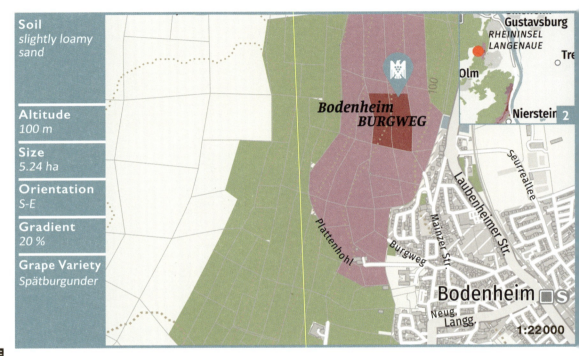

Soil
slightly loamy sand

Altitude
100 m

Size
5.24 ha

Orientation
S-E

Gradient
20 %

Grape Variety
Spätburgunder

VDP.Estates: Kühling-Gillot

The VDP.GROSSE LAGE® BURGWEG is situated north of Bodenheim at an altitude of 100 metres above sea level and has an south to east aspect. Ice age loess and sandy as well as clayey loam comprise the soils in which predominantly Spätburgunder grows. This is also due to the fact that small protective swales have formed at the foot of the slope that are advantageous for Spätburgunder. The slope gradient ranges 20 percent. The VDP.GROSSE LAGE® BURGWEG is a small parcel in the upper centre of the Burgweg vineyard.

History: The first documented mention of the site stems from the year 1364 where it was called "Uf dem Burgwege". It is likely that this was a way for writing "on the mountain paths".

FALKENBERG

Dienheim | Rheinhessen
VDP.GROSSE LAGE®

Soil
calcareous marl

Altitude
140-160 m

Size
2.82 ha

Orientation
E

Gradient
30 %

Grape Variety
Riesling

VDP.Estates: **Brüder Dr. Becker**

The VDP. GROSSE LAGE® FALKENBERG encompasses three parcels in the upper area of the Falkenberg vineyard. It has an east aspect and thus enjoys sunshine from early morning until midday. A neighbouring hill protects the site from cold west winds allowing warmth to collect in the vineyards. The Riesling here roots in deep loess banks and the share of calcareaus marl lend good storage capacity. The parcels of the FALKENBERG GL lay between 140 and 160 metres above sea level and are slightly sloped to steep.

History: The name refers to ownership by the Dukes of Falkenstein.

FRAUENBERG

Nieder-Flörsheim | Rheinhessen
VDP.GROSSE LAGE®

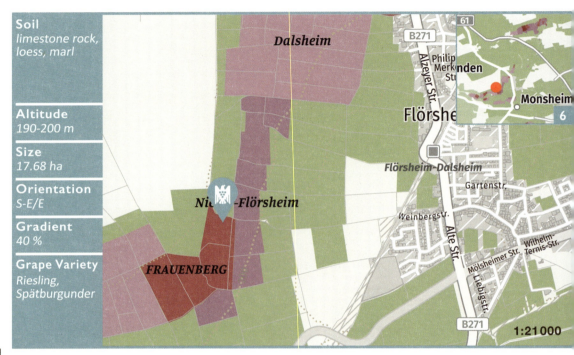

Soil
limestone rock, loess, marl

Altitude
190-200 m

Size
17.68 ha

Orientation
S-E/E

Gradient
40 %

Grape Variety
Riesling, Spätburgunder

VDP.Estates: Battenfeld Spanier, Keller

The VDP.GROSSE LAGE® FRAUENBERG slopes towards Niederflörsheim at a gradient of 40 percent. The vineyard lies between 190 and 200 metres above sea level. The soils include loess, marl, limestone and stony and clayey loam. A unique microclimate is created by the interchange between the warm south to southeast exposition and the cool winds, which benefit a long ripening period. The VDP.GROSSE LAGE® is situated in the upper, steeper parcels of the otherwise relatively flat Frauenberg vineyard.

History: The site was documented 1290 under the name "an frauwenhalten". The vineyard was originally owned by a nuns' convent.

GEIERSBERG

Dittelsheim | Rheinhessen
VDP.GROSSE LAGE®

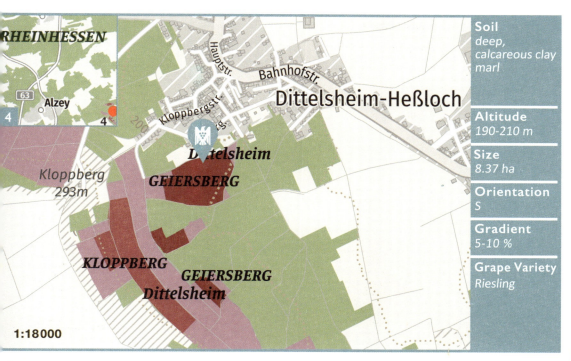

Soil	deep, calcareous clay marl
Altitude	190-210 m
Size	8.37 ha
Orientation	S
Gradient	5-10 %
Grape Variety	Riesling

VDP.Estates: **Winter**

The 8.3-hectare VDP.GROSSE LAGE® GEIERSBERG lies within the significantly larger Geiersberg vineyard. It is the gently sloping foot of the Kloppberg at a 5 to 10 percent gradient. The GEIERSBERG GL lies between 190 and 210 meters above sea level. The vines grow in deep calcareous clay marl. The predominant varieties are Riesling and Spätburgunder.

History: Birds of prey were called "Geier" in the middle ages. The site is named for the presence of raptors here.

GLÖCK

Nierstein | Rheinhessen
VDP.GROSSE LAGE®

Soil
light loess loam

Altitude
80 m

Size
1.96 ha

Orientation
S-SE

Gradient
30 %

Grape Variety
Riesling, Spätburgunder

VDP.Estates: Staatliche Weinbaudomäne Oppenheim

The VDP.GROSSE LAGE® GLÖCK is located on the south end of the Roter Hang in a south to southeast exposition. The 2-hectare vineyard is not significantly marked by the typical red clayey slate of the region, but rather by light loess loam soils and sandy, clayey loam. It lies on 80 metres above sea level and has a moderate slope of 30 percent. The GLÖCK GL nears the Rhine River in the east, which enhances solar radiation through reflection from the water. In addition to this it is nestled in the slope and protected from wind. The old walls that surround the site store warmth, which benefits the vines. The GLÖCK GL is planted mostly with Riesling.

History: The GLÖCK GL is among the oldest vineyards in Germany. The site was first mentioned in a deed of donation in the year 742. It was likely named after the bell of the mountain chapel St. Killian that lies on the hill top.

HEERKRETZ

Siefersheim | Rheinhessen
VDP.GROSSE LAGE®

Soil
rhyolite

Altitude
180-280 m

Size
17.26 ha

Orientation
SE-SW

Gradient
30-80 %

Grape Variety
Riesling

VDP.Estates: Wagner-Stempel

The VDP.GROSSE LAGE® HEERKRETZ is among the most highly elevated sites of Rheinhessen. The vineyard slopes toward the southwest and southeast at 180 to 280 metres above sea level and a gradient of 30 to 80 percent. The HEERKRETZ GL is quite craggy and possesses several convex swales and wind-exposed slope parcels. The site is completely exposed to the Appelbach Valley weather to the southwest. The soil structure is dominated by rhyolite and parts of the slope exhibit melaphyric rock and limestone bands. The HEERKRETZ GL is planted predominantly with Riesling.

History: The name comes from "Kratzen" (to scratch) and highlights the difficult labour required in the vineyards. "Heer" (army) points to the old soldier road in the valley at the foot of the vineyard.

HERRENBERG

Oppenheim | Rheinhessen
VDP.GROSSE LAGE®

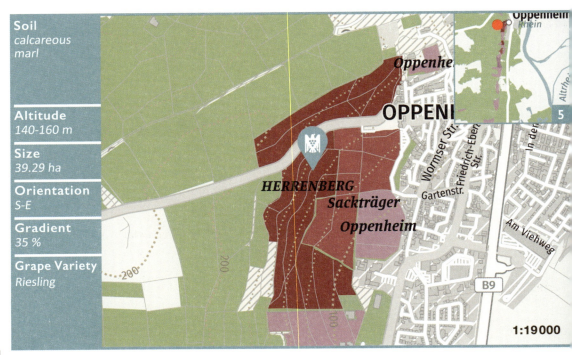

Soil
calcareous marl

Altitude
140-160 m

Size
39.29 ha

Orientation
S-E

Gradient
35 %

Grape Variety
Riesling

VDP.Estates: Rappenhof, Staatliche Weinbaudomäne Oppenheim

The VDP.GROSSE LAGE® HERRENBERG is located slightly above Oppenheim on the side of the village that looks away from the Rhine. The sun's full potential comes into play in this wind-protected site with an east to south aspect. The vines, predominantly Riesling, grow in calcareous marl with relatively high clay content. The HERRENBERG GL rises from 140 to 160 metres above sea level with a moderate slope gradient of 35 percent.

History: The name is based on the possession of a spiritual or temporal lord. It is assumed that these were the lords of Dalberg.

HIPPING

Nierstein | Rheinhessen
VDP.GROSSE LAGE®

Soil
red slate

Altitude
80-174 m

Size
12.28 ha

Orientation
E/SE

Gradient
60-120 %

Grape Variety
Riesling

VDP.Estates: Gunderloch, Keller, Kühling-Gillot, Schätzel, St. Antony

The VDP.GROSSE LAGE® HIPPING is located on an exposed section of the Roter Hang between Nierstein and Nackenheim at an altitude of 80 to 174 metres above sea level. The steep site has a 60 to 120 percent slope that descends towards the Rhine (which is quite wide in this section) with a southeast exposition. The VDP.GROSSE LAGE® is located in the upper part of Rotliegendes (red weathered clayey slate). The lake-like broadening of the Rhine, the intense morning sun, and the highly weathered red slate strongly influence the microclimate. Predominantly Riesling grows in the HIPPING GL.

History: The HIPPING was called "Hupbuhl" in 1550. It is assumed that this was a hill where goats grazed as "Hippe" means goat in Middle High German and "Buhl" is a hill.

HÖLLBERG

Siefersheim | Rheinhessen
VDP.GROSSE LAGE®

Soil
rhyolite

Altitude
150-220 m

Size
7.31 ha

Orientation
SE-S

Gradient
20-50 %

Grape Variety
Riesling

VDP.Estates: **Wagner-Stempel**

The Siefersheimer Horn protects the VDP.GROSSE LAGE® HÖLLBERG from the wind from the west. The site is located on a forested slope north of Siefersheim at 150 to 220 metres above sea level. The HÖLLBERG GL covers until 50 percent slope gradient and has a southeast to south exposition. The soils are comprised of Rhyolite and are planted predominantly with Riesling.

History: The location was mentioned in 1532 by the name "in der helle". Hell denotes a slight slope. This name is very common in West central Germany.

HORN

Ingelheim | Rheinhessen
VDP.GROSSE LAGE®

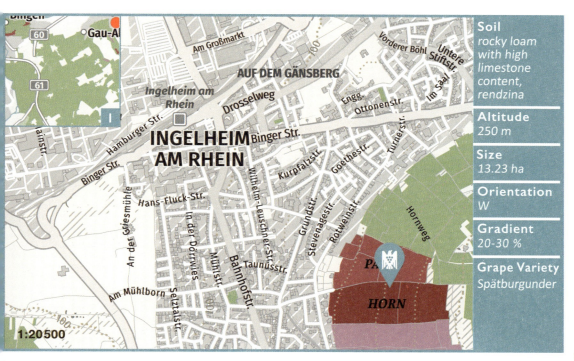

Soil
rocky loam with high limestone content, rendzina

Altitude
250 m

Size
13.23 ha

Orientation
W

Gradient
20-30 %

Grape Variety
Spätburgunder

VDP.Estates: J. Neus

Two VDP.GROSSE LAGE® are located adjacent to one another at the foot of the Mainzer Berg, the PARES GL and the significantly larger HORN GL. The west facing slopes rise visibly above the town of Ober-Ingelheim. The 13 hectares of rocky loam with high limestone content stretch from 250 metres above sea level. As it is the tradition in Ingelheim, Spätburgunder is the predominant grape variety. The climate is characterized by the foothills of the Taunus- and Hunsrück protected Rhine Valley.

History: The location was first mentioned in 1570 by the name "am Horn". Horn is a common name in Rheinhessen for the protruding mountains.

HUBACKER

Flörsheim-Dalsheim | Rheinhessen
VDP.GROSSE LAGE®

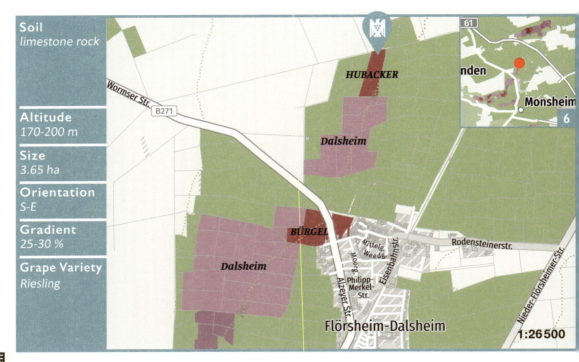

Soil
limestone rock

Altitude
170-200 m

Size
3.65 ha

Orientation
S-E

Gradient
25-30 %

Grape Variety
Riesling

VDP.Estates: **Keller**

Located within the Hubacker vineyard, the VDP.GROSSE LAGE® HUBACKER comprises predominantly the southeast exposed "Oberer Hubacker" parcel. The site lies in the wind-protected rain shadow of the Donnersberg at 170 bis 200 metres above sea level. The vines grow on limestone blocks interspersed with loam and slightly stony loamy clay. Hugh Johnson describes the site as "an unspectacular hill with perfect soil and climate conditions". The main variety is Riesling.

History: The vineyard name can be traced back to the Dalsheim ledger of 1490 that reports of five "Huffe", later called "Hube", which was a measure of land area. "Acker" is an agricultural field.

KIRCHBERG

Bingen | Rheinhessen
VDP.GROSSE LAGE®

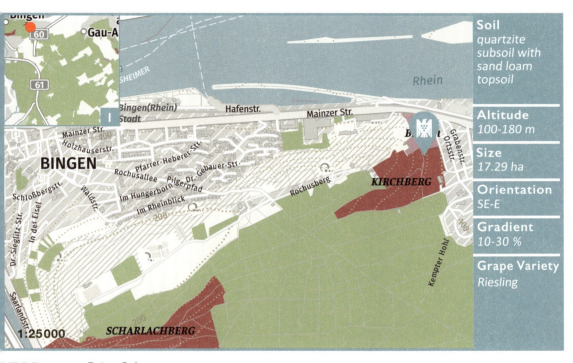

Soil
quartzite subsoil with sand loam topsoil

Altitude
100-180 m

Size
17.29 ha

Orientation
SE-E

Gradient
10-30 %

Grape Variety
Riesling

VDP.Estates: Prinz Salm

The VDP.GROSSE LAGE® KIRCHBERG is located below the Chapel of St. Rochus in Bingen. It has a southeast to east exposition and lies at 100 to 180 metres above sea level. The VDP.GROSSE LAGE® singles out the parcels of the Kirchberg vineyard that drop north and northeast toward the Rhine River and Rheingau. The weathered rock is planted primarily with Riesling. The climate is dry and windy, particularly in the upper area. The vineyard slopes at 10 to 30 percent.

History: The first documentation of the site "im Kirchberg" stems from the year 1726. The responsible church was probably the neighbouring Kempten parish church.

KIRCHENSTÜCK

Hohen-Sülzen | Rheinhessen
VDP.GROSSE LAGE®

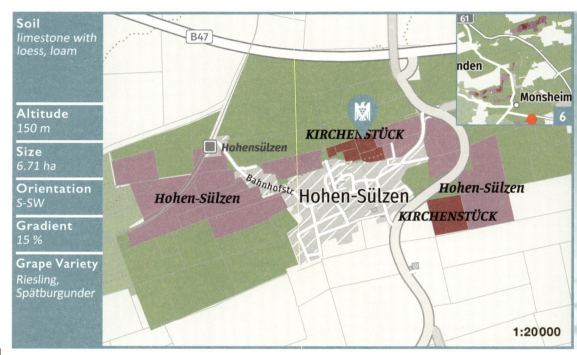

Soil
limestone with loess, loam

Altitude
150 m

Size
6.71 ha

Orientation
S-SW

Gradient
15 %

Grape Variety
Riesling, Spätburgunder

VDP.Estates: **Battenfeld Spanier**

The VDP.GROSSE LAGE® KIRCHENSTÜCK is directed south and southwest. The site lies on 150 metres above sea level. The predominant variety is Riesling. The vines root mostly in limestone with loess. The VDP.GROSSE LAGE® is only a small piece of the Kirchenstück vineyard and encompasses the parcels "Hinter der Kirche", "Am Griebelsteinchen" and "Am Täubertspfad".

History: The site was documented under the name "iuxta Kirchenstücke" in 1297. It was likely a piece of land that served to finance the monastery kitchen, but in any case carries the term for a property of the church.

KIRCHSPIEL

Westhofen | Rheinhessen
VDP.GROSSE LAGE®

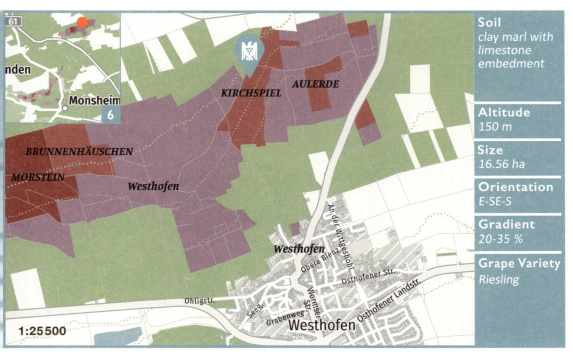

Soil
clay marl with limestone embedment

Altitude
150 m

Size
16.56 ha

Orientation
E-SE-S

Gradient
20-35 %

Grape Variety
Riesling

VDP.Estates: K. F. Groebe, Keller, Wittmann

The VDP.GROSSE LAGE® KIRCHSPIEL is a prime parcel located in the steeper part of the Kirchspiel vineyard that climbs up to a 35 percent gradient to 150 metres above sea level. Surrounded by a chain of hills that protects it from west winds, the GL KIRCHSPIEL opens like an amphitheatre. The site possesses good and homogenous soil and climate conditions and with its south to east exposition, vines benefit from the early morning sun. The soil is clay marl with limestone embedments and weathered calcareous loam. In deeper horizons, one finds predominantly limestone. The VDP.Vinters' parcels are planted predominantly with Riesling

History: The Kirchspiel was first documented as "Kyrsbühel" in 1348. In his book "Der Weinbau in der Provinz Rheinhessen, im Nahethal und Moselthal" (1834), the viticulture specialist Johann Philipp Bronner classified the site (together with the Auler=Aulerde) as outstanding.

KLOPPBERG

Dittelsheim | Rheinhessen
VDP.GROSSE LAGE®

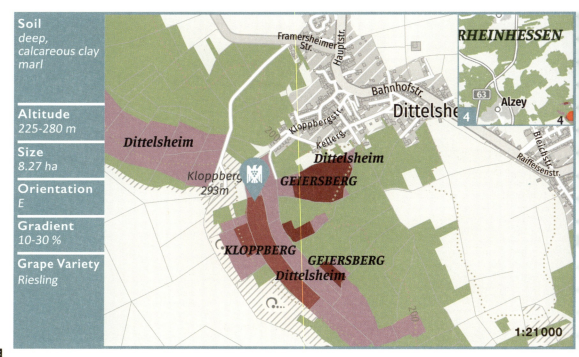

Soil
deep, calcareous clay marl

Altitude
225-280 m

Size
8.27 ha

Orientation
E

Gradient
10-30 %

Grape Variety
Riesling

VDP.Estates: Winter

The VDP.GROSSE LAGE® KLOPPBERG has an east exposition at an altitude of 225 to 280 metres above sea level. This makes the KLOPPBERG GL among the highest vineyards of Rheinhessen. The slope gradient ranges between 10 and 30 percent. The vines are planted in deep calcareous clay marl and the main variety is Riesling.

History: The name "Klopp" first appeared in documents dating 1537. The name can be traced to the Middle High German word "klupf", which refers to the top of a hill.

KRANZBERG

Nierstein | Rheinhessen
VDP.GROSSE LAGE®

Soil
calcareous loess

Altitude
125–129 m

Size
0.79 ha

Orientation
E-SE

Gradient
20 %

Grape Variety
Spätburgunder

VDP.Estates: St. Antony

The slopes of the VDP.GROSSE LAGE® KRANZBERG drop east and southeast towards the Rhine River and Nierstein and approach the Nierstein mountain church. Its soil is comprised of calcarous loam over limestone and sandy-clayey loam subsoil. The site is for the most part a slope, but not steep. The climate of the KRANZBERG GL is, above all else, determined by its direct solar radiation, which is further amplified by the Rhine River, which yet also simultaneously transports cool air. The KRANZBERG GL lies between 125 and 129 metres above sea level. Predominantly Riesling grows on the slopes.

History: The location was mentioned in 1418 by the name "off the Crausberge". It is assumed that the description of the individual situation relates to a person name.

KREUZ

Oppenheim | Rheinhessen
VDP.GROSSE LAGE®

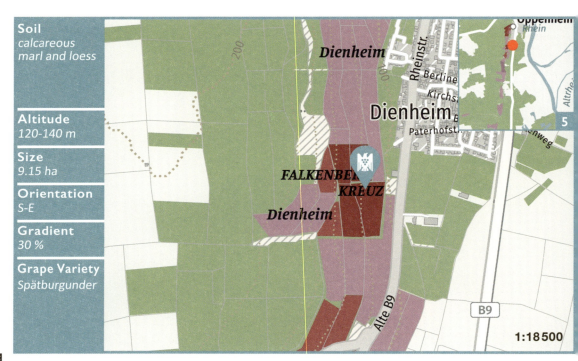

Soil
calcareous marl and loess

Altitude
120-140 m

Size
9.15 ha

Orientation
S-E

Gradient
30 %

Grape Variety
Spätburgunder

VDP.Estates: Kühling-Gillot

The VDP.GROSSE LAGE® KREUZ is nestled in the soft hilly landscape between Oppenheim and Dienheim somewhat more distanced from the Rhine River. The site possesses deep loess banks and calcarous marl at its core, which are interspersed with limestone fractions. With only 30 percent slope gradient, the KREUZ GL is a fairly flat site. It has a south to east aspect and is planted predominantly with Spätburgunder.

History: Kühling-Gillot calls the KRANZ GL the "site of the pope". The 1999 Spätburgunder once served as the sacramental wine for Pope Benedict XVI. Since then, the red wine from the KREUZ GL is considered the Châteauneuf-du-Pape of Rheinhessen. The KREUZ GL is probably named for the tall sandstone cross (Kreuz) that stands at the foot of the vineyard.

LECKERBERG

Dittelsheim | Rheinhessen
VDP.GROSSE LAGE®

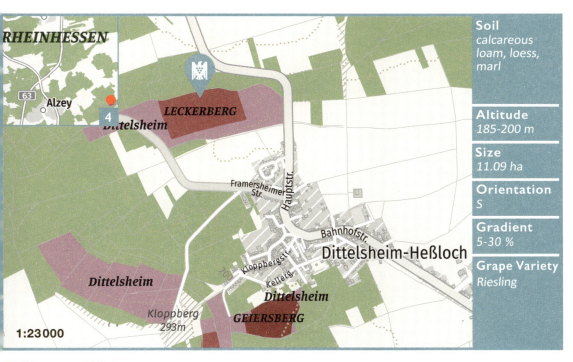

Soil
calcareous loam, loess, marl

Altitude
185-200 m

Size
11.09 ha

Orientation
S

Gradient
5-30 %

Grape Variety
Riesling

VDP.Estates: Winter

The slope of the VDP.GROSSE LAGE® LECKERBERG has a south aspect. With up to 200 metres above sea level, it is among the higher elevated sites in Rheinhessen. It drops down to 185 metres at slop gradients between 5 and 30 percent. The slope is terraced and offers a view to the Upper Rhine Plain. The soils are comprised of calcareous loam, loess, and marl. Riesling and Spätburgunder are the predominant varieties in the LECKERBERG GL.

History: The site was first officially documented with the name "im Leckerberg" in the year 1562. The name could stem from the Lecksteine (licking stones) that were hung outdoors for the game in this area.

LIEBFRAUENSTIFT-KIRCHENSTÜCK

Worms | Rheinhessen
VDP.GROSSE LAGE®

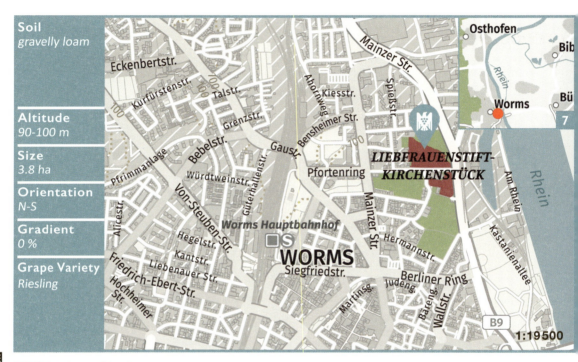

Soil
gravelly loam

Altitude
90-100 m

Size
3.8 ha

Orientation
N-S

Gradient
0 %

Grape Variety
Riesling

VDP.Estates: **Gutzler**

The VDP.GROSSE LAGE® LIEBFRAUENSTIFT-KIRCHENSTÜCK is located in the middle of the city of Worms and surrounds the eponymous Liebfrauen Church. The flat vineyard lies at 90 to 100 metres above sea level and is enclosed by a wall that protects it from wind. The city contributes to a rather warm climate. The soil is comprised of gravelly loam with a share of Rotliegend sandstone as well as some lightly sandy loam. Sand and gravel remaining from the old Rhine riverbed is found in deeper horizons. Mostly Riesling is cultivated in the LIEBRRAUENSTIFT-KIRCHENSTÜCK GL.

History: The etymological root of the name of the vineyard is "Liebfrauenmilch".

MORSTEIN

Westhofen | Rheinhessen
VDP.GROSSE LAGE®

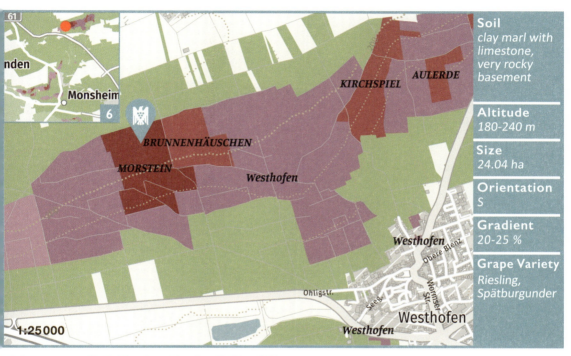

Soil
clay marl with limestone, very rocky basement

Altitude
180-240 m

Size
24.04 ha

Orientation
S

Gradient
20-25 %

Grape Variety
Riesling, Spätburgunder

VDP.Estates: K. F. Groebe, Gutzler, Keller, Wittmann

The Morstein vineyard rises majestically above the Rhine glacial valley and at its heart, between 180 and 240 metres above sea level, is the impressive VDP.GROSSE LAGE® MORSTEIN. The 20 to 25-percent-gradient slope faces due south and stretches into Gundersheim to the west and up to a high plateau. The upper soil horizon of the GL MORSTEIN is heavy clay marl with limestone embedments. Vines struggle to root in this soil, but deep below the surface is a limestone aquifer that provides vines with a good source of minerals and nutrients, even during prolonged dry spells. The vegetation period in the MORSTEIN GL is relatively long and grapes can ripen late. Predominately Riesling and Spätburgunder grow here.

History: The Morstein was first mentioned as "Marsten" in documentation of the Cistercian Otterberg Monastery receiving it as a gift in 1282. The name probably comes from a rock border marker, a "Marstein".

ÖLBERG

Nierstein | Rheinhessen
VDP.GROSSE LAGE®

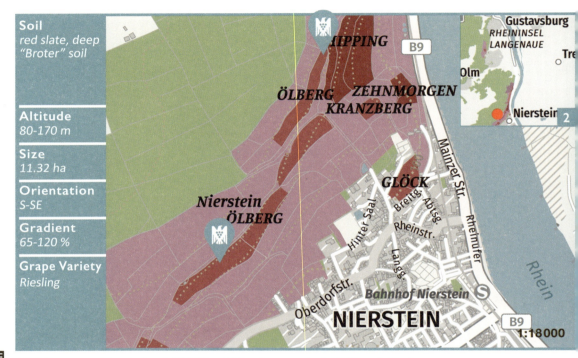

Soil
red slate, deep "Broter" soil

Altitude
80-170 m

Size
11.32 ha

Orientation
S-SE

Gradient
65-120 %

Grape Variety
Riesling

VDP.Estates: Gunderloch, Kühling-Gillot, Rappenhof, Schätzel, St. Antony, Staatliche Weinbaudomäne Oppenheim

VDP.GROSE LAGE® ÖLBERG is situated a little farther from the Rhine River above Nierstein. The site has a south to southeast aspect and belongs to the famous Roter Hang (Red Slope), which turns slightly away from the Rhine at this point. The soil in the best parcels of the Niersteiner Ölberg stems from the Rotliegend sequence of rock strata, a clay slate coloured red by its iron oxide content, characterising the regional landscape. Its structure is often highly fissured, which allows vines to root deeply. The ÖLBERG GL is at an altitude of 80 to 170 metres above sea level It includes steep parcels of the hillside with a slope gradient of 65 to 120 percent. The ÖLBERG GL benefits from intense solar radiation due to its south-facing aspect and steepness, but is also occasionally exposed to strong winds. The prevalent grape variety is Riesling.

History: It is presumed that the Ölberg (Oil Mountain) was named for the oily texture of its wines.

ORBEL

Nierstein | Rheinhessen
VDP.GROSSE LAGE®

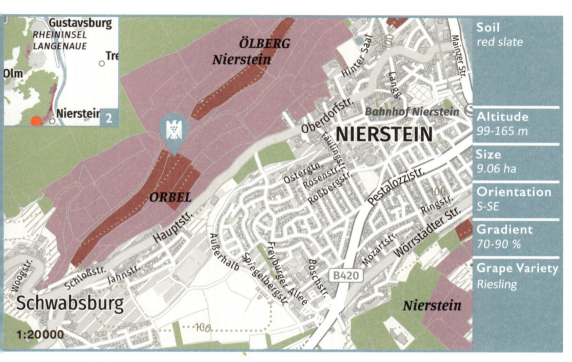

Soil	red slate
Altitude	99-165 m
Size	9.06 ha
Orientation	S-SE
Gradient	70-90 %
Grape Variety	Riesling

VDP.Estates: St. Antony

The VDP.GROSSE LAGE® ORBEL is the vineyard on the Rote Hang (Red Slope) that is the farthest away from the Rhine River. It is the last VDP. GROSSE LAGE® on this chain of hills and forms the southwest border. This steep site with up to 90 percent slope above the Nierstein hamlet of Schwabsburg is also dominated by the vermilion red coloured Rotliegend rock that lends the Roter Hang its name. The ORBEL GL faces south and vines benefit from maximum solar radiation. The Rhine simultaneously provides cool air and functions as a climate regulator for the ORBEL GL. The primary grape variety is Riesling.

History: The land parcel named Orbel was first mentioned in the village chronicles in the year 1386.

PARES

Ingelheim | Rheinhessen
VDP.GROSSE LAGE®

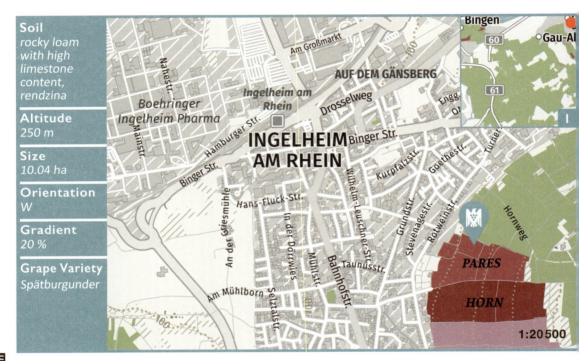

Soil
rocky loam with high limestone content, rendzina

Altitude
250 m

Size
10.04 ha

Orientation
W

Gradient
20 %

Grape Variety
Spätburgunder

VDP.Estates: J. Neus

The 10-hectare VDP.GROSSE LAGE® PARES is located on the west slope of the Mainzer Berg above the town of Ober-Ingelheim. Mostly Spätburgunder grows on rocky loam with high limestone content at 250 metres above sea level. The PARES has a slope gradient of 20 percent. The Rhine Valley marks its climate.

History: The Name Pares probably comes from the Middle High German name "parit", which means horse. This area could possibly been a pasture for animals to graze.

PATERBERG

Nierstein | Rheinhessen
VDP.GROSSE LAGE®

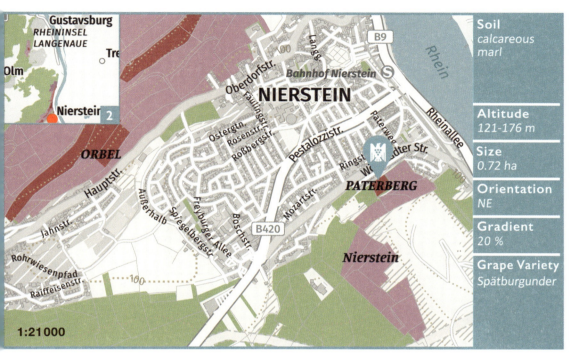

Soil
calcareous marl

Altitude
121-176 m

Size
0.72 ha

Orientation
NE

Gradient
20 %

Grape Variety
Spätburgunder

VDP.Estates: St. Antony

The VDP.GROSSE LAGE® PATERBERG is located between Nierstein and Oppenheim and extends inland from the Rhine waterfront. The site rises toward the northeast from 121 to 176 metres above sea level. The soil consists partially of calcarous marl, the tertiary marine deposits of a calcareous algae reef, and in part from loess. Spätburgunder is the predominant variety cultivated in the PATERBERG GL.
History: Pater is the synonym for monk; the site was once owned by a monastery.

PETTENTHAL

Nierstein | Rheinhessen
VDP.GROSSE LAGE®

Soil
red slate

Altitude
90-170 m

Size
20.62 ha

Orientation
E-SE

Gradient
70-100 %

Grape Variety
Riesling

VDP.Estates: Gunderloch, Keller, Kühling-Gillot, Rappenhof, Schätzel, St. Antony, Staatliche Weinbaudomäne Oppenheim

The VDP.GROSSE LAGE® PETTENTHAL is, along with the HIPPING GL, one of the core vineyards of the Roter Hang. It is situated halfway between Nierstein and Nackenheim with an east to southeast exposition directly overlooking the Rhine. A small section even faces due south toward the sun. The PETTENTHAL GL lays between 90 and 170 metres above sea level and rises above the flat foot of the slope and increases to a very steep 100 percent in the upper reaches. Particularly in the steep section, the soil is comprised of iron-rich clayey slate with a fine-grained texture – the red soil that gives the Roter Hang its name. The light reflected by the Rhine River amplifies the solar radiation and influences the microclimate here, particularly because the sunshine arrives early due to an opening toward the Upper Rhine Plain. The east aspect helps protect the site from cold winds. The main variety is Riesling.

History: The cadastre name exists since 1753.

ROTHENBERG

Nackenheim | Rheinhessen
VDP.GROSSE LAGE®

Soil
coarse grained red clayey slate, scant topsoil, solid rock near surf.

Altitude
90-140 m

Size
8.38 ha

Orientation
E-S/E

Gradient
75-120 %

Grape Variety
Riesling

VDP.Estates: Gunderloch, Kühling-Gillot, Staatliche Weinbaudomäne Oppenheim

The VDP.GROSSE LAGE® ROTHENBERG is the most northerly of the top sites on the so-called Roter Hang (Red Slope). The Roter Hang descends eastward toward the Rhine stretching from Nackenheim in the north to Nierstein in the south. Its name comes from the clayey slate soil (Rotliegend) with a bright red colour derived from its iron oxide content. The ROTHENBERG GL has a south to east exposition. The morning and midday sun reaches the site through an opening towards the Upper Rhine Plain and influences the microclimate of the ROTHENBERG GL bringing warmth that can remain throughout the day. The nearby Rhine River acts as a reflector, offering additional light to the steep slope. With a slope of up to 120 percent, the ROTHENBERG GL is one of the steepest parts of the Roter Hang.

History: This site was first mentioned as "in dem Rode" in 1364. This could certainly point to the colour of the soil (rot), but it could also be that the slope had just been cleared (gerodet).

SACKTRÄGER

Oppenheim | Rheinhessen
VDP.GROSSE LAGE®

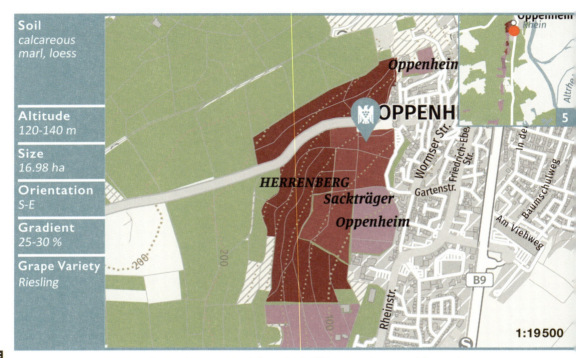

Soil
calcareous marl, loess

Altitude
120-140 m

Size
16.98 ha

Orientation
S-E

Gradient
25-30 %

Grape Variety
Riesling

VDP.Estates: Kühling-Gillot, Rappenhof, Staatliche Weinbaudomäne Oppenheim

The VDP.GROSSE LAGE® SACKTRÄGER is nestled in a well-protected convex site on the scarped ridge of the Rhine Rift Valley that opens east to south toward Oppenheim. This site is sloped with a 25 to 30 percent gradient. Vines grow on a windblown deposit of ice age loess over loam and deep calcareous marl. The soil is easily warmed and in the summer, together with the mild-tempered Rhine winds, the sheltered SACKTRÄGER GL turns into a hot kettle. The preferred variety for this site is Riesling.

History: The site name was first documented in 1541 and stems from the guild of sack carriers (Sackträger). Sack carriers brought shiploads of goods from the Rhine into the city. The guild probably defended one of the towers in the vicinity.

SCHARLACHBERG

Bingen | Rheinhessen
VDP.GROSSE LAGE®

Soil
quartzite slate subsoil with sandy loam topsoil

Altitude
100-220 m

Size
31.73 ha

Orientation
S-SE

Gradient
20-50 %

Grape Variety
Riesling

VDP.Estates: Kruger-Rumpf, Prinz Salm, Wagner-Stempel

The VDP.GROSSE LAGE® SCHARLACHBERG is located north of Bingen-Büdesheim and nearly reaches the Nahe River on its west end. It has a south and to a lesser extent southeast aspect and its weathered slate rock is heterogeneously scarlet red (scharlach) coloured due to its high iron oxide content. The vineyard is located between 100 and 220 metres above sea level at gradients that vary between a steep 50 percent and 20 percent. The rocky soils put vines here at an advantage in wet years. In addition to this, the winds from the Hunsrück have a drying effect, which helps keep grapes dry in autumn and make a late harvest possible. The main grape variety is Riesling.

History: This site first appeared in documents dating 1248 with the name "vocatur scarlachen" (named scarlet). The name stems from the scarlet red colour of soils containing iron oxide.

SCHLOSS WESTERHAUS

Ingelheim | Rheinhessen
VDP.GROSSE LAGE®

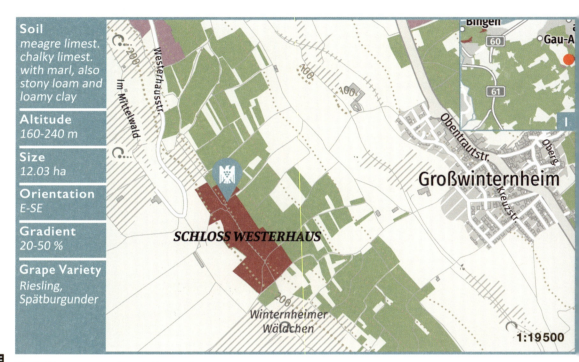

Soil
meagre limest. chalky limest. with marl, also stony loam and loamy clay

Altitude
160-240 m

Size
12.03 ha

Orientation
E-SE

Gradient
20-50 %

Grape Variety
Riesling, Spätburgunder

VDP.Estates: Schloss Westerhaus

The VDP.GROSSE LAGE® SCHLOSS WESTERHAUS is a sloped site located below the eponymous castle. While hugging the Westerberg, it faces east to southeast and is protected from cold west winds. The 12 hectares of vine rows lay at 160 to 240 metres above sea level, which protects from autumn fog banks that collect in the Selz Valley at the foot of the slope. The soil is comprised mostly of meagre limestone and calcareous marl, but stony loam and loamy clay are also found. SCHLOSS WESTERHAUS GL is planted predominantly with Riesling.
History: The first documented mention of the vineyard stems from the year 1408. The vineyard is a Monopole site of the VDP.Estate Schloss Westerhaus.

TAFELSTEIN

Dienheim | Rheinhessen
VDP.GROSSE LAGE®

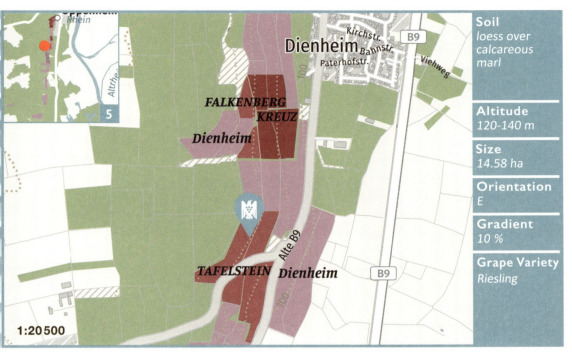

Soil
loess over calcareous marl

Altitude
120-140 m

Size
14.58 ha

Orientation
E

Gradient
10 %

Grape Variety
Riesling

VDP.Estates: Brüder Dr. Becker

The VDP.GROSSE LAGE® TAFELSTEIN is located on the slope overlooking the Rhine River south of Oppenheim. The vineyards face east and have a moderate slope of 10 percent. The TAFELSTEIN GL borders the upper, somewhat steeper single-vineyard Tafelstein parcels. Riesling grows on deep loess over loam and calcareous marl. The soils have good water storage capacity.

History: The name stems from "Tafelgut", the wineries that served as a source of income for the aristocracy.

ZEHNMORGEN

Nierstein | Rheinhessen
VDP.GROSSE LAGE®

Soil
calcareous marl

Altitude
94-124 m

Size
1.21 ha

Orientation
E

Gradient
20-30 %

Grape Variety
Riesling

VDP.Estates: St. Antony

The tiny VDP.GROSSE LAGE® ZEHNMORGEN comprises 1.2 hectares of vines that nearly reach the bank of the Rhine. Although this site sits on the lower Roter Hang (Red Slope), the typical regional clay and sandstone, which is coloured red due to iron oxide content, is not found here. Instead, heavy, large limestone rocks that dominate the subsoil break the surface of the clay. The site extends from the flat bank of the Rhine River at 94 metres up to more inclined sites at 124 metres above sea level. This east-facing slope is the first to greet the morning sunshine. The Rhine serves as a reflector of the sun and simultaneously transports cool air into the ZEHNMORGEN GL. The main grape variety is Riesling.

History: The name reflects the site's historic measure of area, ten (zehn) morgen. The vineyard today is only half as big.

ZELLERWEG AM SCHWARZEN HERRGOTT

Mölsheim | Rheinhessen
VDP.GROSSE LAGE®

Soil
limestone

Altitude
170-250 m

Size
11 ha

Orientation
S-SE

Gradient
40 %

Grape Variety
Riesling

VDP.Estates: Battenfeld Spanier

The VDP.GROSSE LAGE® ZELLERWEG AM SCHWARZEN HERRGOTT surrounds the west side of Mölsheim, nearly on the border to the Pfalz. Its highest point is located at 250 metres in a south-southeast direction in the Zeller Valley. Light winds are constant in the Zeller Valley and the drying of wet grapes is accelerated. The Donnersberg Mountain to the west provides large diurnal temperature fluctuations. Nights carry cool air from the Palatinate Forest through the valley. Loess and marl dominate the soil.

History: According to historic chronicles, the Schwarzer Herrgott site is one of the oldest vineyards in Germany. The name stems from a weathered cross that was erected by St. Philipp von Zell in the 8th century.

SAALE – UNSTRUT

Along the river valleys of the Saale and Unstrut, in the southern part of Saxony-Anhalt, is Europe's northernmost quality wine-growing region. Proud castles, the Saale-Unstrut-Triasland nature reserve and, of course, the terraced vineyards are the main features of the thousand-year-old landscape around Freyburg, Naumburg and Bad Kösen.

In the Middle Ages, this Central German wine-growing region boasted 10 000 ha (nearly 250 000 acres) of vines and numbered among Germany's largest vineyard areas. Today, vines are cultivated only in southern Saxony-Anhalt and northern Thuringia. With 770 hectares of vines in total and only 6 hectares of classified VDP.GROSSE LAGE® vineyards Saale-Unstrut is one of Germany's smaller regions.

Region:	VDP.GROSSE LAGE®:
770 ha	6.1 ha
VDP.Wineries:	VDP.GROSSE LAGE® Sites:
2	2

SACHSEN

Region:	VDP.GROSSE LAGE®:
500 ha	16 ha
VDP.Wineries:	VDP.GROSSE LAGE® Sites:
2	4

With nearly 500 hectares of vines, Sachsen is even smaller then its neighbour Saale-Unstruth. Its steep, primarily terraced vineyards line the Elbe Valley from Pillnitz, south of Dresden, to Radebeul, Meissen and Diesbar-Seusslitz.

Sachsen is influenced by a continental climate. Despite winter temperatures that can dip to -28°C (-18°F), the annual average temperature is 9.3°C (49°F). This, and the region's annual average of 1570 hours of sunshine, provide excellent growing conditions for vines. Continuous stimuli challenge the vines to assertthemselves, be it the constant fluctuation between warm days and cool nights or the succession of sunshine, rain and wind.

The special character of the wines is also influenced by the various soils and geological formations in the Elbe Valley such as carboniferous granite and syenite, the latter often covered by a layer of sandstone, loess, clay and sand.

EDELACKER

Freyburg | Saale-Unstrut
VDP.GROSSE LAGE®

Soil
shell limestone

Altitude
115-220 m

Size
0.491 ha

Orientation
S-SSE

Gradient
45 %

Grape Variety
Grauburgunder, Riesling, Weißburgunder,

VDP.Estates: **Lützkendorf, Pawis**

The VDP.GROSSE LAGE® EDELACKER is a historic, terraced vineyard that lies in the protected gorge of the Unstrut River. The vineyard faces south to south-southeast and rises at a steep 45 percent slope gradient from 115 to 220 metres above sea level. The dry stone terrace walls store the warmth of the abundant sunshine and release it into the vines at night. The pale shell limestone soils also reflect the sunlight and intensify solar radiation in this vineyard. The vineyard lies in the rain shadow of the Harz Mountains and enjoys a sub-continental climate.

History: The vineyard terraces were built in the Middle Ages.

HOHE GRÄTE

Karsdorf | Saale-Unstrut
VDP.GROSSE LAGE®

Soil
quartzite, Keuper, shell limestone

Altitude
110-220 m

Size
5.61 ha

Orientation
S-SSW

Gradient
10-45 %

Grape Variety
Grauburgunder, Riesling, Silvaner, Traminer, Weißburgunder

VDP.Estates: Lützkendorf

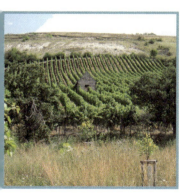

The VDP.GROSSE LAGE® HOHE GRÄTE lies on a massive, exposed layer of quartzite and gypsum marl. Gypsum continues to be mined at the local Karsdorf limestone quarry. The soils are highly mineral and the white colour reflects the sunlight into the vines, intensifying the solar radiation. The south to south-southwest facing site has an up to 45 percent slope gradient and already benefits fully from sunshine throughout the day. The GL HOHE GRÄTE is protected from the wind. It is relatively dry and temperatures are warm in summer and mild in winter. The vineyard lies at 110 to 220 metres above sea level and is a monopole vineyard of the VDP.Estate Lützkendorf.

History: The name HOHE GRÄTE most likely goes back to the Middle High German word Gret, which also has the meaning alp. The original spelling was GRETE.

KÖNIGLICHER WEINBERG

Pillnitz | Sachsen
VDP.GROSSE LAGE®

Soil
weathered granite

Altitude
125-170 m

Size
4.52 ha

Orientation
SSW

Gradient
30 %

Grape Variety
Grauburgunder, Riesling, Weißburgunder

VDP.Estates: Klaus Zimmerling

The VDP.GROSSE LAGE® KÖNIGLICHER WEINBERG lies above the Pillnitz Castle. It drops from its highest point at 170 metres above sea level down to 125 metres at a moderate incline of 30 percent. The vineyard faces south-southwest toward the Elbe River. Riesling is the predominant variety and grows on weathered granite. The Elbe Valley offers vineyard slopes good protection in a very northern location. Days are also longer and the sunshine is able to warm the dark granite soil in this GL quite well.

History: The vineyard above the Pillnitz Castle was planted nearly two centuries ago under the reign of Frederick Augustus I., King of Saxony. The vineyard was laid out with a route system for delivery, waterways – both above ground and underground, and a press house. A little church dedicated to the Holy Spirit is also located in the vineyard.

SCHLOSS PROSCHWITZ

Proschwitz, Rottewitz, Zadel, Diesbach-Seußlitz | Sachsen
VDP.GROSSE LAGE®

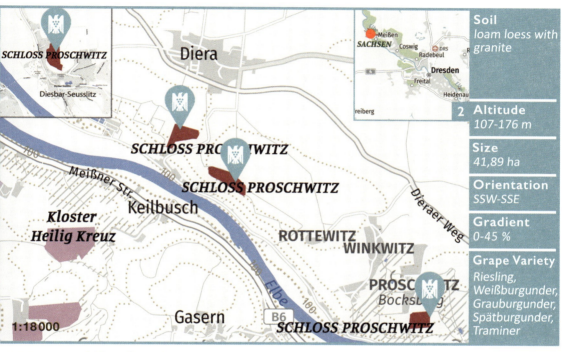

Soil
loam loess with granite

Altitude
107-176 m

Size
41,89 ha

Orientation
SSW-SSE

Gradient
0-45 %

Grape Variety
Riesling, Weißburgunder, Grauburgunder, Spätburgunder, Traminer

VDP.Estates: Schloss Proschwitz - Prinz zur Lippe

The VDP.GROSSE LAGE® SCHLOSS PROSCHWITZ lies above the scarped ridge of the Elbe Valley. The vineyards have a south-southeast to south-southwest exposition and are gently to steeply sloped with an up to 45 percent gradient. The soil is comprised of an up to six meter deep layer of decomposed loess over red granite. It has good available water capacity and warms well and homogenously in the sun exposed site. The vines are planted between 107 and 176 metres above sea level.

History: Dr. Georg Prinz zu Lippe re-purchased the vineyard in 1990. The property was confiscated from his family in 1945 without compensation.

Region:	VDP.GROSSE LAGE®:
11500 ha	1690 ha
VDP.Wineries:	VDP.GROSSE LAGE® Sites:
18	50

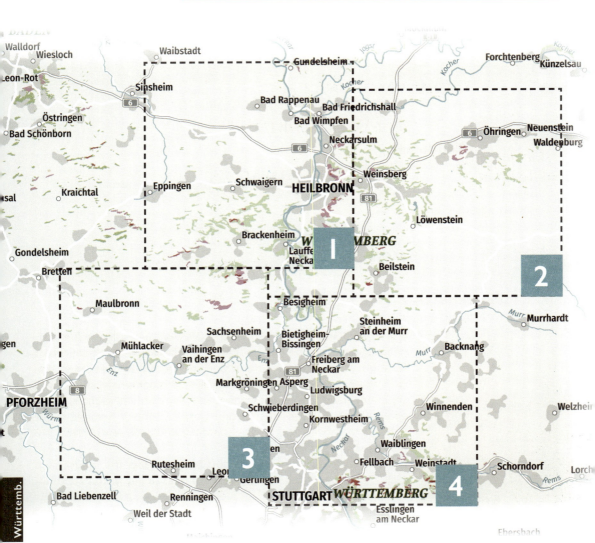

WÜRTTEMBERG

The Neckar River runs through the heart of the Württemberg wine-growing region. From its upper course near Tübingen to its confluence with the Rhine near Heidelberg, it shapes a landscape that is both charming and inviting. For 250 romantic kilometers (155 miles) it winds its way through the Jurassic soils of the Swabian Alb and the keuper near Stuttgart, then cuts its way northward through shell-limestone in a series of deep bends. In the course of several million years, together with its tributaries, the Kocher, Jagst, Murr, Enz and Rems rivers, the Neckar has created a contemporary, regional viticultural landscape that is at once unique and extraordinarily diverse.

Württemberg's vines grow primarily on deep, weathered, warm, red keuper soils that are the deposits of an ancient sea. Thanks to layers of gypsum keuper and coloured marl, which are naturally rich in minerals and nutrients, the Rems Valley, the Bottwar Valley, the Stomberg and the Zabergäu, as well as the areas near Heilbronn and the Hohenlohe, are particularly fertile.

The steep slopes in the narrow bends of the middle Neckar Valley, as well as along the Enz, Jagst and Kocher rivers, consist primarily of fossil-rich shell limestone. The small terraced vineyards, supported by heat-retaining, natural stone walls, bear witness to Württemberg's centuries-old viticultural tradition.

ALTENBERG

Schnait | Württemberg
VDP.GROSSE LAGE®

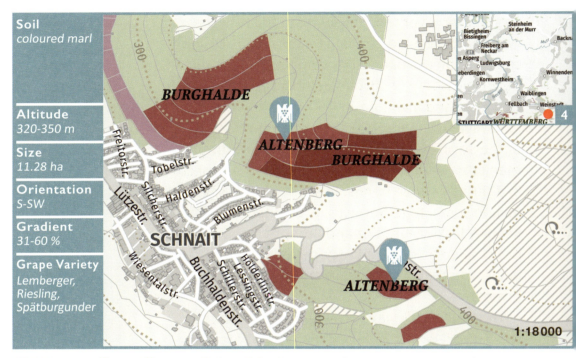

Soil
coloured marl

Altitude
320-350 m

Size
11.28 ha

Orientation
S-SW

Gradient
31-60 %

Grape Variety
Lemberger,
Riesling,
Spätburgunder

VDP.Estates: Jürgen Ellwanger, Rainer Schnaitmann

The parcels of the VDP.GROSSE LAGE® ALTENBERG lie with a south to southwest aspect on the slopes above the village Schnait in a side valley of the Rems River. The soil is heavy coloured marl with a high pH-value. The vineyard rises at a moderately steep gradient of 30 to 60 percent from 320 to 350 metres above sea level.

ALTENBERG

Strümpfelbach | Württemberg
VDP.GROSSE LAGE®

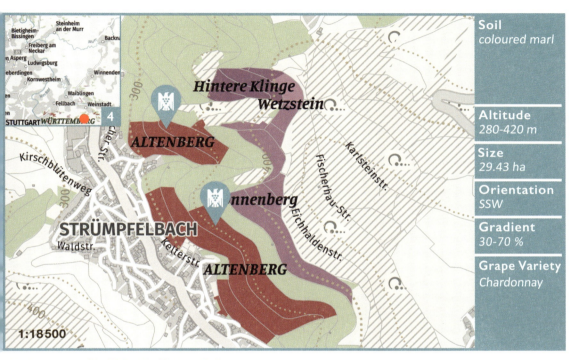

Soil
coloured marl

Altitude
280-420 m

Size
29.43 ha

Orientation
SSW

Gradient
30-70 %

Grape Variety
Chardonnay

VDP.Estates: Karl Haidle, Rainer Schnaitmann

With a slope gradient of up to 70 percent, the VDP.GROSSE LAGE® ALTENBERG is among the very steepest sites in Württemberg. This vineyard spreads along the slope above the village Strümpfelbach at an elevation of 280 to 420 metres above sea level. The soil of this site in the Rems Valley is heavy, coloured marl. The vineyard faces south-southwest and the vines benefit from sunshine throughout the day.

BERG

Hebsack | Württemberg
VDP.GROSSE LAGE®

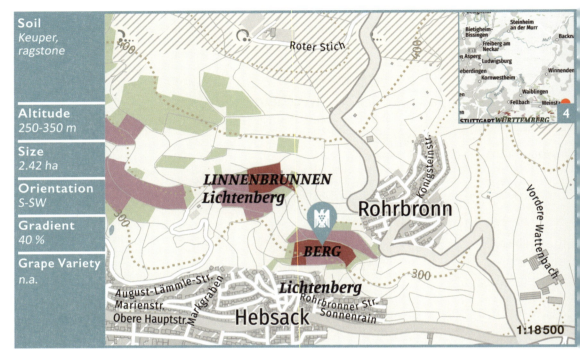

Soil
Keuper, ragstone

Altitude
250-350 m

Size
2.42 ha

Orientation
S-SW

Gradient
40 %

Grape Variety
n.a.

VDP.Estates: Jürgen Ellwanger

The south to southwest-facing VDP.GROSSE LAGE® BERG is a prime parcel within the VDP.ERSTE LAGE® Lichtenberg. It rises from 250 to 350 metres above sea level with a slope gradient of 40 percent. The vines root in Keuper marl and pebbly sandstone, which has good water storage capacity and warms easily.

BROTWASSER STEINGRUBE

Stetten | Württemberg
VDP.GROSSE LAGE®

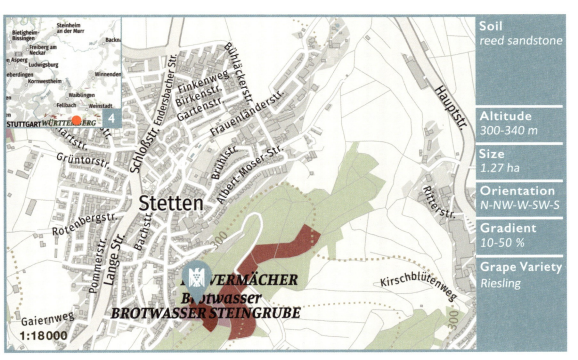

Soil	reed sandstone
Altitude	300-340 m
Size	1.27 ha
Orientation	N-NW-W-SW-S
Gradient	10-50 %
Grape Variety	Riesling

VDP.Estates: Herzog von Württemberg

The terraces of the VDP.GROSSE LAGE® BROTWASSER STEINGRUBE climb from 300 to 340 metres above sea level at a steep 50 percent slope gradient. The vineyard wraps around the mountain slope below the Yburg fortress ruin, turning from south to southwest, west and northwest to the coolest parcels on the north side. The clayey sandstone warms easily and the vines usually have "warm feet". The GL BROTWASSER STEINGRUBE is a monopole vineyard of the Herzog von Württemberg.

History: The name "Brotwasser" (bread water) can be traced back to a Stetten court lady in the 17th century who liked to fill her water jug with wine from this vineyard and use it to soften her bread.

BURG WILDECK HERRSCHAFTSBERG

Burg Wildeck | Württemberg
VDP.GROSSE LAGE®

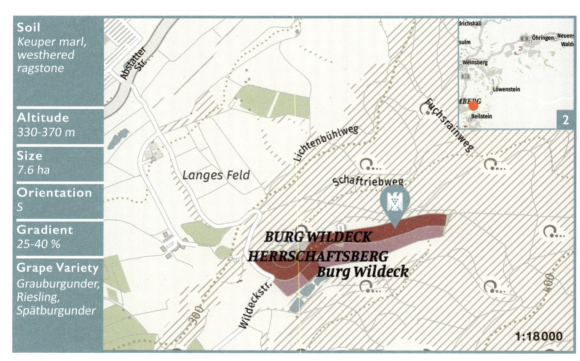

Soil
Keuper marl, westhered ragstone

Altitude
330-370 m

Size
7.6 ha

Orientation
S

Gradient
25-40 %

Grape Variety
Grauburgunder, Riesling, Spätburgunder

VDP.Estates: **Staatsweingut Weinsberg**

Due to its elevated position at 330 to 370 metres above sea level just below a medieval fortress, the VDP.GROSSE LAGE® BURG WILDECK HERRSCHAFTSBERG has a rather cool microclimate. The vegetation period begins and ends a little later than average and the yields are naturally reduced by the lower temperatures. The soils are Keuper marl and weathered gravel. The slope gradient ranges from a moderate 25 percent to steeper 40 percent. The wines from this vineyard climate exhibit good aroma intensity and robust acid structure.

Information: The Burg Wildeck vineyard is the birthplace of the Dornfelder grape variety. The first documentation of vine cultivation in this site stems from the year 1653.

BURGHALDE

Beutelsbach | Württemberg
VDP.GROSSE LAGE®

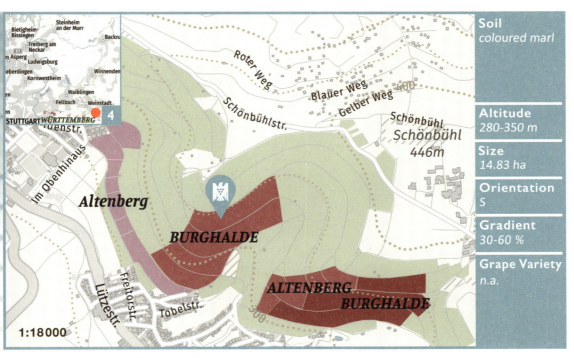

Soil
coloured marl

Altitude
280-350 m

Size
14.83 ha

Orientation
S

Gradient
30-60 %

Grape Variety
n.a.

VDP.Estates: Jürgen Ellwanger, Rainer Schnaitmann

The VDP.GROSSE LAGE® BURGHALDE is located in the hills between Schnait and Beutelsbach in a side valley of the Rems Valley. It profits from its protected position as well as its south aspect, that affords direct position to the sun. The result is a mild microclimate in which the warmth of the day is stored well. The vineyard drops from 350 to 280 metres above sea level at a moderately steep to steep 30 to 60 percent gradient. The vines are rooted in heavy sandy loam from coloured marl.

History: The Burghalde was first mentioned in documents dating 1600 and carried the name Halde until 1971.

BURGHALDE

Schnait | Württemberg
VDP.GROSSE LAGE®

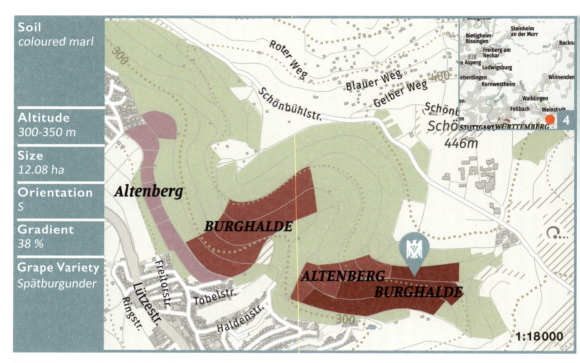

Soil
coloured marl

Altitude
300-350 m

Size
12.08 ha

Orientation
S

Gradient
38 %

Grape Variety
Spätburgunder

VDP.Estates: Karl Haidle, Rainer Schnaitmann

The VDP.GROSSE LAGE® BURGHALDE lies in a side valley of the Rems Valley near Stuttgart. Its protected position brings a mild microclimate in which the warmth of the day is stored well. The vineyard drops toward the wine village Schnait from 350 to 300 metres above sea level at a moderately steep 38 percent gradient. The south aspect affords direct exposition to the sun. The soil is heavy sandy loam from coloured marl.

History: The Burghalde was first mentioned in documents dating 1600 and carried the name Schnaiter Halde until 1971.

EILFINGERBERG KLOSTERSTÜCK

Maulbronn | Württemberg
VDP.GROSSE LAGE®

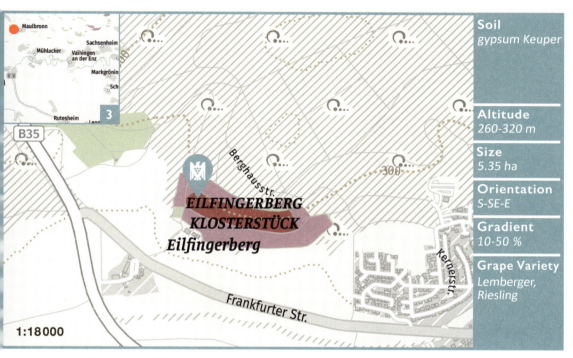

Soil
gypsum Keuper

Altitude
260-320 m

Size
5.35 ha

Orientation
S-SE-E

Gradient
10-50 %

Grape Variety
Lemberger, Riesling

VDP.Estates: Herzog von Württemberg

The VDP.GROSSE LAGE® EILFINGERBERG KLOSTERSTÜCK is the filet parcel located in the heart of the Eilfingerberg vineyard. The vineyard enjoys a mild climate protected by the forest at the top of the mountain. It rises from 260 to 320 metres above sea level at a steeper incline of up to 50 percent that faces south to southeast. Vines root in mineral-rich, calcareous gypsum marl with an easily warmed top soil of sandy clay. The GL EILFINGERBERG KLOSTERSTÜCK is a monopole vineyard of the VDP.Estate Herzog von Württemberg. History: The name stems from "elf finger", which translates to "eleven fingers". This eleventh finger is something the Cistercian monks at the Maulbronn Monastery desired so they could taste more of this vineyard's wine during Lent. Licking wine from a finger was the only method allowed to taste a wine during Lent at the monastery. The Cistercians were the first to plant this vineyard 850 years ago.

FORSTBERG

Oberstenfeld | Württemberg
VDP.GROSSE LAGE®

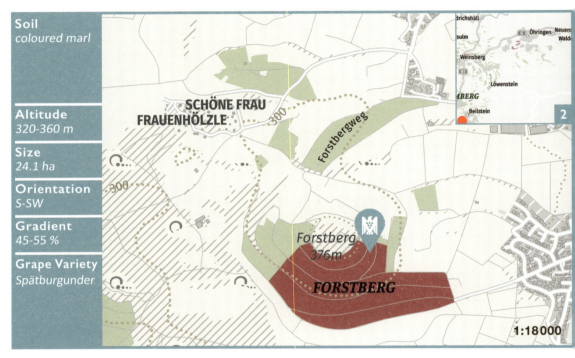

Soil
coloured marl

Altitude
320-360 m

Size
24.1 ha

Orientation
S-SW

Gradient
45-55 %

Grape Variety
Spätburgunder

VDP.Estates: Dautel

The VDP.GROSSE LAGE® FORSTBERG is a south to southwest facing vineyard slope of the Forstberg mountain that is turned slightly away from Oberstenfeld. The forested mountaintop shields the vineyard from brisk north winds. The vineyard is fairly elevated and rises at a 45 to 55 percent gradient from 320 to 360 metres above sea level. This imparts the wines from this site a certain cool elegance. The coloured marl and stony loam and clay are fairly heavy and have good water availability.

GAISSBERG

Pfaffenhofen | Württemberg
VDP.GROSSE LAGE®

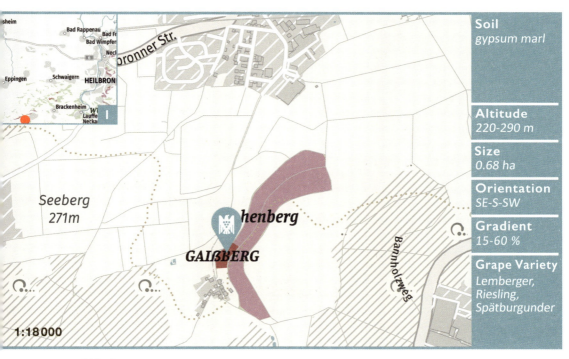

Soil
gypsum marl

Altitude
220-290 m

Size
0.68 ha

Orientation
SE-S-SW

Gradient
15-60 %

Grape Variety
Lemberger, Riesling, Spätburgunder

VDP.Estates: **Wachtstetter**

The VDP.GROSSE LAGE® GAISSBERG is a parcel within the Hohenberg vineyard that lies above the Rodbachhof near Pfaffenhofen. It is fairly steep and rises from 220 to 290 metres above sea level at up to a 60 percent slope incline. The GL GAISSBERG faces southwest and benefits particularly from the midday and afternoon sun. Its protected position near Pfaffenhofen and its gypsum marl soils make it one of the warmest and most fertile sites in Württemberg.

GIPS MARIENGLAS®

Untertürkheim | Württemberg
VDP.GROSSE LAGE®

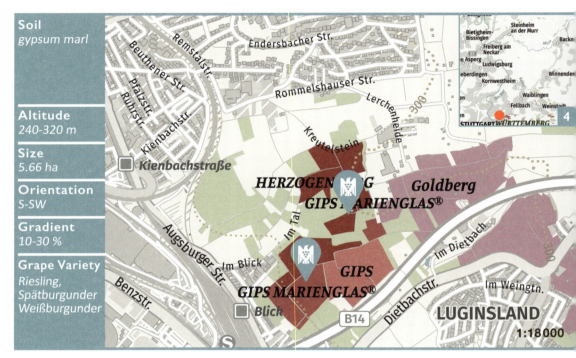

Soil
gypsum marl

Altitude
240-320 m

Size
5.66 ha

Orientation
S-SW

Gradient
10-30 %

Grape Variety
Riesling,
Spätburgunder
Weißburgunder

VDP.Estates: Aldinger

The VDP.GROSSE LAGE® GIPS MARIENGLAS® lies in front of the GL GIPS closer to the Neckar River above Untertürkheim. An unusually warm microclimate distinguishes this site. The vegetation period begins around a week earlier than other vineyards in the vicinity. The reason for this is that the GL GIPS MARIENGLAS® lies protected in a valley basin that diverts cold air away from it. The gypsum marl soil also stores warmth well, which is enhanced by the vineyard's sunny south and southwest aspect. The GL rises from 240 to 320 metres above sea level at a slope gradient of 10 to 30 percent.

Information: The site was named by VDP.Estate Aldinger for its unique soil composition. "Marienglas" is the German name for selenite, the purest and most prized form of gypsum. It is transparent and because its crystals can easily be split into thin sheets, it was historically used as a substitute for glass, particularly for pictures of St. Mary – thus the name Marienglas

GIPS

Untertürkheim | Württemberg
VDP.GROSSE LAGE®

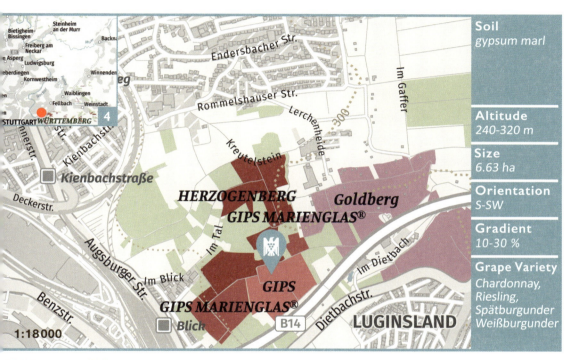

Soil
gypsum marl

Altitude
240-320 m

Size
6.63 ha

Orientation
S-SW

Gradient
10-30 %

Grape Variety
Chardonnay, Riesling, Spätburgunder, Weißburgunder

VDP.Estates: **Aldinger**

A very special microclimate distinguishes the VDP.GROSSE LAGE® GIPS. The vineyard lies protected in a valley basin that opens toward the Neckar River. The rising cold air from the river flows left and right from the valley opening. The gypsum marl soil stores warmth well, which is enhanced by the vineyard's sunny south and southwest aspect. The advantageous climatic conditions of the GL GIPS bring an earlier start to the vegetation period compared to other vineyards in the vicinity.

Information: The name of the vineyard stems from the high share of gypsum (Gips) in the soil. Vintners discovered these gypsum layers more than 200 years ago. This material was also quarried in the vicinity until the beginning of the 1970s. The VDP.Estate Aldinger decided to recultivate this vineyard in 1974 and named the site after the soil.

GÖTZENBERG

Kleinbottwar | Württemberg
VDP.GROSSE LAGE®

Soil
Keuper

Altitude
230-260 m

Size
0.38 ha

Orientation
S-SW

Gradient
50 %

Grape Variety
Spätburgunder

VDP.Estates: **Graf Adelmann**

The VDP.GROSSE LAGE® GÖTZENBERG rises up the slope of the Benning Mountain from 230 to 260 metres above sea level at a 50 percent gradient. The tiny 0.4-hectare GL faces south to southwest and offers a microclimate that is similar to GL SÜSSMUND and GL OBERER BERG. The subsoil is deep Keuper marl that has good water availability. The topsoil is easily warmed sandy clay that contributes to the mild microclimate of this GL.

GÖTZENBERG

Uhlbach | Württemberg
VDP.GROSSE LAGE®

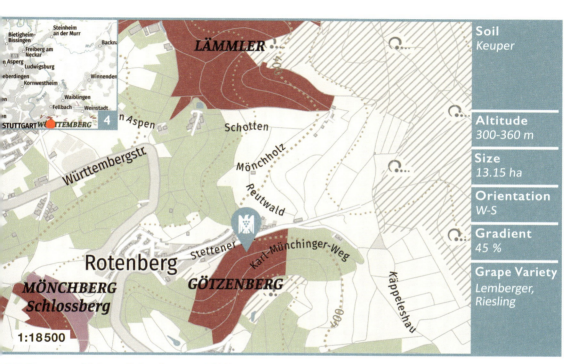

Soil Keuper

Altitude 300-360 m

Size 13.15 ha

Orientation W-S

Gradient 45 %

Grape Variety Lemberger, Riesling

VDP.Estates: Rainer Schnaitmann, Aldinger

The VDP.GROSSE LAGE® GÖTZENBERG is located in the bowl of a small closed side valley of the Neckar in the Stuttgart district Uhlbach. Easily warmed, fossil-rich sandstone of the Stuttgart formation dominates the south-southeast facing vineyards. The protected convex location, protected from the north and east winds, also contributes to the microclimate. The warm thermals created on sunny days provide good aeration in the vineyard and sweep moisture away from the vine canopy and grapes. This combination often makes a particularly long ripening period possible. The slopes of the GL GÖTZENBERG climb from 300 to 360 metres above sea level at a 45 percent gradient.

History: The name Götzenberg comes from an antique place of worship from the Hallstatt era that was discovered in 1820.

HERZOGENBERG

Untertürkheim | Württemberg
VDP.GROSSE LAGE®

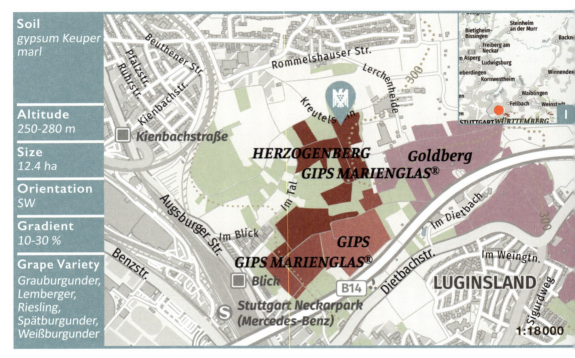

Soil
gypsum Keuper marl

Altitude
250-280 m

Size
12.4 ha

Orientation
SW

Gradient
10-30 %

Grape Variety
Grauburgunder, Lemberger, Riesling, Spätburgunder, Weißburgunder

VDP.Estates: Wöhrwag

The VDP.GROSSE LAGE® HERZOGENBERG lies on the slopes that rise east of Untertürkheim. At 250 to 280 metres above sea level, it is a little more highly elevated than the neighbouring GL GIPS and is thus slightly cooler. As it is usual for the sites around Untertürkheim, the soil is gypsum marl. The vines grow on a rather flat to slightly hilly slope with a 10 to 30 percent gradient.

HIMMELREICH

Gundelsheim | Württemberg
VDP.GROSSE LAGE®

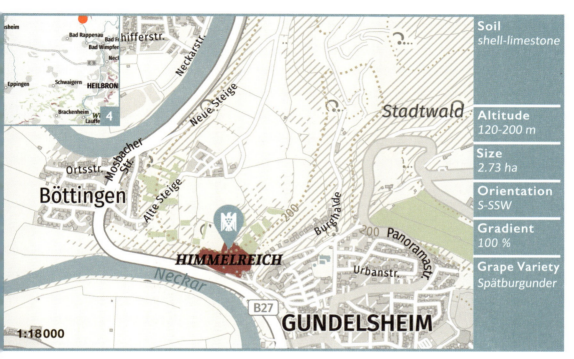

Soil
shell-limestone

Altitude
120–200 m

Size
2.73 ha

Orientation
S-SSW

Gradient
100 %

Grape Variety
Spätburgunder

VDP.Estates: Staatsweingut Weinsberg

The VDP.GROSSE LAGE® HIMMELREICH is the prime 3-hectare parcel in the heart of the eponymously named vineyard that has a very steep slope gradient of up to 100 percent. The imposing terraced south to south-southwest facing site has battens, stairs, and dry stone walls up to six metres high—it rises impressively above the German Order Castle Horneck in Gundelsheim above the Neckar River. The walls warm quickly in summer and provide a continuously warm climate with little temperature fluctuation. Mostly Spätburgunder and Riesling grow on deep, fertile soils of weathered shell limestone with some loess deposit.

History: The renowned German viticulturist Johann Philipp Bronner wrote about the Himmelreich in 1837: "This marvellous south-southwest vineyard possesses all prerequisites for exceptional viticulture. Slope, exposition, and soil unite under the most advantageous conditions."

HUNGERBERG

Winterbach | Württemberg
VDP.GROSSE LAGE®

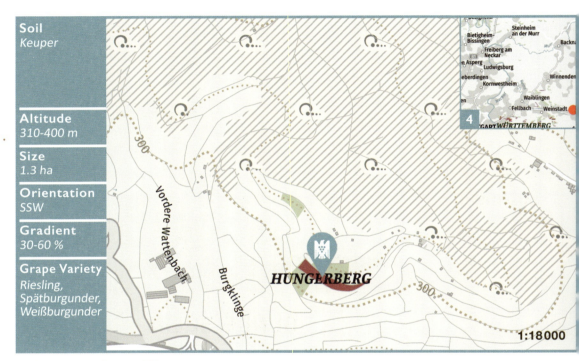

Soil
Keuper

Altitude
310-400 m

Size
1.3 ha

Orientation
SSW

Gradient
30-60 %

Grape Variety
Riesling, Spätburgunder, Weißburgunder

VDP.Estates: Jürgen Ellwanger

The VDP.GROSSE LAGE® HUNGERBERG lies at 310 to 400 metres above sea level and has a south-southwest exposition. The 1.3 hectare site is very steep with an up to 60 percent gradient. The loamy shell limestone and weathered Keuper is interspersed with bands of sandy loam. Mostly Riesling and Weißburgunder grow here.

KÄSBERG

Mundelsheim | Württemberg
VDP.GROSSE LAGE®

Soil
shell-limestone

Altitude
190-280 m

Size
0.44 ha

Orientation
W-SW-S-SE

Gradient
50 %

Grape Variety
Spätburgunder

VDP.Estates: Herzog von Württemberg

The VDP.GROSSE LAGE® KÄSBERG lies between 190 and 280 metres above sea level above the Käsbergkanzel, a striking rocky face on a bend of the Neckar River where the Käsberg, Rozenberg and Felsengarten vineyards are located. With its shape and numerous small terraces, the site resembles an amphitheatre. The convex topography has a west to southeast aspect that captures and intensifies the sunlight. This is further enhanced by a 50 percent slop gradient so that high temperatures can develop in the GL KÄSBERG. The shell limestone and clayey loam provide vines with good water availability.

LÄMMLER

Fellbach | Württemberg
VDP.GROSSE LAGE®

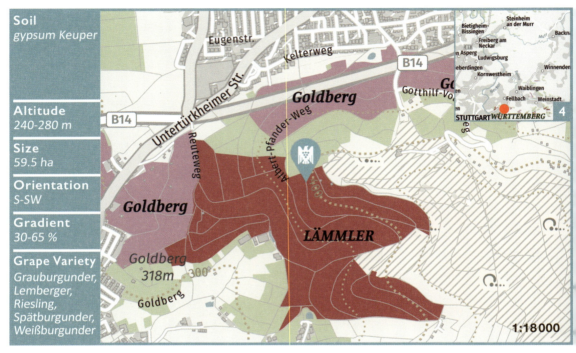

Soil
gypsum Keuper

Altitude
240-280 m

Size
59.5 ha

Orientation
S-SW

Gradient
30-65 %

Grape Variety
Grauburgunder, Lemberger, Riesling, Spätburgunder, Weißburgunder

VDP.Estates: Aldinger, Heid, Rainer Schnaitmann,

The south exposition and protected convex shape provides the VDP. GROSSE LAGE® LÄMMLER with a warm climate that is advantageous for the ripening of grapes. Cool evening breezes from the neighbouring Schurwald hills ensure crisp freshness and aroma. The GL is sloped to steep and climbs from 240 to 280 metres above sea level with up to a 65 percent gradient. Soils include weathered Keuper, Stuttgart formation sandstone and, and coloured marl. The soil within the vineyard varies in heaviness and lime content. Predominantly Pinot varieties, Lemberger, and Riesling grow in the GL LÄMMLER.

History: The name can be traced to the family Lämmle who were the owners of the 3-hectare vineyard for centuries. The historic border of the vineyard is about the same as the VDP.GROSSEN LAGE® LÄMMLER.

LINNENBRUNNEN

Hebsack | Württemberg
VDP.GROSSE LAGE®

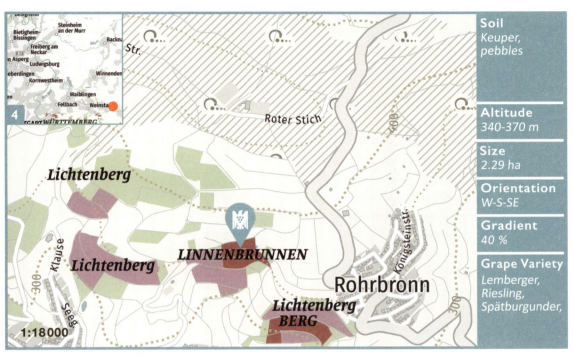

Soil
Keuper, pebbles

Altitude
340-370 m

Size
2.29 ha

Orientation
W-S-SE

Gradient
40 %

Grape Variety
Lemberger, Riesling, Spätburgunder,

VDP.Estates: Jürgen Ellwanger

High retaining walls traverse the VDP.GROSSE LAGE® LINNENBRUNNEN and together with the easily warmed Keuper marl and pebbly sandstone, they help provide a warm microclimate. The slope has a natural water spring and marl soil also has good water availability for vines. The GL LINNENBRUNNEN faces south and southwest between 340 and 370 metres and is rather steep with a 40 percent gradient.

MICHAELSBERG

Cleebronn | Württemberg
VDP.GROSSE LAGE®

Soil
coloured marl

Altitude
335-385 m

Size
10.15 ha

Orientation
S

Gradient
40-50 %

Grape Variety
Lemberger

VDP.Estates: Dautel

The VDP.GROSSE LAGE® MICHAELSBERG is located on the south facing slope of the Michaelsberg mountain. The free-standing cone is noted for its cool nights in summer and persistent aeration. The top of the mountain and the neighbouring Stromberg protect the vines from cold winds from the north and east. Couloured marl, calcareous Keuper shale interchanges with heavy clay and marl. With a steep 40 to 50 percent gradient that rises from 335 to 385 metres above sea level, this is a demanding vineyard to maintain.

History: Wine cultivation in this vineyard can be traced back to the 8th century.

MÖNCHBERG "BERGE"[1]

Stetten | Württemberg
VDP.GROSSE LAGE®

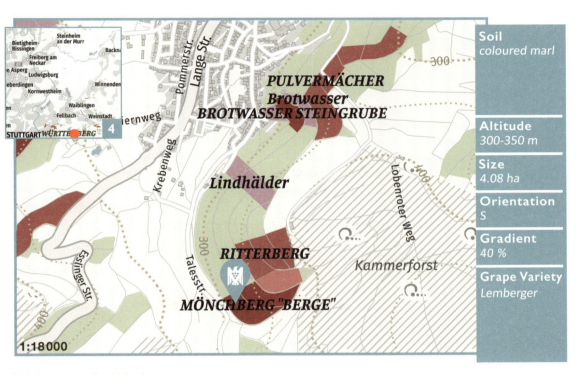

Soil
coloured marl

Altitude
300-350 m

Size
4.08 ha

Orientation
S

Gradient
40 %

Grape Variety
Lemberger

VDP.Estates: Karl Haidle

The VDP.GROSSE LAGE® MÖNCHBERG "BERGE"[1] is a historic prime parcel within the Mönchberg vineyard. The thickly forested hilltop and the surrounding Schurwald hills protect this south facing slope from cold west and east winds. The Mönchberg is among the warmest vineyards in the region. The soil is mostly coloured marl. It is well aerated and warms easily.

MÖNCHBERG "GEHRNHALDE"[1]

Stetten | Württemberg
VDP.GROSSE LAGE®

Soil
coloured marl, reed sandstone

Altitude
300-350 m

Size
3.32 ha

Orientation
S-SE

Gradient
25 %

Grape Variety
Lemberger

VDP.Estates: Karl Haidle

Coloured marl and Keuper gypsum marl determine the heavy soils of the VDP.GROSSE LAGE® MÖNCHBERG "GEHRNHALDE"[1]. This provides good water availability and simultaneously predestines the site for the planting of red wine varieties that have a preference for these soils. The vineyard lies between 300 and 350 metres, well protected by the Schurwald Mountains. The 25 percent grade slope faces southeast and east. The GL MÖNCHBERG GEHRNHALDE is among the oldest Lemberger vineyards in the Rems Valley.
Information: The name "Gernhalde" is locally pronounced as "Geiernhalde", which translates to "vulture pile". The site is also locally called "Stoffelkopf", which means "knucklehead".

MÖNCHBERG "ÖDE HALDE"[1]

Stetten | Württemberg
VDP.GROSSE LAGE®

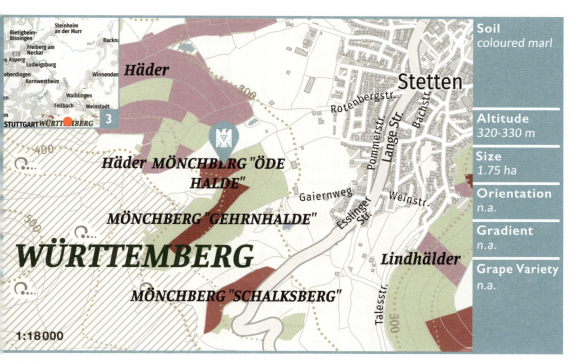

Soil
coloured marl

Altitude
320-330 m

Size
1.75 ha

Orientation
n.a.

Gradient
n.a.

Grape Variety
n.a.

VDP.Estates: Beurer

The VDP.GROSSE LAGE MÖNCHBERG "ÖDE HALDE"[1] is a parcel within the Mönchberg vineyard. It spreads along the slope of the Schurwald mountain Kernen toward the little city of Stetten. The Schurwald Mountains protect this east and southeast facing site from west and east wines, thus providing a warm microclimate. The coloured marl soil is heavy and has good water storage capacity as well as sub-layers with good water availability.

History: "Mönchberg" translates to "Monk Mountain" and as one would suspect, the vineyard once belonged to a monastery of the Catholic Church.

MÖNCHBERG "SCHALKSBERG"[1]

Stetten | Württemberg
VDP.GROSSE LAGE®

Soil
coloured marl

Altitude
310-320 m

Size
3.82 ha

Orientation
E-SE

Gradient
n.a.

Grape Variety
Lemberger

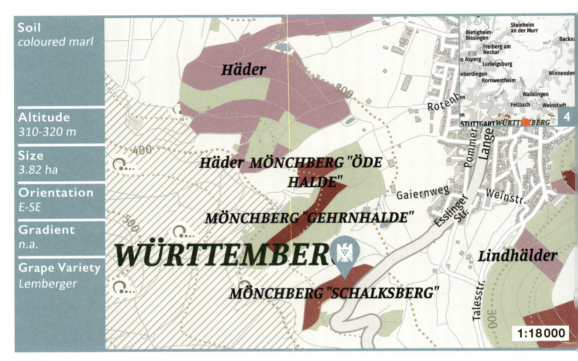

VDP.Estates: Beurer

The VDP.GROSSE LAGE® MÖNCHBERG "SCHALKSBERG"[1] lies west of Stetten below Kernen Mountain, which belongs to the Schurwald range of forested mountains near Stuttgart. The soil of this east and southeast facing vineyard is calcareous gypsum marl and coloured marl. The Lemberger vines that grow here are over 40 years old and have developed deep roots to reach water and nutrients deep below the earth surface.

MÖNCHBERG

Untertürkheim | Württemberg
VDP.GROSSE LAGE®

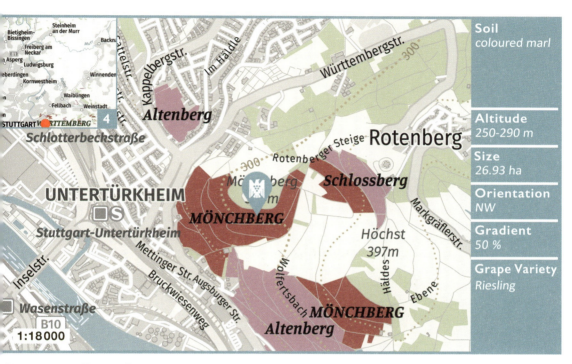

Soil
coloured marl

Altitude
250-290 m

Size
26.93 ha

Orientation
NW

Gradient
50 %

Grape Variety
Riesling

VDP.Estates: Rainer Schnaitmann, Herzog von Württemberg

The VDP.GROSSE LAGE® MÖNCHBERG lies southeast of Untertürkheim below the peak of the eponymous mountain. The vineyard slope faces northwest toward the Neckar River. It rises from 250 to 290 metres above sea level at a steeper 50 percent gradient. The coloured marl soil is heavy and has good water storage capacity.

History: The vineyard originally belonged to the Zwiefalten Monastery, thus the name Mönchberg, which translates to "Monk Mountain". The House of Württemberg became the owner of this site in the year 1671.

MÜHLBERG

Pfaffenhofen | Württemberg
VDP.GROSSE LAGE®

Soil
gypsum Keuper

Altitude
220-290 m

Size
8.02 ha

Orientation
SE-S-SW

Gradient
15-60 %

Grape Variety
Lemberger,
Riesling,
Spätburgunder

VDP.Estates: **Wachtstetter**

The VDP.GROSSE LAGE® MÜHLBERG is a parcel within the Hohenberg vineyard that is located on the south slope of the Heuchelberg above the Zaber River. Keuper soils and a mild, protected climate make this mostly south-southwest facing vineyard near Pfaffenhofen one of the most fertile in Württemberg. Grey-purple gypsum marl with a high share of sandy clay in the subsoil comprises a mineral-rich foundation that is not too heavy, which makes it easy for vines to develop good root systems. The GL MÜHLBERG is rather steep and rises from 220 o 290 metres above sea level at a 60 percent slope gradient.

NIEDERNBERG

Besigheim | Württemberg
VDP.GROSSE LAGE®

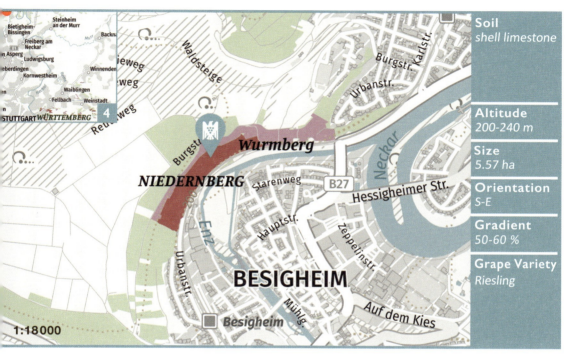

Soil	shell limestone
Altitude	200-240 m
Size	5.57 ha
Orientation	S-E
Gradient	50-60 %
Grape Variety	Riesling

VDP.Estates: **Dautel**

The VDP.GROSSE LAGE® NIEDERNBERG is located on a bend of the Enz River that flows around Besigheim. The Enz is a tributary of the Neckar River. The vineyard has a south to east aspect and some sections benefit from the earliest sunshine, where in other parts of the site, vine leaves and grapes bathe in the sunlight the entire day. Sunshine is further enhanced by the steep 50 to 60 percent slope gradient. The vineyard rises from 200 to 240 metres above sea level. The vines of the GL NIEDERNBERG root in shell limestone.

OBERER BERG

Kleinbottwar | Württemberg
VDP.GROSSE LAGE®

Soil
Keuper

Altitude
220-280 m

Size
7.94 ha

Orientation
S-SW

Gradient
35-50 %

Grape Variety
Lemberger

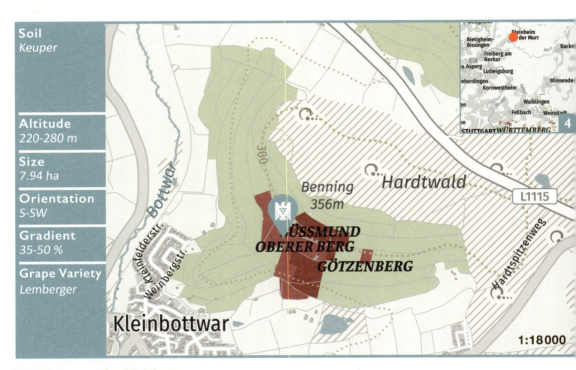

VDP.Estates: Graf Adelmann

The VDP.GROSSE LAGE® OBERER BERG lies on the south slope of the Benning Mountain 220 to 280 metres above sea level. The south to southwest aspect provides vines with direct sunshine the entire day. The up to 50 percent slope gradient further intensifies the solar radiation. The Keuper marl soil is deep and provides good water availability.

OCHSENBERG

Pfaffenhofen | Württemberg
VDP.GROSSE LAGE®

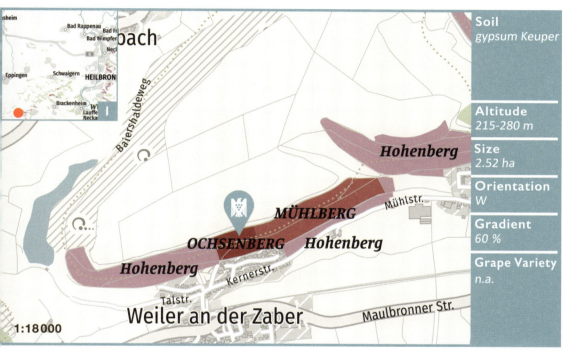

Soil
gypsum Keuper

Altitude
215-280 m

Size
2.52 ha

Orientation
W

Gradient
60 %

Grape Variety
n.a.

VDP.Estates: **Wachtstetter**

The VDP.GROSSE LAGE® OCHSENBERG is a parcel within the Hohenberg vineyard that is essentially an extension of the GL MÜHLBERG toward the west. The vineyard drops at a steep 60 percent gradient from 280 to 215 metres above sea level. The village of Weiler and the Zaber River lie at its foot. The west aspect allows plenty of sunshine throughout the day. The grey-purple gypsum marl with a share of sandy clay is rich in minerals and calcium carbonate. Like the other vineyards surrounding Pfaffenhofen, the GL OCHSENBERG is among the most fertile and warm sites in Württemberg.

PULVERMÄCHER "BERGE"[1]

Stetten | Württemberg
VDP.GROSSE LAGE®

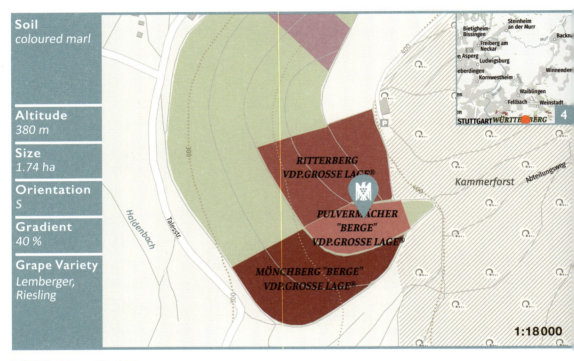

Soil
coloured marl

Altitude
380 m

Size
1.74 ha

Orientation
S

Gradient
40 %

Grape Variety
Lemberger, Riesling

VDP.Estates: Beurer

The VDP.GROSSE LAGE® PULVERMÄCHER "BERGE"[1] is a parcel within the Pulvermächer vineyard. It lies at 380 metres above sea level and has a south aspect that allows it to benefit from sunshine throughout the day. The Kammerforst forest and the surrounding Schurwald mountains shield the site from cold winds from the west and east. The easily warmed gravelly soil of coloured marl is well drained and aerated.

PULVERMÄCHER

Stetten | Württemberg
VDP.GROSSE LAGE®

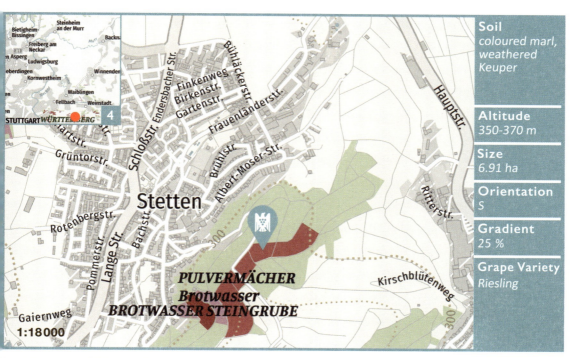

Soil
coloured marl, weathered Keuper

Altitude
350-370 m

Size
6.91 ha

Orientation
S

Gradient
25 %

Grape Variety
Riesling

VDP.Estates: **Aldinger, Beurer, Karl Haidle**

The partially terraced VDP.GROSSE LAGE® PULVERMÄCHER vineyard is located at 350 to 370 metres above sea level in a wind-protected side valley of the Rems Valley just below the prominent Yburg Castle ruin near Stetten. The fossil-rich coloured marl and weathered Keuper of this site warm easily. The vineyard terrace walls of this south-facing vineyard also collect the warmth of the day.

History: The Pulvermächer vineyard was first mentioned in documents dating 1650. The name loosely translates to "Pulveriser" and is a very old term for an explosives expert, which can be traced to the neighbouring quarry where rock blasting took place.

RITTERBERG

Stetten | Württemberg
VDP.GROSSE LAGE®

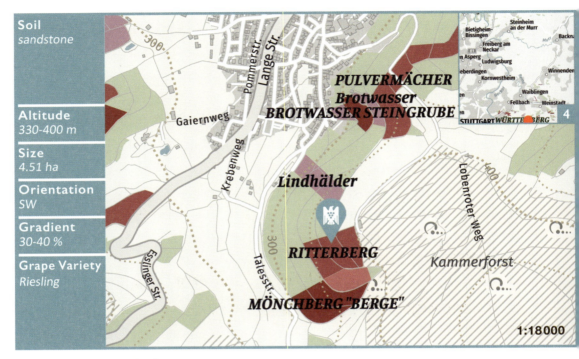

Soil
sandstone

Altitude
330-400 m

Size
4.51 ha

Orientation
SW

Gradient
30-40 %

Grape Variety
Riesling

VDP.Estates: Karl Haidle

The VDP.GROSSE LAGE® RITTERBERG lies in the centre of the slope of the Kammerforst mountain at 330 to 400 metres above sea level, south of the little wine city Stetten. The slope gradient ranges from 30 to 40 percent. Sandstone and sandy clay comprise a well-drained soil that warms easily. Vines must drive their roots deep to find sufficient water reserves. The site faces southwest and benefits from warm sunshine from midday until sunset.

ROTER BERG

Schozach | Württemberg
VDP.GROSSE LAGE®

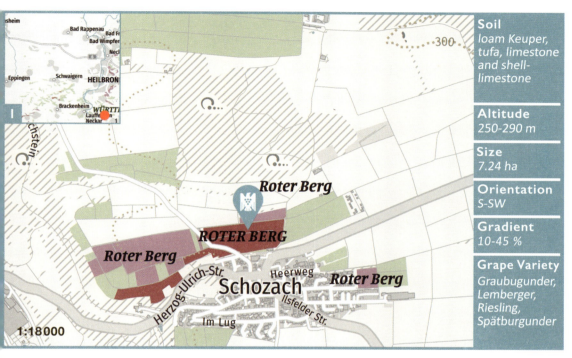

Soil
loam Keuper, tufa, limestone and shell-limestone

Altitude
250-290 m

Size
7.24 ha

Orientation
S-SW

Gradient
10-45 %

Grape Variety
Graubugunder, Lemberger, Riesling, Spätburgunder

VDP.Estates: Graf von Bentzel-Sturmfeder

The 7-hectare VDP.GROSSE LAGE® ROTER BERG has a south to southwest aspect that faces the wine village Schozach. It rises at an up to 45 percent slope gradient from 250 to 290 metres above sea level. The microclimate of the GL ROTER BERG can tend to extremes. Due to thermal air masses, it can heat up tremendously during the day and then cool again significantly at night.

History: The name of this site comes from the red colour of the porous soil, which is comprised of Keuper marl with shell limestone intercalations

RUTHE

Schwaigern | Württemberg
VDP.GROSSE LAGE®

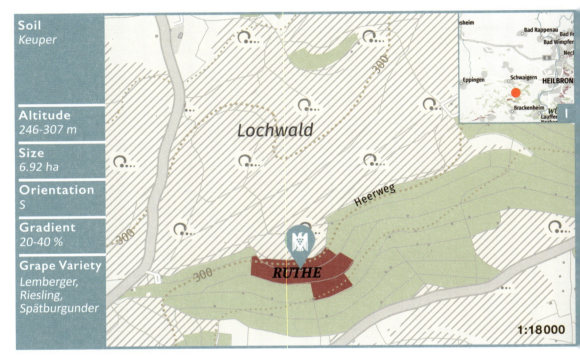

Soil
Keuper

Altitude
246-307 m

Size
6.92 ha

Orientation
S

Gradient
20-40 %

Grape Variety
Lemberger, Riesling, Spätburgunder

VDP.Estates: **Graf Neipperg**

The partly terraced VDP.GROSSE LAGE® RUTHE is moderately steep with a 20 to 40 percent gradient. The Siegelsberg protects vines from cold north and west winds. The south exposition and location at 246 to 307 metres above sea level enhances solar radiation in the vineyard. This promotes early flowering and a long ripening period for highly ripe grapes. The soil is Gipskeuper with coloured marl in the upper area. Predominantly Riesling and Lemberger are cultivated here.

History: The Ruthe was first mentioned in 1385. The name can linguistically be traced back to the clearing of the slope together with the Schlossberg.

SCHEMELSBERG

Weinsberg | Württemberg
VDP.GROSSE LAGE®

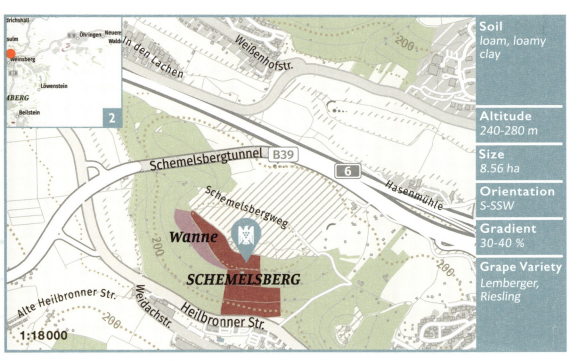

Soil
loam, loamy clay

Altitude
240-280 m

Size
8.56 ha

Orientation
S-SSW

Gradient
30-40 %

Grape Variety
Lemberger, Riesling

VDP.Estates: **Staatsweingut Weinsberg**

The VDP.GROSSE LAGE® SCHEMELSBERG is located above the city of Weinsberg. It climbs the south to south-southwest facing slope to the peak of the eponymous hill from 240 up to 280 metres above sea level. The soil is heavy with loam and loamy clay with good water storage capacity. The slope is fairly steep with a 30 to 40 percent gradient. The site is a monopole vineyard of the VDP. Estate Staatsweingut Weinsberg, who also use the site for research purposes.

Information: A "schemel" is a footstool and this refers to the shape of the Schemelsberg hill. The Schemelsberg vineyard was first mentioned in a document from the 14th century.

SCHEUERBERG "ORTHGANG®"

Neckarsulm | Württemberg
VDP.GROSSE LAGE®

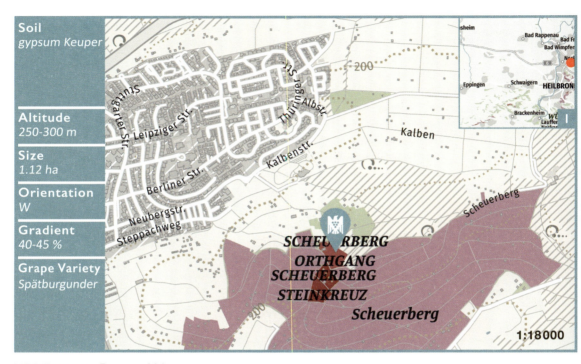

Soil
gypsum Keuper

Altitude
250-300 m

Size
1.12 ha

Orientation
W

Gradient
40-45 %

Grape Variety
Spätburgunder

VDP.Estates: **Drautz-Able**

The VDP.GROSSE LAGE® SCHEUERBERG "ORTHGANG®" is the very highest section of the Scheuerberg vineyard that lies at 250 to 300 metres above sea level. With its west aspect, it collects sunshine and warmth from midday to sunset, which is further enhanced by its rather steep 40 to 45 percent slope gradient. The convex wedge shape of the Scheuerberg protects the site from storms and functions like a weather shield that directs storm fronts either toward the Odenwald or Weinsberger Valley. The soil of the GL SCHEUERBERG "ORTHGANG®" is heavy gypsum marl. Its high share of calcium carbonate makes it predestined for red wine grape varieties, in particular Spätburgunder.

History: Wine has been cultivated on the Scheuerberg Mountain since the end of the 13th century. The word "Scheuer" is a word used in Swabian dialect that stems from the Old German words "Schiur" or "Sciura", which translates to "shelter".

SCHEUERBERG "STEINKREUZ®"

Neckarsulm | Württemberg
VDP.GROSSE LAGE®

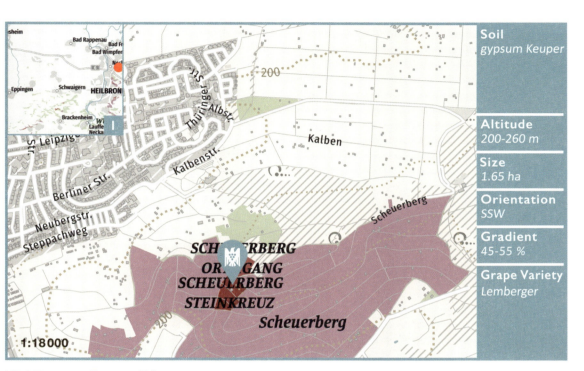

Soil
gypsum Keuper

Altitude
200-260 m

Size
1.65 ha

Orientation
SSW

Gradient
45-55 %

Grape Variety
Lemberger

VDP.Estates: **Drautz-Able**

The VDP.GROSSE LAGE® SCHEUERBERG "STEINKREUZ®" lies in the upper section of the Scheuerberg vineyard. The site's solar radiation is ideal due to its south to southwest aspect and steep 45 to 55 percent slope gradient. The Scheuerberg landscape contributes in other ways as well. Its convex wedge shape functions like a watershed and directs rainstorms either toward the Odenwald Valley or the Weinsberger Valley. The soil of this GL is heavy, very calcareous gypsum marl, which lends the wines plenty of power. The high share of calcium carbonate makes this vineyard ideal for the cultivation of red wine varieties.

SCHLIPSHÄLDE

Bönnigheim | Württemberg
VDP.GROSSE LAGE®

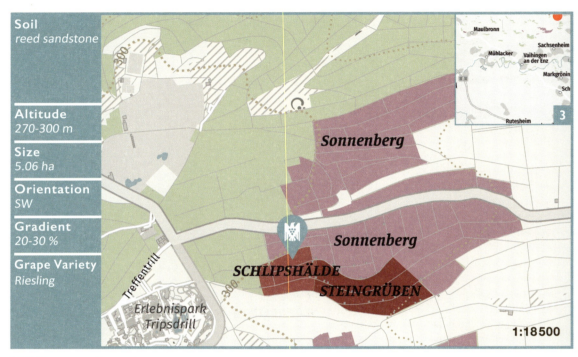

Soil
reed sandstone

Altitude
270-300 m

Size
5.06 ha

Orientation
SW

Gradient
20-30 %

Grape Variety
Riesling

VDP.Estates: **Dautel**

The VDP.GROSSE LAGE® SCHLIPSHÄLDE is a cadaster parcel within the Sonnenberg vineyard near Bönnigheim. The southwest slope rises from 270 to 300 metres above sea level. Reed sandstone and calcareous Keuper shale determines the soil of the 5-hectare vineyard. Predominantly Riesling grows in the GL SCHLIPSHÄLDE; the vines were planted in 1971.

SCHLOSSBERG

Neipperg | Württemberg
VDP.GROSSE LAGE®

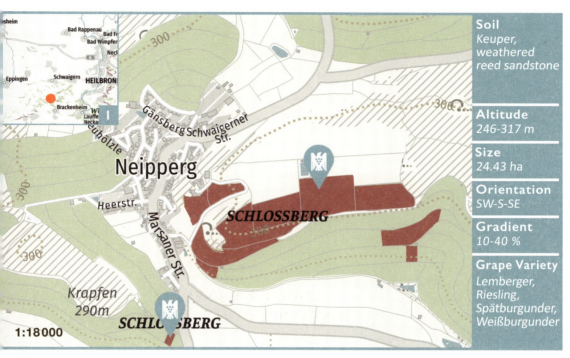

Soil
Keuper, weathered reed sandstone

Altitude
246-317 m

Size
24.43 ha

Orientation
SW-S-SE

Gradient
10-40 %

Grape Variety
Lemberger, Riesling, Spätburgunder, Weißburgunder

VDP.Estates: Graf Neipperg

The VDP.GROSSE LAGE® SCHLOSSBERG comprises a 10 to 40 percent slope of the Burgberg (the home mountain of the Neipperg family) that ends in a high plateau. The vineyard has a southeast, south and southwest exposure. The section that is terraced possesses deep, nutrient-rich Keuper with some loess pockets and is planted with Lemberger and Riesling. The 24 hectares of the GL SCHLOSSBERG lie at 246 to 317 metres above sea level.

History: The Schlossberg (Castle Mountain) was cleared and planted with vines at the beginning of the 13th century.

SCHLOSSWENGERT

Hohenbeilstein | Württemberg
VDP.GROSSE LAGE®

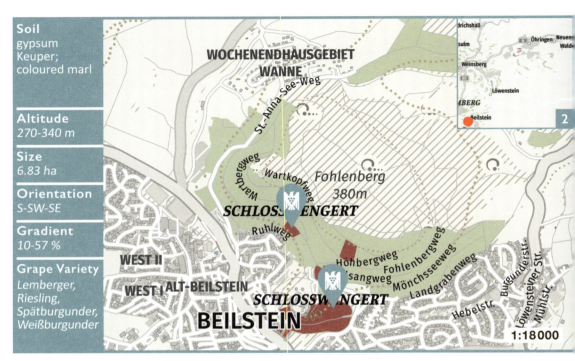

Soil
gypsum Keuper; coloured marl

Altitude
270-340 m

Size
6.83 ha

Orientation
S-SW-SE

Gradient
10-57 %

Grape Variety
Lemberger, Riesling, Spätburgunder, Weißburgunder

VDP.Estates: Schlossgut Hohenbeilstein

The vineyard slopes of the VDP.GROSSE LAGE® SCHLOSSWENGERT wrap around the mountain of the Hohenbeilstein fortress from the southwest to south to southeast. The slope rises from 270 to 340 metres above sea level at a steep gradient of up to 57 percent. Sections of the vineyard are braced with dry stone terrace walls. The walls warm easily in the sun and contribute to the vineyard's warm microclimate. Vines root in calcareous Keuper gypsum marl and coloured marl. The GL SCHLOSSWENGERT is a monopole vineyard of the VDP.Estate Schlossgut Hohenbeilstein.

SCHUPEN

Bönnigheim | Württemberg
VDP.GROSSE LAGE®

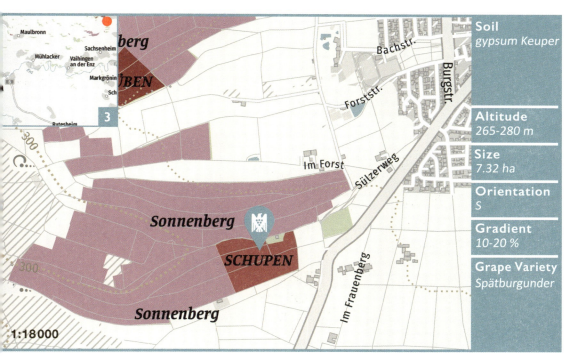

Soil
gypsum Keuper

Altitude
265-280 m

Size
7.32 ha

Orientation
S

Gradient
10-20 %

Grape Variety
Spätburgunder

VDP.Estates: Dautel

The VDP.GROSSE LAGE® SCHUPEN is a prime southeast facing parcel within the Sonnenberg vineyard located southwest of Bönnigheim. The Spätburgunder vines grow on highly calcareous Gipskeuper and weathered limestone. The soils are clayey and heavy. The vineyard is sloped to steep with up to 20 percent gradient. The GL SCHUPEN is well protected from wind and warms easily.

STAHLBÜHL

Heilbronn | Württemberg
VDP.GROSSE LAGE®

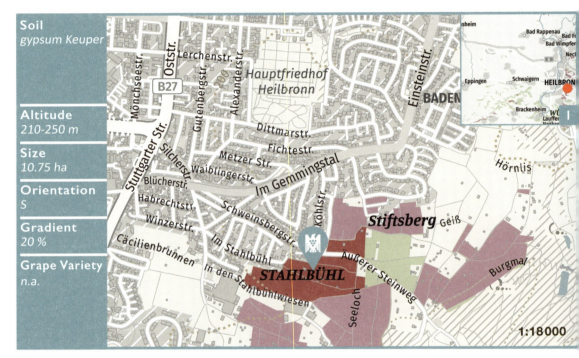

Soil
gypsum Keuper

Altitude
210-250 m

Size
10.75 ha

Orientation
S

Gradient
20 %

Grape Variety
n.a.

VDP.Estates: Schlossgut Hohenbeilstein, Kistenmacher-Hengerer

The VDP.GROSSE LAGE® STAHLBÜHL is located in the middle section of the Stiftsberg vineyard that surrounds Heilbronn. This site rises directly from the edge of the city at 210 to 250 metres above sea level at a moderate 20 percent slope gradient that faces south. The soil is predominantly very calcareous gypsum marl, which excels not only with good water availability but abundant minerals.

STEINGRUBE

Pfaffenhofen | Württemberg
VDP.GROSSE LAGE®

Soil
gypsum Keuper, reed sandstone

Altitude
220-290 m

Size
9.58 ha

Orientation
SE-S-SW

Gradient
15-60 %

Grape Variety
Lemberger, Riesling, Spätburgunder

VDP.Estates: **Wachtstetter**

The VDP.GROSSE LAGE® STEINGRUBE is a parcel within the Hohenberg vineyard that is located above Pfaffenhofen at the foot of the Scharrenberg. The parcel rises from the edge of the city at 220 up to 290 metres above sea level. It turns from south-east to south to southwest. Gypsum Keuper and sandy clay under a very meagre top layer dominates the soils, particularly in the upper parts of this site. Vines must thrust their roots deep to find sufficient water and minerals.

STEINGRÜBEN

Bönnigheim | Württemberg
VDP.GROSSE LAGE®

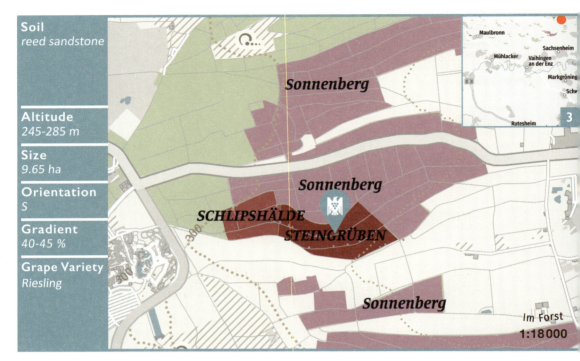

Soil
reed sandstone

Altitude
245-285 m

Size
9.65 ha

Orientation
S

Gradient
40-45 %

Grape Variety
Riesling

VDP.Estates: Dautel

The VDP.GROSSE LAGE® STEINGRÜBEN lies in a wind-protected south-facing site between the villages Cleeborn and Bönnigheim. The vineyard rises from 245 to 285 metres above sea level at a 40 to 45 percent gradient, which contributes positively to solar radiation and warmth. The soil is fossil-rich sandstone from the Stuttgart Formation.

STIFTSBERG "HUNSPERG®"

Heilbronn | Württemberg
VDP.GROSSE LAGE®

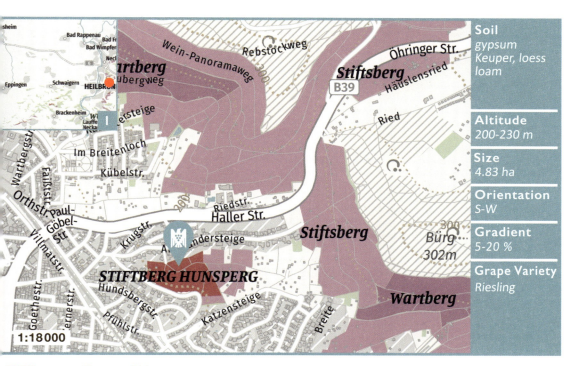

Soil
gypsum Keuper, loess loam

Altitude
200-230 m

Size
4.83 ha

Orientation
S-W

Gradient
5-20 %

Grape Variety
Riesling

VDP.Estates: Drautz-Able

The VDP.GROSSE LAGE® STIFTSBERG "HUNSPERG®" is located in the northern section of the Stiftsberg vineyard on a hill that reaches into the city. The typical gypsum marl of Heilbronn with high calcium carbonate content and a share of loess loam comprises a soil with good water storage capacity. The site has a moderate 5 to 20 percent slope gradient and turns from the south toward the west. The vineyard lies at 200 to 230 metres above sea level.

History: The Stiftsberg vineyard was first mentioned under the name "Stifteberch" in documents dating the year 1281, which indicated Stift Comburg as the owner. The gypsum content in Stiftsberg is so high that this material has occasionally been quarried here.

STIFTSBERG KLINGE

Heilbronn | Württemberg
VDP.GROSSE LAGE®

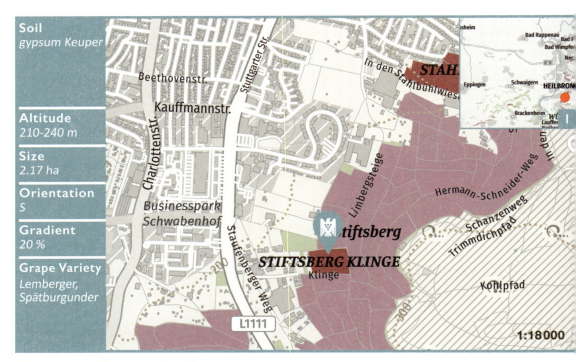

Soil
gypsum Keuper

Altitude
210-240 m

Size
2.17 ha

Orientation
S

Gradient
20 %

Grape Variety
Lemberger, Spätburgunder

VDP.Estates: Kistenmacher-Hengerer

The VDP.GROSSE LAGE® STIFTSBERG KLINGE is a 2-hectare parcel within the 325-hectare EL Stiftsberg. It is located in the southern section that stretches along the hills around Heilbronn. The site faces south. The gypsum Keuper marl that dominates the soil is very calcareous and has good water storage capacity. The vineyard rises moderately at a 20 percent gradient from 210 to 240 metres above sea level.

History: The Stiftsberg vineyard was first mentioned under the name "Stifteberch" in documents dating the year 1281, which indicated Stift Comburg as the owner. The gypsum content in Stiftsberg is so high that this material has occasionally been quarried here.

SÜSSMUND

Kleinbottwar | Württemberg
VDP.GROSSE LAGE®

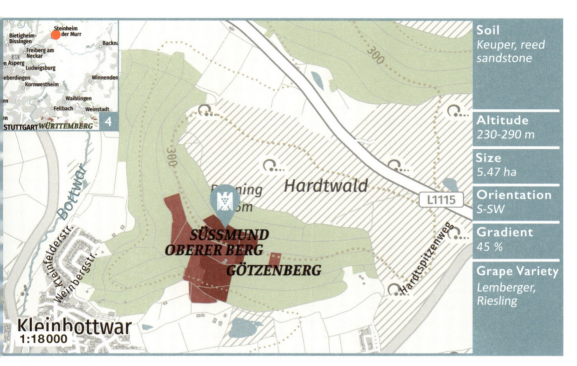

Soil
Keuper, reed sandstone

Altitude
230-290 m

Size
5.47 ha

Orientation
S-SW

Gradient
45 %

Grape Variety
Lemberger, Riesling

VDP.Estates: **Graf Adelmann**

The VDP.GROSSE LAGE® SÜSSMUND lies on a south to southwest facing slope above the village Kleinbottwar. The forest at the peak of the Benning Mountain protects the vineyard and helps provide a mild climate that results in wines with good intensity and high extract. The slope rises from 230 to 290 metres above sea level at a 45 percent gradient, which insures vines good exposure to sunlight. The sandy clay over calcareous Keuper marl warms easily and offers good water availability. The GL SÜSSMUND is a monopole vineyard of the VDP. Estate Graf Adelmann.

Information: The name "Süssmund" means "sweet mouth" and refers to the outstanding quality of this vineyard's wines. The wines historically brought prices three or four times higher than others in the same village. The site was already well known in the 16th century.

VERRENBERG

Verrenberg | Württemberg
VDP.GROSSE LAGE®

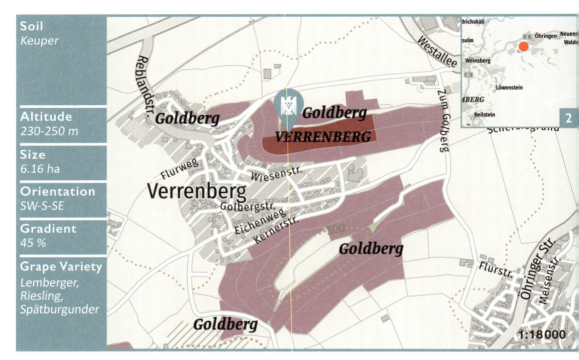

Soil
Keuper

Altitude
230-250 m

Size
6.16 ha

Orientation
SW-S-SE

Gradient
45 %

Grape Variety
Lemberger, Riesling, Spätburgunder

VDP.Estates: Fürst Hohenlohe Oehringen

The VDP.GROSSE LAGE® VERRENBERG has unusual soils for the Hohenlohe Plain: Keuper sandstone, shell limestone, and gypsum Keuper. The steep 45 percent slope faces southwest, south and southeast and rises from 230 to 250 metres above sea level. It lies in a wind protected convex and solar radiation is high. This promotes an early budbreak and a long ripening period for the grapes. The GL VERRENBERG is planted predominantly with Lemberger, Spätburgunder, and Riesling.

History: The Verrenberg site was first mentioned in documents dating 1260. The eponymous village was named after this vineyard.

WARTBERG SONNENSTRAHL®

Heilbronn | Württemberg
VDP.GROSSE LAGE®

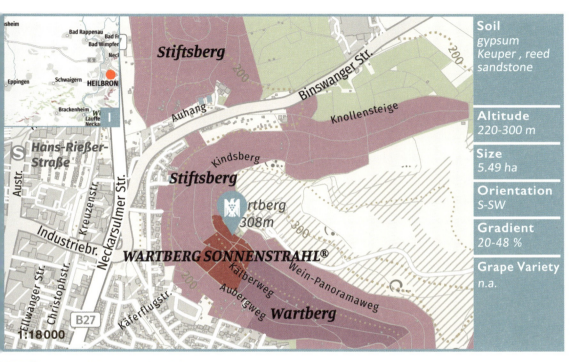

Soil
gypsum Keuper, reed sandstone

Altitude
220-300 m

Size
5.49 ha

Orientation
S-SW

Gradient
20-48 %

Grape Variety
n.a.

VDP.Estates: Kistenmacher-Hengerer

The VDP.GROSSE LAGE® WARTBERG SONNENSTRAHL® is a vineyard located above Heilbronn on the eponymous mountain at 220 to 300 metres above sea level. The site faces south and southwest toward the Neckar River at a steep 48 percent slope gradient, thus benefitting from good light intensity and growing conditions. The subsoil is calcareous, mineral-rich gypsum marl, which is covered by a layer of easily warmed sandy clay that also influences the microclimate of the GL WARTBERG SONNENSTRAHL® positively.

The VDP.REGIONAL OFFICES

VDP.AHR
VDP.Weingut Deutzerhof
Hans Lüchau
Deutzerwiese 2 | 53508 Mayschoß
Phone: +49 (0) 2643 - 7264
E-Mail: info@weingut-deutzerhof.de

VDP.BADEN
Timo Renner
Neunkircherstraße 16 | 79241 Ihringen
Phone: +49 (0)7668 - 2004992
E-Mail: info@vdp-baden.de

VDP.FRANKEN
Jutta Hemberger
Gräfenneuses 21 | 96160 Geiselwind
Phone: +49 (0)9556 - 981029
E-Mail: info@vdp-franken.de

VDP.MITTELRHEIN
Jochen Ratzenberger
Blücherstraße 167
55422 Bacharach
Phone: +49 (0)6743 - 1337
E-Mail: weingut-ratzenberger@t-online.de

VDP.NAHE
Linda Anspach
c/o Weingut Emrich-Schönleber
Soonwaldstr. 10a | 55569 Monzingen
Phone: +49 (0)6751 - 2733
E-Mail: info@vdp-nahe.de

VDP.MOSEL-SAAR-RUWER
Fabian Theiß
Gartenfeldstraße 12a | 54295 Trier
Phone: +49 (0)651 - 75041
E-Mail: grosserring@vdp-mosel.de

VDP.PFALZ
Carina Sperber & Juliana Mocha
Weinstraße 35 | 76833 Siebeldingen
Phone: +49 (0)6345 - 9594403
E-Mail: info@vdp-pfalz.de

VDP.RHEINGAU
Mathias Ganswohl
Mühlberg 5 | 65399 Kiedrich
Phone: +49 (0)6123 - 676812
E-Mail: info@vdp-rheingau.de

VDP.RHEINHESSEN
Anne Rothermel
Taunusstraße 61 | 55118 Mainz
Phone: +49 (0)6131 - 9456516
E-Mail: info@vdp-rheinhessen.de

VDP.SACHSEN-SAALE-UNSTRUT
Ramona Marschall
c/o Weingut Schloss Proschwitz |
Dorfanger 19 01665 Zadel ü. Meißen
Phone: +49 (0)3521 - 767613
E-Mail: ramona.marschall@schloss-proschwitz.de

VDP.WÜRTTEMBERG
Diana und Dietmar Maisenhölder
Nebelhornstraße 30 | 70327 Stuttgart
Phone: +49 (0)711 - 6937460
E-Mail: info@vdp-wuerttemberg.de

The VDP.ESTATES

AHR

VDP.Weingut J. J. Adeneuer
Max-Planck-Str. 8
53474 Bad Neuenahr-Ahrweiler
E-Mail: JJAdeneuer@t-online.de
www.adeneuer.de
Phone: +49 (0)2641 - 34473

VDP.Weingut Deutzerhof -
Cossmann-Hehle
Deutzerwiese 2
53508 Mayschoß/Ahr
E-Mail: info@deutzerhof.de
www.deutzerhof.de
Phone: +49 (0)2643 - 7264

VDP.Weingut H.J. Kreuzberg
Schmittmann-Str. 30
53507 Dernau
E-Mail: info@weingut-kreuzberg.de
www.weingut-kreuzberg.de
Phone: +49 (0)2643 - 1691

VDP.Weingut Meyer-Näkel
Friedensstr. 15
53507 Dernau, Ahr
E-Mail: weingut@meyer-naekel.de
www.meyer-naekel.de
Phone: +49 (0)2643 - 1628

VDP.Weingut Nelles
Göppinger Str. 13 a
53474 Heimersheim
E-Mail: info@weingut-nelles.de
www.weingut-nelles.de
Phone: +49 (0)2641 - 24349

VDP.Weingut Jean Stodden
Rotweinstr. 7 - 9
53506 Rech/Ahr
E-Mail: info@stodden.de
www.stodden.de
Phone: +49 (0)2643 - 3001

BADEN

VDP.Weingut Bercher
Mittelstadt 13
79235 Vogtsburg-Burkheim
E-Mail: info@weingutbercher.de
www.weingutbercher.de
Phone: +49 (0)7662 - 90760

VDP.Weingut Blankenhorn
Basler Strasse 2
79418 Schliengen
E-Mail: info@gutedel.de
www.gutedel.de
Phone: +49 (0)7635 - 8200-0

VDP.Weingut Freiherr von
und zu Franckenstein
Weingartenstr. 66
77654 Offenburg
E-Mail:
weingut@weingut-von-franckenstein.de
www.weingut-von-franckenstein.de
Phone: +49 (0)781 - 34973

VDP.Weingut Dr. Heger
Bachenstr. 19
79241 Ihringen
E-Mail: info@heger-weine.de
www.heger-weine.de
Phone: +49 (0)7668 - 205

The VDP.ESTATES

VDP.Weingut Heitlinger
Am Mühlberg 3
76684 Östringen-Tiefenbach
E-Mail: info@weingut-heitlinger.de
www.weingut-heitlinger.de
Phone: +49 (0)7259 - 91120

VDP.Weingut Bernhard Huber
Heimbacher Weg 19
79364 Malterdingen
E-Mail: info@weingut-huber.com
www.weingut-huber.com
Phone: +49 (0)7644 - 1200

VDP.Weingut Franz Keller
Badbergstraße 23
79235 Vogtsburg-Oberbergen
E-Mail: keller@franz-keller.de
www.franz-keller.de
Phone: +49 (0)7662 - 93300

VDP.Weingut Andreas Laible
Am Bühl 6
77770 Durbach
E-Mail: post@andreas-laible.com
www.andreas-laible.com
Phone: +49 (0)781 - 41238

VDP.Weingut Lämmlin-Schindler
Müllheimer Str. 4
79418 Schliengen-Mauchen
E-Mail: weingut@laemmlin-schindler.de
www.laemmlin-schindler.de
Phone: +49 (0)7635 - 440

VDP.Weingut Markgraf von Baden
Schloss Salem
88682 Salem
E-Mail: weingut@markgraf-von-baden.de
www.markgraf-von-baden.de
Phone: +49 (0)7553 - 81281 (Zentrale)

VDP.Weingut Michel
Winzerweg 24
79235 Vogtsburg-Achkarren
E-Mail: info@weingutmichel.com
www.weingutmichel.com
Phone: +49 (0)7662 - 429

VDP.Weingut Robert Schätzle -
Schloss Neuweier
Mauerbergstr. 21
76534 Baden-Baden/ Neuweier
E-Mail: kontakt@weingut-schloss-neuweier.de
www.weingut-schloss-neuweier.de
Phone: +49 (0)7223 - 96670

VDP.Weingut Burg Ravensburg
Am Mühlberg 3
76684 Östringen-Tiefenbach
E-Mail: info@weingut-heitlinger.de
www.weingut-burg-ravensburg.de
Phone: +49 (0)7259 - 91120

VDP.Weingut Salwey
Hauptstr. 2
79235 Vogtsburg-Oberrotweil
E-Mail: weingut@salwey.de
www.salwey.de
Phone: +49 (0)7662 - 384

The VDP.ESTATES

VDP.Weingut Schlör
Martin-Schlör-Straße 22
97877 Wertheim-Reicholzheim
E-Mail: info@weingut-schloer.de
www.weingut-schloer.de
Phone: +49 (0)499342 - 4976

Privatweingut H. Schlumberger (VDP)
Weinstraße 19
79295 Laufen
E-Mail: info@schlumbergerwein.de
www.schlumbergerwein.de
Phone: +49 (0)7634 - 8992

VDP.Weingut Seeger
Rohrbacher Str. 101
69181 Leimen
E-Mail: info@seegerweingut.de
www.seegerweingut.de
Phone: +49 (0)6224 - 72178

Staatsweingut Freiburg (VDP)
Merzhauserstraße 119
79100 Freiburg
E-Mail: staatsweingut@wbi.bwl.de
www.staatsweingut-freiburg.de
Phone: +49 (0)761 - 40165 4310

VDP.Weingut Stigler
Bachenstr. 29
79241 Ihringen
E-Mail: info@weingut-stigler.de
www.weingut-stigler.de
Phone: +49 (0)7668 - 297

VDP.Weingut Wöhrle
Weinbergstr. 3
77933 Lahr
E-Mail: info@woehrle-wein.de
www.woehrle-wein.de
Phone: +49 (0)7821 - 25332

FRANKEN

VDP.Weingut Johann Arnold
Lange Gasse 26 - 28
97346 Iphofen
E-Mail: mail@weingut-arnold.de
www.weingut-arnold.de
Phone: +49 (0)9323 - 89833

VDP.Weingut Wilhelm Arnold
Friedensstr. 4-6
97236 Randersacker
E-Mail: info@arnoldwein.de
www.arnoldwein.de
Phone: +49 (0)931 - 708326

VDP.Weingut Benedikt Baltes
Wilhelmstraße 107
63911 Klingenberg am Main
E-Mail: info@weingut-benedikt-baltes.de
www.weingut-benedikt-baltes.de
Phone: +49 (0)9372 - 2438

VDP.Weingut Bickel-Stumpf
Kirchgasse 5
97252 Frickenhausen
E-Mail: info@bickel-stumpf.de
www.bickel-stumpf.de
Phone: +49 (0)9331 - 2847

The VDP.ESTATES

VDP.Weingut Bürgerspital zum Hl. Geist
Theaterstr. 19
97070 Würzburg
E-Mail: weingut@buergerspital.de
www.buergerspital.de
Phone: +49 (0)931 - 3503441

Fürstlich Castell'sches
Domänenamt (VDP)
Schlossplatz 5
97355 Castell
E-Mail: weingut@castell.de
www.castell.de
Phone: +49 (0)9325 - 60163

VDP.Weingut Michael Fröhlich
Bocksbeutelstr. 41
97332 Escherndorf
E-Mail: info@weingut-michael-froehlich.de
www.weingut-michael-froehlich.de
Phone: +49 (0)9381 - 2847

VDP.Weingut Rudolf Fürst
Hohenlindenweg 46
63927 Bürgstadt
E-Mail: info@weingut-rudolf-fuerst.de
www.weingut-rudolf-fuerst.de
Phone: +49 (0)9371 - 8642

VDP.Weingut Glaser-Himmelstoß
Langgasse 7
97334 Nordheim
E-Mail: info@weingut-glaser-himmelstoss.de
www.weingut-glaser-himmelstoss.de
Phone: +49 (0)9381 - 4602

VDP.Weingut Bernhard Höfler
Albstädter Str. 1
63755 Alzenau-Michelbach
E-Mail: info@weingut-hoefler.de
www.weingut-hoefler.de
Phone: +49 (0)6023 - 5495

VDP.Weingut Juliusspital Würzburg
Klinikstr. 1
97070 Würzburg
E-Mail: weingut@juliusspital.de
www.juliusspital.de
Phone: +49 (0)931 - 3931400

VDP.Weingut Fürst Löwenstein
Schlosspark 3
63924 Kleinheubach
E-Mail: weingut@loewenstein.de
www.loewenstein.de
Phone: +49 (0)9371 - 9486600

VDP.Weingut Rudolf May
Im Eberstal 1
97282 Retzstadt
E-Mail: info@weingut-may.de
www.weingut-may.de
Phone: +49 (0)9364 - 5760

VDP.Weingut Roth
Büttnergasse 11
97355 Wiesenbronn
E-Mail: info@weingut-roth.de
www.weingut-roth.de
Phone: +49 (0)9325 - 902004

The VDP.ESTATES

VDP.Weingut Johann Ruck
Marktplatz 19
97346 Iphofen
E-Mail: post@ruckwein.de
www.ruckwein.de
Phone: +49 (0)9323 - 800880

VDP.Weingut Horst Sauer
Bocksbeutelstraße 14
97332 Escherndorf
E-Mail: mail@weingut-horst-sauer.de
www.weingut-horst-sauer.de
Phone: +49 (0)9381 - 4364

VDP.Weingut Rainer Sauer
Bocksbeutelstraße 15
97332 Escherndorf
E-Mail: info@weingut-rainer-sauer.de
www.weingut-rainer-sauer.de
Phone: +49 (0)9381 - 2527

VDP.Weingut Egon Schäffer
Astheimer Str. 17
97332 Volkach-Escherndorf
E-Mail: info@weingut-schaeffer.de
www.weingut-schaeffer.de
Phone: +49 (0)9381 - 9350

VDP.Weingut Schmitt's Kinder
Am Sonnenstuhl 45
97236 Randersacker
E-Mail: weingut@schmitts-kinder.de
www.schmitts-kinder.de
Phone: +49 (0)9931 - 7059197

VDP.Weingut Gregor Schwab
Bühlstraße 17
97291 Thüngersheim
E-Mail: info@weinschwanken.de
www.weinschwanken.de
Phone: +49 (0)9364 - 89183

VDP.Weingut Zur Schwane
Erlachhof 7
97332 Volkach
E-Mail: weingut@schwane.de
www.schwane.de
Phone: +49 (0)9381 - 71760

VDP.Weingut Schloss Sommerhausen
Hauptstraße 25
97286 Sommerhausen
E-Mail: info@sommerhausen.com
www.sommerhausen.com
Phone: +49 (0)9333 - 260

Staatlicher Hofkeller Würzburg (VDP)
Residenzplatz 3
97070 Würzburg
E-Mail: hofkeller@hofkeller.bayern.de
www.hofkeller.de
Phone: +49 (0)931 - 3050923

VDP.Weingut am Stein, Ludwig Knoll
Mittlerer Steinbergweg 5
97080 Würzburg
E-Mail: mail@weingut-am-stein.de
www.weingut-am-stein.de
Phone: +49 (0)931 - 25808

The VDP.ESTATES

VDP.Weingut Störrlein Krenig
Schulstr. 14
97236 Randersacker
E-Mail: info@stoerrlein.de
www.stoerrlein.de
Phone: +49 (0)931 - 708281

VDP.Weingut Paul Weltner
Wiesenbronner Straße 17
97348 Rödelsee
E-Mail: info@weingut-weltner.de
www.weingut-weltner.de oder
www.weltnerwein.de
Phone: +49 (0)9323 - 3646

VDP.Weingut Hans Wirsching
Ludwigstr. 16
97346 Iphofen
E-Mail: info@wirsching.de
www.wirsching.de
Phone: +49 (0)9323 - 87330

VDP.Weingut Zehnthof, Theo Luckert
Kettengasse 3
97320 Sulzfeld
E-Mail: luckert@weingut-zehnthof.de
www.weingut-zehnthof.de
Phone: +49 (0)9321 - 23778

MITTELRHEIN

VDP.Weingut Bastian
Erbhof "Zum grünen Baum"- Oberstr. 63
55422 Bacharach
E-Mail:
info@weingut-bastian-bacharach.de
www.weingut-bastian-bacharach.de
Phone: +49 (0)6743 - 9312530

VDP.Weingut Toni Jost
Oberstr. 14
55422 Bacharach
E-Mail: weingut@tonijost.de
www.tonijost.de
Phone: +49 (0)6743 - 1216

VDP.Weingut Lanius-Knab
Mainzer-Str. 38
55430 Oberwesel
E-Mail: weingut@lanius-knab.de
www.Lanius-Knab.de
Phone: +49 (0)6744 - 8104

VDP.Weingut Matthias Müller
Mainzer Str. 45
56322 Spay
E-Mail: info@weingut-matthiasmueller.de
www.weingut-matthiasmueller.de
Phone: +49 (0)2628 - 8741

VDP.Weingut Ratzenberger
Blücherstr. 167
55422 Bacharach
E-Mail: weingut-ratzenberger@t-online.de
www.weingut-ratzenberger.de
Phone: +49 (0)6743 - 1337

MOSEL

VDP.Weingut Clemens Busch
Kirchstraße 37
56862 Pünderich
E-Mail: weingut@clemens-busch.de
www.clemens-busch.de
Phone: +49 (0)6542 - 1814023

The VDP.ESTATES

VDP.Weingut Dr. Fischer-Hofstätter Weis
c/o Weingut Nik Weis
Urbanusstraße 16
54314 Leiwen
E-Mail: info@weingut-doktor-fischer.com
www.weingut-doktor-fischer.com
Phone: +49 (0)6507 - 93770

VDP.Weingut Le Gallais
54459 Wiltingen/Saar
E-Mail: egon@scharzhof.de
Phone: +49 (0)6501 - 16676

VDP.Weingut Forstmeister
Geltz-Zilliken
Heckingstr. 20
54439 Saarburg
E-Mail: info@zilliken-vdp.de
www.zilliken-vdp.de
Phone: +49 (0)6581 - 2456

VDP.Weingut Grans-Fassian
Römerstr. 28
54340 Leiwen
E-Mail: weingut@grans-fassian.de
www.grans-fassian.de
Phone: +49 (0)6507 - 3170

VDP.Weingut Fritz Haag
Dusemonder Str. 44
54472 Brauneberg/Mosel
E-Mail: info@weingut-fritz-haag.de
www.weingut-fritz-haag.de
Phone: +49 (0)6534 - 410

VDP.Weingut Willi Haag
Burgfriedenspfad 5
54472 Brauneberg/Mosel
E-Mail: info@willi-haag.de
www.willi-haag.de
Phone: +49 (0)6534 - 450

VDP.Weingut Haart
Ausoniusufer 18
54498 Piesport/Mosel
E-Mail: info@haart.de
www.haart.de
Phone: +49 (0)6507 - 2015

VDP.Weingut Heymann-Löwenstein
Bahnhofstr. 10
56333 Winningen, Mosel
E-Mail: info@hlweb.de
www.hlweb.de
Phone: +49 (0)2606 - 1919

VDP.Weingut von Hövel
Agritiusstr. 5-6
54329 Konz-Oberemmel/Saar
E-Mail: info@weingut-vonhoevel.de
www.weingut-vonhoevel.de
Phone: +49 (0)6501 - 15384

VDP.Weingut Karthäuserhof
Karthäuserhof
54292 Trier-Eitelsbach
E-Mail: mail@karthaeuserhof.com
www.karthaeuserhof.com
Phone: +49 (0)651 - 5121

The VDP.ESTATES

VDP.Weingut Reichsgraf von Kesselstatt
Schlossgut Marienlay
54317 Morscheid
E-Mail: info@kesselstatt.de
www.kesselstatt.com
Phone: +49 (0)6500 - 91690

VDP.Weingut Knebel
August-Horch-Str. 24
56333 Winningen
E-Mail: info@weingut-knebel.de
www.weingut-knebel.de
Phone: +49 (0)2606 - 2631

VDP.Weingut Peter Lauer
Trierer Straße 49
54441 Ayl
E-Mail: info@lauer-ayl.de
www.lauer-ayl.de
Phone: +49 (0)6581 - 3031

VDP.Weingut Schloss Lieser -
Thomas Haag
Am Markt 1
54470 Lieser
E-Mail: info@weingut-schloss-lieser.de
www.weingut-schloss-lieser.de
Phone: +49 (0)6531 - 6431

VDP.Weingut Dr. Loosen
St. Johannishof
54470 Bernkastel-Kues
E-Mail: drloosen@drloosen.de
www.drloosen.com
Phone: +49 (0)6531 - 3426

VDP.Weingut Maximin Grünhaus
Hauptstr. 1
54318 Mertesdorf
E-Mail: verwaltung@vonschubert.de
www.vonschubert.de
Phone: +49 (0)651 - 5111

VDP.Weingut Josef Milz
Brückenstraße 4
54349 Trittenheim
E-Mail: milz@milz-laurentiushof.com
www.milz-laurentiushof.com
Phone: +49 (0)6507 - 2300

VDP.Weingut Egon Müller-Scharzhof
54459 Wiltingen/ Saar
E-Mail: egon@scharzhof.de
www.scharzhof.de
Phone: +49 (0)6501 - 17232

VDP.Weingut Nik Weis - St. Urbans-Hof
Urbanusstr. 16
54340 Leiwen
E-Mail: info@nikweis.com
www.nikweis.com
Phone: +49 (0)6507 - 93770

VDP.Weingut Von Othegraven
Weinstr. 1
54441 Kanzem/Saar
E-Mail: info@von-othegraven.de
www.von-othegraven.de
Phone: +49 (0)6501 - 150042

The VDP.ESTATES

VDP.Weingut Piedmont
Saartalstr. 1
54329 Konz-Filzen/Saar
E-Mail: piedmont-weingut@t-online.de
www.piedmont.de
Phone: +49 (0)6501 - 99009

VDP.Weingut Joh. Jos. Prüm
Uferallee 19
54470 Bernkastel-Wehlen
E-Mail: info@jjpruem.com
www.jjpruem.com
Phone: +49 (0)6531 - 3091

VDP.Weingut S.A. Prüm
Uferallee 25-26
54470 Bernkastel-Kues | Wehlen
E-Mail: info@sapruem.com
www.sapruem.com
Phone: +49 (0)6531 - 3110

VDP.Weingut Schloss Saarstein
54455 Serrig/Saar
E-Mail: weingut@saarstein.de
www.saarstein.de
Phone: +49 (0)6581 - 2324

VDP.Weingut Willi Schaefer
Hauptstr. 130
54470 Graach/Mosel
E-Mail: info@weingut-willi-schaefer.de
www.weingut-willi-schaefer.de
Phone: +49 (0)6531 - 8041

Stiftungsweingut Vereinigte Hospitien (VDP)
Krahnenufer 19
54290 Trier
E-Mail: weingut@vereinigtehospitien.de
www.vereinigtehospitien.de
Phone: +49 (0)651 - 9451210

VDP.Weingut Wwe Dr. H. Thanisch,
Erben Thanisch
Saarallee 31
54470 Bernkastel-Kues
E-Mail: sofia@thanisch.com
www.thanisch.com
Phone: +49 (0)6531 - 2282

VDP.Weingut Van Volxem
Zum Schlossberg 347
54459 Wiltingen
E-Mail: office@vanvolxem.com
www.vanvolxem.com
Phone: +49 (0)6501 - 16510

VDP.Weingut Dr. Wagner
Bahnhofstr. 3
54439 Saarburg
E-Mail: info@weingutdrwagner.de
www.weingutdrwagner.de
Phone: +49 (0)6581 - 2457

VDP.Weingüter Geheimrat J. Wegeler -
Gutshaus Mosel
Martertal 2
54470 Bernkastel-Kues
E-Mail: wegeler-bks@t-online.de
www.wegeler.com
Phone: +49 (0)6531 - 2493

The VDP.ESTATES

NAHE

VDP.Weingut Dr. Crusius
Hauptstraße 2
55595 Traisen
E-Mail: info@weingut-crusius.de
www.weingut-crusius.de
Phone: +49 (0)671 - 33953

VDP.Weingut Schlossgut Diel
Burg Layen 16
55452 Rümmelsheim
E-Mail: info@diel.eu
www.diel.eu
Phone: +49 (0)6721 - 96950

VDP.Weingut H. Dönnhoff
Bahnhofstr. 11
55585 Oberhausen/Nahe
E-Mail: weingut@doennhoff.com
www.doennhoff.com
Phone: +49 (0)6755 - 263

VDP.Weingut Emrich-Schönleber
Soonwaldstr. 10 a
55569 Monzingen
E-Mail: weingut@emrich-schoenleber.de
www.emrich-schoenleber.de
Phone: +49 (0)6751 - 2733

Gut Hermannsberg (VDP)
Ehemalige Weinbaudomäne
55585 Niederhausen
E-Mail: info@gut-hermannsberg.de
www.gut-hermannsberg.de
Phone: +49 (0)6758 - 92500

VDP.Weingut Kruger-Rumpf
Rheinstraße 47
55424 Münster-Sarmsheim
E-Mail: info@kruger-rumpf.com
www.kruger-rumpf.com
Phone: +49 (0)6721 - 43859

VDP.Weingut Prinz Salm
Schlossstraße 3
55595 Wallhausen
E-Mail: info@prinzsalm.de
www.prinzsalm.de
Phone: +49 (0)6706 - 9444-0

VDP.Weingut Joh. Bapt. Schäfer
Burg Layen 8
55452 Rümmelsheim
E-Mail: schaefer@jbs-wein.de
www.jbs-wein.de
Phone: +49 (0)6721 - 43552

VDP.Weingut Schäfer-Fröhlich
Schulstr. 6
55595 Bockenau
E-Mail: weingut-schaefer-froehlich@t-online.de
www.weingut-schaefer-froehlich.de
Phone: +49 (0)6758 - 6521

PFALZ

VDP.Weingut Acham-Magin
Weinstraße 67
67147 Forst a.d.W.
E-Mail: info@acham-magin.de
www.acham-magin.de
Phone: +49 (0)6326 - 315

The VDP.ESTATES

VDP.Weingut Geh. Rat Dr. v. Bassermann-Jordan
Kirchgasse 10
67146 Deidesheim
E-Mail: info@bassermann-jordan.de
www.bassermann-jordan.de
Phone: +49 (0)6326 - 6006

VDP.Weingut Friedrich Becker
Hauptstr. 29
76889 Schweigen
E-Mail: wein@friedrichbecker.de
www.friedrichbecker.de
Phone: +49 (0)6342 - 290

VDP.Weingut Bergdolt - Klostergut St. Lamprecht
Dudostr. 17
67435 Neustadt-Duttweiler
E-Mail: info@weingut-bergdolt.de
www.weingut-bergdolt.de
Phone: +49 (0)6327 - 5027

VDP.Weingut Bernhart
Hauptstr. 8
76889 Schweigen
E-Mail: info@weingut-bernhart.de
www.weingut-bernhart.de
Phone: +49 (0)6342 - 7202

VDP.Weingut Reichsrat von Buhl
Weinstr. 18-24
67146 Deidesheim
E-Mail: info@von-buhl.de
www.von-buhl.de
Phone: +49 (0)6326 - 96500

VDP.Weingut Dr. Bürklin-Wolf
Weinstraße 65
67157 Wachenheim a.d.W.
E-Mail: bb@buerklin-wolf.de
www.buerklin-wolf.de
Phone: +49 (0)6322 - 95330

VDP.Weingut A. Christmann
Peter-Koch-Str. 43
67435 Gimmeldingen
E-Mail: info@weingut-christmann.de
www.weingut-christmann.de
Phone: +49 (0)6321 - 66039

VDP.Weingut Fitz-Ritter
Weinstraße Nord 51
67098 Bad Dürkheim a.d.W.
E-Mail: info@fitz-ritter.de
www.fitz-ritter.de
Phone: +49 (0)6322 - 5389

VDP.Weingut Knipser
Hauptstraße 49
67229 Laumersheim
E-Mail: mail@weingut-knipser.de
www.weingut-knipser.de
Phone: +49 (0)6238 - 742

VDP.Weingut Kranz
Mörzheimer Straße 2
76831 Ilbesheim
E-Mail: info@weingut-kranz.de
www.weingut-kranz.de
Phone: +49 (0)6341 - 939206

The VDP.ESTATES

VDP.Weingut Philipp Kuhn
Großkarlbacher Str. 20
67229 Laumersheim
E-Mail: info@weingut-philipp-kuhn.de
www.weingut-philipp-kuhn.de
Phone: +49 (0)6238 - 656

VDP.Weingut Herbert Meßmer
Gaisbergstr. 5
76835 Burrweiler
E-Mail: messmer@weingut-messmer.de
www.weingut-messmer.de
Phone: +49 (0)6345 - 2770

VDP.Weingut Theo Minges
Bachstraße 11
76835 Flemlingen
E-Mail: info@weingut-minges.com
www.weingut-minges.com
Phone: +49 (0)6323 - 93350

VDP.Weingut Georg Mosbacher
Weinstr. 27
67147 Forst
E-Mail: info@georg-mosbacher.de
www.georg-mosbacher.de
Phone: +49 (0)6326 - 329

VDP.Weingut Müller-Catoir
Mandelring 25
67433 Haardt
E-Mail: weingut@mueller-catoir.de
www.mueller-catoir.de
Phone: +49 (0)6321 - 2815

VDP.Weingut Münzberg - Gunter Keßler
Böchinger Straße 51
76829 Landau-Godramstein
E-Mail: wein@weingut-muenzberg.de
www.weingut-muenzberg.de und:
www.fuenf-winzer.de
Phone: +49 (0)6341 - 60935

VDP.Weingut Pfeffingen
Pfeffingen 2
67098 Bad Dürkheim a.d.W.
E-Mail: Pfeffingen@t-online.de
www.pfeffingen.de
Phone: +49 (0)6322 - 8607

VDP.Weingut Ökonomierat Rebholz
Weinstraße 54
76833 Siebeldingen
E-Mail: wein@oekonomierat-rebholz.de
www.oekonomierat-rebholz.de
Phone: +49 (0)6345 - 3439

VDP.Weingut Rings
Dürkheimer Hohl 21
67251 Freinsheim
E-Mail: info@weingut-rings.de
www.weingut-rings.de
Phone: +49 (0)6353 - 2231

VDP.Weingut Karl Schaefer
Weinstr. Süd 30
67098 Bad Dürkheim
E-Mail: info@weingutschaefer.de
www.weingutschaefer.de
Phone: +49 (0)6322 - 2138

The VDP.ESTATES

VDP.Weingut Georg Siben Erben
Weinstr. 21
67146 Deidesheim a. d. W.
E-Mail: info@weingut-siben.de
www.weingut-siben.de
Phone: +49 (0)6326 - 989363

VDP.Weingut Siegrist
Am Hasensprung 4
76829 Leinsweiler
E-Mail: wein@weingut-siegrist.de
www.weingut-siegrist.de
Phone: +49 (0)6345 - 1309

VDP.Weingut Dr. Wehrheim
Weinstraße 8
76831 Birkweiler
E-Mail: wein@weingut-wehrheim.de
www.weingut-wehrheim.de
Phone: +49 (0)6345 - 3542

VDP.Weingut von Winning
Weinstr. 10
67146 Deidesheim
E-Mail: weingut@von-winning.de
www.von-winning.de
Phone: +49 (0)6326 - 966870

RHEINGAU

VDP.Weingut Fritz Allendorf
Kirchstr. 69
65375 Oestrich-Winkel
E-Mail: Allendorf@Allendorf.de
www.Allendorf.de
Phone: +49 (0)6723 - 91850

VDP.Wein- und Sektgut Barth
Bergweg 20
65347 Eltville Hattenheim
E-Mail: mail@weingut-barth.de
www.Weingut-Barth.de
Phone: +49 (0)6723 - 2514

VDP.Weingut Diefenhardt
Hauptstr. 9 - 11
65344 Eltville-Martinsthal
E-Mail: weingut@diefenhardt.de
www.diefenhardt.de
Phone: +49 (0)6123 - 71490

VDP.Weingut August Eser
Friedensplatz 19
65375 Oestrich-Winkel
E-Mail: mail@eser-wein.de
www.eser-wein.de
Phone: +49 (0)6723 - 5032

VDP.Weingut Friedrich Fendel
Marienthaler Str. 46
65385 Rüdesheim
E-Mail: info@friedrich-fendel.de
www.friedrich-fendel.de
Phone: +49 (0)6722 - 90570

VDP.Weingut Joachim Flick
Straßenmühle
65439 Flörsheim-Wicker
E-Mail: info@flick-wein.de
www.flick-wein.de
Phone: +49 (0)6145 - 7686

The VDP.ESTATES

VDP.Weingut Freimuth
Am Rosengärtchen 25
65366 Geisenheim-Marienthal
E-Mail: info@freimuth-wein.de
www.freimuth-wein.de
Phone: +49 (0)6722 - 981070

Hochschule Geisenheim University (VDP)
Kirchspiel
65366 Geisenheim
E-Mail: weinverkauf@hs-gm.de
www.hs-geisenheim.de/weingut
Phone: +49 (0)6722 - 502173

VDP.Weingut Hamm
Hauptstr. 60
65375 Oestrich-Winkel
E-Mail: info@hamm-wine.de
www.hamm-wine.de
Phone: +49 (0)6723 - 2432

VDP.Weingut Prinz von Hessen
Grund 1
65366 Geisenheim-Johannisberg
E-Mail: weingut@prinz-von-hessen.de
www.prinz-von-hessen.com
Phone: +49 (0)6722 - 409180

Domäne Schloss Johannisberg (VDP)
Schloss Johannisberg
65366 Geisenheim-Johannisberg
E-Mail: info@schloss-johannisberg.de
www.schloss-johannisberg.de
Phone: +49 (0)6722 - 70090

VDP.Weingut Johannishof
Grund 63
65366 Johannisberg
E-Mail: info@weingut-johannishof.de
www.weingut-johannishof.de
Phone: +49 (0)6722 - 8216

VDP.Weingut Jakob Jung
Eberbacher Str. 22
65346 Erbach
E-Mail: info@Weingut-Jakob-Jung.de
www.Weingut-Jakob-Jung.de
Phone: +49-6123 - 900620

VDP.Weingut Graf von Kanitz
Rheinstr. 49
65391 Lorch
E-Mail: info@weingut-kanitz.de
www.weingut-kanitz.de
Phone: +49 (0)6726 - 346

VDP.Weingut Kaufmann
Rheinallee 6
65347 Eltville-Hattenheim
E-Mail: info@kaufmann-weingut.de
www.kaufmann-weingut.de
Phone: +49 (0)6723 - 2475

VDP.Weingut August Kesseler
Lorcher Str. 16
65385 Rüdesheim-Aßmannshausen
E-Mail: info@August-Kesseler.de
www.August-Kesseler.de
Phone: +49 (0)6722 - 9099200

The VDP.ESTATES

VDP.Weingut Baron Knyphausen
Erbacher Straße 28
65346 Eltville-Erbach
E-Mail: weingut@baron-knyphausen.de
www.baron-knyphausen.de
Phone: +49 (0)6123 - 790710

VDP.Weingut Krone Assmannshausen
Niederwaldstrasse 2
65385 Rüdesheim-Assmannshausen
E-Mail: info@weingut-krone.de
www.hotel-krone.com
Phone: +49 (0)6722 - 2525

VDP.Weingut Peter Jakob Kühn
Mühlstr. 70
65375 Oestrich
E-Mail: info@WeingutPJKuehn.de
www.weingutpjkuehn.de
Phone: +49 (0)6723 - 2299

VDP.Weingut Künstler
Geheimrat-Hummel-Platz 1 a
65239 Hochheim
E-Mail: info@weingut-Kuenstler.de
www.weingut-Kuenstler.de
Phone: +49 (0)6146 - 83860

VDP.Weingut Leitz
Theodor-Heuss-Str. 5
65385 Rüdesheim
E-Mail:johannes.leitz@leitz-wein.de
www.leitz-wein.de
Phone: +49 (0)6722 - 48711

VDP.Weingut Georg Müller Stiftung
Eberbacher Straße 7-9
65347 Eltville-Hattenheim
E-Mail: info@georg-mueller-stiftung.de
www.georg-mueller-stiftung.de
Phone: +49 (0)6723 - 2020

VDP.Weingut Prinz
Im Flachsgarten 5
65375 Hallgarten
E-Mail: info@prinz-wein.de
www.prinz-wein.de
Phone: +49 (0)6723 - 999847

VDP.Weingut Balthasar Ress
Rheinallee 7
65347 Eltville-Hattenheim
E-Mail: info@balthasar-ress.de
www.balthasar-ress.de
Phone: +49 (0)6723 - 91950

VDP.Wein- & Sektgut F.B. Schönleber
Obere Roppelsgasse 1
65375 Oestrich-Winkel
E-Mail: info@fb-schoenleber.de
www.fb-schoenleber.de
Phone: +49 (0)6723 - 3475

VDP.Weingut Josef Spreitzer
Rheingaustr. 86
65375 Oestrich-Winkel
E-Mail: info@weingut-spreitzer.de
www.weingut-spreitzer.de
Phone: +49 (0)6723 - 2625

The VDP.ESTATES

Hessische Staatsweingüter Kloster Eberbach (VDP)
Kloster Eberbach
65346 Eltville am Rhein
E-Mail: weingut@kloster-eberbach.de
www.kloster-eberbach.de
Phone: +49 (0)6723 - 60460

VDP.Weingut Schloss Vollrads
65375 Oestrich-Winkel
E-Mail: info@schlossvollrads.com
www.schlossvollrads.com
Phone: +49 (0)6723 - 660

VDP.Weingut Achim von Oetinger
Rheinallee 1
65346 Eltville-Erbach
E-Mail: info@von-oetinger.de
www.von-oetinger.de
Phone: +49 (0)6123 - 62528

VDP.Weingüter Geheimrat J. Wegeler - Gutshaus Rheingau
Friedensplatz 9 - 11
65375 Oestrich-Winkel
E-Mail: info@wegeler.com
www.wegeler.com
Phone: +49 (0)6723 - 99090

VDP.Weingut Robert Weil
Mühlberg 5
65399 Kiedrich
E-Mail: info@weingut-robert-weil.com
www.weingut-robert-weil.com
Phone: +49 (0)6123 - 2308

VDP.Weingut Domdechant Werner
Rathausstr. 30
65239 Hochheim
E-Mail: weingut@domdechantwerner.com
www.domdechantwerner.com
Phone: +49 (0)6146 - 835037

RHEINHESSEN

VDP.Weingut Battenfeld Spanier
Bahnhofstraße 33
67591 Hohen-Sülzen
E-Mail: kontakt@battenfeld-spanier.de
www.battenfeld-spanier.de
Phone: +49 (0)6243 - 906515

VDP.Weingut Brüder Dr. Becker
Mainzer Str. 3-7
55278 Ludwigshöhe
E-Mail: weingut@brueder-dr-becker.de
www.brueder-dr-becker.de
Phone: +49 (0)6249 - 8430

VDP.Weingut K. F. Groebe
Mainzer Straße 18
67593 Westhofen
E-Mail: info@weingut-k-f-groebe.de
www.weingut-k-f-groebe.de
Phone: +49 (0)6244 - 4523

VDP.Weingut Gunderloch
Carl-Gunderloch Platz 1
55299 Nackenheim
E-Mail: info@gunderloch.de
www.gunderloch.de
Phone: +49 (0)6135 - 2341

The VDP.ESTATES

VDP.Weingut Gutzler
Roßgasse 19
67599 Gundheim
E-Mail: info@gutzler.de
www.gutzler.de
Phone: +49 (0)6244 - 905221

VDP.Weingut Keller
Bahnhofstr. 1
67592 Flörsheim-Dalsheim
E-Mail: info@keller-wein.de
www.keller-wein.de
Phone: +49 (0)6243 - 456

VDP.Weingut Kühling-Gillot
Ölmühlstraße 25
55294 Bodenheim
E-Mail: info@kuehling-gillot.de
www.kuehling-gillot.de
Phone: +49 (0)6135 - 2333

VDP.Weingut J. Neus
Bahnhofstr. 96
55218 Ingelheim/Rh.
E-Mail: info@weingut-neus.de
www.weingut-neus.de
Phone: +49 (0)6132 - 73003

VDP.Weingut Rappenhof
Bachstr. 47-49
67577 Alsheim
E-Mail: weingut.rappenhof@t-online.de
www.weingut-rappenhof.de
Phone: +49 (0)6249 - 4015

VDP.Weingut Schätzel
Oberdorfstraße 34
55283 Nierstein
E-Mail: weingut@schaetzel.de
www.schaetzel.de
Phone: +49 (0)6133 - 5512

VDP.Weingut St. Antony
Wilhelmstr. 4
55283 Nierstein
E-Mail: info@st-antony.de
www.st-antony.de
Phone: +49 (0)6133 - 509110

Staatliche Weinbaudomäne Oppenheim (VDP)
Wormser Str. 162
55276 Oppenheim
E-Mail: info@domaene-oppenheim.de
www.domaene-oppenheim.de
Phone: +49 (0)6133 - 930305

VDP.Weingut Wagner-Stempel
Wöllsteiner Straße 10
55599 Siefersheim
E-Mail: info@wagner-stempel.de
www.wagner-stempel.de
Phone: +49 (0)6703 - 960330

VDP.Weingut Schloss Westerhaus
Westerhaus
55218 Ingelheim
E-Mail: info@schloss-westerhaus.de
www.schloss-westerhaus.de
Phone: +49 (0)6130 - 6674

The VDP.ESTATES

VDP.Weingut Winter
Heilgebaumstr. 34
67596 Dittelsheim-Heßloch
E-Mail: info@weingut-winter.de
www.weingut-winter.de
Phone: +49 (0)6244 - 7446

VDP.Weingut Wittmann
Mainzer Str. 19
67593 Westhofen
E-Mail: info@wittmannweingut.com
www.wittmannweingut.com
Phone: +49 (0)6244 - 905036

SAALE-UNSTRUT

VDP.Weingut Lützkendorf
Saalberge 31
06628 Naumburg, OT Bad Kösen
E-Mail: info@weingut-luetzkendorf.de
www.weingut-luetzkendorf.de
Phone: +49 (0)34463 - 61000

VDP.Weingut Pawis
Auf dem Gut 2
06632 Freyburg/OT Zscheiplitz
E-Mail: info@weingut-pawis.de
www.weingut-pawis.de
Phone: +49 (0)34464 - 28315

SACHSEN

VDP.Weingut Schloss Proschwitz - Prinz zur Lippe
Dorfanger 19
01665 Zadel über Meißen
E-Mail: weingut@schloss-proschwitz.de
www.schloss-proschwitz.de
Phone: +49 (0)3521 - 76760

VDP.Weingut Klaus Zimmerling
Bergweg 27
01326 Dresden-Pillnitz
E-Mail: info@weingut-zimmerling.de
www.weingut-zimmerling.de
Phone: +49 (0)351 - 2618752

WÜRTTEMBERG

VDP.Weingut Graf Adelmann
Burg Schaubeck
71711 Steinheim-Kleinbottwar
E-Mail: weingut@graf-adelmann.com
www.graf-adelmann.com
Phone: +49 (0)7148 - 921220

VDP.Weingut Aldinger
Schmerstr. 25
70734 Fellbach
E-Mail: info@weingut-aldinger.de
www.weingut-aldinger.de
Phone: +49 (0)711 - 581417

The VDP.ESTATES

VDP.Weingut Graf von
Bentzel-Sturmfeder
Sturmfederstr. 4
74360 Ilsfeld-Schozach
E-Mail: weingut@sturmfeder.de
www.sturmfeder.de
Phone: +49 (0)7133 - 960894

VDP.Weingut Beurer
Lange Straße 67
71394 Kernen-Stetten i.R.
E-Mail: info@weingut-beurer.de
www.weingut-beurer.de
Phone: +49 (0)7151 - 42190

VDP.Weingut Dautel
Lauerweg 55
74357 Bönnigheim
E-Mail: info@weingut-dautel.de
www.weingut-dautel.de
Phone: +49 (0)7143 - 870326

VDP.Weingut Drautz-Able
Faissstr. 23
74076 Heilbronn
E-Mail: info@drautz-able.de
www.drautz-able.com
Phone: +49 (0)7131 - 177908

VDP.Weingut Jürgen Ellwanger
Bachstr. 21
73650 Winterbach
E-Mail: info@weingut-ellwanger.de
www.weingut-ellwanger.de
Phone: +49 (0)7181 - 44525

VDP.Weingut Karl Haidle
Hindenburgstr. 21
71394 Kernen im Remstal
E-Mail: info@weingut-karl-haidle.de
www.weingut-karl-haidle.de
Phone: +49 (0)7151 - 949110

VDP.Weingut Heid
Cannstatter Straße 13
70734 Fellbach
E-Mail: info@weingut-heid.de
www.weingut-heid.de
Phone: +49 (0)711 - 584112

Schloßgut Hohenbeilstein (VDP)
Schlossstr. 40
71717 Beilstein
E-Mail: info@schlossgut-hohenbeilstein.de
www.schlossgut-hohenbeilstein.de
Phone: +49 (0)7062 - 937110

VDP.Weingut Fürst Hohenlohe
Oehringen
Wiesenkelter 1
74613 Öhringen-Verrenberg
E-Mail: brand@verrenberg.de
www.verrenberg.de
Phone: +49 (0)7941 - 94910

VDP.Weingut Kistenmacher-Hengerer
Eugen-Nägele-Straße 25
74074 Heilbronn
E-Mail: info@kistenmacher-hengerer.de
www.kistenmacher-hengerer.de
Phone: +49 (0)7131 - 172354

The VDP.ESTATES

VDP.Weingut Graf Neipperg
Schloss
74193 Schwaigern
E-Mail: info@graf-neipperg.de
www.graf-neipperg.de
Phone: +49 (0)7138 - 941400

VDP.Weingut Rainer Schnaitmann
Untertürkheimer Straße 4
70734 Fellbach, Württ
E-Mail: info@weingut-schnaitmann.de
www.weingut-schnaitmann.de
Phone: +49 (0)711 - 574616

Staatsweingut Weinsberg (VDP)
Traubenplatz 5
74189 Weinsberg
E-Mail: staatsweingut@lvwo.bwl.de
www.lvwo-weinsberg.de
Phone: +49 (0)7134 - 504-0

VDP.Weingut Wachtstetter
Michelbacher Str. 8
74397 Pfaffenhofen
E-Mail: info@wachtstetter.de
www.wachtstetter.de
Phone: +49 (0)7046 - 329

VDP.Weingut Wöhrwag
Grunbacher Str. 5
70327 Stuttgart-Untertürkheim
E-Mail: info@woehrwag.de
www.woehrwag.de
Phone: +49 (0)711 - 33 16 62

VDP.Weingut Herzog von Württemberg
Schloss Monrepos
71634 Ludwigsburg
E-Mail: weingut@hofkammer.de
www.weingut-wuerttemberg.de
Phone: +49 (0)7141 - 221060